Make Your Own Acoustic Guitar

Melvyn Hiscock

NBS
PUBLICATIONS

First published NBS Publications 2010

First Edition

NBS Publications
7 Church Green
Dunsfold
Surrey
GU8 4LT

A catalogue record for this book is available from the British Library.

ISBN 978-0-9531049-2-5

Typeset by NBS Publications

Edited by Robert Zealley

Printed and bound in Singapore by Craft Print International Ltd.

Contents

Chapter 1

Basics

Many years ago my book *Make Your Own Electric Guitar* was released to an unsuspecting public. Since then many thousands of people have read it and seem to agree that the approach to the subject I used, totally by accident, was more or less right. The book was never intended to be a strict 'follow my rules and make this guitar' type of book, but more of an investigation into how guitars are made and how to apply those methods yourself. I tried to cover all the possible combinations of features on the guitars and the ways that these could be made, whether with a fully equipped workshop or with just the bare minimum of tools. I also wanted to pose some of the more frequently asked questions and answer them in a manner that was simple to understand, and to apply those answers to the task in a manner that made it clear **why** you were doing something as well as **how**.

Now, I have decided the time is right to apply the same sort of approach to the making of acoustic guitars. I have been making acoustics for some years and it is a different type of activity to making solid-bodied electrics. A lot of the basic theory behind the instruments is the same, but solid-bodied guitars are designed to be made in the most mechanised way possible, whereas acoustic guitars rely on far more handwork and so are, in some ways, more satisfying to make.

Over the past 20 or so years much has been written about all types of guitars, and a lot has been written about the theories behind making acoustic guitars. This can range from complex mathematical theories on the nature of vibration in different types of wood through to subjective thoughts on the properties of different types of glue, and I do not intend to repeat a lot of it here. I will, however, make reference to it and attempt to suggest how to access this material, how best to use it, and in some cases which kinds of information to ignore completely.

With the amount of information available it would be all too easy to lose sight of the principal goal, which is to make a good-sounding, good-playing and attractive acoustic guitar. Since much of this information can be very technical, confusing and in some cases contradictory, it often serves only to act as a smokescreen, and in the worst cases can put people off from attempting to do the one thing that it should be helping.

With this in mind, I will tell two stories. The first relates to my good friend and the excellent acoustic guitar maker Dave King, of Dave King Acoustics in England. He believes that it is simply not necessary to pay attention to any of the overtly technical information that is available, since if you make a guitar from the right materials, you put it together properly and you pay attention to what you are doing while you are doing it, then you will make a good-sounding and good-playing instrument that will be better than most commercially available guitars: but, he stresses, the key is good materials and good workmanship. Dave also makes excellent guitars.

The second example is a gentleman I met at the 2001 Oshkosh airshow. He was working on his company's exhibition stand and we got talking. He found that I have an interest in guitars and then told me he was a bluegrass player and that he had made his own guitar. Under the watchful eye of a local maker he made a guitar with only limited woodworking skills. He was coached throughout and he told me there were some wonderful moments, such as when he realised that the endless sanding he had been doing was highlighting the grain of the wood in a way he had not experienced before. He has made the grand total of one guitar and it remains his principal instrument despite his having other, factory-produced guitars. Perhaps he proved Dave King's comments.

SO, WHAT IS A GUITAR?

In order to understand how to make a guitar you need to understand the basic principles of how it works and a little of its history, so that you can understand why the shape and style has evolved into what we now all accept as a guitar

In the beginning there were the banging things

The earliest forms of musical accompaniment were percussive. Banging two rocks, two sticks or, for the more adventurous, two dinosaurs together would make some sort of sound that could accompany chanting, singing or, in the case of the dinosaurs, bleeding.

The Parts of the Guitar

| Body | Neck | Head |

Lower bout
Bridge
Soundhole
Waist
Upper bout
Soundhole inlay
Fingerboard overhang
Fingerboard
Nut
Frets

Binding
Purfling
Fingerboard position markers
Fingerboard binding
Machine heads

Bridge pins
Lower bout
Saddle
Waist
Scratchplate
Upper bout

The next stages were blowing and plucking. Blowing down reeds, hollow logs or similar items would lead to everything from penny whistles to bass saxophones: plucking a string stretched between two points would lead to everything from the piano to the double bass.

The two problems with plucking strings are that you can only get one note and that the vibration of the string is not very loud. Therefore stringed instruments evolved so that the number of strings varied and a means of amplifying the vibration had to be found. Attaching one end of the string to a hollow box of some form causes the surface of the box to vibrate and this moves a greater volume of air than the string could on its own, therefore producing a louder noise.

SPECIALISATION AND DEVELOPMENT

The stringed instrument has, as I have already mentioned, developed across a wide family of instruments and many of that family have become very specialised. Both the piano and guitar rely on exactly the same mechanism to produce sound, that is to say the vibrating string acts on a soundboard made of softwood. The piano has one or more strings for each note on the keyboard. The guitar usually has just six strings

and the additional notes are found by shortening the string against raised frets. The violin family has no frets, so the string is shortened by simply pressing it with the finger. Most of the violin family are played with a bow that allows the player to keep the string vibrating all the time that the bow is moving: this enables the player to keep the note vibrating much longer than its natural decay.

Within the family of fretted instruments there is a wide variety, such as lutes, mandolins, bouzoukis, the various styles of guitar and the banjo. All of these have evolved in a broadly similar way from the very earliest plucked instruments.

The basic form of all these instruments is the same: they have some sort of box onto which the string is attached. One face of this box will have the string passing over it and the vibration of the strings will be transmitted to that face by the strings either being anchored to it, or passing over a raised bar so that the downward pressure of the vibrating string will cause the face of the box to vibrate. The other surfaces of the box provide structural support for the tension in the strings and help to project the sound of the vibrating top away from the player. A hole is often cut into the vibrating face as this has been found to assist the projection of the sound.

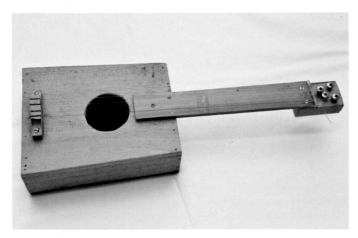

The most basic box can become a stringed instrument. My father threw this together for his youngest granddaughter who loved it. This was only ever designed to be something a three year old could thrash around on and not break, but it still produced a sound.

The other half of the instrument is the neck. This supports the string as it passes over the fretboard and at one end there is a means of altering the tension of the string to keep it, or them, in tune.

Since the strings on any instrument are under tension, the structure of the instrument needs to be strong enough to withstand this. However, the stronger and heavier it is, the less it will vibrate, so all stringed instruments are a compromise between having the soundbox light enough to vibrate efficiently and having it strong enough to withstand the tension of the strings.

This has affected the design of instruments. Many of the mandolin family have rounded backs to project the sound and to give structural strength. The guitar is generally made with a waisted shape that provides adequate structural strength and allows the instrument to sit comfortably on the knee.

THE HISTORY ASPECT

Guitars today owe much of their design to the work of three people. The first of these was Antonio de Torres Jurado, who lived from 1817 to 1892. Known simply as Torres, he is rightly considered to be the father of the modern classical, or Spanish, guitar. He pioneered ways of bracing the top and shaping the body that gave a good sound with sufficient structural strength, and many of his designs are still copied by makers from all over the world.

The guitar was not one of the most popular instruments in the 17th and 18th centuries. Little music was specifically written for it and it did not have the power and projection to hold its own in an orchestral situation. Therefore it developed as a solo instrument, or one that could accompany singers.

Christian Frederick Martin, who lived from 1796 to 1873, began his instrument-making career in his native Germany and moved to the United States in 1833. His

Antonio de Torres.

Christian Frederick Martin.

early guitars were small-bodied and typical of instruments built in Europe before the influence of Torres changed everything. Martin worked in New York after arriving in the USA, but in 1839 he moved to Nazareth in Pennsylvania and started a small factory. After his

Orville Gibson.

death in 1873 and that of his son in 1888, his grandson Frank Henry Martin took over and many innovations were incorporated into the guitars. During the 1920s Martin started making steel-strung instruments that were louder and stayed in tune better than the gut-stringed instruments before them. Because of the higher tension in steel strings, the instruments had to be stronger and Martin pioneered their X-Bracing system, generally referred to as cross bracing, that has been copied by most other makers. Martin also introduced the Dreadnought guitar with a much larger body that gave greater volume. This too has been copied by many makers.

The last of the truly influential makers was Orville Gibson. He was born in 1856 and he applied violin-making principles to the manufacture of guitars. He reasoned that an arch-topped guitar would have a greater internal volume that an equivalent flat-topped guitar and could be made to be louder. By the time he died in 1918, his company was gaining a reputation for fine work that continued into the 1920s, with the introduction of the first f-hole guitars and such innovations as the adjustable truss rod.

There has been further development since the 1930s, but most of what we know of guitars stems from the work of these three people and the development that was done by their successors.

Some of that development has centred on adding new materials to the art of guitar making. The most noticeable of these were the work of the Ovation company, which made guitars with round backs made from a type of fibreglass. They also worked on the Adamas series of guitars that had carbon fibre-impregnated tops. These guitars recorded well and some people swear by them, but to others they lacked the charm of an all-wooden instrument. Since then other makers have experimented with various synthetic materials, but part of the problem is that they will, by their very nature, sound different and people are used to guitars sounding a particular way. It is a little like the chicken and egg: which came first? Did people make guitars from wood because that is what provided the sound they wanted, or did they make them from wood and then get used to the sound they created? Of course, they made guitars from wood as that was the only suitable material at that time but our ears can now tell us that is what is 'right'. Modern materials can be used, and may well become more common in the future, but they may never have the little idiosyncracies that make wood so appealing.

THE BIG DILEMMA

Much of the complexity of the acoustic guitar stems from the fact it is trying to do two jobs at once, and each opposes the other.

The first thing it has to do is sound good, for which it needs to be light enough to resonate nicely. The problem is that it needs to do this with strings attached, and the strings impart a lot of stress into the wood. If you make it light enough it can collapse when you put the strings on, but if you make it strong enough to withstand any tension you care to throw at it, it may sound terrible.

There are two accepted ways around this, one of which is outside the scope of this book. You can arch the top and carve it from one piece of wood (as Orville Gibson used to do), making the top similar, in some ways, to an eggshell that has enormous strength due to its shape. You need very little in the way of bracing inside and you get a greater internal volume – and so the potential for a louder guitar – but the top may not be vibrating at its optimum. The arch-top guitar has become an instrument in its own right and to cover all its aspects would require another book – I may write it one day, but not before I have taken a deep breath and have my personal masseur, therapist and nutritionist by my side. For the moment I will concentrate on what is known as the flat-top acoustic.

The flat-top is what many people associate with an acoustic guitar: the familiar shape with a round sound-hole and a top that may actually be flat (but more of that later). On these guitars the top is braced against the pull of the strings by a number of wooden struts glued in underneath, which support the top and take

Top bracing.

some of the loads from the strings. They also divide the top into smaller segments that will each vibrate differently from their neighbours as they are under differing tensions – those in front of the bridge may be in compression and those behind in tension – and are generally of different shapes and sizes. I have seen it written that the bracing struts do not transfer the vibration of the string. I am not an engineer but common sense makes me think that if a strut is beneath the bridge and the bridge is where the vibration is starting, the strut will also vibrate and therefore has to transmit some of that vibration to other parts of the top.

It all starts to get complex now

The top will also be vibrating and since it is a different thickness and mass from the struts, it may well vibrate at a slightly different rate. It will also vibrate across its width and length, and some of these vibrations may well be accentuated or damped by those in the struts. The divisions of the top caused by the strutting arrangement may also cause conflicts in phasing, and the fact that the top is attached to the sides may well alter the vibration in these areas, which in turn may well affect the vibration of other parts of the top and cause conflicts.

Many years ago I saw an experiment on British TV where a guitar top was excited by a given frequency and the areas of vibration were filmed so that the frequency

Factors affecting a guitar's sound

Body size
Body shape
Depth of body
Guitar top wood choice
Guitar top density
Guitar top thickness
Bracing thickness
Density of bracing wood
Position of bracing
Position of soundhole
Scale length
Material chosen for back and sides
Density of back and sides
Thickness of back and sides
Arching of back
Arching of top
Position of bridge
Type of strings used
Height of frets
Type of truss rod or neck strengthening fitted
Thickness of neck wood
Fingerboard wood
Fret wire
Angle of headstock
Height of strings relative to body
Height of bridge saddle
Bridge material
Saddle material
Nut material
Weight of machine heads
Neck join

response on any part of the top was known for any frequency of vibration. The idea was that guitar tops could be tailored to give exactly the frequency response required. Whilst this sounded sensible on the outside, some alarm bells were ringing in my non-technical but occasionally common-sense brain.

The experiment measured types of bracing but appeared to make no allowance for the difference in structure of any one piece of wood. Even two pieces from next to each other in the same tree will have different structures and different characteristics. Not only that, it missed one very important point (which I have to admit amazed me) and that was that the top was not attached to a guitar and was not under string tension when tested, so how could the results be useable? It is a little like flight-testing an aeroplane without leaving the ground.

A good friend of mine is a very, very clever mathematician. He is also a guitarist and has an excellent collection, and we have great fun disagreeing on some points. He maintains that you can accurately predict and model, mathematically, the response in any piece of wood. Whilst this may be true, I still argue that the differences between any two pieces of wood, the differences in how two different guitar tops are constructed, such as the integrity of the glue join and the amount of pressure used to clamp it, and countless other factors ranging from atmospheric pressure to how much sleep you have had and from the integrity of the neck join to your blood-sugar level, can all make a significant difference to how a guitar sounds to you. For example, many years of using woodworking machines and hammering in frets has damaged the top end of my hearing. Any guitar will sound slightly different to me than to someone with perfect hearing. These factors outweigh the value of any mathematical prediction and so make a normal subjective assessment of the guitar far more valuable. It is all too easy to get caught up in technicality for the sake of technicality when it is usually not needed, and is sometimes of dubious value.

EASY OR NOT?

One simple fact about making an acoustic guitar is that you are likely to spend as much time making jigs and forms as you will the guitar, and the tools and items you buy to help you will probably cost more than the guitar. This is a simple fact and there are no real ways

---

Will I Make a Mistake?

Yes you will. If you don't you will be very rare. Mistakes happen to people who have been making guitars for many years; it is part of the job. The frequency of mistakes tends to lessen as people learn what they are doing, so a first guitar can be a minefield. This is the reason for my suggesting using medium-grade and cheaper wood: if you do foul up then it will cost you less, but you will still end up with a guitar that will look and sound good if you manage to avoid the worst of those mistakes!

Most mistakes are not terminal. For example, whilst a side that breaks when being bent will have to be replaced, a small crack on the back of the guitar can easily be glued, and that may not even be noticeable when the guitar is completed.

---

around it. If you are making one guitar then you simply have to accept that you need to gear up to make several in order just to make the one. Of course, if you decide to make some more, than the investment in tools and jigs will pay off. Either way, you will get a great deal of satisfaction from doing the job properly, and the only way to do the job properly is to use the right tools and to prepare properly. These will be described as we go along but an overview of most of the tools required is in Chapter 3.

The processes of making acoustic guitars can scare some people away, but if you are a reasonable proficient woodworker there is no reason why you cannot make a reasonable guitar. Bending the sides tends to scare people, but this is not the hardest part of the process – simple things like maintaining the alignment of the guitar will take up more time and brainpower. Making anything is 90 per cent common sense and 10 per cent acquired skill. If you plan correctly, work carefully and measure everything at least twice before you cut it, then making an acoustic guitar is relatively straightforward.

At the end of the construction section in *Make Your Own Electric Guitar* I wrote 'All there is left to do is plan your next guitar', and the same can apply to making an acoustic. You can make a good, viable and fine-sounding instrument on your first attempt, but you will learn as you go and the seed to experiment may be sown, and then further guitars will begin to answer the questions you set for yourself. It is satisfying, it is fun and you get to play with the results.

Chapter 2
Design

As was stated in the previous chapter, the factors affecting the sound of a guitar are many and varied, and to worry about each and every one can use up too much otherwise essential sleeping time. It is simply impossible to deal with all of this, especially on a first guitar, so I would recommend choosing a design that is straightforward and use materials that are good quality and that you know will produce an interesting guitar. I would not recommend making a first guitar from an exotic, wildly figured wood as there can be all sorts of problems in dealing with these (as will be described later). Choosing something that is easily available and relatively cheap is a good way to start.

The guitars in this book vary from a commercially available kit, one made from totally reclaimed materials to one made from figured wood, but I suggest straight-grained maple or sycamore for a first guitar as it is cheap and is easy to bend for the back and sides. Mahogany or a good mahogany substitute is a good choice for the neck, rosewood for the fingerboard – as it is easier to fret than ebony – and a middle-grade top of whatever wood is best value.

DESIGNING YOUR GUITAR

The simplest way of designing your guitar is to draw it out on a large piece of paper. You could do the work on a computer, using any one of the computer-aided design packages that are available, but you need to question what advantages you will be getting. It may be much faster, and more fun, to use pen and paper. There is nothing wrong in using a computer, but you will be working at a reduced scale whereas working with pen and paper at full size will show mistakes and anything that is mis-proportioned faster than a computer will.

Guitar Shape

Now, you could cheat and simply copy the design of an existing guitar that you know sounds good. However, guitar designs are the property of whoever

A note on length conversions

Conversions from imperial to metric can cause problems. One inch is 25.4 mm, so 25½ inches is 647.7 mm. If you are making your guitar using entirely metric measurements it is just as easy to round up the scale length to 650 mm. The small extra length is going to make very little difference to the feel and sound of the guitar.

The same applies when describing tools and drill bits, for example. A ⅛ in drill bit is 3.175 mm but this is not a size that is found, a 3 mm is going to be fine to do the same job. Throughout this book metric to imperial conversions will be to what is most convenient, so a drill size will be to the nearest commonly available size rather than an exact mathematical conversion. This will explain why some conversions vary slightly through the book, some will be exact for the purposes of explanation and others will be approximate as a guide to tool sizes.

designed them, so copying them should not be done without the relevant permissions. Even if you do copy, let us say for example, a 1932 Martin then your guitar is very unlikely to sound just like a 1932 Martin. It might sound broadly similar, but your own personality will come through and your guitar will sound like your guitar, no-one else's. David Russell Young, a fine builder who has now retired, was interviewed by Tom Wheeler for his *Guitar Book* (Harper & Row, 1974). He stated that he once shared a workshop with another maker and as an experiment they both made identical guitars using the same materials and design, but both came out sounding different as each maker had built in his own sound.

The shape of the guitar is an important part of the design but it is not difficult to design your own – just don't get too daunted by the thought. There is a lot of information to hand and you are unlikely to do anything drastically wrong if you follow some basic guidelines. If you begin to worry about the mathematical implications of increasing the size of the lower bout

This wonderful old Martin OO was photographed at the Martin factory in 2004 where it was in for repair and is typical of the small, parlour guitars of the early 20th century.

(the curve in the main body) by $^1/8$ in (4 mm) then you might just be worrying a little too much. Design it, make it and listen to it – that is the best way.

SIZE

Choosing a size is partly a matter of preference. Many early guitars were quite small and sounded very good; the problem was that they did not produce a lot of volume and so larger guitars were made to help cut through in a band situation. The Martin Dreadnought and the Gibson J-200 are good examples of this thinking. During the 1970s it seemed that the 'jumbo' acoustic guitar was most popular, but more recently many people have rediscovered smaller-bodied guitars. They may not cut through in a band setting when having to compete with other instruments, but when recorded they sound very good and they can now be amplified more successfully than they could in the 1970s. For some people this has come as an unpleasant development. When 'everyone' wanted larger-bodied guitars there was a hard core of players who appreciated the benefits of smaller guitars. They are now finding the prices of small guitars rising.

A good source of information on various guitars designs is Tom Wheeler's book *American Guitars* (Harper Perennial, 1992). This has a lot of photographs of guitars from all sorts of manufacturers and can be used as a starting point for your own design. There is nothing to stop you adapting the design of a cheap 1929 Sears and Roebuck guitar and seeing what it sounds like if you make it with a 14-fret neck instead of a 12-fret and use a more robust bracing than the transverse braces that were commonly used on guitars of this class (*see* page 15). I have also known of people who have drawn around two or more guitars and then averaged out the differences to make a new shape. This is equally valid.

You will probably have an idea of roughly what size you want your guitar to be, whether it is large, like a J-200, small like a Martin OO or in between somewhere. This, however, is not the most important measurement for your new guitar.

Scale Length

The distance from the edge of the body, where the neck joins, to the bridge saddle (where the string stops vibrating) defines the available space for the soundhole and fingerboard extension, and is partly determined by the scale length of the string. The scale length is the overall length of the string, from the bridge to the top nut. You will need to decide if the neck join is going to happen at the 12th or 14th fret position on the neck and how many actual frets your fingerboard will have extending over the face of the instrument, but the actual measurements are set by the scale length. This is, therefore, the point where you should start your design.

The scale length will normally be between 24 in (610 mm) and 26 in (660 mm), although slightly longer and slightly shorter are also used. A shorter scale length will give a lighter feel than a longer one if the same strings are used, as they do not have to be tensioned as much to reach a given note. On the other hand, the longer scale length is often thought to sound better because the tighter strings respond better. Reaching for difficult chord shapes is easier with a shorter scale length, but many players feel the advantages of the longer scale length, in terms of feel and tone, outweigh the easier playability and opt for a longer scale.

Many guitars are built with what has become a standard scale length of 25$^1/2$ in (648 mm) and it is easy to find pre-cut fingerboards for this scale. Martin guitars most commonly have a 25.4 in (645 mm) board and

Ease of measurement

Throughout this book I have listed measurements in both imperial and metric forms. Both have their merits and if I was to be totally honest I will admit I use both. Many accepted 'standard' measurements on guitars are in inches and fractions, as much design work was done in the United States and this is the preferred method. Therefore a scale length is often listed as 25½ inches (as an example) yet it is easier to work out the fret positions and to mark them, if you are working by hand, as a decimal fraction of an inch. So referring to the scale as 25.5 inches gives a first fret position of 1.431 inches from the nut which is far easier to deal with than trying to calculate how many 32nds, 64ths, or 128ths of an inch it is! The Martin company always show their scale lengths in tenths of an inch and so both styles are shown in the book. Use whatever is most convenient for you.

Pre-cut guitar fingerboards. These were photographed at Touchstone Tonewoods and have excess that needs to be trimmed from behind the nut position.

these are available from some suppliers, most notably Martin themselves.

Many of Gibson's guitars have a shorter scale that is often quoted as being 24³/4 in (628 mm) although this is not the case – it is actually nearer 24⁵/8 in (625 mm). Many replacement boards are cut to the full 24³/4 in, and while fitting these to a new guitar will not be a problem, replacing an old Gibson board on a guitar under repair can create some surprises.

24³/4 in boards are often quite a nice feature on smaller-bodied guitars, which benefit from the slightly decreased treble response from the strings.

Longer scales have been used: Gibson's first J200s had a 26 in (660 mm) scale and specialist guitars, such as seven-string guitars or acoustic basses, will have longer scales. It is not difficult now to find suppliers of pre-cut fingerboards for almost any scale. However, if you prefer to do everything yourself, working out the

Your Very Own Scale Length Calculator

The features of each spreadsheet program will vary but I have used two different programs and the procedure is very similar for both. You will need four columns and as many rows as frets, plus one or two for headings, etc.

Enter the numbers '1' to whatever you choose as your last fret into cells A3 and downwards. Column B is headed 'fret' for the fret-to-fret distances, column C 'nut' for the nut-to-fret distances and column D 'remainder'. In cell C2 enter the scale length you wish to use in the measurement system you are most happy with, metric or imperial. In cell B3 enter the sum of C2 divided by 17.817. This will give the distance from the top nut to the first fret. In cell C3 enter the sum C2 minus B3, which will give you the remainder from the first fret to the bridge. In cell D4 enter the sum C3 divided by 17.817, which will give the distance from the first to the second fret.

This set of calculations can be duplicated down these two columns so that all fret positions are calculated. Changing the number of decimal places that the software gives you will also make your life easier as there is no way that you can work to millionths of a millimetre by hand, so why bother having the extra numbers there?

This has long been the standard way of calculating fret positions, but it has one major flaw. If a mistake is made in the marking of one of the fret positions, all subsequent frets will be out by the same amount, compounding the error. The answer is to measure all positions from the nut, which is what the third column is used for. In cell C3 enter the sum of B3 on its own; this simply duplicates the first fret distance from cell B3 in the new cell. In cell C4 enter the sum of C3 plus B4 to give the distance from the nut to the second fret. These calculations can also be duplicated for all fret positions.

Having the individual fret measurements may not be absolutely necessary but can be useful for further double-checking since, when cutting a fingerboard, you can never be too sure of your accuracy. The second column of remainders is also very useful when working out the position of the neck-to-body join. For example, if your body join is at the 14th fret on a 25½ in (650mm) scale guitar, the bridge saddle will be 11.359 in (288.51mm) from the neck join (see Appendix 1).

There will be tiny errors. For example, on the spreadsheet I have set up to remind myself how to do it while I am writing this very passage, I entered the scale length of 650 mm. My 12th fret remainder should have read 325 but reads 324.998. As we have seen, an error of two thousandths of a millimetre is not going to ruin one of my guitars!

As a guide, this very spreadsheet took well under five minutes to set up. Of course, if you do not have access to a spreadsheet and a computer, you may well have to resort to working out your positions in the old-fashioned way, with a calculator and a piece of paper. Or you could use the tables I have included in Appendix 1.

fret positions on any scale length is simple and with a standard spreadsheet programme such as Microsoft Excel it can take less time to do than it does to describe (see box).

A 14 fret neck join.

A 12 fret neck join.

There will be a small error in the calculation but this is so small as to be irrelevant. It will be in the region of a 1,000th of a millimetre, or a 25,000th of an inch, which is a degree of accuracy way outside of what is achievable on a guitar. Even if it were possible to work this accurately, the manufacturing process for fretwire and the finishing of the fret cannot be this accurate; the amount of stretch and shrinkage of the neck due to temperature, the flexibility of the neck and the pressure used to fret each string will change the tuning more than a thousandth of a millimetre of misplaced fret.

TEMPERED TUNING

All fretted instruments and many keyboard instruments have what is known as tempered tuning. It is a strange and bewildering fact, but the mathematics of music do not actually add up. This happens because the mathematical relationship from one note to the next does not work across all keys. Therefore a guitar playing perfectly in tune in the key of C may not be completely in tune when played in E. Piano tuners are taught to allow for this when tuning the instrument so that it is slightly out of tune in some positions yet stands the best chance of being nearly in tune when played in any key. The guitar fingerboard is also designed in this way, but there are times when playing with other instruments will sound slightly odd as these differences are noticed.

Not all people notice this, although some people are very susceptible to it. I remember one customer who came into Giffin Guitars in London when I worked there in the early 1980s, who had perfect pitch and who found the limitations of the standard guitar fretboard very frustrating. It was even rumoured that he had suf-fered considerable anguish over this and that his perfect pitch was more of a curse than a talent.

To overcome some of the problems of tempered tuning there have been attempts to redesign the guitar to play more in tune, regardless of the key being played. One such method that has come to prominence in recent years is the Feiten system, developed by 'Buzz' Feiten – a considerable number of makers who have used the system swear that it is excellent. It is, however, a patented system so the full details are only available if the correct fees have been paid to the patent owner and if you choose to use it you should ensure that these fees are paid. More information will be found by accessing www.buzzfeiten.com.

TWELVE OR FOURTEEN FRET?

Most acoustic guitars will be referred to as having a 12- or 14-fret neck. This is not the total number of frets, as we have already discussed, but the position of the neck-to-body join. For many years it was considered normal to have this at the 12th fret, but this does make access to the upper frets a little more difficult. A move to 14-fret necks was made and some people regard this as a mistake, claiming the tone of 12-fret guitars is better. This may be the case but I have heard good-sounding guitars of both types.

The total number of frets also needs to be decided. On 12-fret guitars this is sometimes as low as 17, although 18 or 19 is more common. Having any more simply pushes the soundhole back towards the bridge. 14-fret guitars often have 19 or 20 frets as the soundhole would otherwise be moved further towards the edge of the body. Once you have decided which to choose, you can start the physical design of your guitar.

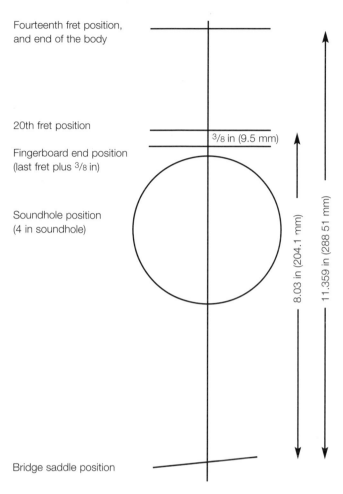

Fourteenth fret position, and end of the body

20th fret position

Fingerboard end position (last fret plus ³/8 in)

Soundhole position (4 in soundhole)

³/8 in (9.5 mm)

8.03 in (204.1 mm)

11.359 in (288.51 mm)

Bridge saddle position

The centre line with neck join position, the end of the board, bridge and soundhole marked. This, when marked onto a large piece of paper, is the beginning of your guitar design.

The soundhole on a Goodall guitar showing the end of the fingerboard hiding the inlay. A nice design touch is the way the curve of the fingerboard end touches the outer ring of the binding.

14.141 in (359.18 mm) from the nut, the remainder being the distance to the bridge. Mark the bridge saddle position, which is the end of your scale length, on the centre line.

The next stage is to mark on the position of the end of the fingerboard. If you have decided on 20 frets, then the distance from the 20th fret to the bridge on a 25¹/2 in scale is 8.03 in (204.01 mm), so measure from the marked bridge saddle position back towards the edge of the guitar and mark this. Do not be tempted to think of this as the end of the fingerboard: it is not, it is the last fret position and so a little extra will be required to support the last fret. This is usually about ³/8 in or approximately 10 mm. Mark this clearly on the centre line as well, and label both marks so you know what they refer to.

PLANNING

You could draw out the complete guitar, with body and neck, but you would need a long piece of paper. Knowing that your body and neck join is at the 12th or 14th fret position means it is easy to calculate the length of the remaining neck so you need only draw out the body, and do another drawing later for the neck.

Start by drawing a centre line. Onto this mark the end of the body. If you have a 12-fret design, the neck-to-body join will be half way along the scale length so divide your scale length by two and measure back this much along the body to find your bridge position. To find the bridge position on a 14-fret neck, or anything other than a 12-fret, use the fretting tables in Appendix 1, or the results of your own calculations, and refer to the 'remainder' column. The entry for the remainder at the 14th fret will be the distance from your neck to body join to the bridge. For example, for a 25¹/2 in scale the distance from the 14th fret to the bridge saddle is 11.359 in (288.51 mm). The 14th fret will be

Soundhole

The next stage is to mark the soundhole. The soundhole will help project the sound of the guitar and its size will make a difference – you do not want to make it too large or too small. There are examples of guitars with small and large soundholes and many of them may sound fine, but for a first guitar it is sensible to err on the side of caution and make one that is roughly between 3¹/2 and 4 in (89 and 101 mm) in diameter, depending on the size of your guitar. It should look obvious if it is out of proportion. The size may be determined for you if you choose to use a pre-manufactured inlay as this will need to be inlaid approximately ¹/4 in (6.3 mm) from the edge of the soundhole.

Some people have used soundholes that are oval or other shapes: they may work, but they can produce other design problems that would need to be dealt with, such as bracing positions. It is much easier to do it simply on your first guitar.

This is one of my favourite guitars, my good friend Susan Mullhaupt's 1955 mahogany Martin OM.

Clearly showing classical guitar influences in its design is this 12-fret Thompson T3.

Martin's square-shouldered Dreadnaught has been copied by many other makers and set a benchmark in guitar design. This is a 1969 D35.

The soundhole is usually positioned so that it is close to the end of the fingerboard. Extending the fingerboard over the soundhole looks bad and having the fingerboard stop very short is not altogether pleasing either. There is another useful trick in positioning the hole close to the board: by having it just short of the board, the soundhole inlay will continue underneath the end of the board and therefore the join on any material that is inlaid around the hole can be hidden.

DRAWING A SHAPE

You can now start to experiment with the shape. A simple internet search while writing this chapter led me to several charts listing the key dimensions of various guitar models. You can use these as a basis for your own design. The overall length is easily chosen, depending on the final size of guitar you require, as is the width at the upper and lower bout. Mark these dimensions onto the plan and then you can start to play with shapes.

The curve of the sides does not need to start at the centre line: it could remain flat for a while and need not even be a radius; it can just as easily be part of an elipse or any other compound curve. Making the sides of the guitar perpendicular to the centre line for a short way actually makes fitting the tail and neck blocks, and indeed the neck, easier. The waist of the guitar can be quite pronounced or fairly shallow. A shallower curve may be easier to bend the wood around, but a tighter waist may look better.

The simplest suggestion I can make is to play around with the shape until it is pleasing to the eye. As already mentioned, it may be possible to improve upon the design by incorporating various mathematical theories into the design, but the advantages will only be small and for a first guitar you will not go far wrong trusting your eye.

There are a few things to watch for. If you are doing this by hand you will only be drawing half of the guitar shape and it may look very different when you mirror it to make the whole shape. Of course, you could try and draw both sides at once but it is far

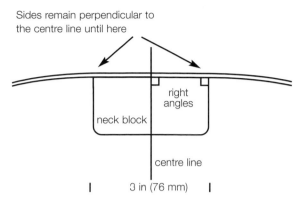

Sides remain perpendicular to
the centre line until here

right
angles

neck block

centre line

| 3 in (76 mm) |

By keeping the sides perpendicular to the centre line for a short
distance the neck block does not have to be shaped to fit the
curve and the neck is easier to fit.

drawing lines until it looks right, then extending the
shape to include both halves and then adjusting until it
looks even better. There is no science involved, just a
careful eye, and it will make a guitar that sounds perfectly acceptable.

Flat or not?

The steel-string acoustic guitar is often referred to as the
flat-top, but there are good reasons why this is not
always in fact the case. Many fine classical guitars are
made with a slightly arched top. This not only allows a
little more air inside the instrument but makes the top
stronger. One only has to think of an eggshell: although
it is quite brittle, it has a lot of strength due to its shape.
The amount of curvature on the top is not great – a
radius of perhaps 25 ft (7.6 m) – is used, but the top will
be able to resist the pull of the strings more than one
that is entirely flat.

easier to draw half the guitar and then fold
it over to duplicate the shape, rather than try
to get the whole shape symmetrical by eye.

A DESIGN STUDY
Body size
A Martin OOO is 19³/₈ in (493 mm) long,
11¹/₄ in (292 mm) across the upper bout,
15 in (382 mm) across the lower bout, and
has a 24.9 in (634 mm) scale. I have decided to use these measurements as a starting
point, but to increase the scale length to
25.4 in (647 mm); therefore I am going to
increase the size of the body slightly. This
will now be 19⁵/₈ in long, 11³/₄ in across
the upper bout and 15⁵/₈ in across the
lower bout.

With a 14-fret neck join and 20 frets,
the fingerboard will extend 3.7 in (94 mm)
over the face of the body – this is made up
of 3.314 in (84 mm) to the last fret plus ³/₈
in (10 mm) for the end of the fingerboard.
The bridge saddle will be 11.314 in (288.2
mm) from the neck join. The first stage is
to draw on the centre line and then add on
the positions of the body, the end of the
fingerboard and the bridge. A line can also
be drawn to show the outer dimensions of
the upper and lower bouts.

With this done I have decided to have
the sides joining and remaining square for
about 1¹/₂ in (38mm). This will give a 3 in
(76 mm) flat section at either end of the
guitar, and the shaping will then start from
there. This will not be noticed once the guitar is completed but will aid fitting the end
blocks.

With the overall dimensions drawn in, it
is time to start sketching. The example
shown on page 14 really is a case of me

A Martin OM28VR.

You could choose to make your guitar with a cutaway but you need to start
with a symmetrical shape and add the cutaway; more details on cutaway
guitars are in Chapter 23. This is an Everett Model L.

The principal dimensions are drawn onto the paper, the dimensions of the body are sketched in and a shape can be drawn. Take care to keep the lines flowing.

With one half drawn, the paper can be folded and the other half traced. A convenient window can be very useful for this.

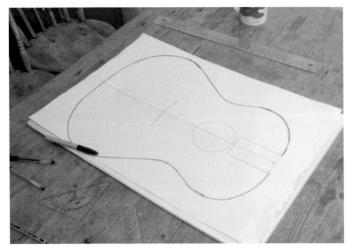

With the paper unfolded, the first attempt at the guitar shape can be seen. This can still be adjusted and played around with until it looks right as long as everything is copied over to both sides.

While the paper, drawing instruments and coffee are all on the kitchen table, the neck plan and side elevation can also be drawn.

The Science of the Guitar Top
— and how to successfully avoid it

The vibration patterns in any guitar top are very complex and are influenced by a number of factors. Fundamental to any understanding of the guitar top is to appreciate the inconsistency of the raw material. Wood is a naturally occurring organic material that, as well as varying from species to species, is affected by the local moisture content of the ground, atmospheric conditions, even the slope of the ground beneath it, and the prevailing winds. Since wood is affected by weather, the annual growth of the tree may vary from year to year. Therefore any guitar top is likely to be unique – even those cut from the same tree may not have the same qualities throughout the plank. All this means that giving a hard-and-fast rule of how to treat all guitar tops is a difficult exercise.

Further complicating this is the fact that a vibrating string produces a very complex signal. The dominant frequency will be the fundamental note, caused by the main end-to-end vibration of the string, but other notes will also be formed in the sub-divided vibration patterns that make up the harmonics.

The top is also divided up into segments that will each have their own fundamental frequency and harmonic range, and each will react differently as different notes are played. Some claim that thinning the bass or treble side of the guitar can alter these specific frequencies, but vibration research on guitar tops shows the vibration patterns at different frequencies to be distributed fairly evenly across the guitar top; they have more to do with the divisions in the top caused by the bracing than with the thickness of the nearest edge of the guitar.

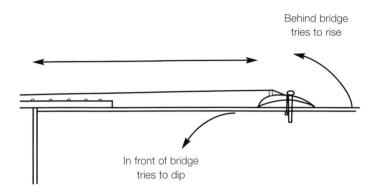

Behind bridge
tries to rise

In front of bridge
tries to dip

The string tension causes the front of the bridge to try to pivot, pushing the area around the soundhole down. The area behind tries to lift as a result of this so the area in front of the bridge is in compression and the area behind in tension.

This has implications for your design, as the arch on the top will mean that the bridge sits slightly higher in relation to the sides. At some point you will need to factor in the angle needed to make the strings the correct height over the bridge; this is done by angling the neck. The amount of angle will be small, probably less than 1 degree, but this will be dealt with later.

BRACING, DESIGN AND PLANNING

The top of the guitar is the heart of the instrument. The top produces the tone of the guitar but it also has to withstand the pull of the strings, so it has a structural function as well as a tonal one. If the top is too thick, it will support the strings but may not vibrate effectively, and if it is too thin it may vibrate well but not be strong enough to withstand the pull of the strings.

In order to make the top thin enough, it is braced by thicker pieces of wood beneath. The positions of the braces will alter the sound of the guitar. There is some argument about how the braces actually work. As previously discussed, some makers say that all of the vibration from the string passes through the bridge and to the top, and that the braces have no part in transferring the vibration to the top. Other makers will say that the braces act to spread the vibration around. The truth has to be somewhere in between: the top will vibrate as a single unit and the braces will have some damping effect on this, but they are also vibrating and, the larger ones especially, have more mass and so could work to spread the vibration from the bridge area to the edges of the guitar.

The braces are going to have a slightly different natural frequency to the top. This will mean that they interact with the top in a very complex way. You could spend many hours, and a lot of money, investigating this and assembling data, but it will only apply to one guitar top. The moment you make another with a dif-

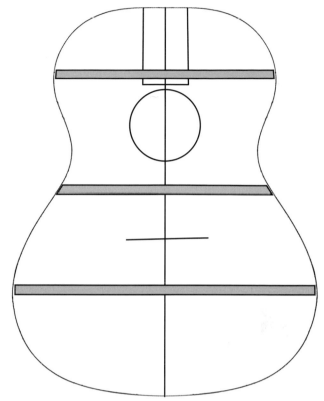

Transverse braces.

ferent set of parts and a slightly different piece of wood, all of the parameters will change slightly. Trying to keep up with all possible changes could send you mad, when all that is important is knowing the general principles; choosing how large and where your braces will be is part of the fun of designing an instrument.

There are conventions about what is considered best. Although some makers have experimented with new designs, some of which have been quite scientifically developed, the conventional designs are more often used as they seem to work. You could try designing something specifically for your guitar, but the best way to get an understanding of how the bracing works and how it affects the stiffness and tone of the top is to start with something conventional, and to leave experiments for later.

The bracing used on classical guitars is entirely unsuitable for steel-strung guitars as it will not withstand the pull of the strings. Some makers in the mid-1800s used simple transverse braces on their instruments. This was also used on some cheap, but well-respected, guitars until quite recently; examples include Stella guitars and the mainstay of the 1960s folk scene, the Harmony Sovereign. I also know of at least one maker of acoustic guitars who used this system and produced some good-sounding instruments, but any guitar braced in this way will have a limited life – I have seen one such guitar that was unplayable after less than ten years of life. The

A scalloped main cross brace from a Martin D28.

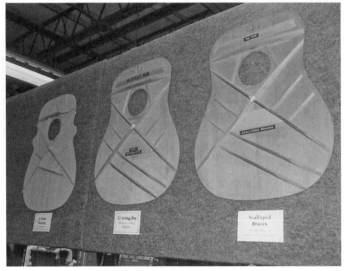

Tops on display at the Martin factory. The one on the right has scalloped bracing, the 12-string top in the centre does not. The Martin X-bracing is also very evident.

CROSS BRACING

During the 1800s the Martin company developed its X-Bracing, or cross bracing, system, which has been adapted and used by almost all other makers. This provides structural rigidity and helps prevent the turning movement of the bridge. Almost all guitars made now have a variation of the X-Bracing system.

Some makers also carve the braces. C.F. Martin was the first company to do this when they offered their D-28 model with scalloped bracing during the 1930s. The braces made for a more lightly braced top, which was appreciated by players who liked the tone of these guitars, but there was a drawback. The lighter-braced top could not support the pull of very heavy strings, which were often what was available at this time, so lighter strings had to be fitted. But these guitars went on to achieve legendary status, and those original examples that are now offered for sale in good condition can fetch very good prices. These are often known as the 'Herringbone' Martins after their distinctive binding. Martin has made reissue versions of the guitar and some makers have also included scalloped bracing on their guitars. If you choose to do this, please remember that you are not going to be able to use a very heavy string.

OTHER BRACING SYSTEMS

Several other systems of bracing have been developed over the years. Perhaps the best known is the Kasha system developed by Dr Michael Kasha in the late 1960s, and initially used by the late Richard Schneider. Kasha reasoned that the conventional fan bracing on nylon-strung acoustic guitars, that had been developed by the maker Torres in the early 19th century, was preventing certain areas on the guitar top from vibrating. He also reasoned that the soundhole should be repositioned onto the upper bout of the instrument as this area provided little in the way of sound. This makes the area between the end of the fingerboard and the bridge stronger and allows that area to generate more sound than would otherwise be the case. He also changed the bridge, making it wider on the treble side and smaller on the bass, to uncouple the upper and lower frequencies

advantage of using a simple transverse bracing is that the top is divided up into larger areas that are able to vibrate quite freely. The problem is that, since the strings are attached to the bridge and pass through the top, the bridge will be trying to twist about its axis. This means that the area behind the bridge can rise and the area in front of the bridge can dip. Since the soundhole is also positioned in front of the bridge, this creates another area of weakness. Transverse bracing is not strong enough to prevent this movement, so I would not recommend it for any guitar.

The bracing used on most guitars now is used for one reason and one reason only, and that is that it works! If you follow tradition and general practice without, of course, slavishly copying a company's own designs, then you are very likely to get a good-sounding and good-working guitar. The trick is to pay attention to the quality of your work. You must ensure that all joins are made correctly and that everything is glued correctly, as a loose brace can be difficult to fix after the guitar is finished and may cause problems with vibration, as well as putting the structural integrity of the top at risk.

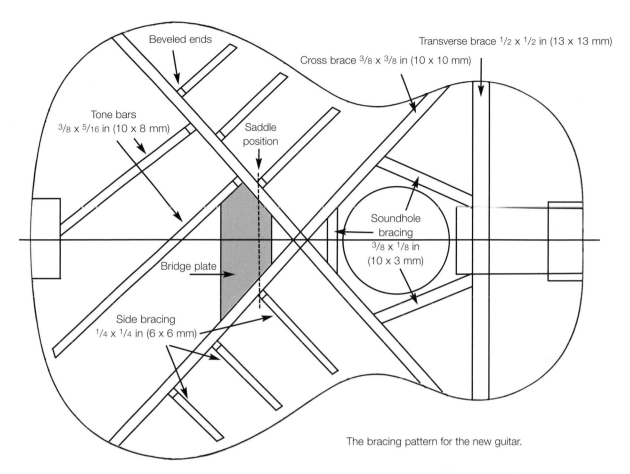

Beveled ends

Transverse brace ¹/₂ x ¹/₂ in (13 x 13 mm)

Cross brace ³/₈ x ³/₈ in (10 x 10 mm)

Tone bars
³/₈ x ⁵/₁₆ in (10 x 8 mm)

Saddle
position

Soundhole
bracing
³/₈ x ¹/₈ in
(10 x 3 mm)

Bridge plate

Side bracing
¹/₄ x ¹/₄ in (6 x 6 mm)

The bracing pattern for the new guitar.

on the guitar to give them more separation. He also made the treble side of the soundboard thicker and the bass side thinner to allow it to better react to those frequencies. Together with a much stiffer neck and neck join, the result was a guitar that was louder than a conventionally braced guitar and many people appreciated the wider frequency response which, they claimed, made the guitars rich in harmonics.

Since then the bracing system has been developed and adapted for use on steel-strung guitars, and Richard Schneider developed the Mark range of guitars for Gibson, which had a version of Kasha bracing, though these did not sell well and were eventually discontinued.

Many builders use the Kasha system or a variation on it, and are very happy with the results, but this is not to suggest that a conventional guitar with cross-bracing pattern is inferior. Kasha's original system relied on the bracings being put into a well-defined pattern that was tailored to the guitar in question. Changing any aspect of this could alter the way in which the different elements worked together and alter the whole response of the top.

Further information on the Kasha bracing system and many other types of bracing can be found by searching the internet, but beware: whilst there is a considerable wealth of good information on the internet, there is also some very dubious information that is based on no research whatsoever. For a first guitar it

is perhaps wiser to use the well-known and trusted X-Bracing; investigating the possibilities of different bracing systems can wait for subsequent guitars.

MAKING IT ALL FIT

If you are using spruce or Douglas fir on a conventional six-string, cross-braced top, the transverse brace is usually largest. Since this supports the end of the fingerboard it is often as large as ⁵/₈ × ¹/₂ in (13 × 16 mm) although I usually make them a little smaller, at about ¹/₂ in square.

The main cross braces are then made to ³/₈ in (10 mm) square to begin with although they may end up being shaped. These can be drawn onto the top plan.

There are two principal areas to concentrate on when designing these for the first time. Firstly, the end that is positioned in the upper bout must not conflict with the transverse brace. It is usual to have the cross braces just touching the transverse, or slightly separate.

The other, equally important, thing to consider is that they should cross far enough back from the soundhole so they are not running right past the edge of the hole, but close enough to it so that there will be room between them to fit the string pins through the top without fouling on either of the braces. This is, after all, why you are drawing things, to avoid any such problems.

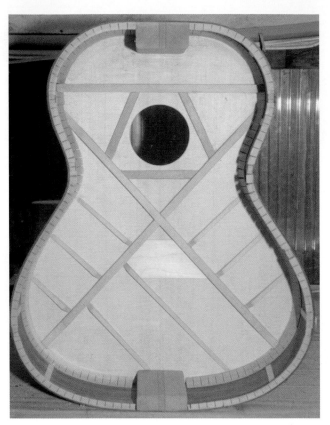

A very similar bracing pattern on a very similar guitar.

When this has been decided mark them onto the drawing and ensure the join between them is right over the centre line.

The bracing in the centre area, behind the bridge, consists of two braces, sometimes known as tone bars, that run from one side of one cross brace almost to the edge of the guitar. These are smaller than the cross braces and I usually make these $^1/4-^5/16$ in (6.5–8 mm) $\times$ $^5/16 - ^3/8$ in (8–10 mm) high. These taper from full depth where they meet the cross brace to nothing where the brace meets the kerfing. They are not butted up against the cross brace but are angled at one end. Traditionally these start on the 'treble' half of the cross brace and go across to the bass. But there is no real reason for this. They could equally well go the other way with little or no effect on the working of the top.

On the outer part of the top, between the cross braces and the edge, are further braces that start at the cross brace and taper out to nothing by the kerfing. I usually make these $^1/4$ in (6.5mm) square. Once again there are traditions that the treble side should be braced stiffer than the bass side, perhaps by having three braces on the treble side against two on the bass side, but remember there has been no real research done into this. After all, the treble frequencies may not just go where you tell them!

The area around the soundhole also needs some strengthening. Some classical guitar makers will add a ring of spruce the same thickness as the top here, perhaps an inch (25 mm) wide. Most steel-string guitar makers use smaller strips such as those seen in the photos and drawings.

Some makers also add another strip between the transverse brace and the neck block to further strengthen this area. This can be seen on the topsat the Martin factory shown on page 16.

The bracing sizes are not set in stone. You may vary these as you wish, the 12-string in Chapter 22 has larger braces because of the extra pull of the additional strings.

You may also not be able to fit everything in as you expect if you make a cutaway guitar. The guitar in Chapter 23 needed to have the transverse brace angled to clear the cutaway and this, in turn, meant the main cross braces needed to be asymmetric.

The main braces on the top, that is to say the transverse brace and the two cross braces, are normally fitted into recesses cut into the kerfing. There is no reason this needs to be the case. There is enough stiffness around the edge of the guitar to allow these to stop at the kerfing, as the smaller braces do. It could be argued this might even allow the top to vibrate a little better but without any proof I am not entering that argument. It does make the top easier to fit although recessing them into the kerfing may make a stronger guitar. I have used both methods with good results but it is a matter of personal choice.

As mentioned above (*see* page 16), there are alternative ways to brace the top. You could design your own bracing. I once made a guitar with an 'A'-frame bracing. There were two braces that ran either side of the soundhole at an angle, joining the neck block but wide enough apart for the strings to fit through the bridge. The transverse brace was fitted over these and smaller braces were added to stiffen the top. The transverse brace supported the end of the fingerboard as normal, with some added strength from the main braces. Because these were running almost in line with the strings, they supported the twisting action of the bridge and the top was able to have larger areas unsupported allowing them to vibrate more freely. It is a good-sounding guitar and as soon as I have finished this book I may well experiment further!

BRIDGE PLATE

The area beneath the bridge is usually reinforced with a plate glued between the braces, which supports the top against the pull of the strings. This is a hardwood piece and the string pin holes in the bridge will be drilled through it. The hardwood also means that the strings have something more solid to sit against in their pin holes.

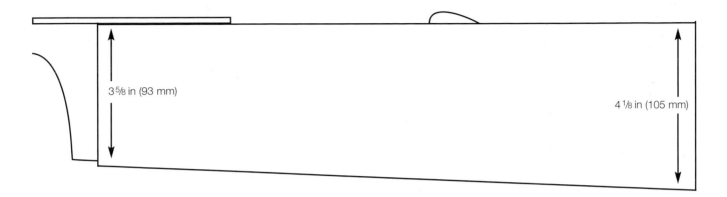

The body taper.

BACK BRACING

The back will also need to be braced, which is usually done with simple cross braces, although you will need to decide how many; some guitars will have four and some, three. These are covered further in Chapter 7.

BODY DEPTH

With the outer body shape finalised, the depth of the body can be decided. This is another area where experimentation can be fun. Most guitars vary between $3^1/2$ in (89 mm) and 5 in (127 mm) at their thickest point. Larger guitars usually have deeper bodies, but not all small guitars will have shallow bodies. The proportions can vary. A deeper body can be harder to make as any discrepancies in how square the body sides are to the top will show up more, and there is no point making a guitar extra deep just for the fun of it. Using a rule of thumb and keeping it around $4–4^1/2$ in (102–114 mm) on most medium-sized guitars will be fine. I have chosen to make this one at $4^1/8$ in (105 mm). A deeper guitar may have better bass response.

The depth of the body refers to the deepest dimension, at the end of the bottom bout. Most acoustic guitar bodies taper to become thinner nearer the neck. One exception is resonator guitars (of which more later) although I do know makers that maintain constant depth on all of their guitars. I am making this one with a depth at the neck of $3^5/8$ in (93 mm).

NECK BLOCKS AND END BLOCKS

The guitar body will need strengthening where the two halves join. In order to do this blocks, known as the end block and neck block, are glued in. The end block protects the weakest part of the guitar from damage and also holds the strap button; it is normally $^1/2$ to $^5/8$ in (12.7 to 15 mm) thick. The neck block is larger, usually 1 in to $1^1/4$ in (25 to 30 mm) thick as it supports the neck. It will also be cut to accept the tenon or dovetail depending on how the neck is fitted. Since the top will be glued onto the blocks this will affect where the bracings

can be positioned. More details on neck and end blocks are in Chapter 8.

NECK DESIGN

The neck has a different set of design problems. None of these are difficult to overcome but the relationship between the neck and the body is the key to the success of the guitar.

Having decided the scale length and the position of the neck-to-body join, the length of the fingerboard section of the neck is already decided. You will need to decide how the neck and body will be joined as any tenon or dovetail will need to be added to the end of the neck, and the length of the head and the position of the nut, and its size, will determine how long the neck will need to be.

The angle of the head, the depth of the neck and the depth of the heel, where the neck joins the body and which will be determined by the body depth, will also need to be considered.

This is something that needs to be drawn full size before starting work.

Other neck details, such as the position and style of the truss rod, if fitted, and how it is anchored and adjusted, the shape of the head and the position of the machine head holes, any head decoration and the actual shape of the head can be decided once the basics are known.

You will need to decide the style of the neck-to-body join. For the guitar in this exercise I am using a simple butt join as used by David Russell Young very successfully for many years, so the neck piece needs to be 14.1 in (360 mm) long to take the fingerboard, plus $^1/4$ in (6.35 mm) for the top nut and at least 7 in (178 mm) for the head, making a total of 21.3 in (544 mm).

If a dovetail or tenon is used then a further 1 in (25 mm) will need to be added to the end of the neck; these dimensions can be added to onto the centre line of the drawing you are making.

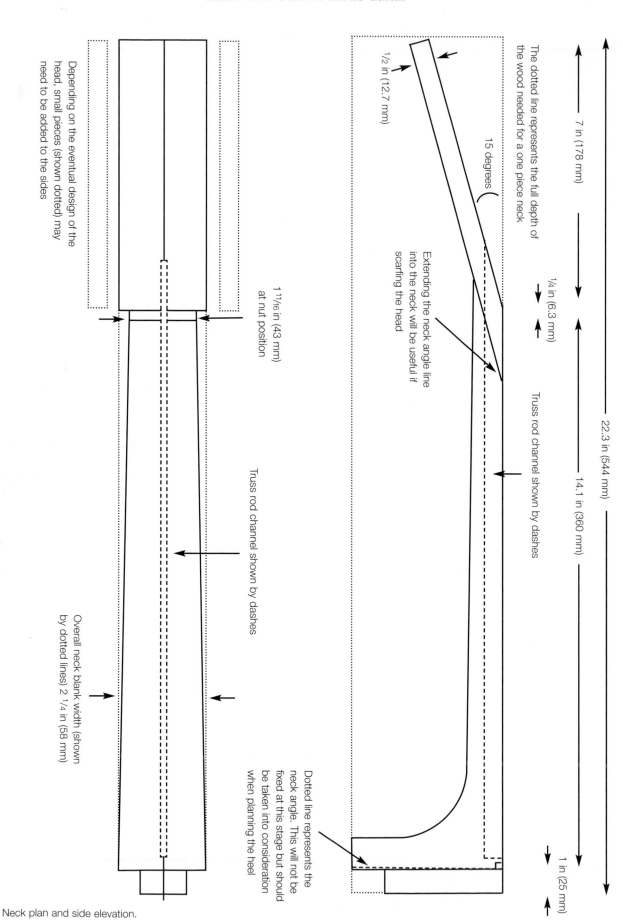

The dotted line represents the full depth of the wood needed for a one piece neck

7 in (178 mm)

22.3 in (544 mm)

14.1 in (360 mm)

1/4 in (6.3 mm)

1 in (25 mm)

1/2 in (12.7 mm)

15 degrees

Extending the neck angle line into the neck will be useful if scarfing the head

Truss rod channel shown by dashes

Dotted line represents the neck angle. This will not be fixed at this stage but should be taken into consideration when planning the heel

Depending on the eventual design of the head, small pieces (shown dotted) may need to be added to the sides

1 11/16 in (43 mm) at nut position

Truss rod channel shown by dashes

Overall neck blank width (shown by dotted lines) 2 1/4 in (58 mm)

Neck plan and side elevation.

Neck width

The fingerboard is tapered to give a wider string spacing nearer the bridge, to give more space when plucking, and narrower at the nut to make fingering chords easier.

The width of the neck and its taper are largely a matter of personal taste. The only real exceptions are classical guitars, that are set by tradition, and guitars with more than six strings. There is nothing to stop you making a seven- or eight-string guitar which will require a wider fingerboard while 12-strings usually have a wider board so that the strings are not all bunched together. This particular author has had to play a 12-string that felt like it had 12 individual strings rather than six pairs.

There are some dimensions that have become standard. Nut widths for six-string guitars are usually around 1 $^{11}/_{16}$ in (43 mm) and 12-strings are usually 1 $^{13}/_{16}$ in (46 mm). The width at the neck join is usually around 2 $^{1}/_{4}$ in (58 mm), although this may vary a little on some guitars. I often go for 60 mm at the body and 42 mm at the nut since it is easy to divide in two and I am quite comfortable working in both metric and inches.

It is not necessary to decide on the actual shape of your head just yet if you allow enough length for it. With the main elements of the plan view decided and marked on the drawing it is time to draw the side elevation of the neck.

The depth of the body at the neck join will determine the depth of the guitar heel and so the depth of the neck blank, if it is to be made from one piece. The first guitar of this style is to be made from reclaimed wood so the neck will be laminated, but it needs to have pieces glued on to make the heel 3 $^{5}/_{8}$ in deep.

It is possible the neck will need to be angled back from the body slightly to allow the strings to be at the correct height at the bridge. This does not have to be decided just yet as the angle will be very small and may not upset the overall geometry of the neck.

On the side elevation draw a line to represent the face of the neck that will sit beneath the fingerboard. Transfer the measurements for the fingerboard length, tenon length (if needed) and the length of the nut and head to this line.

At the neck-to-body join, mark the depth of the body as this will be close to the depth of your heel. It is common practice to extend the heel to the inside edge of the rear binding on the body. Since you should know the depth of your body, marking this onto the heel area is straightforward. You can also start the design of the heel by drawing on the depth of it. The heel is normally between $^{3}/_{4}$ in (19 mm) and 1 in (25 mm) deep and will curve up to meet the underside of the neck. Since you have yet to decide on the actual depth of your neck, mark only the depth of the heel at this point by marking back 1 in (25mm) from your neck join line.

The neck depth will need to be decided. This will affect how easy it is to get your hand around it and do the important playing thing. A neck that is too thick will be uncomfortable but one that is too thin may not support the stress of the strings and may also be uncomfortable to play. I knew a maker, many years ago, who made necks with a very shallow depth on his acoustics and although they had a normal width nut I could not play them: by the time I had wrapped my hand around the neck I felt as if I had too many fingers at the front! Very thin necks can also cause problems in fitting an adjustable truss rod. Curved truss rods and double rods (*see* Chapter 11) need at least $^{3}/_{8}$ in (9.5 mm) thickness and are in danger of appearing out of the back of the neck if it gets too thin.

Most guitar necks reach their thinnest point somewhere between the nut and first fret because they tend to expand from this point to the head and thicken towards the body. The depth at the thinnest point is usually between $^{3}/_{4}$ in (19 mm) and $^{7}/_{8}$ in (22 mm) thick, from the face of the fingerboard to the back of the neck; towards the body they are usually nearer to 1 in (25 mm). The fingerboard accounts for between $^{3}/_{16}$ in (5 mm) and $^{1}/_{4}$ in (6.35 mm), which needs to be taken into consideration when planning the neck. I usually aim for $^{7}/_{8}$ in total at the thinnest point, although some further wood might get removed when the neck is shaped. This needs to be marked on the drawing.

Headstock

The headstock on the guitar is angled back to give a downward pressure for the strings over the top nut; this angle is usually between 10 and 20 degrees. Some old Gibson guitars were made with a 17-degree angle, but this can make the head weaker if the neck is made without a spliced-on headstock. With the grain of the neck all going in one direction, an angled headstock will have grain running through it at an angle, and if there is a recess cut to adjust the truss rod at the head, there will be very little wood holding the headstock onto the guitar; this could cause problems if the head of the guitar is knocked. An alternative is to make the neck with the headstock spliced on so it has grain running parallel to the face of the head – this is covered in Chapter 11. I often use an angle of 15 degrees, but this is just personal choice.

The face of the head can be drawn onto the neck side elevation at whatever angle you choose. For the moment, leave this at about 7 in (178 mm) long for a six-string and 10 in (255 mm) for a 12-string. This may well change when the head is designed, but for the moment this will be fine.

Head Thickness

The next stage is to decide on the depth of your head. This will vary depending on the type and style of machine heads used. Side-mounted machines on a slotted head will require a thicker head than rear-mounted

Measuring the depth for the machine head. The bushing has been screwed part way into the housing and the resulting depth measured. There is enough adjustment on this head to allow a thickness of between $^1/2 - ^5/8$ in (13 — 17 mm).

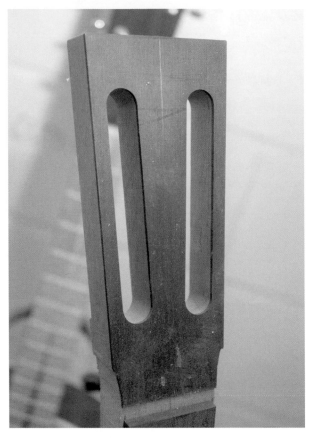

One of Dave King's slotted headstocks under construction.

heads, and the depth required for rear mounted heads can vary. You will need to know what model heads you will be using in order to plan this stage: finding that the head on your finished guitar is too thick or too thin and that your machine heads will not fit properly will not happen if you plan well at this stage.

Many modern machine heads are made with screwed-in bushes. These serve two purposes: they prevent the string post from being pulled back towards the bridge by the string tension and they help to hold the machine head in place. These heads often only have one screw to hold them in place on the rear of the head and this is only to prevent them from turning; the mechanical attachment of the head to the guitar is by tightening the bushing.

There is usually a reasonable amount of adjustment in the bushing but you do not want to have the head too thin, preventing the bush from tightening fully, or so thick that the string post barely protrudes from the face of the head, making stringing difficult. The best thing to do is assemble the bushing onto the machine head and then tighten the bushing about half way. Measure the distance between the underside of the bushing (and its washer if one is fitted) and the inside face of the machine head, and use this as a guide. $^1/2$ in (12.7 mm) is usually enough for most makes, but a little more or less is sometimes needed.

Heads with side-mounted machines are another thing altogether. The head thickness on these will be a little thicker and the depth will be determined by the chosen machine head. Most side-mounted heads come on a metal plate and there needs to be enough thickness on the head to mount this, but the head does not need to be so thick that stringing the guitar, through the slots that will ultimately be cut into the face of the

head, is made difficult. Allowing $^1/16$ in (1.2 mm) either side of the plate will be sufficient.

I know of one maker who prefers this as the head needs to be made thicker to mount this style of machine head and so the area has more mass; he feels that it helps the sound of the guitar and also makes for a stronger headstock, less prone to breaking if the guitar is knocked over.

Mark on the depth of the head and draw this line, extending it all the way to the face of the neck. This not only makes it easier to draw the line in parallel to the face of the head but will give you some useful dimensional marks if you choose to splice on the headstock. The actual head design can come later.

Your main neck design is now done. It is time to start planning the details.

TRUSS ROD

The neck side elevation drawing is useful when planning where your truss rod will go. Clearly if you just use a $^1/4$ in (6.3 mm) square piece of steel in the neck or some carbon fibre then estimating the depth of the rout needed is not really a problem. If you are going to fit a curved truss rod then you need to be able to work out how deep this will be in your neck and allow enough space for it. This is further covered in Chapter 11.

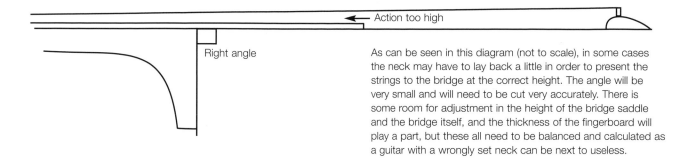

Right angle

As can be seen in this diagram (not to scale), in some cases the neck may have to lay back a little in order to present the strings to the bridge at the correct height. The angle will be very small and will need to be cut very accurately. There is some room for adjustment in the height of the bridge saddle and the bridge itself, and the thickness of the fingerboard will play a part, but these all need to be balanced and calculated as a guitar with a wrongly set neck can be next to useless.

The wedge under the end of the resonator fingerboard. Smaller wedges may be needed on conventional guitars depending on the neck angle.

NECK-TO-BODY JOIN

The neck drawing will also allow you to start properly visualising your neck-to-body join. As mentioned previously, there may be a small angle between the neck and body to allow the correct string height at the bridge.

This neck angle will depend upon a number of factors. After all, nothing in acoustic guitar making is likely to be easy is it? These will include the thickness of the fingerboard and height of the frets, the desired action of the guitar and the thickness of the bridge and saddle.

A bridge that is too thin may not have enough depth to support the saddle, and may be too thin to transmit the string vibration to the top. A thin bridge will also leave the strings very close to the front of the guitar that could then be damaged when the guitar is being played by either a pick or by fingers.

A bridge that is too thick may also not transmit the string vibration well. It will also require more of a neck angle which will mean that the section of fingerboard that runs over the face of the guitar will either have to be supported by a wedge underneath or will have to angle away from the rest of the fingerboard. This is not, generally, a problem as the angle should be very

slight and since the top frets of any acoustic guitar are not played that often, the string being a little higher from the fret will not matter that much.

The fingerboard may well remain totally flat on a guitar with an arched front as the neck angle may match the curve on the top and I have made flat top guitars where there was a very minimal angle and the board did not need shimming. I have also got it wrong and that can be very difficult to put right, so careful planning is essential, as is being able to adjust the fit when the neck actually goes on.

I have said the actual angle is very small and this can be shown quite simply. Whilst sitting here in my spacious medieval mansion writing this (this is not true but I like to imagine), I looked on the Internet and the only figures I could find showed that a 1 degree slope will give a rise of 500 feet over five miles. It will also mean that 1 degree over one mile will give a 100 foot rise. So, since there are 63,360 inches in mile and 1200 inches in 100 feet, dividing 1200 into 63,360 will give a ratio that can be used for any measurement. Therefore the slope will rise 1 inch in 52.8 inches. You can take this further. If you divide the angle by 2, to make one half-degree it will give a rise of $1/2$ in over 52.8 inches and a rise of $1/8$ in over 13.2 inches.

Hypothetically, if we have a guitar with a 26.4 inch scale length (just for the purposes of this exercise) and a 12th fret neck-to-body join then a half-degree neck angle will raise the string at the bridge position by $1/8$ in, which is a lot in guitar making terms. A quarter degree will alter the action by $1/16$ in. It may be fine to design all this on a computer with carefully designed angles but if you cannot work to the accuracy required, and few people actually can if we are honest about it, then your neck-to-body join may need some adjustment when the neck is fitted to allow the action at the bridge to be correct.

Remember also that there may be other factors that can add up to make life interesting. If your mould has been built with a very slight angle between the walls and the face - and it may not even be noticeable to the eye - then this can contribute to a change in the neck angle. Add to this a slight change to the angle caused by sanding the kerfing around the top a little more at the neck end than at the body, a small difference in the flatness, or indeed curve, of the top and then a neck angle cut that is even just $1/16$th of a degree out, then the whole lot can combine to make a larger error. Equally, all of these factors might cancel each other out but you can never be 100 per cent sure at the time the guitar is designed and so you need to allow for this. Design your neck so that you have some leeway in how you will fit it; do not make the heel too thin, as you might need to change the angle very slightly when fitting it, so allow a little extra when planning your neck. This will all get covered in more detail when it is time to fit the neck.

The thickness of the fingerboard can also have a big part to play in this. Working on the figures mentioned earlier, a $1/16$ in (1.25mm) difference in the thickness of the board, which equates to a saddle needing to be $1/16$ in (1.25mm) lower to allow for the difference in board thickness, is the same as a change in neck angle of one quarter of a degree.

There are really no hard and fast rules or definitive lists of ideal measurements that will ensure that your neck-to-body join, the height of the bridge and the various other factors all combine to make the job easy (*see* page 29). There is much in guitar making that resembles trying to design something in three dimensions in mid air with no reference points and this is one of them. I tend to use a fingerboard that is not too thin, usually around $1/4$ in (6.35 mm) at the centre, and initially mark for no neck angle at all (a 90 degree angle at the end of the neck), but this may well change when the neck and body are fitted and I leave some extra wood on the end of the neck in case.

THE HEAD

The head shape can also be decided now. This is an area where some guitars can excel and others fail. Some designs are elegant and simple. Others are either way too fussy or just plain ugly. Whatever shape it ends up, it does need to perform a function. If the strings do not have a clear path to their tuning post they can foul other tuning posts and cause tuning problems.

Bad headstock design is certainly something that will make a good guitar look less appealing. The main factor in determining the length of your headstock is the number and style of tuning machines. These need to be spaced so that the headstock is not too long or too short. Too long may cause balance problems with your guitar as the further away the weight of the machine heads is from the body, the greater moment they will have. Making the head too short also causes problems as the string from one machine head may foul another. If you are using machine heads that are three, or six, on a plate then the problem of choice disappears! It is not surprising that many makers use roughly the same distance between heads as is found on three-on-a-plate sets

Simplistic design can be very stylish.

The head on the 12-string from Chapter 22.

The head on the 'Drunken Farmer' guitar from Chapter 21.

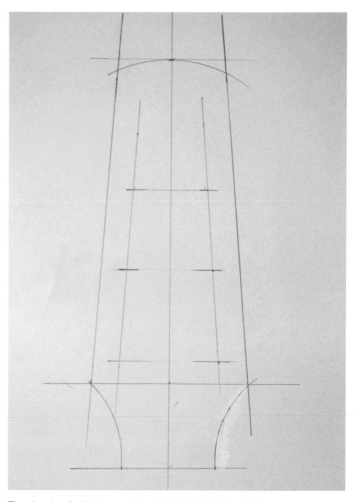

The drawing for the tapered head on the electro-acoustic in Chapter 23.

and this is 1 $^3/_{16}$ in (35 mm) between the centres. A six-string head is usually 6 $^1/_2$ in (153 mm) to 7 in (178 mm) long or 8 in (203 mm) to 9 in (229 mm) long on a 12-string. Needless to say, if making a 12-string with a neck cut from a single piece of wood with a 15 degree angle you will need quite a deep neck blank to achieve this. All of these things need to be worked out before you start cutting innocent pieces of wood.

If it is to be slotted, with side-mounted heads, there is little that can be done to its overall shape. The pitch of the holes needed to accept the three-on-a-plate tuning machines will be decided. The sides have to be straight to accept the tuners, although they could be angled, but the angle cannot be too extreme as otherwise the strings might foul each other on the way to the string post. This really only leaves the top of the head to be a focus for the designer's dreams of immortality. Many classical guitars with slotted headstocks have some very elaborate carving at the top of the head, others remain plain and simple. Plain and simple can often work very well.

The easiest way to design your head is to keep it simple and to plan it on a piece of paper. Remember that if you have drawn a plan view of the neck this will only be accurate for the face of the neck as the angle of the head will make the perspective wrong when trying to make it, so it is better to plan this out separately.

Draw the nut to full size and mark the tuner positions. Allow a little for the diameter of the posts. These are usually about $^3/_{16}$ in (5mm) diameter. From this you can work out if any string is going to get too near to another string post. On the 12-string guitar I have chosen to taper the headstock to bring the tuners closer to the centre of the head so that they do not have to angle away from the nut slot too much. The head on the resonator and the reclaimed wood guitar are both variations on a Martin style head with the addition of the top part being curved instead of the straight line that Martin uses.

Some guitars will have bound and inlaid heads although this does not have to be decided at this stage.

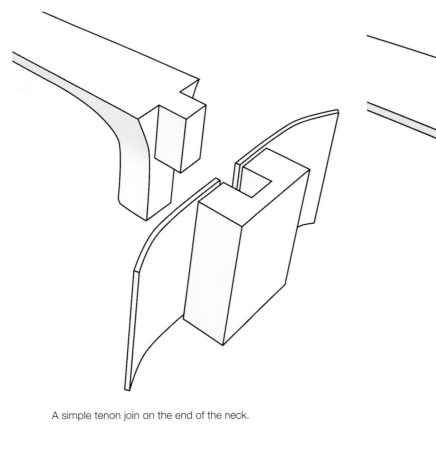

A simple tenon join on the end of the neck.

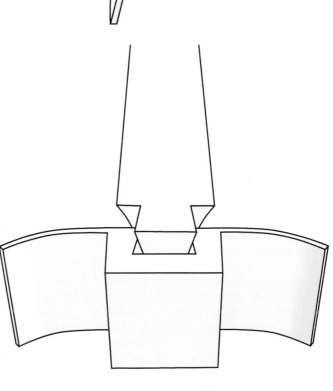

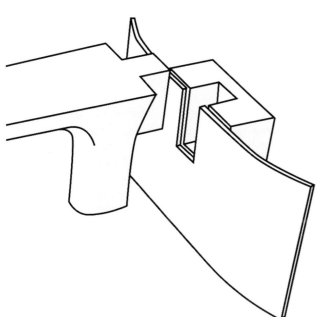

A simple tenon need not go the full depth of the heel. It is designed to help locate the neck in the correct position as well as give some extra gluing area. Bolt-on necks (*see* page 157) often use a version of this join.

Dovetail joins can be very effective on guitars but are not easy to make. They do make gluing the neck easier as they pull themselves together. Many makers go for an easier tenon join.

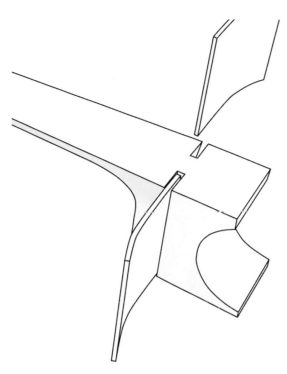

A slipper heel, where the neck block inside the guitar is integral with the neck, is used on some Spanish guitars.

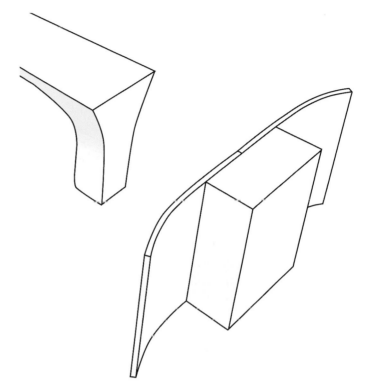

A butt join can be very effective but requires great accuracy in making and assembly.

TYPE OF JOIN

It is now time to turn your attention to the detail of the neck-to-body join.

There are several ways of attaching the neck to the body; some of these are better than others and some perfectly adequate despite seeming a little strange. Most commercially-produced acoustic guitars have a dovetail join of some description. This tapers when viewed from above and from the end and a matching V is cut into the neck block. Many handmade guitars are also made this way and it does give an excellent join but only when made accurately. Any sloppiness in the join will make the join much weaker.

Slipper heel

Many classical or Spanish guitars have what is known as a 'Slipper Heel'. With this method the neck and body of the guitar are constructed together with the neck extending into the guitar body and the guitar sides and top being attached to this. This is said to help the tone of the instrument, and would certainly be better than a badly cut tenon or dovetail, but it does have its disadvantages. Making the guitar in this way means that the body mould must be cut to allow the neck to be fitted as the sides are bent and the whole guitar needs to be manhandled when doing jobs like carving the neck shape. The slipper heel also requires very accurate work. If making a dovetail or tenon it is possible to hold the body and neck together to check the work and

to make any minor adjustments that might be needed. The slipper heel has to be right first time and so careful marking and cutting is essential. Once the neck angle has been cut into the sides it is fixed and no further adjustment is possible.

Butt joined

In more recent years other types of neck to body join have been used. David Russell Young made his guitars with a simple butt join between the body and neck. This is effectively a tenon type join without the tenon! The end of the neck is simply cut flat and then glued to the sides. Young argues (*The Steel Strung Guitar, Construction and Repair*, The Bold Strummer Ltd, 1987) that the extra gluing surface provided by the tenon is not needed as modern epoxy glues are more than strong enough on this type of join. I have made several guitars in this way and have never had a problem. Some critics of this have said that this is recipe for disaster as the neck is permanently fixed to the guitar and will not be removable should the guitar require a neck reset. In this case either the neck or the body will possibly be wrecked should anyone attempt to remove the neck, but Young argues that a guitar made properly should not need a neck reset and it is often badly cut neck tenons that give a little over time that are the very cause of necks moving in relation to the body. The jury may still be deliberating on this. Another reason to reset the neck is when the body has bowed slightly and the bridge has risen. Young also makes his guitars with bulged fronts that are inherently stronger than flat tops and less likely to move. More about this is contained in the section on body design.

Pinned necks

The makers Bill Cumpiano and Jonathan Natelson use a pinned neck join on the guitars they make and this is described in their book *Guitar Making Tradition and Technology* (Rosewood Press, 1987). This starts life as a tenon but instead of being glued they use wooden pins that are pushed into holes on either side of the neck block to hold the neck. The advantage is that the neck is relatively easy to remove for repair, should that be necessary, but also that the body of the guitar and neck can be made and finished separately. The area around the neck heel and body join is notoriously difficult to finish, as lacquer builds up around the join and if too thick can crack, causing unsightly lines. It is also difficult to get into this area to polish the finish to a good gloss. Having the neck and body finished separately can give a better finish in this area of the guitar.

Bolt-on

Some makers are now using bolt-on necks. This has all the advantages of the separately pinned body and neck listed above and is also a little stronger than the pinned method. In this method two captive nuts are fixed into the end of the neck and two bolts pass through the neck block to attach the neck. Providing that all joining faces are perfectly flat there is no reason this cannot be as firm and solid as a conventional glued join.

In all cases the fingerboard is stuck onto the front of the guitar as usual. If a neck removal is required it is far easier to remove this small section than all of the neck.

All of these neck joins are discussed in more detail in Chapter 11.

THE HEEL

The heel of the neck provides a stronger join than would be possible if the neck was much thinner, by allowing it to be glued the full depth of the sides. The shape is a matter of personal taste. Most Spanish (classical) guitars have elegant heels that curve into the side of the body and back out again and are almost triangular when viewed from in front. Many steel-string makers used similar shapes on their guitars but others use less elaborate designs. These are no better or worse structurally. Some are triangular when viewed from the front but do not flare back out like the classical heel. Others are rectangular when viewed from the front. These are often a better bet when making a guitar with a cutaway as the neck shape will blend cleanly into the cutaway.

The heel on a Thompson guitar.

The heel on a cutaway guitar.

The transition from the back of the neck to the heel needs to be decided. Too tight a curve will feel strange and may result in a weaker heel whilst a gentle curve may extend too far into the neck and make the neck feel very fat when playing the upper frets. A radius of 1–1.5 in (25–37mm) is usually fine.

You can now add a little flair to all of the lines at the back of the neck so there are no angles and one plane blends into the others.

DESIGNING THE BRIDGE

The bridge serves to support the saddle and to transmit the string's vibration to the top of the guitar. To do this effectively it needs to be not so big as to damp the top, but not too small either. It also needs to act as the anchor for the strings, so there must be room to drill the six (or however many strings you choose to have) holes in the face of it, and these should not be too close to the saddle position. The material is chosen to be quite dense so that the vibration is transmitted through the bridge rather than being absorbed and damped. The saddle acts as the physical end point of the strings' vibrating length and will be angled slightly (*see* below). Therefore there will need to be enough room on the bridge to allow this, and to allow enough material around the saddle so that it is supported well within the bridge.

The bridge on an acoustic guitar is normally made of rosewood or ebony, although in the past ivory has been used. Of course, ivory is now embargoed as it looks much better on the elephant that it ever could on a guitar – and on the whole elephants prefer to keep their own ivory than donate it to the cause of instrument making.

The bridge shape can vary, but for your first guitar keeping it simple and not unlike many thousands of guitars that have gone before it, is not a bad idea.

Bridge design and neck angle

It is important to understand the relationship between the bridge and the saddle and how this relates to the angle of your neck.

The saddle is made of bone or one of the excellent modern synthetic materials such as Corian or Tusq. It sits in a slot cut into the bridge that keeps it upright against the strings' tendency to try to push it over. There needs to be enough depth in the bridge slot to support the saddle without cutting through it entirely, and enough of the saddle needs to protrude above the bridge to allow the string to 'break' properly. If the saddle is too high, the strings will put a lot of strain onto it and this may crack the bridge in time. If it is too low then there may not be enough angle behind the saddle to stop the small amount of string that passes over the top of the bridge vibrating along with the playing section of the string. This can be the cause of some annoying buzzing on finished guitars.

In practice most guitar bridges are between 5/16 and 7/16 in (7 and 11 mm) high with the saddle being 1/8 to 3/16 in (3 to 5 mm) above this. This gives an overall height of between 7/16 and 5/8 in (11 to 16 mm). A good size to aim for is 1/2 in overall (13 mm).

The actual height is determined by the depth of the fingerboard, the angle of the neck and the desired action of the strings above the fingerboard and the best way to work this out is a full size drawing. The actual measurements may vary a little while you make the guitar as you will need to adjust things as you go but the drawing will be invaluable to help you visualise the problem. This will not only give you the height from the bridge but also the neck angle you may require. I may have mentioned earlier that some aspects of guitar making only fall into place when you do two things together.

The overall depth of the fingerboard will be about 5/16 in (7 mm) including the height of the fret. On your paper, draw a line as long as the distance from the nut to the bridge position and mark onto that the position of the body join, whether it is 12- or 14-fret, and if it is a 14-fret neck add in the 12th fret position too.

Above this, draw another line 5/16 in (7 mm) above it and parallel to it as long as the fingerboard will be. This represents the front face of your fingerboard, frets included. Now you need to add the desired action of your guitar. At the 12th fret position, make a mark 3/32 in (2 –2.5 mm) above the line that represents the face of your fingerboard and frets and draw a line starting at the face of the board at the nut position (using the first fret position would be more accurate but there is very little in it). Join this mark to the one at the 12th fret and extend this all the way to the bridge. This line represents the top string of the guitar (the bass strings will have a slightly higher action) and you will notice the action at the 20th fret is slightly higher than it is at the 12th. This is normal.

At the bridge position, measure down from this line to the line that represents the underside of your fingerboard. You will most likely see this is much less than the 1/2 in (13 mm) total that you require for your bridge height. Therefore in order to have a bridge of a reasonable height, you need to angle the neck back a little.

On your drawing mark 1/2 in (13 mm) down from the line representing your string, at the bridge position, and make a mark. Join this mark to the point where the underside of your fingerboard meets the neck to body join. This line represents the front of your guitar body and you will see that it is angled back from the underside of the fingerboard by a small amount. It is this angle you need to measure and transfer to your neck drawing as the neck angle.

This is likely to be a very small angle indeed but it is one of the most important measurements on the whole guitar. The excellent book included with the Martin kit describes the neck angle as being 1.5 degrees. When it is time to fit the neck it will be marked and cut but may well need some slight adjustment.

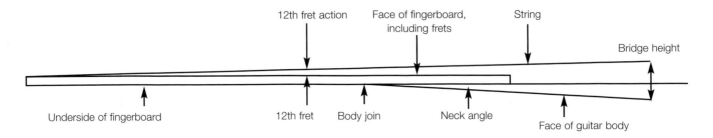

12th fret action   Face of fingerboard,   String
                    including frets

Bridge height

Underside of fingerboard   12th fret   Body join   Neck angle   Face of guitar body

This diagram is not to scale in order to demonstrate
the neck angle and bridge height calculations.

You can also take a measurement from the line that represents the underside of the fingerboard to the line that now represents the face of your guitar body at the bridge position. When you trial fit your neck with the fingerboard still unglued, this is the distance that a straightedge, placed on the face of the neck, will need to be above the guitar body at the bridge position. This may only be $^3/16$ in (4.5 mm) or less.

If your guitar has an arched front the drawing may be a little more complicated but if you have made a former (*see* page 67) to make that curve, this can be used to draw a curved line to represent the face of the guitar in the same way as the straightedge used above.

The bridge shape

The size and shape of your bridge may vary depending upon the style of guitar you are making. Obviously a 12-string guitar will need a larger bridge and some smaller-bodied guitars have correspondingly small bridges. Since the bridge needs to be large enough to hold the saddle and the bridge pins, the position of these may be a good place to start the design.

String spacing

The distance between the pin holes in the bridge is usually between $^7/16$ and $^1/2$ in (11 and 12 mm) and is determined by the width of the fingerboard and its taper. A neck that is almost parallel may have a narrower string spacing at the bridge than one that it is more tapered.

The position of the string pins can be found in two ways. The first is to draw out a plan of your fingerboard and extend this to the bridge position. Mark the width of the fingerboard at the nut and at the body join (this position can be worked out from the scale chart) and draw on the fingerboard. Mark the position of the top and bottom strings. This is usually $^1/8$ in (3mm) from the edge of the nut. Draw on the string position, keeping it parallel to the edge of the fingerboard. The pins are usually between $^1/4$ in (6.5 mm) and $^1/2$ in (12.7 mm) behind the saddle so extend your line past the bridge position marked on your drawing. The bass side of the saddle will be further back towards the pins than the treble side due to the compensation needed to keep the guitar playing in tune (*see* page 170).

Measure between the two string lines at this position to give you the positions of the outer bridge pins. You then need to divide this number by five to give you the distance between each of the pins. Do not be tempted to divide by six; this will give you seven pins. Six pins require five spaces between them.

You could also measure this off the guitar itself, as there is no reason you cannot leave the final design of the bridge until then. This is easier after the neck has been attached to the body or if it can be attached temporarily. The position of the bridge can then be marked on the front (putting some masking tape on the area to protect the top is not a bad idea), and the string positions found and marked as above. The measurements can then be transferred to the bridge drawing.

The width of the saddle also needs to be decided even though the saddle will not be fitted until later. The saddle will extend a small way past the outer strings and so allow between $^1/4$ in (6.3 mm) and $^3/8$ in (9.5 mm) either side. This will determine the minimum width of your bridge.

With the saddle position and pin positions marked the rest of the bridge can be marked. The usual size for a bridge is between 5 and 6 in across (127 to 152 mm). The drawing here is typical of a large-ish bodied six-string but sizes will vary. More detailed information on designing the bridge is found in Chapter 16.

With all of the component parts of the guitar designed it is time to start thinking about cutting pieces of wood: not, to begin with, on the guitar itself but to make the jigs and forms that will be used in the making of it.

Chapter 3
Tools

There are a number of tools that will be required in order to build your guitar that are fairly specific for the job and others that any reasonably well-equipped workshop will have. Some of these will be dealt with as we go through the book, especially if they are specific to one job or can be adapted from other tools. There are, however, some tools and workshop items that will definitely be needed and some of these are things that are always useful.

There is an old saying that 'a bad workman always blames his tools', but you need to have those tools before you can even think about blaming them. If you have the right tools, then you are less likely to have something that you want to blame on something or someone else.

BASIC TOOLS

Access to a good workbench is pretty much essential. You could make a guitar on a portable folding bench, but you will be causing yourself problems: they are simply not rigid enough to support the work, and if your work moves around when you try to do something you will not get a good result. Ideally, the bench should have a good wood vice attached and should have ample area on which you can work. Other tools should, ideally, be within reach and all should be kept tidy. Now I am first to admit that I am not the most tidy person on earth and I can say with the benefit of many, many years' experience that this is not the best way to be. An untidy workbench can cause damage to the guitar as you put things down on top of things that should not be there.

You will need to use some fairly standard woodworking tools. A good quality plane will be very useful when jointing the top and back and can be used to thickness the top too. Among the most useful tools I have are a small Japanese back saw that I use for just about everything, chisels of various sizes, a small smoothing plane and scraper blades, of which more later. I find it impossible to believe anyone can have enough wooden sprung clothes pegs if they are mak-

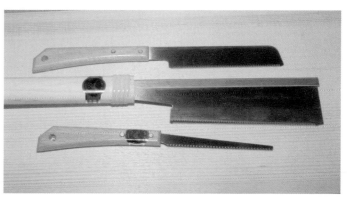

Japanese saws.

One of a number of very useful 3 in (77 mm) clamps I have had for years, and two different sizes of spring clamp. These are extremely cheap and are usually bought from discount tool suppliers.

ing guitars. These are very useful when gluing bindings and I have a number of cheap, small plastic clamps that I use for a variety of jobs. I also have a lot of 3 in (77

Good quality tools will always last. This Gentleman's saw was bought years ago and is very useful in making small tenons.

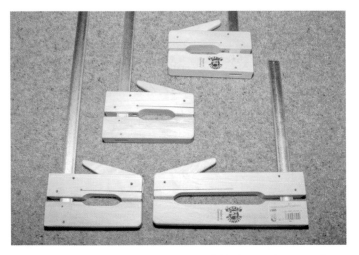

These wooden cam clamps are available from various suppliers and are available with different depths and reaches. The cam operation is very simple.

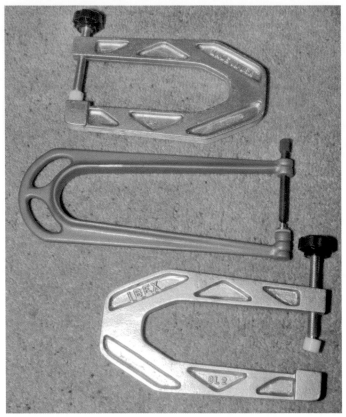

Longer reach clamps can be very useful for gluing bracings into place but are essential when gluing the bridge. The aluminum clamps are light and so do not strain the guitar top as a heavier steel clamp might.

My very un-specialist fretting hammer.

mm) C-clamps that get a lot of use and a couple of slightly larger ones for gluing end blocks. A good-quality plane will be very useful when jointing the top and back, and can be used to thickness the top too. For bending the sides you will need a bending iron of some sort. These are available from guitar parts suppliers, or you can make something yourself, as discussed in Chapter 8.

Fretting the guitar may also require some specialist tools and these too can be bought from parts suppliers, though some can be adapted from normal workshop tools. Flush-cutting end nippers are needed for trimming the fret ends; these can be made by carefully grinding down nippers that can be bought almost anywhere and which normally do not quite cut flush. The only problem with these is that the grinding can heat the metal and make it brittle. Some supply houses will sell specialist hammers for fretting the guitar, but I have been using a simple tack hammer ever since I started making guitars and it works for me. Files will also be needed and these are easily bought.

I also use a lot of good-quality masking tape, various grades of sandpaper and sanding blocks for any number of different tasks. I also use sharp knives for all sorts of jobs, and for neck shaping I tend to use spokeshaves, surforms and cabinet scrapers. The humble cabinet scraper is one of the finest tools ever invented and, if sharpened and used correctly, can save time in sanding and shaping. Scrapers can be bought, but the key to using them is to keep them sharp.

My trusty bending iron that is now well over thirty years old.

Smoothing plane.

A brand new bending iron; these can be expensive but will be safer to use than something home made.

This small plane was bought for me by an old friend at a vintage tool show and is very good for carving braces and the centre trim on the back.

Cabinet scrapers.

I am lucky that I have access to some excellent tools in the workshop, including a thickness sander, planer thicknesser, drill presses and belt sanders, but I do not actually own any of these – they come with the workshop that I rent. When I was starting out I used to ask nicely at various woodworking companies and small jobs were often done for me for just a donation to the company's coffee fund! Even so, these tools are labour-saving devices and whilst they are very good at what they do, all of these jobs can be done by hand if necessary. It just takes little longer and quite a bit more effort.

Useful stuff

One item that has proven very useful is a block of hardwood, in my case maple and wenge, which is about

Sharpening scrapers

You can get a very fine finish with a cabinet scraper, but the finish is dependent on the quality of the finish on the scraper itself. Curved and shaped scrapers will need a variation on the sharpening technique; the key is to prepare an edge on the scraper that is perfectly square to the face of the scraper, and to polish that.

Using a small block of wood to ensure the scraper stays square to the oilstone.

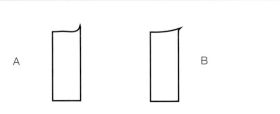

This exaggerated view helps explain what you are trying to do, firstly (A) make a small, sharp lip on the edge of the scraper and then (B) turn it so that it is facing in the direction you need to cut.

Start by filing if necessary and then polish on a fine oilstone so that the face and edge of the scraper are square to each other. They should be free from any deep scratches. One good tip in helping to keep the face and edge square is to use your oilstone in one of the wooden boxes sold to hold them, which usually have a lid. The scraper can be held on the edge of the stone and supported by the base and lid together, so that it is at 90 degrees to the stone.

Using a large diameter drill bit to produce the burr.

With the square end polished, a burr has to be made on one, or both, sides of the polished edge. There are tools sold for exactly this purpose but the handle of a chisel, the shaft of a large-diameter drill bit or the shank of a large screwdriver blade can also be used. The scraper is held so that the edge is supported over the side of the workbench or a lump of hardwood and the burnishing tool is run along the edge to create a burr. The burnisher needs to be moved across the edge as it is moved along, so that the edge of the scraper does not damage the burnisher.

The burr will now be formed but facing in the wrong direction, so it needs to be turned through 90 degrees. Again run the burnisher along the edge, this time attempting to turn the burr so that it is at 90 degrees to the flat face of the scraper, rather than being an extension of it as before.

Clearly, better-quality polishing of the scraper and using a better-quality burnisher will introduce less marks into the scraper and burr, and the resulting edge will produce a finer finish.

Turning the burr.

My very useful sanding stick that has been used for most things in the workshop although I have yet to train it to make coffee.

Cork sanding blocks are very useful; being slightly soft they have a little more give and so are useful for smoothing rather than shaping.

A small hardwood block with some sandpaper stuck on with double-sided tape can be very useful. This one is about 4 by 1 in (100 × 25 mm).

Hardwood sanding blocks with radiused faces are available for sanding fingerboards.

Odd bits of scrap wood can be used as clamping cauls or sanding blocks. I have several small boxes full of pieces like this.

3 in (77 mm) wide, 18 in (457 mm) long and about 1¹/₂ in (38 mm) thick. It has been planed totally flat on one face and has many uses: as a sanding block; for flattening and for shaping fingerboards; to level the top edges of the guitar sides before fitting tops; to knock things into position and as a neck support when fretting. I have also used it as a club to threaten guitars that do not behave as I think they should. This generally has no effect.

A neck support block made from an offcut of mahogany bandsawn to shape and padded with strips of masking tape.

End nippers. Very useful for cutting fret ends.

This small gouge is excellent for cutting truss rod recesses.

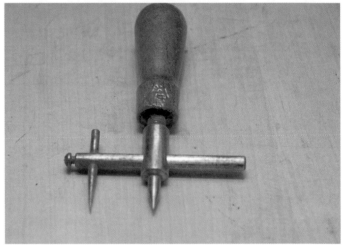

A circle cutter is useful for cutting soundholes or soundhole inlay channels. The blade is sharpened on both sides so that it can be used in either direction.

You will also need a supply of small pieces of wood, in various sizes, that can be used as clamping cauls. These prevent clamps marking the wood you are working on and help to even out the pressure on a glue join. I use a lot of pieces of scrap left over from guitar tops and backs, and also blocks of $1/2$ in (13 mm) and $1/4$ in 6 mm) plywood.

It is a good idea to cut a couple of blocks with a curved recess to support the back of the neck when the guitar is having its final set-up. The set-up will also require a few specialist tools.

Specialist tools

Cutting the nut can be done with specialist nut files, but can also be done with small needle files and saws. I also have a couple of cork sanding blocks that are not only very useful as sanding blocks but are also good for supporting necks as they are soft enough not to damage the wood of the neck.

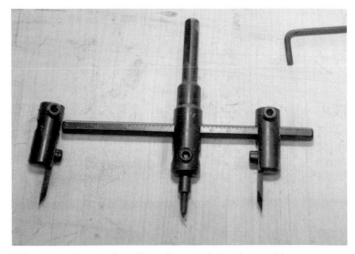

This circle cutter was found in a cheap tool store just as this book was in the final stages of production. It has a long reach and has two cutters, one for each direction.

Fret files are one specialist tool that most guitar makers seem unable to live without. They are available in a variety of sizes and styles.

A wooden-handled purfling cutter. These are based on old violin making instruments and, If used with care, can give excellent results.

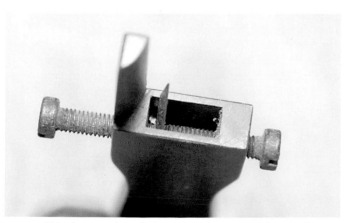

This close-up view of a brass-handled version of the purfling tool shows how the width of the cut can be altered. Two blades are included so that it can be used in both directions around the instrument, which is very useful in not splitting grain.

An alternative to the purfling cutter is to use a small router like this laminate trimmer. This has a very useful tilting base, seen here at 90 degrees to the cutter.

And also tilted to its maximum amount.

The other area where really specialist tools may be required is in finishing the guitar. It is possible to use brush finishes or even to French polish the guitar, but if it is going to be sprayed then it is important to use the correct equipment and to take adequate precautions in dealing with the material. Most paints and lacquers are not good for the respiratory system and some are highly poisonous, so spraying a guitar without adequate ventilation can be dangerous. In some countries it will be illegal to use some of the products mentioned in the book – if you are in any doubt then take professional advice or opt for something different. I have access to a properly ventilated spraybooth with efficient extraction and even so I would not consider using a two-pack lacquer without using a mask with a separate air supply and protective clothing.

With all tools one cannot stress safety too much. Any job will be much easier if the tools are used correctly and it is up to the person using them to ensure

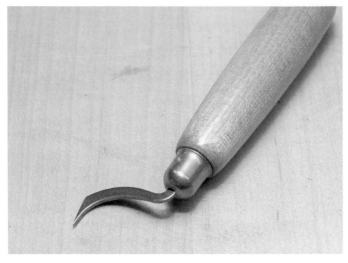

This hook was bought from Touchstone Tonewoods in England and is excellent for clearing waste from soundhole inlay channels.

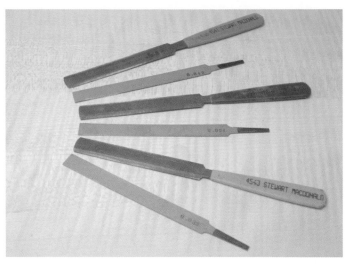

Nut files.

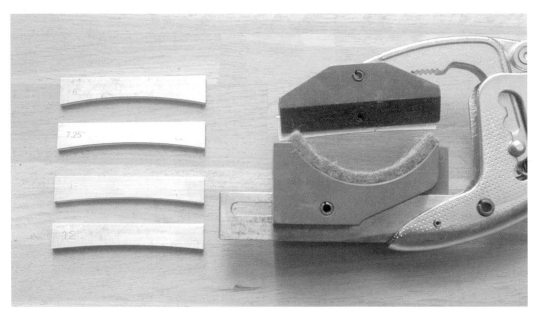

Stewart MacDonald sell this wonderful fret press, known as jaws. The clamping cauls are also available in a fitting that will go into a normal drill press and can be used as a fret arbour, to push them into the board. This makes for a very tidy job.

they know what they are doing. Tools used for any sort of cutting, such as planes and chisels, will work much better if they are sharpened correctly and are kept sharp. This will, obviously, make them more dangerous and maximum care should be exercised when using them. Again, if you have any doubts about your ability to use them, you should seek advice. There is no point in making your dream guitar if it costs you a couple of fingers! All tools are potentially dangerous but none will hurt you if you leave them alone; therefore the deciding factor is whether you choose to use them, and if you do, it is your responsibility to make sure you know what you are doing.

There are some excellent companies now selling tools and parts for guitar makers. Some of these are very simple and very useful, such as the flush-cutting end nippers used (*see* page 36) for trimming the ends of

frets after fitting, while others are much more elaborate. You could spend a lot of money on tools like this only to find that there are cheaper alternatives to do the job. One example is the laminate trimmer used to cut the channels around the edge of the guitar to fit the binding. This is a difficult job to set up on many machines as the back of the guitar is curved and rises and falls around its edge. There are specialist tools available and add-on fittings for other tools, all designed to do this job. However, I have found that with some careful setting up, a tilted base on a commercially available laminate trimmer works just as well as any of the specialised tools that I have seen, and was much, much cheaper. Having said that I would also not be without my tang nippers that I bought from Stewart MacDonald Guitar Shop Supply – a specialist tool that was not cheap but that has saved me a lot of time.

Fret tang cutters are a big timesaver when fretting bound fingerboards.

No prizes for guessing which company supply this excellent fretwire bender.

I will add just one final point. Whilst clever tools might help you get the job done more quickly and may make things a little easier, the job can still be done with basic hand tools. You do not need to use a router to cut the soundhole inlay, you do not need to use a thicknessing sander on the top, back and sides. These jobs can be done in other ways, so don't think that you have to spend a lot of money. You can get as much enjoyment and an equally good guitar if you do things more simply.

Workboards

I find these essential for any number of jobs. You can work directly on the surface of your bench, but I find that a good workboard is just easier. A workboard is also much easier to replace than a bench and so it doesn't really matter if you have to drill holes in it or if you rout into it. I use several that are made from 1.25 in (32 mm) MDF that is heavy enough not to move around when doing many jobs and is thick enough not to distort. These are usually about 3ft (915 mm) square, which gives ample space on which to work. Most of

Guitar moulds.

these will be described as the book progresses and there is nothing to stop you inventing your own.

JIGS AND MOULDS

You will also need a number of jigs and forms and there is one item that is essential: you will need to construct a mould to retain the shape of the guitar while you work on it. The guitar will remain in the mould while the sides are being worked on and up to the point where the top and back are glued on. The mould can be made from plywood, MDF or scrap wood, but it

MDF Warning

Medium Density Fibreboard (MDF) is not pleasant to work. When doing any woodwork you should protect yourself against dust, as breathing in wood dust is not good for you, but MDF is known to be especially nasty stuff and has been linked to some cancers. If you choose to use MDF you MUST ensure that you are working in a way that is safe and minimises your risk of exposure to harmful elements, a dust mask is the bare minimum. MDF can be substituted with other materials, and if you have any doubts about its safety you should not use it.

Cutting to a line

When cutting out the former – or if you are really brave and have a good bandsaw capable of the job – the entire mould, you need to cut very accurately to a line.

A good tip for this is to not try to follow the line. There will be some movement in the bandsaw blade and the blade does cut a small channel, usually somewhere in the region of $3/32$ in (2.3 mm). Therefore if you cut to the line, your cut can vary by this much as it will not be clear whether you are cutting right to the line, or the edges. You could then have as much as $3/16$ in (4.5 mm) difference in the shape of your mould.

If you cut to one edge of the line and align the saw blade with that, you will get a more accurate cut.

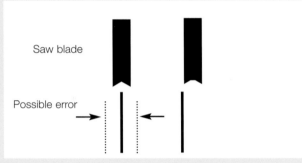

In the above diagram, the left hand saw blade is trying to cut to the line. The dotted lines show the amount of error possible whilst still cutting the line. The right hand example clearly shows that following the edge of the line will give a more accurate cut.

A ball-bearing follower bit was used to match the shape of the former on to the mould.

The guitar shape was first cut into a piece of $3/8$ in (10 mm) plywood and each of the six pieces of MDF that make up the mould were rough cut on the bandsaw.

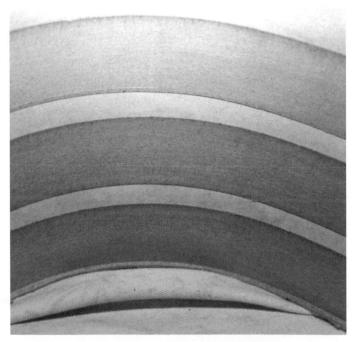

Two passes were needed to remove all of the waste, here the top two have been fully routed and the lower one still has a small ridge that can be sanded or routed away.

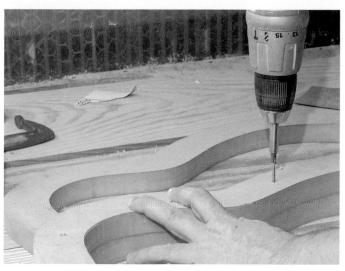

The mould pieces were carefully drilled, glued and screwed together, staggering the screw positions on the inner and outer laminates so that the screws did not touch each other.

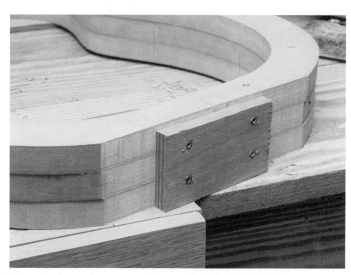

When dry, the ends were sawn to a straight line and end plates were fitted to hold the two halves together. These should not be glued as they need to be removed to split the two halves of the mould at various times.

will need to be accurate and symmetrical. It also needs to be at least 3 in (77 mm) thick as the sides need to be supported and kept vertical while the end blocks are glued in (*see* Chapter 8).

The mould in the photographs was made for the resonator guitar built in Chapter 24. This was built up from three pieces of 1 in (25 mm) MDF each side, making it a total depth of 3 in (77 mm).

The mould is made in two halves that are screwed together with endplates to make up an internal shape, it will need to be about 6 in (152mm) longer and 3 in (76mm) wider than one half of the guitar shape so the final mould can be cut leaving about 3 in (77 mm) all the way round to support the guitar. You could glue up two lots of four pieces of 3/4 in (19 mm) MDF and then bandsaw the shape out of them, but this requires a good bandsaw and accurate sawing. I find it easier to make up a master shape, of half of the guitar shape, from plywood and then use this as a router guide to make sure all the pieces are exactly the same. The former does need to be cut very accurately.

The shape of the guitar half is marked onto each piece of board, making sure they are all in the same position, and then cut out roughly on the bandsaw. The master piece is then screwed onto each piece and the final shape routed with a follower bit. When all have been done the pieces can be screwed and glued together to make the two halves.

Each guitar shape will need a mould of its own, but they are not particularly difficult to make.

Further jigs will be seen as the build chapters progress. These include jigs for sanding the sides to accept the back, cutting the arch on back braces and jigs for routing truss rod channels.

Chapter 4

Glue

There has been much debate over the last few years on the relative merits of different types of glue for use in guitar making. Some people will swear that only a traditionally prepared and applied hide glue should be used. There are certainly arguments for this over and above the mere tradition of the process. Hide glue is less likely to shrink and can be disassembled should the need arise, but it can be difficult to use and is not for the amateur. Pre-prepared hide glue can be obtained in plastic pots as an alternative, but the modern resin glues are very effective.

The most commonly encountered glue is Titebond; this a trade name for a yellow aliphatic resin glue produced by Franklin International. This is an excellent glue and easy to use but other companies make very similar products. Good-quality white glues can also be used although these tend to vary more in quality and strength than the yellow glues. In all cases your guitar parts supplier will normally carry stocks of glue and will be able to advise.

Most of these glues are water-soluble, so excess that squeezes out of the joins can be removed by wiping with a damp cloth. Waterproof versions are also available but it is not necessary to use them; they are designed for things that spend a lot of time immersed in water, such as boats, and they are no stronger than their non-waterproof counterparts. Also, they cannot be disassembled like the non-waterproof glues by using hot water and a palette knife to separate the pieces: once they are stuck it is permanent.

Epoxy

Some makers have suggested using epoxy glues on guitars. These are certainly very strong, but they are not ideal in all cases. The physical properties of the glue are different to those of the white and yellow resin glues, and they are not absorbed into the wood, but leave a film on either side of the join. This makes for a thicker glue line that can remain visible in some circumstances, such as when joining the sides of the top and back. Epoxies are also permanent and, as stated above, there may be times when you want to take your guitar apart.

Just some of the types of glue you can use on a guitar. Titebond original is a very good woodworking glue; the liquid hide glue is recommended by some makers who prefer the similarity to old hide glues. In the centre is a two-pack cyanoacrylate that uses an aerosol spray catalyst and, in the foreground, is a plastic cement that can be used to fix plastic bindings.

One time that epoxy can be used is if you decide to use a butt join on the neck (*see* page 27). This was recommended by David Russell Young in his book *The Steel Strung Guitar, Construction and Repair* (The Bold Strummer Ltd, 1987) which is well worth reading. He argues that a guitar with an epoxied, butt-joined neck will be at least as strong and probably stronger than a guitar with a dovetail.

Some people react badly to epoxies, which can cause irritation and skin problems. In all cases, read the manufacturer's safety information and, if necessary, wear disposable rubber gloves when gluing. Epoxy can be difficult to remove from where it has squeezed from joins, but often a damp cloth will suffice. Cleaning

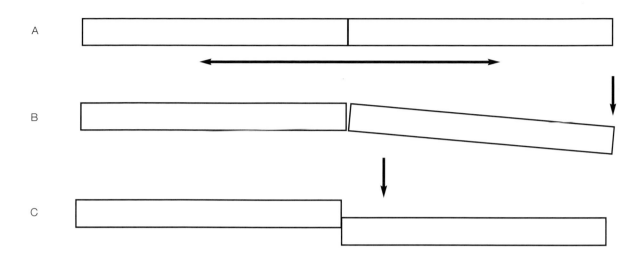

residue on hands should be done with plenty of soap and water.

Cyanoacrylate

For other applications there are a number of glues that are very useful. Superglue (cyanoacrylate) can be very useful for a number of tasks, so long as you appreciate its properties and limitations. It cannot be used for structural work as it has good tensile strength but limited shear strength, so whilst you may be able to pull on a join and not break it, you can usually twist it apart. This makes it ideal for things such as top nuts that do require to be removed from the guitar from time to time; fixing them in place with cyano will hold them perfectly well, but a sharp blow from a hammer onto a piece of wood held next to the nut will break the join and should not damage the wood underneath, which would be the case if something like epoxy were used.

There are several types of cyanoacrylate available, with some being more liquid than others. In some cases they do not work well on porous surfaces, such as wood, unless the surface has been dampened with a moist cloth. They require limited clamping but they will bond to organic material and this, of course, includes you. Therefore great care must be taken not to get covered in the stuff, as you can find yourself attached to all manner of things. The glue does give off fumes so it is also essential that you wear eye protection when using cyanoacrylates, as injuries to the eyes can be very severe if the glue is accidentally splashed into them.

GENERAL GLUING TIPS

Some woods take better to being glued than others. Rosewood, for example, is very oily so wiping the area to be joined with some alcohol or spirit can remove some of the oil and make the glue join a little stronger,

In the diagram above, A represents tensile strength. Superglues are very good in this respect. B shows bending strength and C shows shear strength. Superglues are less good in this respect but this is useful when gluing parts that may need to come apart, such as top nuts.

but the spirit must be allowed to evaporate fully before gluing starts.

Some schools of thought suggest that faces should be scuffed before gluing to give a greater area for the glue to work on. This is a long-established practice, but there are positive and negative aspects to it. Scuffing the surface will produce dust that, far from helping the join, will harm it. Many modern glues are designed to work on flat surfaces, so scuffing them means that slightly less of the surface is in direct contact. Some years ago I read a US Department of Forestry report on scuffing before gluing that concluded that in most applications it was not necessary and had no benefits over conventional gluing. Whilst preparing this book I have searched for a reference to this and failed to find it!

If the two pieces you are going to glue are properly prepared they will be close-fitting with no gaps. The glue will then form a very thin layer between the two parts. It is important that the glue layer is uniform, and not too thick or too thin. Spreading the glue as evenly as possible before assembling the pieces will help, and a careful watch while clamping the pieces will show some glue seeping out of the join. This is a good thing: seepage shows that the glue has penetrated the whole area of join and may also show if your clamping is uneven! It is important not to use too much pressure when gluing – you do not want to squeeze all of the glue from the join. As long as the two pieces are firmly held and not slipping they should be fine. Overclamping may also distort or damage the wood.

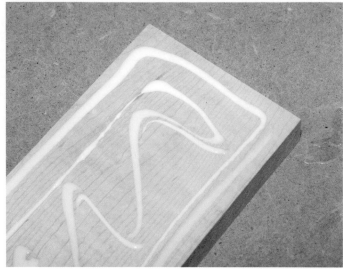

A little glue can go a long way. This is more than enough to give a thin film over the entire surface.

Using some cellulose thinners on this piece of rosewood shows how much oil can be lifted off in one pass.

This neck laminate was glued with veneers between the laminates. A thin film was put onto one surface for each join.

TEMPERATURE AND GLUE

Some glues do not react well to changes in temperature. Epoxies, and other glues to a lesser extent, tend to get very thick when it is cold, and hard to mix. In an ideal world this will never matter as you would have a temperature-controlled workplace with ideal conditions for woodwork all year round, but in the real world – the one that most of us inhabit – this is not always the case. If it is really cold it is not a good idea to be gluing anything, as the properties of the glue may be affected. When it is too warm the glue may be easier to spread, but it may also harden and become unuseable far more quickly.

Glue residue

It is important to clean excess glue from around the joins before it sets. Once it has set it is not only far more difficult to remove, but can also damage the

Using a damp paper towel to remove the glue that has seeped out from under a bridge.

Cutting a drinking straw at an angle.

wood. The glue is, after all, designed to grip the wood, and chipping a chunk of set glue from around a join can take small pieces of wood with it.

Most glues can be cleaned up with a damp rag. This should not be too wet, but just damp enough to lift the glue. Several passes may be required and this will get rid of the majority of the glue. However, some may remain in the corners of joins; this is particularly the case when gluing the top braces. Getting right into the corners can be difficult, so scraping the glue away is a good idea. The best tool for this is the humble drinking straw. These can be cut to make a scoop that will get right into the corner and pull out the glue. It is then a simple job to clean the rest with a damp cloth or paper towel. Once the glue is set, the area around the join may still need a little light sanding to remove the final evidence.

Using the straw to get into the angle between the brace and the back and remove the glue. A light wipe with a damp paper towel may be all that is needed to clean this completely.

Chapter 5
Wood

A maple tree.

As you get further into making an acoustic guitar, it becomes clear that it is a very complex and interesting instrument. It is structurally very light but possesses a lot of strength. This is down to how the instrument has evolved, and the choice of wood plays a big part in this.

The wood that you chose to make your guitar from will not only determine how it will sound, but will also affect how easy it is to make.

The back and sides of the guitar provide some structural rigidity to support the top but also act as soundwoods in their own right, influencing the tone of the guitar. There have been, and always will be, arguments about just how *much* they effect the sound but the type of wood *will* make some difference. Some people have claimed that the back of the guitar does little for the sound other than act as a reflector for the soundwaves to propel them out of the soundhole. However, all the parts of the guitar vibrate, the back included, so it is logical to deduce that it has an affect on the sound, even if that is only to dissipate some of the strings' energy, although the density of the wood does seem to have an effect on how the sound is projected from the guitar.

The top of the guitar is traditionally made of a soft-wood such as spruce although all-mahogany guitars have been made, such as Gibson's LGO, and makers have also used woods such as koa for tops. They are not to everyone's taste, although I have played several guitars with hardwood tops that are really very pleasant, and in the main softwood is normally used.

SOURCING THE WOOD

The popularity of guitar making has meant that it is now far easier to get the right woods than it was twenty or thirty years ago. Back in the bad old days you would need to not only find your source of wood but quite possibly have it cut to size or do that yourself. Now specialist instrument makers suppliers take all the hard work out of this. Guitar tops, backs and sides, necks and fingerboards can be bought easily and relatively cheaply. (If you have any doubt about this, try sourcing the wood yourself and having it cut!)

Suppliers will also gladly advise you about what is best for your project. You can buy the most expensive woods they have but for a first guitar this is not sensible. For a first guitar it is not necessary to buy the very best materials. Remember that you are more likely to make mistakes on your first instrument and those mistakes are easier to bear when they are not causing too much damage to your bank balance. We have already covered that a well-made guitar from average materials will sound every bit as good and perhaps better than a badly made one from good materials. Many cheap guitars made in the 1930s sounded excellent!

Because the wood for the guitar made in Chapter 21 was reclaimed from small boards and sawn, there is some rising grain in the top which is shown by the different reflection of light from one side to the other.

Just a small part of the stock of tops at Touchstone Tonewoods in England.

TOPS

Ideally, the top should be inspected before buying but this is not always possible. Not everyone has the luxury of a guitar parts supplier within easy reach and so it is sometimes necessary to buy from a distance. All of the companies that I know of will do their utmost to provide the best possible parts or wood for the budget that is available. However, you must let them know what you are after. There is no point expecting a high quality top if you are only willing to spend minimum money. Also you should let the supplier know what type of guitar you will be making. There is no point buying any old guitar top if you want to make a large-bodied guitar. You can well find your top being not big enough and this wastes time and money, equally you do not want to buy a nice wide piece of wood and waste a large amount of it. As just stated, don't buy the very best, they will have often have lesser quality wood that is perfectly acceptable, and some people chose to cut their own tops, backs and sides or even use reclaimed wood. It is also not essential that you have a two-piece top, many fine violins are made with three or four-piece tops and they sound great.

One of the better-known instrument wood suppliers in the UK, and an old friend, is David Dyke who not only converts his own wood but will also buy ready-cut wood from larger suppliers that might not normally be available to the smaller volume maker. Dave very generously gave me considerable time, and a nice lunch, while I was preparing this chapter.

I could give my own opinions but they are just that, opinions, so I will leave most of the information in here to Dave as he has a wealth of experience not just as a supplier but also as a maker himself.

"When I buy soundboards they are often already cut and have been graded. If I look at a pile of tops that are listed as top grade often only about 5–10 per cent of that wood is actually top grade. The problem is that some suppliers simply have too much wood to look at and so time is a factor. You can often find top grade tops in the next grade down and they will be considerably cheaper.

What you are looking for in a top is stiffness across the board and straight grain. Split tops will be better. Splitting the wood ensures the grain is as parallel to the face of the board as possible. Not everyone splits the wood as it is time consuming and more wasteful but sawing tops can mean the grain rises and falls. This is evident on a top as the light will reflect differently from each side. Think of a mown lawn, or one of the tennis courts at Wimbledon. Although the grass is all one colour, they will appear to be striped as the mowing machine will lay the grass in alternate directions and the light will reflect differently. It is the same with wood. If the grain is slightly diagonal through the board then each side will reflect the light slightly differently and this will show as a change in colour.

David Dyke preparing to split a top from a western red cedar log.

The splitting tool is a knife blade at 90 degrees to the handle and this is hit enthusiastically with a large hammer to split the wood.

Looking down the freshly split top.

Surfacing the split face of the board.

Since the surfaced side was split any saw cut will now be parallel with the grain.

The freshly cut top ready to go into stock.

Medullary rays on a sitka spruce top.

A rough cut spruce soundboard. There is some minor damage but this is not deep and will be lost in thicknessing.

If you hold the two halves of the top with the light behind you and tilt them you may see a slight change in colour between the sides that will not be evident when you look at them directly.

This can also cause problems when making the guitar. On a split top it should be possible to plane in either direction. A sawn top may have some rising grain and so the plane will be fine in one direction but will lift the grain when planing in the other direction. This is not so much of a problem if you are able to drum sand the top, but hand planing is going to be the way most people have to go.

Stiffness across the top is easy to judge as slightly flexing each piece will show that some are stiffer than others. A good sign is to look for medullary rays, these run perpendicular to the grain and are a good sign. If you can see these, the top will be as stiff as possible.

You also need to look for anything that might ruffle the surface, like fluffy grain. This can deaden the top but you can also test for this quite simply by tapping the top. Hold it in your fingers at a point about one third of its length and on the edge and tap it with your knuckles. If it is sparkly and bright sounding it will probably make a good top."

TYPES OF WOOD GENERALLY USED FOR TOPS

Dave Dyke recommends Sitka spruce for steel string guitars but not really for nylon-string ones as it is a dense and strong wood and takes more energy to get it vibrating properly. It is still available in large pieces but is getting 'worryingly endangered'. An alternative is European spruce; this is sometimes known as German spruce although it is not generally grown there but is processed there. This is generally grown at higher altitudes, close to the tree line, and in Switzerland it is a managed wood. Dave Dyke says that it seems to work well with most types of instrument and seems to be more responsive than Sitka spruce and so for a light finger picking style guitar it would probably be better, with Sitka being better for a harder, strummed sound.

Yellow cedar can also be good as can Adirondac spruce, which is sometimes known as red spruce. It is probably easier to find in the US but European makers are finding it in short supply. Another American wood that can be superb, if you can get it, is redwood. This not only sounds superb and is good to work but also has a great colour.

Bearclaw figuring.

Woods that are much easier to obtain include Douglas fir, which will make good guitar tops except that it is prone to developing resin spots as it ages. These do not alter the sound of the wood but look unsightly, although if you were making a guitar that was to be finished in a solid colour this may be fine. The wood is cheap and good quality.

Western red cedar is also a good choice for tops. Since it is available in large sizes and is naturally straight-grained it splits very well and has consistent grain. It is a good choice for a first guitar as it planes well, but it is easily dented or marked if knocked. If you are careful it can make very good guitar tops and is quite cheap compared to some other woods.

Bearclaw

Bearclaw is a disturbance in the grain that is often quite sought after for guitar tops. It generally goes across the grain and can vary in appearance. It can take the form of short marks across the grain or it can look like clouds. It is also not always symmetrical. David Dyke is characteristically honest when he says "I am perfectly

Quarter Sawn

Quarter sawn is a term used a lot in guitar-making literature but is often slightly misunderstood.

Wood is at its strongest when the growth rings run through the plank in the same direction of any load. If the growth rings in the wood are perpendicular to the face of the plank, the fibres will be arranged in such a way that they sit above each other and will be stronger than if they are parallel to the face of the plank.

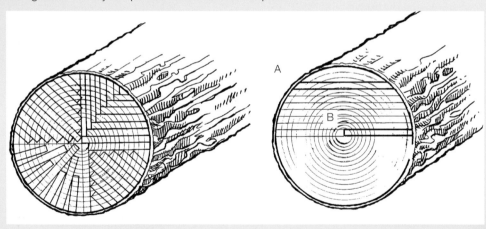

The diagram on the left shows three versions of quarter sawing. It can be seen this is quite wasteful and needs careful setting up, which is expensive in time. Through and through sawing produces planks that are slab sawn (A) and quarter sawn (B). This is a far more economical way to saw the log.

Quarter sawing a log produces the maximum amount of wood with the grain perpendicular to one face of the plank but is wasteful. Most woodyards chose not to cut in this way but simply slice through the log, known as slab sawing. This does produce some wood with the growth rings perpendicular to one face of the plank but it also produces a lot with growth rings running in all other directions.

In general guitar making, quarter sawn is more often used to describe the quality of the grain in any one piece of wood rather than to refer to how it was cut. If the growth rings run perpendicular to one face of the board, it is generally called quarter sawn.

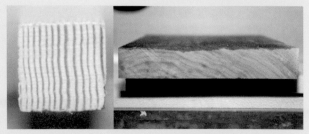

The wood on the left has the growth rings running vertically and would normally be referred to as 'quarter sawn' while the wood on the right clearly shows the grain at various angles to the surfaces.

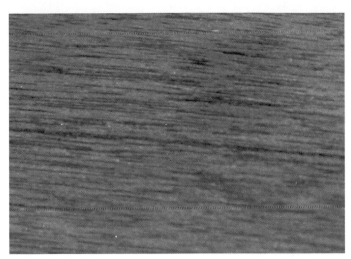

Good quality mahogany can be hard to find but is a pleasure to work. Alternatives, many of them very good, are available.

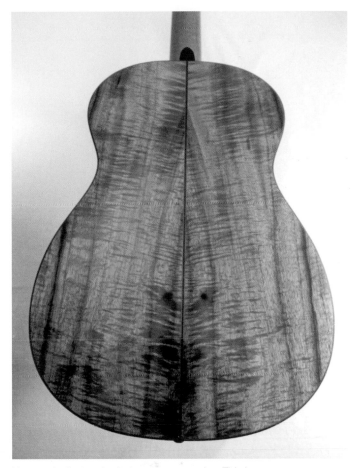

Koa can look stunning but can be expensive. This is on a Goodall guitar.

Indian rosewood. Backs and sides are sold as sets but it is wise to sort and get a good match.

happy to accept it makes the best tops but I have no idea how it forms." What is does appear to do is stiffen the board across the grain and that is a good thing.

BRACING

The wood used for bracing is traditionally the same as for the top although this does not need to be the case. I tend to use Douglas fir as it is easy to get close grained and straight pieces. David Dyke recommends that bracings should be from split wood rather than sawn for the same reasons as for the top. Bracings should also be quarter sawn and guitars traditionally have the grain running vertically through the brace, although Lute makers have the grain parallel with the top.

One wood that has been used successfully, but is now under threat, is cocobolo. It is a nicely figured wood that makes good guitars but beware, like some other woods, for example paduak, the excellent colour it has when first cut will change. Some woods will alter in colour due to light or exposure to air. Cocobolo does change to a deep brown and remains a good looking wood.

Flame maple and sycamore have always been favouites.

Quilted maple will be expensive and can be hard to work.

BACKS AND SIDES

Backs and sides can be made from a variety of woods. It is very important that the sides are quarter sawn. Flat sawn sides will simply not stay flat when they are bent and they may take on a cupped shape. Slab sawn wood is also more likely to shrink across its width and this is far from ideal!

For many years the accepted woods for guitar back and sides were rosewood, mahogany and, to a lesser extent, maple. Trade embargoes to protect certain species have meant that some woods are almost impossible to find and those woods that do get legally released for sale can be extremely expensive. Rio rosewood is one example. Many very fine guitars have been made of this over the years and it also looks superb but it is now hard to find. The downside of this is that not only is it difficult, and in some cases illegal, to get but you cannot get the quality that was available years ago. This makes alternative woods even more viable.

As Dave Dyke says, "Indian rosewood is an alternative that has also been used for years and supplies are still good. It can also be good value but it has to be dried properly. It is very dense and so any deviation in the grain after the guitar is built can lead to the wood bending or cracking the struts as the forces in the wood will be so great. It has enormous potential for tension if it is not properly dried. It is a very bright and lively wood and if you run it through your fingers you can sometimes hear it 'sing'."

Mahogany is now also not as straightforward as it once was. Honduras mahogany is now hard to find and expensive. Apart from being a good wood tonally, it is also relatively easy to work. There are a number of other woods in the mahogany family and not all of these share the same characteristics. As Dave Dyke says "It is important to know your mahoganies as there are so many variations. It is best to choose something that is easy to work

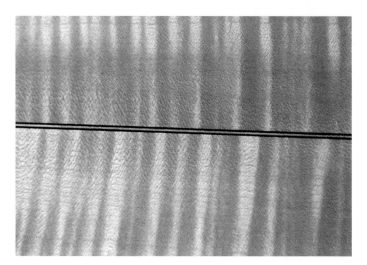

Backs are usually bookmatched so that the grain mirrors.

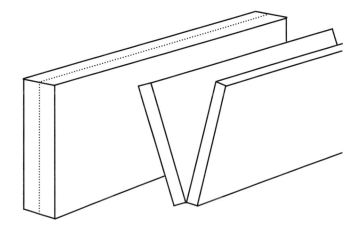

Bookmatching is achieved by cutting the wood and opening out the two halves as if they were a book.

Flame

There is no doubt that figured woods can make very attractive guitars. They can, however, add a level of complexity that is not suitable for a first timer. The problem comes because of how the figure is formed in the wood. The most common form of figure seen on instruments is a flame across the grain; this can happen in many different woods and as I write this my own acoustic that has a nice flamed mahogany neck, is just a few feet away. Maple and sycamore can often have very impressive flame and it is necessary to understand how the flame affects the wood.

We have seen that rising or falling grain on a top can alter the apparent colour as the light reflects differently off the grain and this is the case with a flame. It is best to think of flame as a slight waviness in the grain. The grain will not rise and fall much and so may be completely contained by the thickness of the side for a light flame, but if it is a wild flame it may amount to almost diagonal grain through the side which can weaken it. Bending flame maple sides can be done, but it must be done with care and is usually best after some experience.

The edge of this board of quilted maple clearly shows the waviness of the grain.

and is not endangered. African mahoganies can be a little furry and that tends to make a deader sounding guitar, although sometimes still very useable. This can also make it more difficult to work; some mahoganies do not plane well and work better if thickness sanded."

One of the mahogany family that I have used is sapele. Sapele can also have a very nice colour, often starting out looking very red but changing to a deep brown as it is exposed to light, but you have to choose it very carefully. It is subject to interlocked grain, where the fibres seem to go in all directions at once, and this can make it very difficult to bend.

There are alternative woods and some of these can be surprisingly nice, not just in terms of how they look but also how they work and sound. Dave Dyke's current favourite is walnut. It is very easy to bend and comes in a variety of colours and the grain can often be stunning. Cherry is also good but it is hard to find pieces big enough for two-piece backs although this does not have to be a problem as multi pieces can be used.

Whatever wood is chosen Dave says "If I am choosing sides they *have* to be perfect. What may be acceptable on a back is not going to be acceptable in the sides. The grain needs to be even, straight and have no knots. For a first guitar I would recommend straight mahogany or maple or walnut if you can get it. Avoid the temptation of buying figured woods, especially maple (*see* box) as they can produce a whole new set of problems. Also be prepared to try unusual woods if they have the right characteristics." For the 12-string in Chapter 22, Dave supplied me with pearwood which has been excellent.

Rosewood, mahogany, maple and walnut backs and sides at David Dyke's.

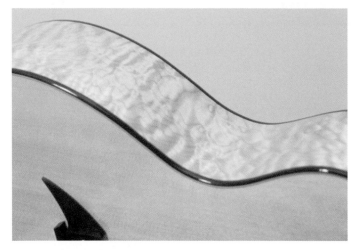

Quilted maple sides can look stunning but will be difficult to bend, and expensive if you break one bending it.

Brazilian cedar neck blanks at Touchstone Tonewoods.

This maple neck laminate, with a subtle flame, was found in a pile of boards sold for building work proving that it is always worth searching any stocks as good wood often turns up.

NECKS

Finding good wood for necks depends on how it is cut and used. For one-piece necks the favoured wood was Brazilian mahogany. "Brazilian was wonderful and is now not available; they were big trees and so it was easy to get perfectly quarter-sawn and straight wood. Now other woods are often used. Spanish cedar is often used as a replacement for mahogany, and maple and walnut are very good too." I have also used Douglas fir which is cheap and plentiful and has a good stiffness to weight ratio. Because of the way the tree grows, it is often easer to find maple with the grain more suited to making vertically laminated necks. For a first guitar a laminated neck is the best option, using one of the mahoganies, walnut or maple.

FINGERBOARDS

Fingerboards are normally rosewood or ebony. The dense black of a good ebony board is visually very good. Dave Dyke recommends not scrimping on the board. You need to find something that is quartered and has a straight grain. It also needs to be hard enough to take the wear and to hold the frets. Brazilian rosewood, long favoured by makers, is now very hard to find as it is a threatened species but there are alternatives. As for the sides, Indian rosewood can be used and some of the other rosewoods, such as Mexican rosewood, and ebony alternatives such as Macassar ebony are available.

BRIDGES

Bridges are usually made from the same materials as the fingerboard and they need to be dense to transfer the vibration of the string to the top effectively. Most wood suppliers will cut blanks from the same wood as the fingerboards; the waste from the fingerboard cutting is often ideal for bridges and so supplies should not be a problem.

DRYING

There are stories that the violin-maker Stradivarius used to choose his wood by tapping the trunks of spruce trees to see which trees sounded best. This is absolute tosh. A tree, like many other living things, contains a significant amount of water. Tapping on the trunk of a living tree will tell you precisely nothing

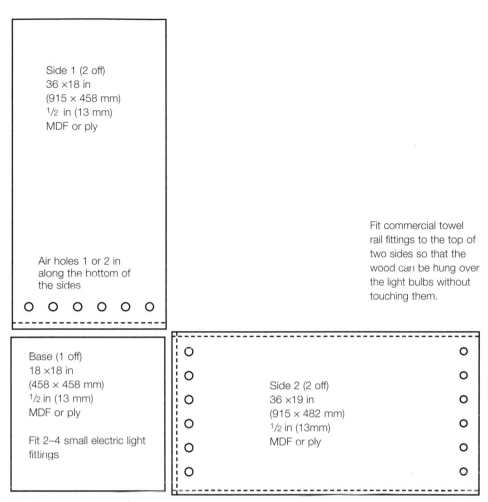

Side 1 (2 off)
36 ×18 in
(915 × 458 mm)
1/2 in (13 mm)
MDF or ply

Air holes 1 or 2 in
along the bottom of
the sides

Fit commercial towel
rail fittings to the top of
two sides so that the
wood can be hung over
the light bulbs without
touching them.

Base (1 off)
18 ×18 in
(458 × 458 mm)
1/2 in (13 mm)
MDF or ply

Fit 2–4 small electric light
fittings

Side 2 (2 off)
36 ×19 in
(915 × 482 mm)
1/2 in (13mm)
MDF or ply

A drying box is easy to make. Simply make an open ended box with holes around the base to allow air to circulate and fit several small low-wattage light bulbs on the base. The sizes quoted here are not definitive; 36 in height should be enough for most guitar sides to hang without touching the light bulbs and the width just needs to be enough to allow air to circulate around all of the parts being dried. Remember that in some countries it may be mandatory to have an electrician check all installations.

about the wood inside, and all you will learn is that you can hurt your knuckles assaulting trees with your fists.

Because trees are full of water, the wood needs to be dried. In times gone by this would be done by storing the planks for years while the water naturally evaporated. This is known as air drying and is obviously not very economical as if you dry your wood for, let us say, ten years, then you not only need to hold ten years worth of stock, but also need to estimate what the demand will be in future years.

Commercially, wood is usually dried in a kiln, which accelerates the drying and allows the process to be controlled. Not all the water is removed, as completely dry wood would crack and split, so about 8–10 per cent moisture remains.

Another alternative is vacuum drying where the air is pumped out of the container holding the wood and, as the pressure drops, the moisture in the wood boils away due to the boiling point of any liquid falling as the pressure is reduced. This is an expensive way of doing

things but it works very well, particularly with woods that are not as suited to kiln drying. Maple, for example, is very dense and in a kiln the outside tends to dry before the inside, with the outside 'case hardened'. The difference in tension between the outer and inner can cause distortion when the plank is split open. Larger pieces are also quite hard to dry. Vacuum drying works the other way, with the internal moisture getting released more effectively and so vacuum drying can make for a more stable wood.

DIY DRYING

It is possible that you may not choose to buy your wood already cut or you may have concerns about its seasoning, but drying wood yourself is not a great problem and is fairly straightforward. Dave Dyke says that "If it does not move after you have sawn it, it should be OK, but it will need time to stabilise nevertheless." However, you might want to be doubly sure, even with wood you have bought ready cut, and there are ways you can dry wood at home.

One way is to hang the wood over a radiator. Ideally it should be between two halves of a radiator and suspended so that there is free air around it and the heating is not just from one side. Air circulation is very important. It is possible the wood might move but this will be a sign that it was probably not that good anyway; if the wood is good, it should take to being dried like this.

It is also not necessary to dry sides like this, only the tops and back will need it as the sides will get wet when they are bent and the act of bending will dry the sides.

It is possible to make a simple drying box. Since the sides will not need drying the box can be made just deep enough to dry the top and back. Make a box from thick plywood or MDF (*see* above) that is open on the top and has several low wattage light bulbs at the bottom. There will also need to be holes around the bottom to allow air to enter and circulate upwards as it heats.

Humidity can be a problem when drying wood and so a small de-humidifier in the room is not a bad idea, although it is possible to get small crystal dehumidifier that would fit inside the bottom of a light bulb-heated drying box. These are available from hardware stores and pull a surprising amount of moisture from the air.

As a rough guide, a freshly cut top from a new log would need about a week of drying in this manner; backs would need longer as the wood is denser. It is important that you check regularly to ensure that things are not getting too hot; light bulbs can produce a lot of heat.

In all cases, it is easier to dry woods that have already been cut so do not be tempted to buy a piece of wood to cut your backs and sides from and dry it before it is cut; you will get a better result if the wood is dried in smaller pieces.

Air drying sycamore at David Dyke's. There is nothing to stop you doing this at home if you have the time.

Chapter 6

Tops

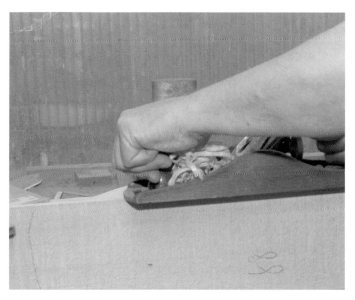

Planing the edges of the top prior to gluing.

Holding the join up to daylight will show where it will need more attention.

One of the annoying things about making acoustic guitars is that there are many small things that need to be glued and it is often necessary to wait while things dry out. On the other hand, one of the enjoyable things about making acoustic guitars is that there are so many small things that need to be glued that you can leave something and get on with another part of the guitar while you are waiting. So even the downside of making acoustic guitars has a good side!

This means there is no real order to how you make most of the guitar. You do not start with the top, then make the back, then the sides and so on, but you get as far as you can on one piece before having to wait for something to dry. Then, while waiting, you can do another part of the guitar. To write a book like this would be incredibly complicated and confusing, so I am dividing the parts of the guitar into separate chapters, but I would urge anyone reading the book to be a little flexible.

I normally start with the top. There is no pressing reason for this; it is just habit on my part and makes no difference to the guitar. But it is generally not very long

before I am also working on the back, the sides and so on. You could start with the sides, or the back, or the neck. In fact, pretty much the only thing that you cannot actually begin a guitar with is the finish.

THE TOP

The design work so far has concentrated on the overall shape of the top, where and what size the soundhole will be, where the bridge will end up, roughly where the bracings will be and how they will interact. Putting it all together to make a top is where the fun starts and we also start thinking a little more deeply about how the parts of the guitar work together.

The first stage is to examine the top for quality and grain direction. This will be very important as you come to work on it. The relative straightness of the wood should also be assessed: if the top has warped it should not be used as no amount of bracing is going to remove the warp. If you have not started work on it then you should be able to return it to the supplier.

57

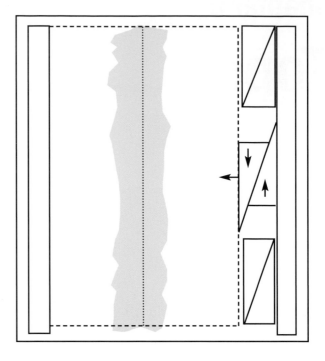

A diagram of the top gluing board. The top is represented by the dotted lines, the centre line sits over the area that has been waxed and the wedges apply pressure to the edges of the board as they are pushed apart.

Using a household candle to wax the area of the join to stop the top from sticking to the workboard.

If the wood is straight it needs to be joined. Tops are generally two-piece bookmatched. When opened out, the grain pattern should match on both sides. All tops will show some difference in the number of grain lines across the top from one side to the other, and they should be joined so that the closest grain lines are in the centre.

The sides should be held together and placed in a vice so that the joining surface can be planed. It is important that this is done accurately and the join is both flat and square to the face of the board. It is easy to remove too much from one end or the centre, and joining wood like this will cause problems and may lead to a split in the guitar top at a later date.

Some makers recommend sanding the edges of the boards to get them flat, by fixing sandpaper to a flat board and pushing the pieces along to get the edges straight. There are some good points about this, but it is necessary to keep the pieces vertical and to avoid rocking them as they are moved. It is all too easy to introduce a curve into the edge that should be straight by using too much pressure at one end of the board. Sanding the edges can also introduce dust into the join. If using this method it is a good idea to wipe the edges of the board with a damp cloth to remove the dust and let them dry out before gluing.

As the edges of the board are planed, or sanded, the join can be held together and held up to the light. It will be obvious where any gaps are.

Once a near-perfect mating has been achieved the top can be joined. It will need to be under some pressure while the glue dries, but too much pressure can compress the top or squeeze the glue out of the join so that it is dry and does not bond properly. The best way to join a top for a novice is to use a workboard. The centre of the board, where the glue line will lie, should be coated with wax; this is to stop the top from sticking to the workboard. Using an ordinary candle as a drawing stick will achieve this nicely, and it will be evident when the entire area is covered. A bar should also be fixed to the workboard – preferably with screws so that it can be removed for other work to be done on the same board – so that it lies along the outer side of the top when the centre is aligned with the waxed area. Small wedges should also be made by taking a piece of thin hardwood, $1/4 \times 4 \times 2$ in ($6 \times 100 \times 50$ mm), cut diagonally across its centre.

This will make two wedges that when forced together will expand and can be used to press the two sides of the top together. Make at least three sets of these.

Another bar can be screwed to the board so that is about 1 in (25.4 mm) outside the outer edge of the other half of the side.

One side should then be placed on the board against the first bar and with the inside edge safely over the

Tapping the wedges together to apply pressure to the top. It is important not to apply too much and force the top to bend. Just enough to make the glue seep from the join is sufficient.

waxed line. If it extends past the wax it will stick to the board so make sure enough wax is in place. The other side can then have thin bead of glue added along the edge before it is placed on the workboard. Both sides will need to be held down onto the board so that they do not flex, but not so hard that they will not move under the pressure of the wedges.

The wedges can then be inserted into place and forced together until some glue can be seen seeping out of the join. If the glue does not seep there is either not enough pressure or not enough glue, or your join was not very good. Do not force all the glue out of the line, but just let it begin seeping.

When all of the wedges are in place the top join should be showing a little glue seepage along its whole length. This can then be cleaned off with a damp cloth or sponge and set aside until the glue is set, which is usually overnight. It is, however, advisable to keep an eye on this to make sure that nothing moves and the wedges remain in place, and tightly wedged.

Another way of achieving the same result is to position the top on the board with a small strip of wood beneath the join. While this is in place, put small nails along the edges so they hold the board lightly together. When the strip of wood is removed, and the centre pressed down, the nails exert pressure on the sides and hold the join together. The thickness of the wood strip will determine how high the centre is held off the board before gluing and how much pressure is exerted. If the sides of the board appear to be under too much pressure, for example if they are trying to flex, then use a thinner piece of wood. A dry run of things is essential. Once the right amount of pressure has been determined, the join can be glued and the centre weighted to hold it down while the glue dries. Remember, of course, to wax the board under the join before you apply glue.

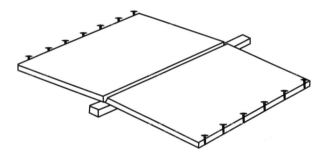

The centre batten method of clamping a top or back. This is very simple but does need careful setting up as the sides may try to buckle when the batten is removed if the batten is too thick. I find that $1/2$ in (13mm) is usually sufficient, but do a trial run first.

The top also needs to be checked to make sure it is sitting flat on the workboard for its whole length and that both sides are aligned with no high or low points.

If one side is slightly thicker than the other, which can happen if they are rough cut, one side may be slightly proud of the other, but as long as the underside of both pieces is flat on the workboard and the step is even this is not a problem, as the step can be removed when the top is thicknessed. Most guitar tops are cut to be quite thick and getting a finished top of the correct thickness is possible. The top for the electro-acoustic guitar in Chapter 23 was quite rough-looking, having been in store at home for ages. This looked pretty rough after it had been glued, but when thicknessed proved to be really good.

A particularly uneven top could be roughly evened before being glued. However, it is not wise to completely thickness the two halves before they are glued

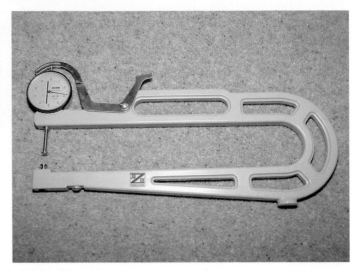

A measuring gauge. A simple one such as this will only be good enough to check the edges and so is fine on tops and backs that have been through a thicknesser, but a longer reach one will be needed if you are thicknessing by hand.

Most guitar parts suppliers will sell something like this thicknessing gauge.

Sanding the board on the 12-string guitar in Chapter 22.

as there will may be a little unevenness in the gluing; removing this may make the top too thin.

When the top is finally dry, it needs to be thicknessed. As already discussed this is done quickest using a thicknessing sander, but if you do not have access to one of these it will need to be thicknessed by hand.

TOP THICKNESS

Guitar tops vary in thickness from 0.1 in (2.5 mm) to 0.15 in (3 mm). This figure will vary with the type of wood used for the top and with the qualities of the particular piece of wood chosen. The top can be thicknessed by hand, but if it is possible to get access to a commercial sanding machine the task will be much easier and much more accurate.

Beware of people who tell you that tops should alter in thickness so that the centre is thinner than the edges. It is all too easy to measure a guitar top and assume that a slight decrease in thickness at the edge was intentional and that the designer or maker had had this in mind. I have heard people quoting exact thicknesses that should be aimed for and this is total rubbish. As we have already seen, quoting the figure for one piece of wood will not be correct for another.

One also has to consider why the top may be thinner at the edges. If this difference it not great it could be simply that the edges got more sanding as the bindings were sanded down flush with the top!

However, some people have taken complete guitars and have sanded the edges down and are convinced they have made them sound better. They may well have done so, but it can also be that they expect to make them sound better and so are convinced they do – a sort of 'Emperor's New Clothes' state of affairs – and it may just be that removing the finish from the top has made the difference. The finish is something we will come to later and which can have a definite effect on the guitar.

The top is already thin, so planing it is going to be difficult. It will need to be held to prevent it sliding across the workbench as it is thicknessed, but this may be difficult. Putting a stop on the workbench may not work as the stop would need to be very low to prevent it being hit by the plane, so it may be too low for the top to actually sit against it rather than rising up and over it. The top is also very thin and so may buckle while it is being planed, which can cause all sorts of problems and may even cause it to break. One way around this is to clamp the top to a thick workboard.

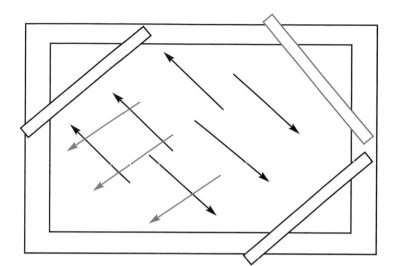

Start with the top clamped to the board as shown by the red marks and plane in the direction of the red arrows, then reclamp in the blue position to plane in the direction of the blue arrows, finally to the green position and so on around the board. By being careful, using a sharp plane and measuring between each stage, the board can be thicknessed quite well. Planing away from the clamps also ensures the board is in tension and is not likely to collapse on itself.

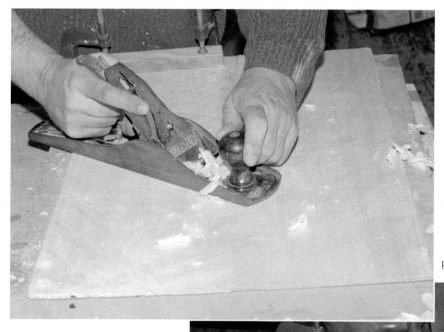

Planing in one direction ...

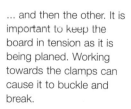

... and then the other. It is important to keep the board in tension as it is being planed. Working towards the clamps can cause it to buckle and break.

The workboard needs to be thick enough not to distort so that the top can be thicknessed accurately.

The top will need to be thicknessed in stages, with part of the top being used to clamp it to the workbench while the other is worked on. In this way different areas of the top will be worked on at any one time and changed around so that the work gets spread around.

The plane used must be very sharp and you need to be aware that the bookmatched nature of the top means that planing in one direction along the grain may well be fine on one half but may be against the lay of the grain on the other, so the plane may try to pull chunks out. The best way to rough-finish the top is to set the plane for a fine cut and plane at an angle across the grain. If the plane digs in at any time, stop and change direction as you do not want to be planing against the grain, which could ruin the top. By moving around the board, unclamping and reclamping sections as you go, you should be able to get an even thickness. This can be measured with a simple thicknessing gauge like the one in the photo, although if you want to get clever and be very accurate, then you will need to buy a specialist guitar top-measuring gauge.

Planing to an exact thickness is not what is required. Some makers argue that tops should be so many millimetres or fractions of an inch thick, but the optimum thickness will depend on the individual piece of wood. Check it regularly and flex it. You don't want a top that is too flexible but you don't want one that is too stiff, so what is the optimum? Other factors such as the grain layout and how dense the wood is will make a difference, too. Judging this is the sort of thing that can only be learned by feel. David Russell Young quotes in *The Steel String Guitar, Comstruction and Repair* that he made spruce tops between 0.1 and 0.12 in (2.5 and 3 mm) but he also would thin the top further by hand if he felt it was too stiff. The magic word there was 'felt': you can only gain this by experience, but if the top is relatively flexible and rings slightly when tapped with the finger, the chances are that it will make a fine-sounding guitar.

With the top roughly planed, the planing marks can be removed by even finer cuts with a very sharp plane, by scraping or by sanding. If sanding you need to be careful to apply even pressure as it is all too easy to push harder in one place and remove more wood than in others. This should not affect the guitar too badly, unless you manage to make one part way too thin with overly coarse paper, but it is better to avoid this if you can.

The top should be sanded down with 320 grit paper so that it has a fine finish, and this should be done on both sides. Good finish on the inside of the guitar is every bit as important as good finish on the outside.

Of course, I cheat and use a power sander, but I still get the final thickness by feel rather than by measuring and I still finish by hand.

THE SOUNDHOLE AND INLAY

With the guitar top still in its rectangular form, the shape of the top can be marked on in pencil. Drawing on the shape on both sides of the top is a good idea, but you need to ensure that the two sides match!

With the overall shape drawn, the position of the bridge, fingerboard overhang and soundhole can be marked. This should be known from your design work so transfer the information over onto your piece of wood, checking that you have not made any errors. Remember, measure at least twice before you cut anything.

From the drawing you should be able to show on the front of the guitar the position of your bridge, the position for the end of the fingerboard and where the soundhole will be. You can also mark on the underside of the top the brace positions, the soundhole position and where the bridge will be so that you can ensure your bridge plate is in the right place!

The first stage in making the top is to mark the soundhole itself and then install the decorative inlay around it.

Soundholes

Do not cut the soundhole at this point. The first stage is to mark it and then check all your dimensions.

The inlay around the soundhole is largely decorative and you could, if you so desired, just paint on a design. However, people have got used to seeing guitars with inlays around the soundhole and it can add considerably to the look of the guitar. Early stringed instruments, such as lutes, had an intricate design of fretted wood in the soundhole. This was often very attractive but could represent weeks of work as each part had to be cut by hand.

Many classical guitars have a rosette and although these can be ordered from parts suppliers, many makers choose to make their own as it adds their own signature to their instruments. The rosette is made from strips of coloured wood that are glued together into a square block. This is then sliced into sections that are then shaped to make a circle and inlaid into a recess cut into the guitar top. This is time-consuming but enjoyable work and there is nothing to stop a rosette being added to a steel-strung guitar, although they are not common. The more usual form of inlay is concentric lines and patterns inlaid into the top around the hole. These can be as simple as different layers of fibre through to elaborate bought or prepared designs and rings of abalone or pearl.

In all cases the materials should be prepared first. Soundhole inlays can be bought ready to install and these could well be the ideal choice for a first guitar, but lengths of binding strip, as used around the edges of the guitar, can be used to make up custom inlays. The most simple would be a single three-ply line of binding

A small selection of available soundhole inlays.

The simplest inlays can be very effective; this is on my favourite 1950s Martin.

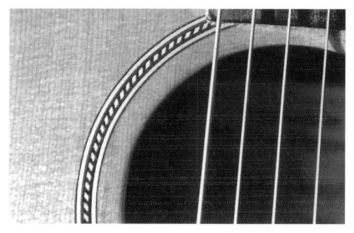

Still very simple, this is a commercially available inlay that just needs to have a channel cut.

A very effective and simple looking, but complicated to make, inlay on a Breedlove. This has a binding to the inside of the soundhole, inlaid segments that were all individually fitted and an outer inlaid ring.

The inlay on this Collings guitar is far more complicated with inlay strips and abalone.

material inlaid into a suitable channel. More complex designs simply require larger, or more, channels to be cut into the guitar top. The practice of inlaying more complex designs is covered later, but a simple herringbone design, as in the photo above, simply needs a circular channel $1/4 \times 1^1/16$ in (6.3×27 mm) cut around the soundhole.

With cutting the channel to accommodate the inlay, as with all things, there is an easy way and a hard way. The easiest is to use one of the small routers, such as

Using the Dremel router with a ¹/8 in (3mm) bit.

The Dremel is centred with a pin inserted through the top into the workboard below.

the Dremel, with its circle-cutting attachment. It is best to practise on a piece of scrap first, as any mistakes on the actual top are going to be very costly. It may not be possible to cut the entire ¹/4 in (6.3 mm) width in one pass, so the router needs to be set so that it is cutting the inside radius of the channel.

Some router bits are not ideal for this job as they can cause the edges of the hole to feather, as the fibres in the wood do not cut cleanly. Using specialised bits, available from many guitar makers' suppliers, is a better option. These often have a downward spiral cut which is better for slicing through the fibres and, as the cut is going downwards, does not lift them at the edge of the channel.

With the first cut made, it is a simple job to extend the radius and cut the outer part of the channel. If there is any excess wood still in the middle, this can be dealt with on a third pass.

If the channel is smaller than any available router bits, or you do not have access to the router, then it is not out of the question to cut these channels by hand. You will need a means of cutting a circular hole, and these are available from guitar parts suppliers, but it is possible to make your own if you have any engineering ability. You will need a centre point, an adjustable arm and a blade that can cut the channel edges. The one in the photographs was bought second hand and has seen some service in its time. As well as making many guitar soundholes and inlay channels it has been used to cut holes in aviation plywood, but that is another story! The black circle cutter shown on page 36 was bought in a discount tool store for less than the price of a beer.

If using a cutter, the outer edges of the channel will need to be cut taking care not to cut all the way through the top. The excess should then be removed carefully with small, sharp chisels. Take your time doing this as a good finish will do wonders for the look

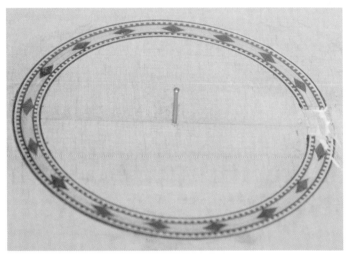

An inlay freshly glued into the recess. The missing space will be covered by the guitar fretboard.

of your guitar but careless work will look careless, no matter what you do to disguise it.

Once the channels are cut, the inlay can be glued in. The inlay should sit so that it is almost flush with the guitar top. Being below this level is not a good idea as the whole top would need to be thinned down just to accommodate the inlay. If it is very proud then it will need a lot of trimming to become flush with the top. This can damage the inlay, as it can pull out from its slot if you are trying to remove too much, and you will undoubtedly remove some wood from the top in the area of the soundhole while sanding. As with all parts of the building process, the more care you take with preparation, the better the end job will be.

With the soundhole inlay/rosette in place and sanded flush you can cut out the soundhole using either the router or the circle cutter. The edges of the soundhole

Using the trusty old circle cutter, pictured on page 36.

The blade on the circle cutter is double edged so that it will cut in either direction. This is very useful when cutting against the grain in a guitar top as it stops the grain from lifting.

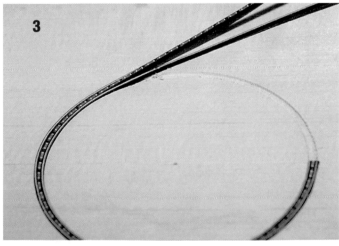

The inlays on the 12-string in Chapter 22 were inserted together and then thin superglue was used to fix it in place by capilliary action.

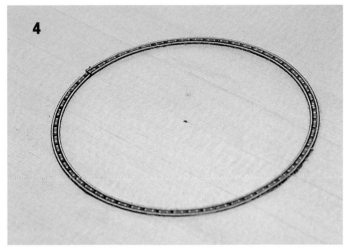

The inlay in place and ready to be sanded down.

It is a good idea, if using a hand cutter, to cut the soundhole from both sides of the board. This will give a cleaner cut. Drilling through the centre point with a $1/16$ in (1.5 mm) drill will help locate the cutter in the right place.

With the hole cut out the inside edges can be gently sanded.

Cutting the shape of the reclaimed wood guitar from Chapter 21.

will need some tidying to remove sharp edges. This can be done with sandpaper but be careful not to remove too much: guitar tops are usually quite soft and when sanding any edge it is possible to overdo things. This is not a job for 60 grit paper!

You can now also cut out the shape of the guitar – be careful to keep any offcuts, which will be useful in future years if you need to do any repairs. The shape can be cut using a bandsaw or carefully by hand. If you are using a bandsaw you will need to use a fine-tooth blade as otherwise the saw blade may pull small pieces out. The top is very soft and the grain will, in some places, be relatively coarse so small pieces could be pulled out by a coarse blade. It is best to leave between $^1/4$ in (6.3 mm) and $^3/8$ in (9.5 mm) outside your lines, rather than to cut right on the line. If you are unlucky and you do pull some fibres out, you may well find that the damage will be covered by the binding when that is fitted.

BRACE YOURSELVES . . .

Choosing the style and size of bracing was covered in Chapter 2; it is now time to cut and fit it.

Braces can be rough cut from larger stock and planed to size by hand or you can pass suitable lengths through a power planer to get them to size. The largest are the ones that form the cross bracing and the one that goes across the top in front of the soundhole. This is known as the transverse brace. It is possible to make the smaller braces from the waste from the larger ones, or from larger pieces cut down to size. I have to admit that many of mine come from other things made in the workshop.

When gluing anything on the guitar it is essential that the wood is protected from compression damage

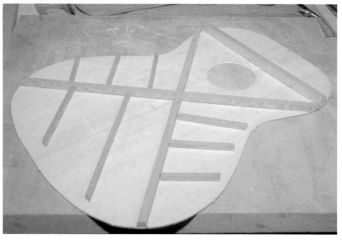

Rough cut braces, placed on the top ready for gluing.

with clamping cauls as discussed in Chapter 3. This is doubly important on the top of the guitar as, since you are clamping the braces to the underside of the top, any damage caused by the clamp could well appear on the face of your guitar – this is generally not a good idea. Before gluing any part, especially when dealing with the top, make sure that everything you need to complete the job is close at hand and that you do a dry, non-glued trial run to make sure it will all work when done for real.

The first brace to be fitted is the transverse brace. Even with a guitar with a slightly arched top this will be straight as the area around the top bout will not be arched. The transverse brace can be glued into place, clamped and the glue join cleaned before being left to dry. While this is drying the other braces can be prepared.

Measuring fifteen feet from a fixed point in the workshop to make the back arch.

Using a fifteen foot long piece of wire with a loop in the end to support a pencil. Marking the top arch is the same, it just uses more wire!

Bracing cutting list

Transverse   12-14 inches $5/8$ x $1/2$ in (16 x 13 mm)

Cross braces   18-20 inches $3/8$ x $3/8$ in (10 x 10 mm)

Centre bracing   18 inches $3/8$ x $5/16$ in (10 x 8 mm)

Edge bracing   18 inches $1/4$ x $1/4$ in (6 x 6 mm)

Soundhole bracing 10-12 inches $3/8$ x $1/8$ in (10 x 3 mm)

Additional top brace (if req.) 10 inches $3/4$ x $1/8$ in
(19 x 3 mm)

The above lengths are only guides. Measure the total length of each type of brace and prepare more than you need. All will need to be cut to their exact length when being fitted.

The Martin kit in Chapter 20 has the braces pre-cut. The brace has been pre-shaped which means there will be a small gap where the curved section on the second brace runs through the straight cut in the lower one.

If you have chosen to arch the top of the guitar, the cross braces will need to be shaped to hold the top in place. The amount of arch is not great, usually about a 25 ft (7.6 m) radius. You can mark this onto a former by tying a pencil 25 ft along a piece of string, anchoring the other end and using the pencil to mark your work. In these modern days, however, it is possible to use one of a number of easily accessible computer-aided design (CAD) programs that will produce exactly the right curve for you. It is worth making a jig either to use with a router to cut the braces or as a former to mark the wood so that the excess can be sanded or cut away. The curve could be cut by hand onto each brace using a template as a guide, but it is important that the curve is even and the same on both braces and that it does not angle across the bottom of the brace. It is possible to put a twist into the brace that may impart all sorts of stresses into the top.

The braces of the reclaimed wood guitar in Chapter 21. These have been cut and trial fitted but are not, at this stage, glued.

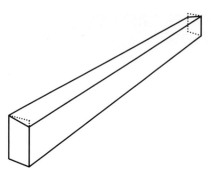

It is important there is no twist in the brace. This diagram shows a brace that has a twist which is evident if you look at the ends.

This useful little jig allows me to rout the bottom of a piece of wood to a curve. The piece can then be run through a saw to give braces with evenly curved bases.

Since the cross bracing intersects near the centre, the braces need to be cut to fit into each other where they cross. Merely cutting one and butt-joining it to the sides of the other is not really acceptable and will not give the support needed at this point, even with modern glues. It is far better to cut a recess in both so they slot into one another.

Since the position of all the braces has been marked on the reverse of the top, the first of these should be placed on to ensure that it has not been cut too short (this has been known although I, of course, have never done it ...). The position where the other half of the cross brace intersects can be marked with pencil; the second brace can then be placed into position and the process repeated. Using a square on the top of the brace (the part that has not been radiused!), the marks on the top of the brace can be extended down the sides. At half the depth of the brace a mark can be made. On one brace the top half will need to be removed and on the other the bottom half to make a join. The excess is cut away using a fine saw and the join cleaned so that it is firm without being too tight. It is also wise to double-check that you are removing the material from the right half of the brace. It has happened (perhaps even during the writing of this book) that a brace was cut incorrectly and so would not fit with the other.

It is also important that you glue the braces in place in the right order. Gluing on the one that has the excess cut away nearest the bottom first will make it impossible to glue the other into place. It is also important, if the brace is curved, that the caul under the clamp allows for this so that the brace takes up the correct shape. You can use one curved caul that runs the length of the brace or a series of smaller ones to even out the pressure.

There are some alternatives to gluing braces one at a time and waiting for each one to dry before removing the clamps and doing the next one. The simplest answer is to have more clamps, but this is not practical as they are heavy and can put a lot of strain on the top.

You could use a vacuum bag for the job as discussed in the Martin Factory tour in Chapter 25. Vacuum bags are great for a number of things. They work by enclosing what you need to glue in a sealed bag and removing all the air. Since atmospheric pressure is 15 psi at sea level on a standard atmospheric day, this can exert a lot of pressure. They are great for veneering, for example, as the pressure is so even. However, getting all the bits of a guitar top into a bag, keeping them in the correct place as the air leaves and the pressure is applied, and supporting any curved braces is bad enough before you then have to think about how you remove any excess glue that seeps out (or you need to ensure that exactly the right amount of glue is applied). You need to keep the pressure on for some time as the glue will dry more slowly, not being able to react to air as it normally does.

If you do choose a vacuum bag there is also the problem of finding a bag big enough to take the whole guitar top. It is sometimes easier to use two pieces of plastic and a lot of Gaffa tape or to try another method. Needless to say, vacuum bags are not as effective if you live on a 10,000 ft mountain as the air pressure is considerably lower.

An alternative is a bar system. This is very simple but does need a jig to be made. What you are aiming to do is use the downward pressure of a number of bent dowels or sticks to hold all the pieces down.

You need to make a box that has a floor and a roof but no sides. The floor needs to be big enough to take the guitar top and the height of the box needs to be enough to allow a reasonable length of dowel, as dowels that are too short will not bend easily. The jig

A simple open box for using the bar system of clamping.

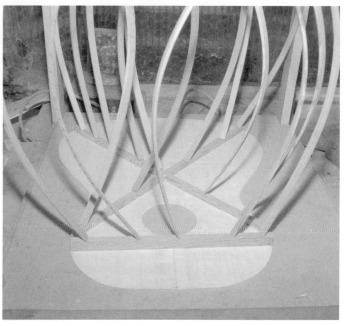

The only limit to the number of braces you can glue at one time is the amount of space you need to position the sticks and whether you can get to the joins to clean the glue residue.

brace

clamping caul

As can be seen from the exaggerated diagram (*above*), having a curved clamping caul with the curved brace means the top has to conform to the shape. This can be seen in action on a back brace which has a tighter radius (*right*).

in the photos is made with a base that is 24 in (635 mm) × 18 in (458 mm) and a height of 24 in (635 mm). Getting exactly the right length of dowel is a case of trial and error, and will depend on the material of the dowels you are using and their diameter. You do not want to have to bend them too much to get them into place, and if they are too long they will be difficult to keep vertical above where they are clamping and may exert a side pressure on the glue join that will cause it to slip. As with other clamping methods, do a trial run first.

Carving the taper on the smaller braces on the electro-acoustic in Chapter 23. This is being done with a very sharp chisel and a lot of care is needed to prevent marking the top.

Some additional bracing is required around the soundhole.

A maple bridge plate on a spruce top.

If the cross braces are curved, you will also need to support the underneath of the top (the face of the top) using a curved clamping caul. If you don't, you will simply be bending the braces to conform to the surface shape of the base beneath the top rather than bending the top to fit the brace, so the dowels will need to be cut to allow for the depth of the caul, the top and the brace.

It is important that all excess glue is cleaned away using a pointed-front drinking straw, as described in Chapter 4.

With the main braces in place, the smaller ones can be glued in. Each should be left until the glue has hardened, which depends on the glue used but is usually several hours, before unclamping and gluing the next. If you have a totally flat top you can glue a number of pieces at one time, as the only thing that limits you is

the number of dowels you have and the ease of access past dowels you have already installed. Working from the centre outwards solves this, and will let you clean the glue from around the braces using a damp cloth and a pointed drinking straw.

Bracing shape

The braces do not have to be left in their rectangular form; they can be rounded over or carved (*see* page 16) as on the Herringbone Martins. The main cross braces are usually tapered towards the edges where they join the sides for about the last 2 in (50 mm). This is so that they are more easily fitted to the linings and, since the edges of the top are supported by the guitar sides, the braces need not be so large here. The smaller braces are also tapered to nothing as they approach the

---

Tap tuning

If you look hard enough on the Internet you can find all sorts of information on tap tuning guitar tops and how to get the 'correct' vibration patterns and this does have some academic interest. The problem with a first guitar is that you have to know what you are looking for before you can find it. Some makers swear that tap tuning the top and back of their guitars will enable them to tailor the tone of the guitar by listening out for the specific frequency of the top and adjusting it to one that is required. Others are less enthusiastic about it. I know of one maker who claims that all of his tops seem to have about the same tap tone regardless of what wood he makes them from and how he braces them, and he does have a lot of experience. Instead of looking for a specific resonant frequency he makes his tops so that they sound bright and alive when he taps them. Others insist that a top should be tuned to a particular frequency and do so by removing wood from areas of the top or from the braces until they are satisfied.

I have no doubt that when you have made many guitars you will understand what you are looking for when tap tuning or trying to 'tailor' a guitar top.

This will not be so obvious on a first guitar. My good friend Dave King says that he made at least forty guitars before he was satisfied he knew what he was hearing when he was tapping guitar tops. For a first guitar it is best to avoid getting too hung up on this and to concentrate on making a guitar as accurately and tidily as you can from good materials.

---

sides, but they do not slot into the kerfing, instead stopping short of it.

All braces can be shaped so they are not rectangular. Some makers also like to shape the braces so they are curved in profile. This can be done after they have been glued with some careful chisel work or with a knife, finishing up with sandpaper and being very careful not to slip and dig into the top. It is also a very good idea to frequently check under the top when you are working on it, to make sure that there are no stray items underneath that could damage the face of the guitar. Shaping can also be done before the braces are glued but the rounded shape may make clamping more difficult and the area around the join on the main cross braces should be left rectangular so there are no gaps around it.

The bracings will also need to be sanded to remove any marks made when assembling and to give them a smooth finish. Keeping the inside of the guitar tidy is not essential but does look much better.

There are several other smaller items that will need to be added. The soundhole is supported by some smaller braces or by an internal ring which simply stops the soundhole distorting. These can be made from small strips of wood and are shown in the photographs.

The last item is the bridge plate. This is often made of rosewood or maple and, as discussed earlier, it is not a good idea to use softwood as the wood has to stop the ends of the strings from coming through the top. If the top of the guitar is arched the edges of the bridge plate may need to be sanded to fit. The amount needed will not be great, but a snug fit is very desirable. With this complete the bridge plate can be glued into place using either the dowels or clamps.

The mould can be placed over the top and the final lengths of the transverse and cross braces marked for length. If, at this stage, the sides are not in the mould, the thickness of them will need to be taken into account when marking the lengths. The braces can then be carefully cut to length, taking a lot of care not to damage the top.

With this done the top can be finally cleaned up and placed to one side ready to be fitted to the sides.

Chapter 7
Backs

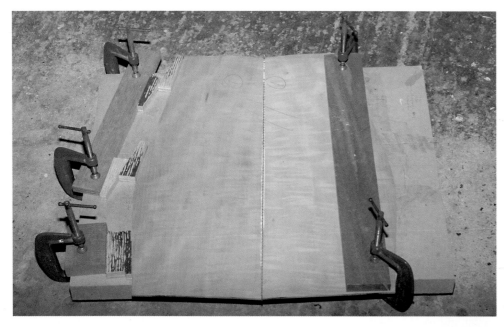

Gluing the back for the 12-string guitar in Chapter 22. Since this was not a rectangular board some adaptation of the gluing jig was needed. The wood is pearwood.

Gluing the two pieces of the back is done in the same way as for the top, the only difference being that there is usually some form of trim inlaid along the centre join. This usually matches the bindings and a variety of styles can be obtained from guitar makers' suppliers. You do not actually need to do this – there are many fine guitars that have no centre line inlay – but it does look good and is not that hard to fit.

Some guitars may have a three-piece back as some types of wood are hard to find in widths suitable for a two-piece back. In most cases each join has some form of inlay.

The simplest form of line – a simple line made of a contrasting veneer – is, if anything, the hardest to fit as it is fiddly. It may be only 1/16 in (1.5 mm) thick or even less, and making a piece that is long enough to go between the two halves of the top and only as wide as the back thickness can be tricky. The large pre-prepared inlays are thicker and so easier to handle. A simple black/white/black line can be added using purfling material and, since this is usually sold in lengths that will go all around the sides of a guitar, you may have enough left over to bind either side of your end inlay (*see* page 105).

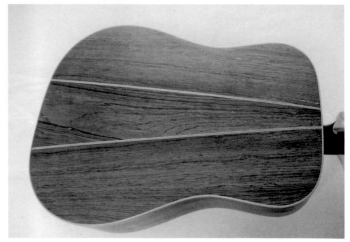

A three-piece Brazilian rosewood back on a 1969 Martin D35.

These inlay pieces are often the same thickness as the back but sometimes may be a little thinner. This may not be the case after the back is thicknessed, but it

The inlay placed between the two halves of a rosewood back before gluing. The difference in thickness between the back wood and the inlay means you must be careful to ensure the inlay sits flat on the workboard and lines up with at least one face of the back.

Passing the back for the reclaimed wood guitar in Chapter 21 through a thicknessing sander.

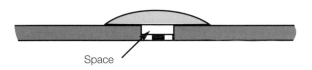

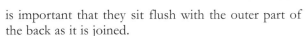
Space

If there is an air gap under the back trim it is advisable to fill it as it could lead to an unstable back.

Using a cabinet scraper to get the back smooth after sanding.

is important that they sit flush with the outer part of the back as it is joined.

If the back halves are supplied rough-cut it is a good idea to part-thickness them before gluing so that they have at least one flat side. They will then sit onto the workboard and, if the inlay you are using is thinner than the two pieces for the back, it can be positioned right against the board so that it remains in line with the two back pieces.

If the back trim is glued level as to the outer surface as possible, subsequent thickness sanding will quickly make this flush. The inside may be different as, if the trim is thinner than the finished back, there may be a gap between the inlay and the trim strip that covers it (*see* above). Simply covering this gap with the trim will leave a gap beneath that could result in an unstable back and so filling the gap, either with another piece of trim or with a suitably sized strip of wood, will make the join more stable.

Once the two halves of the back are glued they can be thicknessed. Again this can be done by hand, although machine sanding will be more accurate and easier. Back thicknesses will depend on the material. The back has some effect on the tone of the guitar but

obviously not as much as the top. The usual thicknesses for backs are 0.09 in (2.1 mm) to 0.1 in (2.3 mm). The back needs to be flexible enough to fit the shape dictated by the sides and the curved bracing, but thick enough not to be too weak and to split. The ideal thickness will depend on the wood being used and I have to admit I rarely measure, preferring to work by feel. If it is flexible yet still strong, that is good enough. I am also lucky to have access to a thicknessing sander, so life is a little easier: I can remove a little at a time and feel and stop when it feels right.

With the back suitably thicknessed, it can be sanded smooth on the inside to give a good finish, the outside being dealt with later, and the shape can be marked on from the mould. Remember to leave a little extra around the edges so that the back will overlap the sides by a small amount. It can then be cut out. If using a bandsaw for this it is wise to use a fine-tooth blade, as

Lining up the centre trim.

Carving the centre trim to shape using a small plane and being very careful not to mark the back.

Gluing the centre trim onto the Martin kit using a very large piece of maple to weigh it down.

Sanding the back trim.

Cleaning the glue from the centre strip as it is clamped with the bar system.

with the top, so that the grain does not tear out along the edges.

The positions of the back braces can be marked, taking care to keep them at 90 degrees to the centre line.

Before the back braces are fitted, the back join is covered by a centre trim. This is a thin piece of wood, often as little as $1/2 \times 1/8$ in (12.7 × 3 mm) that is glued over the join to strengthen and support it. The grain on this trim is usually perpendicular to the grain on the back and can be made from scrap wood left over from the top or from other guitars. Some makers use softwood – the Martin kit in Chapter 20, for example, uses spruce – but other woods can be used. They are usually contrasting, like a rosewood trim on a maple guitar or a maple trim on rosewood or mahogany.

The centre trim will need to be made up from a number of pieces, as it is basically a very short but very wide piece, given the orientation of the grain. This gives two things to consider. The various pieces are

The back braces ready for shaping and fitting.

The back bracing cut to length and placed into position.

Using a chisel to remove the waste on the centre trim for the back brace to sit flush.

The curve on the underside of the back braces can be cut on a bandsaw. The underside can then be tidied using sand paper on a 15 feet radius sanding jig.

The back trim has been slotted to accept the cross braces and the first has been glued on. This has a curved clamping caul underneath and the cauls on the two inner clamps are shaped to allow for the pre-carved brace.

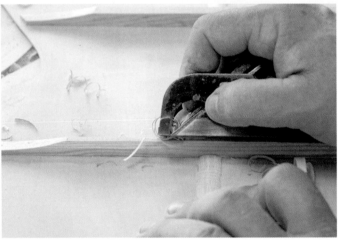

Carving the brace to shape using a very sharp small plane. This can be done before or after the ends are shaped.

The shaped back brace.

The back braces are tapered to $^1/_8$ in (3 mm) where they slot into the kerfing. I use a sharp chisel to carve a gentle curve.

When cutting the curve on the ends of the braces it is worth remembering that if the last section is to fit into a recess carved in the kerfing (*see* page 94), it will need to remain flat for the depth of the recess.

going to need to be joined, and so it is a good idea to hide the joins at the positions of the cross braces, and the pieces must be made and fitted accurately so the trim remains parallel and glued straight along its length.

The trim can be held down using the bar system or with clamps or even with weights but once dry it should be shaped into a curve across its width. This can be done with chisels or a small plane but needs to be done carefully as the chisel can slip off and mark the back wood. The final stage is to finish sand the trim.

Like the top, the back is braced although the bracing pattern is far simpler. Three or four cross braces are fitted and these can be made from spruce or something similar. The back will usually be arched, although this is not the case with all guitars. The Gibson J45 and Epiphone Texan of the 1950s, which was essentially the same guitar, had flat backs and they sound fine. An arched back is technically better, but if you have any doubts about making one then a flat back will do.

The shape is created by arching the back braces. The radius of the back is usually about 15 ft (4.5m). As with the top, if you are curving the bracing it is important to keep the amount of curve even and the bottom face square to the sides. As with the top, getting this wrong can create all sorts of stresses into the brace that could cause it, in time, to break away from the back.

Once this is done the markings showing the positions of the cross braces can be extended across the trim and the trim cut away to fit the brace. The cross braces can then be glued on using the same system as you used for the top braces, either clamps or bars, and the excess glue can be removed.

Some makers like to shape the bracings so that they are pointed in profile but others leave them rectangular. As with the top there is argument about whether there is any benefit in tone from doing this, but it is largely a matter of taste. If you wish to shape them, this should be done carefully with chisels or with a small plane and the braces should then be finished with sandpaper. Remember that people will look into the soundhole of your guitar, so finish everything well.

Like the top braces, each end of the brace will also need to be shaped so that it will fit into a small recess in the kerfing of the guitar.

As with the top, position the mould over the back, linging up the centre line accurately, and mark the lengths of the back braces.

The back is now ready to be fitted to the sides which, of course, will now need to be made.

Chapter 8
Sides

Thickness sanding sapele sides. These ended up being used to make the sound ring for the resonator guitar in Chapter 24.

The sides of the guitar serve several main functions. They support the top, giving it extra strength as part of the box structure of the guitar, they define the depth of the soundbox, or body, and they act as part of the structure to reflect the sound of the guitar through the soundhole.

Bending sides is something that many new makers fear, but it is not as daunting as one might expect. The sides of the guitar are traditionally made from the same wood as the back: this is not 'set in stone', and you could experiment if you wanted, but normally the same wood looks better. Some woods are easier to bend than others but all woods need to have the correct orientation of the grain, otherwise they can distort and split.

As discussed in Chapter 5, the sides need to be quarter sawn with the growth rings running through the wood perpendicular to the face. It would be easier to bend them if they were sawn with the growth rings parallel to the face, but this does not give enough support to the wood: they will usually distort across their width, rendering the sides useless, and this is something that cannot be put right. Bending against the strongest direction of the grain is harder but will give a more stable side.

Guitar sides are also usually bookmatched. It is very easy to get these mixed up so that the grain ends up opposing rather than matching. If you are sawing the board yourself it is a good idea to mark them when they have been opened out so they remain bookmatched – drawing an arrow on will show which end is which. If you have bought your sides then they ought to be together so the grain matches, but they should be checked and the matching faces found and then marked. Obviously, marking bookmatched sides should not be done with anything that will leave a permanent mark on the sides; chalk or pencil will be fine.

The sides may come from a supplier already thick-nessed, but if you have to prepare them it is best to find somewhere that can machine sand them to thickness. You could plane and sand them by hand, using a variation on the method used on the top (*see* page 61) but you may get variations in the thickness that can make bending interesting. I am fortunate to have access to a thicknessing sander and I sand the sides gradually to a thickness of about $1/10$ in (2.5 mm). This thickness will depend on the wood being used as each has its own characteristics. Straight-grained maple, for example, bends very well and so can be a little thicker than some other woods. I tend to use feel as much as measurement

The sides for the reclaimed wood guitar in Chapter 21 laid out to show the bookmatched grain. The arrows show which line represents the top.

to tell when a side is thin enough but this is, of course, not possible for a first guitar.

Throughout this process the sides need to be worked together so they remain the same thickness and special attention needs to be paid to ensure they do not get flipped over and so get 'out of bookmatch'.

The machine sanding will leave the sides with some sanding marks that can be removed with finer grades of sandpaper. There is little point in sanding the sides to a good finish at this stage though, as the bending process will raise the grain as the sides are wetted and the bending iron will leave some marks. I sand with 120 grit to remove any obvious marks and any grain that may be a little fluffy, as can happen on some woods such as cherry. With the sides prepared, they can be marked for cutting.

Start by again checking that your sides are book-matched – you really cannot do this too often! Put them together into the vice and plane one edge so that it is flat. Now you can make sure not only that your marks show the grain orientation, but also which side is planed. If you do this on the inside the marks will be visible when you bend and place them in the mould.

The next stage is to mark the back taper onto the sides. Both the top and the back may have some degree of arch, which will need to be allowed for on the sides, but for the purposes of marking out it can be assumed that the top surface of the sides is flat and the bottom is tapered. As we have seen, most guitars have a body that is deeper at the bottom end than it is at the neck.

The arching of the top and back means that the sides will be slightly shallower at the edge of the top bout as they will curve away from the neck block. This can be roughly catered for by leaving the last few inches of the side parallel, up to the apex of the top bout, and this will be adjusted when the back is fitted.

CAD design of acoustic guitar back arches

CAD designing the shape required for the sides for a guitar with an arched back is not straightforward. The shape of the guitar would need to be plotted and the sides extended upwards. A 50 ft (7.62 m) diameter globe would then need to be drawn and a section of this overlaid onto the top, and the points where it touches the sides of the guitar plotted. The side would then need to be expanded out and the shape noted. It may be much easier just to make it and cut it to fit.

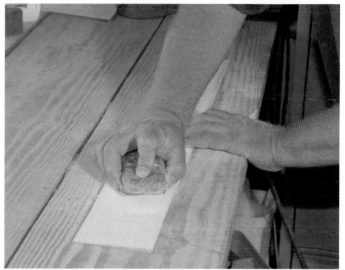

Hand sanding a maple side to remove marks made by the thicknessing sander.

If you have access to CAD software, you could work out the exact shape the sides will be when the back is about to be fitted, but cutting the sides to the exact shape is not wise as there may be some movement when they are fitted into the mould (*see* alignment box on page 128). It is far easier to make them slightly oversize and make the top and back fit, as described later, than it is to try to be too clever at this stage – although the sides could be cut roughly to shape, which may save time later.

If you are to make more than one guitar it may be an idea to plan the taper for your side and make a jig – from thin ply or sheet aluminium – that can be used to mark the sides without having to draw each one separately. This can also be useful if you are just making one guitar as measuring one side differently to the other, which can happen, could be a minor disaster. Again, you could use the measurements from an existing guitar to allow for the curve on the back and make a jig for it, but there is still plenty of room for error as the side making process is far from being precision engineering, and small movements of any one part may ruin your carefully planned shape.

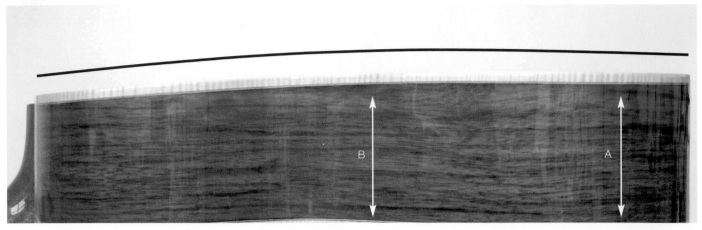

The shape of the guitar side can be very complex. The back of the guitar is domed, therefore is not only curved across its width, as shaped by the back braces, it is also curved along its length. This is denoted by the upper curved black line above the body in this photograph. Since the guitar is circular, the dome will not touch the body evenly all the way around. The outer parts will be closer to the edges of the dome whilst the waist will be nearer the centre, where the dome is higher. In this photograph the guitar was placed face down and level and it can be seen that although the body is tapered, the depth of the body is similar from the edges of the lower bout (point A) to close to the waist (point B).

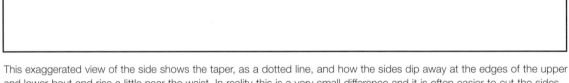

This exaggerated view of the side shows the taper, as a dotted line, and how the sides dip away at the edges of the upper and lower bout and rise a little near the waist. In reality this is a very small difference and it is often easier to cut the sides as shown in the diagram below and adjust them when fitting the back.

Bandsawing the sides.

Waxing one end of the mould.

The body mould is designed to split into two halves: having separate halves makes it easier to fit the sides as they are being bent. When fitting the end blocks there is a risk of glue seeping through the join between the two sides and gluing your sides firmly into the mould. To prevent this you should wax the inside of the mould, using a candle, around the area where the two halves join.

The last few years have seen improvements in the equipment available to makers, with thermostatically controlled bending irons and jigs becoming available, but in the dim and distant past, or over 20 years ago, often the only option was a length of steel tube of roughly 2–3 in (50–75 mm) diameter heated either by an electric element or by a gas flame. This is still a perfectly good method if nothing else is available, but since the heat is not easily controllable, the sides may not bend properly or could get scorched. This is not the end of the world on the insides of the guitar as much of the scorching could be sanded off, but since scorching often damages the wood quite deeply, removing all the damage by sanding could weaken the side. The alternatives are to put up with an ugly mark, or paint the guitar, or scrap it and start again. It is also very important to remember that naked flames and wood are not the best of friends, so a lot of care must be taken when using a gas flame.

Electric bending irons that are thermostatically controlled and designed especially for musical instruments are available, but they can be quite expensive. It is theoretically possible to design your own using an electric heating element, a potentiometer and a suitable piece of steel tube but I strongly advise you NOT to do this. The sides will be wet when applied to the iron, and incorrectly assembled electrical equipment and water can be a dangerous, even lethal, combination. If you choose to go this route you are responsible for your own safety. Remember that all countries have very strict rules relating to this sort of thing in order to prevent accidents: do not mess around with a botched-up design.

I use an old electric bending iron that had seen previous service with the excellent guitar maker Roger Giffin. This is usually set at maximum heat as that is how I have had best results.

With the jig finished, the shape can be transferred onto the sides. Open them up like a book and lay the straight edges together. Place the jig onto one side so that it is in the right direction with its straight edge along the join. Mark one side and then simply flip the jig over so that it is the mirror image of itself. This way the two sides will have the same grain pattern.

It is wise to leave a little extra at either end so that the sides can be trimmed to fit. I leave the bottom bout end as measured and add about $^1/_2$ in (12.7 mm) to 1 in (25.4 mm) at the neck end. This allows for any slight variations in the shape as the bending is done. Any slight gaps at the end block caused by the side moving slightly in the mould will be lost when the end inlay (*see* page 105) is fitted. This is also because I work from the end block when shaping sides, but that is just a matter of preference and you can do whatever feels most natural as you work.

To cut the sides out I tend to use the bandsaw with a fine-toothed blade and once this is done and the edges are cleaned up, the sides can be prepared for bending.

BENDING

There are several methods of bending sides. Some involve quite complicated jigs and produce excellent results, or you can do it by hand. The trick is to heat the wood so that the moisture in it heats and allows the wood to bend without breaking. Depending on the type of wood and the amount of heat and moisture, some quite sharp bends can be made. Sharper bends are helped if the wood is supported to prevent 'breakout': this occurs when fibres in the wood do not all bend, and some separate. This can be enough to render your sides useless.

WETTING THE SIDES

Different makers have differing ideas about how wet the sides of the guitar need to be before they are bent. Some will even claim that they prefer to bend them dry. All methods are valid if they work: there is no right way or wrong way. I will show what works for me and some other makers and then let you make up your own mind as to which you think may work best for you.

In the past I have soaked the sides in a bath of water for at least an hour before attempting to bend them. I have found that soaking for longer can distort them,

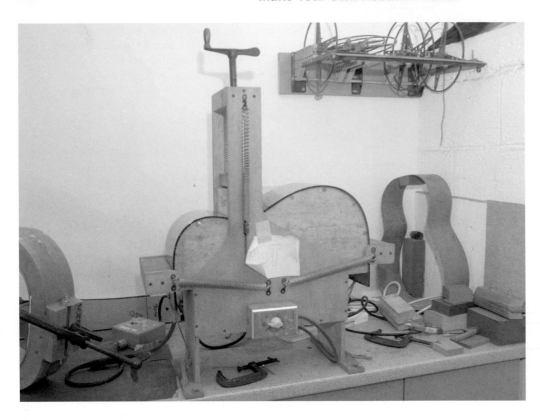

Plans for a side bender such as this can be had from several sources. The sides are soaked and then bent to shape on the former whilst being heated. This one belongs to Dave King and he leaves sides in for 24 hours so that the shape is fixed.

depending on the type of wood, and dark woods can stain the bath. This does not affect your guitar making but can affect how nice you need to be to your partner for some time. You generally need to be much nicer to them if the stain is from rosewood rather than mahogany as the stain is worse. I also used to keep a water spray – a small spray used for watering plants is fine – to keep the sides wet as I bent them. Nowadays, however, I do not bother to soak at all: I use the water spray alone, having found that spraying the sides liberally before bending them is sufficient. The late Irving Sloan, who wrote one of the better books on making classical guitars (*Classic Guitar Construction*, Sterling Publishing 1984), used to recommend boiling guitar sides for some time before placing them into the mould. He also used to build the guitar inside a mould as usual, but had a jig to bend the sides that had slightly more curve than the finished sides so that any spring-back, which does happen to varying degrees depending upon the wood type, was allowed for.

Some makers use heated jigs that produce excellent and, as much as wood allows, consistently accurate results, and these are not that difficult to make. Again, the late Irving Sloan's excellent book on making classical guitars provides details and some of the guitar parts companies offer kits or plans to make something similar.

The basic jig is made from two pieces of plywood that are a slightly exaggerated version of the shape of half the guitar, to allow for the spring-back when the sides are being bent, so the final shape approximates that of the guitar. These two pieces are held apart by cross slats so the jig is wide enough to take both sides

at once. There is also some form of adjustable clamping arrangement to pull the sides down into the jig, and a form of heater to heat the sides. This may be simple light bulbs (remembering what was said above about the proximity of electrical power and water). The details of each design may differ slightly, but the end result is the same: the sides get bent together using a combination of heat and moisture. Plans for these bending jigs are available from some guitar-makers' supply companies. It is possible that the sides will come out of the jig and not fit exactly into the mould, so it might be necessary to adjust the shape using a normal bending iron.

If you are making a guitar with a cutaway it may be wise to consider a way of soaking the cutaway pieces more than the rest of these sides as the radii needed may be considerably tighter. The Martin factory still hand-bend many of their cutaway guitars rather than relying on jigs, and sides can be found in the factory with one end in a container of hot water while they are waiting for one of the craftsmen to bend the cutaway.

If you are using a bending iron without the help of a jig, you could start by trying to bend the sides of your guitar or you could practise on some scrap wood. Side bending is not that difficult with a little practice. It is, of course, always better to practise on scrap than on the sides of your guitar, and you will notice that there is a limit beyond which you cannot bend. You will also get a feel for the material you are working on and how much pressure you need to exert to get a bend started. Try various pieces to see how smooth you can make the bend and how tight you can make it before you get

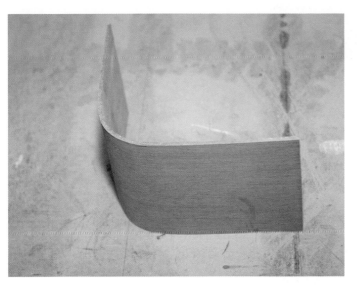

A short test piece on the bench. This went easily to 90 degrees but would have split if bent any further without more soaking.

Bending the sides on the 12-string from Chapter 22. The mould is easily to hand to check shape and just beyond the bending iron is the water spray the author uses. This held fabric softener in a previous life.

problems. It is important to keep the wood moving so that any bends are gradual and not to let the area being heated dry out too much. The water in the wood is turned to steam and it is this that softens the fibres so they can be bent. As the wood is held against the iron the steam will be seen coming from the wood and it will eventually dry out as all the moisture converted. Try other materials to see how different they are. I have always found that straight-grained mahogany has a lot of spring and so needs more work to bend it into the correct shape than, say, rosewood.

Figured woods, such as flamed maple, are something different entirely. The nature of the figure will mean that the grain is not as straight as it would be on many other woods, so you may be trying to bend the wood when the grain is actually quite short and running through the wood at an angle. This can be a recipe for disaster as the strain of bending will take the path of least resistance and this short grain may separate.

In these cases the wood will need to be supported as it is bent. The normal way is to hold it in place with a backing sheet of metal, which can be bought from guitar makers' suppliers, or a thin sheet of stainless steel or aluminium can be used. This needs to be a material that is thin and that will not deform as it is bent. There are various types of alloys that will allow this, and as long as the material is quite springy you should be OK.

It is important in all cases to keep the bends at right angles across the wood. Holding the side against the iron at an angle can cause all sorts of twists. You will also get a feel for how the guitar shape develops around the mould. The curves are not always even: they flatten out in places and completely reverse in others, so careful reference to the side of the mould is essential.

Using a commercially available strap to support the sides while bending.

Small splits in the sides, such as this one, are not the end of the world and can be easily repaired. This was glued and clamped and since it did not extend too far, it was removed when the binding channel was cut.

Sides marked ready to be cut to length.

Once both sides are bent, the mould can be reassembled.

It is worth taking time on bending the sides. Get them as close to a perfect fit around the mould as you can. It is very important to hold it to shape while the wood cools: whilst it is still hot the side will remain very springy. As it cools some of that spring will be lost and it will retain its shape better. The Irving Sloan jig, referred to above, keeps the wood bent past the point where it is required so that the spring-back when it is cool is roughly what is required for it to fit the mould. When bending by hand it is necessary to keep the wood bent in the same way until it cools and reference to the mould can be made. The wood will try to spring back, but when you have the side as close to the correct shape as possible you can clamp it into the mould. You should find that it touches all the way around. If there are areas where the sides do not seem to want to fit exactly, no matter what you do, don't worry at this stage. It may be that your chosen shape just has some uneven curves and it is the mould that is the problem, not the sides. As long as any gaps are the same on both sides of the guitar then there will be little problem.

Sides clamped into the mould.

The sides of the guitar designed in Chapter 2 are made to be straight where the body joins the neck and so the neck block does not need shaping to fit the curve of the sides.

Allow the sides to dry out thoroughly and then you can trim them to length. They need to be flush with the part of the mould that will butt up against the other part when the mould is put back together.

NECK AND TAIL BLOCKS

The next stage is to screw both sides of the mould back together, which should give you two nice symmet-rical guitar sides held in place with clamps. You then need to make and glue in the end blocks. One of these is designed to take the neck; the other adds strength to the bottom end of the guitar and allows for the fitment of a strap button.

The neck and tail blocks are usually made of mahogany as it is easy to shape. The tail block is often made with the grain running parallel to the top surface of the guitar while the neck block is made with the

Cutting kerfing by hand. The back stop was positioned so that placing the previous cut on the edge of the board, and cutting to the edge of the backstop, produced evenly spaced kerfing.

grain perpendicular to the front of the guitar. The size and type of neck block may vary with the type of neck join you are making, which is covered elsewhere, but the blocks should be made so they are fractionally oversize and protrude more at the back of the guitar that the front. If the guitar has an arched top it will require the end block to be shaped. Both blocks will need to be shaped at the rear to accommodate the arch on the back. In practice I find that leaving approximately $1/8$ in (3 mm) at the end block and neck is plenty. The blocks should also be fitted so they are perfectly square to the top edge of the guitar and do not slip as they are glued, ending up at an angle.

If you have made the area around the neck join square to the centre line as discussed on page 13, then the block can be flat on both sides. If your guitar shape is curved all the way round, the block will need to be shaped to allow for this.

Once the glue is dry, it is the ideal time to place the mould over the top and the back to mark the bracing lengths since the thickness of the sides is easy to see. The bracing will then fit neatly when the top and back are glued.

KERFING

With the blocks glued into place it is time to add the kerfing. This increases the gluing area available to fit the top and the back and strengthens the edges of the guitar. It can be bought from guitar makers' supply shops or can be made. The most commonly used wood is a mahogany substitute, although other woods are equally good – I have used pine on the guitar made from reclaimed materials in chapter 21. The only thing to remember is that cut-outs will be made in some parts and so the grain needs to be relatively tight so

These kerfing strips are bought ready cut and save a lot of time.

that it can be worked well. It also needs to be bent to shape.

Many classical guitars are built with continuous strip that is bent in the same way as the sides. Often maple or sycamore is used for this as it bends easily, but the thickness required makes it harder to bend than the sides. On most other guitars the kerfing is slotted so that it forms a continuous line of blocks held together by a thin strip left uncut. You can leave the kerfing rectangular, but most people choose to taper it so that it is triangular when viewed from the end, with the thinnest side away from the surface being glued

The kerfing is usually made to $1/4 \times 1/2$ in (6.3 × 12.7 mm) with the slots cut anywhere between $1/2$ and $1/4$ in (12.7 and 6.3 mm) apart. Smaller pieces will be easier to

The glued kerfing. This has been glued in short sections to allow for the shape of the back. Gluing a series of flat pieces onto a curved surface is never ideal but with care a good job can be done.

glue as the slotted kerfing will be a series of flat pieces, never forming a true curve. Since these are being attached to a curved surface, the gluing surface is never ideal. Smaller segments will sit better on a curved surface but will be harder to handle and more likely to break, especially when being cut.

If you have access to a table saw with a thin blade, making kerfing with regular cuts is easy. You can set the saw so that it cuts the material to within $1/16$ in (1.5 mm) of the table or even fractionally less, and then insert a small pin into the backboard of your saw table roughly $3/8$ in (9.5 mm) from the saw blade. Make the first cut across the board and then move it so that the pin sits into the saw cut. Make the next cut and then move that along. You will end up with even cuts across the wood. It is theoretically possible to use a piece of wood wide enough to make all four lengths of kerfing that you will need, and then cut the strips out and shape them after they have been slotted. In practice, however, this is a bit difficult to do by hand as the blocks can break off as they are being worked. It is easier, and probably not much slower, to shape the wedge section into your wood and then cut the slots onto each piece in turn. With the pin acting to ensure that all cuts are the same distance apart, the end result will be fine.

It is not that much harder to cut the kerfing by hand as was done for the guitar in Chapter 21. The kerfing was held up against a stop on the workboard and the slots cut with a small saw. As each piece was cut, the kerfing was moved along until the saw cut matched a pencil mark on the workboard. By moving this up each time, each segment was the same width.

The kerfing is glued to the inner edges of the top and back, running from one end block to the other. The first stage is to cut your piece to length. The kerfing can be held in place with ordinary clothes pegs to conform to the shape of the guitar, so that it can be

accurately measured. Start at the neck block and work back to the end block. This is not essential, but the kerfing around the neck block on the back of the guitar will be seen through the soundhole and so it pays to keep this as tidy as possible. Do not succumb to the temptation to cut all four pieces to the first length you measure. The pieces for the top and back are almost certainly going to be different lengths and you may have some variation in your shape.

The kerfing is glued into place with the sides in the mould. It is normal practice to bend the sides into the mould with the top surface flush with one face of the mould. This makes it easier to judge whether you have the shape of the sides correct, so before you can glue the kerfing you need to slide the sides through the mould so that the top is proud. Needless to say, if your sides and end blocks were being held in place with clamps these will need to be removed and you will need to ensure that the top surface is proud of the mould by an equal amount all the way around. It is also essential that the sides have not twisted in any way, and that can be seen if the centre line of the guitar is out of place. Once this is done you can clamp the sides back into place if you wish, but often all that is needed is some way of keeping the waist of the guitar pressed into the mould.

One way is to cut a dowel and wedge the sides. Cut a piece of $1/2 \times 1/2$ in (12.7 × 12.7 mm) wood, and pretty well any type of wood will do, about $3/8$ in (9.5 mm) shorter than the distance between your two sides at the waist of the guitar. Make up two wedges that are about $1/2$ in (12.7 mm) wide and $3/8$ in (9.5 mm) deep at one end, tapering evenly to nothing. You can then hold your wooden strip in place and the two wedges will allow you to press it into position without the fear of one end slipping – which would be the case if only one wedge was used.

Turnbuckles, of the type used to tension cables, can also be used if the ends are ground flat and they are

You can use wedges and a wooden bar to hold the waist in the mould. This is less robust than a turnbuckle and shaped blocks as it can fall out when the guitar is moved. Care is needed not to use too much pressure on the sides.

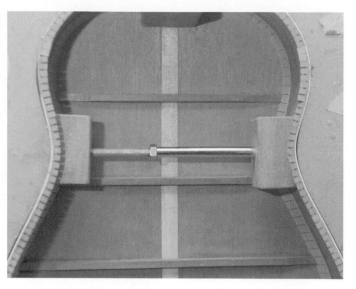

I borrowed this idea for a waist brace from my good friend Dave King; he uses a simple tensioner made from studding and a tube pushing on two wooden blocks.

The component parts of a simple waist brace. A metal tube, a short length of commercial studding, one nut and one washer and two shaped blocks to distribute the load against the sides.

pushing into recesses in shaped blocks that are made to match the curve of the inside of the waist. The turnbuckle can then be opened out to spread the waist.

Making your own version of a turnbuckle is not difficult. The version in the photo above was taken from a design Dave King uses. This is very simple to make. You need a short length of steel tubing (I think the tubing I use is an old bathroom towel rail) and inside this a short length of threaded studding, as found in many hardware stores, is inserted. This is adjusted simply with a nut of the correct thread pushing against a washer.

Each end then pushes against a recess in the shaped blocks that rest against the inside of the waist.

The kerfing is then glued and then held in place with some form of clamp while it dries. You could use small G-clamps, but these will be heavy and expensive. A far better option is to buy a lot of ordinary wooden clothes pegs and some thick elastic bands. Place the bands around the 'clamping' end of the peg so there is more force holding the ends together and then use these as simple clamps. This is a very common way of doing this job and clothes pegs are certainly still used at the Martin factory (*see* page 267). You may need to bolster them in some places with some small spring clamps, but as long as there is a little glue seepage from either side of your kerfing then it is clear there is glue in the join. With all the clamps (pegs) in place you can clean any excess glue off with a damp cloth and with a drinking straw cut into a point.

When both top sides of the body are kerfed, the sides can be released and slid back through the mould so that the back kerfing can be applied. The kerfing helps to keep the sides in shape, but you still need to take care that the sides do not slip through the mould at an angle.

Gluing the kerfing for the back of the guitar is, in most cases, a little more complex. Since the guitar tapers and the kerfing is slotted vertically it will not conform to the shape of the sides without some gaps. Added to this, the shape of the sides needs to accommodate the curve of the back. To remain at full depth all along the back, the kerfing would have to twist and bend in three directions! Clearly this is not possible and there are various ways around it.

Ordinary clothes pegs, and the odd cheap spring clamp, are ideal for clamping the kerfing into place.

The kerfing on the back of this guitar has been left slightly proud to allow for the arching of the back.

The first is to cut a kerfing with angled slots in some places to cater for the taper of the sides, a twist to allow the kerfing to glue flush with the sides, and variable depth to allow for the shape of the sides. Clearly this is complicated and a non-starter! Another way is to glue the kerfing on and accept that there will be some gaps as the wood tries to match the taper of the back and this, too, is far from ideal. The normal methods are to glue the kerfing round and leave it proud of the sides so that it can be cut back when the back is fitted. This way the kerfing will end up shorter around the neck area than at the end block. Alternatively, the kerfing can be cut into smaller lengths which are attached so that they are stepped in order to allow for the differences in height that the kerfing needs to have to accept the shape of the back. This will show on the inside of the guitar but is better than some of the alternatives.

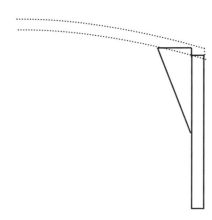

This exaggerated view shows why the kerfing can be slightly proud of the back.

The kerfing on the inside of a cutaway can be difficult to fit.

Another solution might be to separate all the parts of the kerfing so that each triangular piece is glued individually. This is fine in theory, but in practice it is hard to get the pieces to line up correctly and is very time-consuming. I tried it on the maple guitar seen in some of the photographs and was not happy as the kerfing only needs to slip very slightly when being glued to look terrible inside the guitar. If using this method, it is not even essential for the gap to be the width of the saw cut, since as long as there is enough area to hold the top in place then spacing them a little wider should cause no problems. I am also sure that some people may argue this would allow the top to vibrate a little better, although the amount of top that would be able to vibrate would be almost too small to measure.

It is also worth noting that, since both the top and back may have some curve across them, placing the kerfing so that it is flush with the edge of the top surface of the sides may not be ideal. It is better to allow a little even height to protrude, perhaps as little as $1/16$ in (1.5 mm), as this can be cut back as the sides are fitted. It is better to remove some of the kerfing than more of the sides.

CUTAWAYS

Kerfing around the inside of a cutaway can have its own problems. The tight curve around the inside of the cutaway is one thing, but the extreme curve on the inside of the horn is designed to make life interesting. For the inside of the cutaway, I find it easier to cut individual pieces and shape the rear of them so that they

sit flush against the side, but for the inside of the horn they will need to be trimmed on the outside, too, so that they do not touch. This is covered in more detail in Chapter 23.

SIDE BARS

Guitar accidents happen. This is a fact of life and whilst many of them are inconsequential some can write off a guitar instantly. In most cases the damage can be fixed – after all if you can make a guitar you can replace any part of it, but this is time-consuming and frustrating. You can also build into your guitar a means by which damage can be limited in certain circumstances.

Impacts to the edge of the guitar can cause splits in the sides and, since the sides are fairly thin and the grain runs along them, the split may extend a considerable way around the guitar. In some cases this can be repaired but in others the only alternative may be a completely new side. Making and fitting sides is enough for any sane person without having to remove an old one first. The alternative is to add something to the sides of the guitar that would help prevent a crack from extending too far.

For the crack to happen in the first place, the stress from the impact on the side must be along the grain. For the split to occur the stress needs to move the side enough to break open the grain. If the side can be held in place damage should be minimised.

The easiest way to do this is to add side bars to the inside of the guitar. These are small pieces of wood that are glued so that their grain runs perpendicular to that on the sides. They are placed a few inches apart

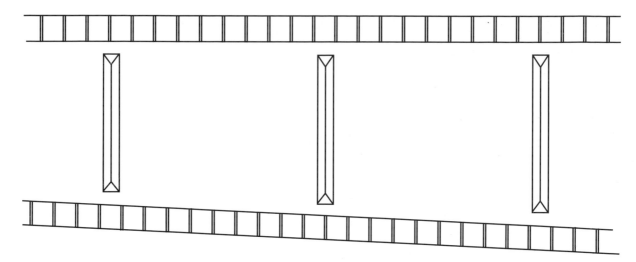

Side bars are designed to stop a crack in the side of the guitar
from spreading too far.

Maple side bars cut for a rosewood guitar. These are cut to
length in pairs.

Using spring clamps and a wooden caul to glue the bar.

Marking the position of the side bar using a square from the top
of the guitar.

and need only be as thick as the side itself. You could
even make them from the same material as the sides –
from scrap that is left over, for example – or you could
use another wood. Maple is often used as it is strong
and close-grained, and so supports the side well. On
guitars made of rosewood, mahogany or any other
dark wood, the contrasting maple does not look bad at
all and also shows that care has been taken with the
internal strength of the instrument.

The bars are made of $^1/_4 \times ^1/_{16}$ in (6.3 × 1.5 mm) or
$^3/_{32}$ in (2.4 mm) strips cut to fit evenly within the sides.
Allowing between $^1/_4$ in (6.3 mm) and $^1/_8$ in (3 mm)
between the end of the side bar and the kerfing is fine.
The side bars can be fitted with the body out of the
mould as the shape will be a little more stable with the
kerfing added but it will still be very flexible. This can
cause problems if the body does not go back into the
mould in the exact same position from which it came
out, so great care is required, but it does mean the

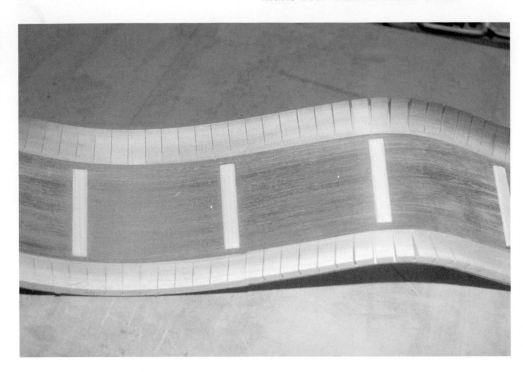

The finished side bars and kerfing.

strips can be glued into place and clamped over the sides of the guitar. Once dry they can be gently shaped with a sharp chisel and sand paper. They need not be too close together, about 3 in is usually enough, and they should prevent any crack in the sides from extending all the way around the guitar.

Once the side bars are all in and shaped, the sides can go back into the mould and the wedge can be replaced at the waist to hold everything in place while the top and back are fitted. Alternatively you may wish to fit the end inlay before returning the sides to the mould.

End inlay

The end inlay covers the join between the two sides at the end block and is a V-shaped inlay. Fitting at this time does make it easier to hold the guitar while the recess is being cut, as the end block can be held in a vice, but be aware that the guitar body is, of course, still very flexible at this point. You may wish to wait to fit the end inlay until after the top and back have been glued (see page 105). Neither way is right or wrong; do it whenever it feels right for you.

Chapter 9
Fitting the Top and Back

With the top and back made, the sides complete in the mould and the kerfing in place, it is time to fit the top and back.

If you have chosen to use a totally flat top, and even a flat back, fitting is quite straightforward; and it is not particularly difficult if you have chosen to curve the top or back or both.

The most important part, as we have already discussed is that the top and back are aligned with the neck. Since the neck is not fitted at this point you need to ensure that the joins between the sides, at the neck block and end block, are along the centre line of the guitar. If the centre lines of the top and back also line up with these then it will be much easier to line the neck up, knowing the body centres are all in agreement.

Before fitting the top it is a good idea to inspect the inside of the guitar again, to ensure that it is as tidy and clean as possible before attempting to glue the top. It is very difficult to deal with sanding or carving braces or even removing glue spots after the top is fitted and next to impossible after the back is fitted. Gently sand everything so any marks are gone and all pieces are smooth. Then remove the dust, using a brush or an airline. Dust caught between the saw cuts on the kerfing may combine with glue to form an ugly and hard-to-remove 'porridge': this will not harm the guitar but it is better if it is not there.

FITTING THE TOP

Traditionally the transverse and cross bracings are fitted into recesses in the kerfing, and the bracing construction in Chapters 7 and 8 has this in mind. In Chapter 2 we did discuss the possibility of fitting the bracing inside the kerfing and not slotting this at all.

The brace positions are marked onto the sides while the top is face down on a workboard. These marks are then transferred to the kerfing which needs to be slotted to accept the braces. These marks on the sides were made before the kerfing was fitted and are a good double check.

The main braces, as we have seen, are usually cut down to 1/8 in (3 mm), or sometimes less, before the recesses in the kerfing are cut. This, in reality, does not give that much extra strength. Since the top and the back are supported by the sides and the kerfing, this part of the guitar is already quite strong.

If making a guitar without recessing the braces, they can be angled rather than curved down (*see* page 76). There would, in this instance, be more mass supporting

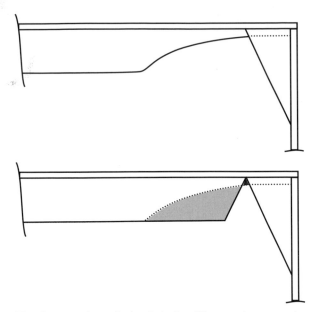

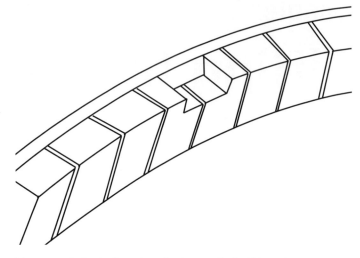

The recess in the kerfing where the brace will sit will have to be cut carefully, Where the recess has to be cut partly into the kerfing it is quite common for small pieces to become dislodged.

The diagrams above demonstrate the differences in recessed and non-recessed braces. The upper diagram shows a standard recessed brace with the recess in the kerfing shown by the dotted line. The lower diagram shows an inset brace. The small red shaded area is the only place where there is less material holding and the grey shaded area shows the additional bracing that can support the edge of the top.

Cutting the recess with a small chisel.

the top further towards the edge of the guitar and it could be argued that the top could vibrate more freely a little further out towards the edges. The fact that both the top and the back would be easier to fit is an additional bonus.

If you choose to go the traditional route, you will need to mark the kerfing for the recesses.

The bracing should have been marked and cut to length, although if you are using the short bracing method this is best done after the kerfing is fitted; if you have not already done so, you will need to trim the main braces so they fit inside the sides and cut a recess into the kerfing to accept the brace.

Place the sides in the mould with the top upwards and with the sides a little proud of the mould, roughly 1 in (25 mm) should be fine. Place the top onto the body with its centre line perfectly aligned with the centre of the body. It may be an idea to tape it into place as if it moves when you are marking the brace positions, all of your careful alignment will disappear. You will be able to see where the braces will fit into the kerfing and these positions can be marked. You should mark six positions: one at either end of each cross brace and one at either end of the main cross brace.

Remove the top and extend the marks on the sides over onto the face of the kerfing and then use a long straight edge to join up the relevant pairs of pencil marks. You should have 12 marks, two for each end of

each brace. It is a good idea to also mark these positions on the inside of the kerfing.

As a good double check you can also place the guitar face down on the workbench or workboard, making sure that nothing is going to mark it, and place the sides, complete with the mould, over it, so that the centre line of the body lines up with the centre of the top; double check from the inside that the brace positions line up with the marks on the kerfing. You can also double-check that all other bracing does, indeed, finish before it reaches the kerfing.

With the top removed, you will see that the recesses that you need to cut to take the ends of the braces will almost certainly cross one or more of the saw cuts in the kerfing. This material will need to be removed carefully to avoid any breakout, and this is made easier if your kerfing material is relatively fine-grained.

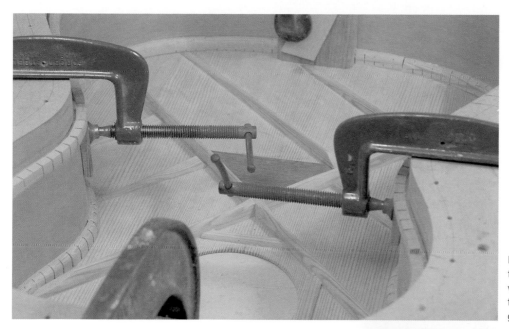

It is a good idea to place the top face down on the workboard and double check the fit inside the guitar before gluing the top into place

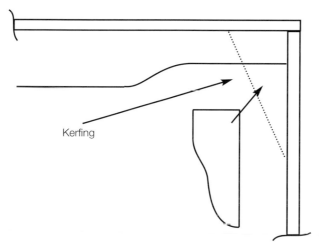

David Russell Young suggests extending the transverse brace down the sides a little with an additional piece.

Kerfing

Using the sanding stick to level the sides on a flat-topped guitar. Careful checking with a straight edge is also essential.

These recesses can then be cut using whatever method you are comfortable with. Some makers insist on doing this by hand with knives and chisels, while others quite happily remove the bulk of the material with a small router. There is no right way and wrong way, but it is important not to damage the sides of the guitar, and to make the recesses as neat as possible.

With the recesses cut the top can be test-fitted. It is important that all parts fit correctly and that the recesses are neither too shallow nor too deep. These may need some adjustment as the top fitting progresses, as an arched top will mean the sides may have to be altered slightly to accommodate the shape of the top, and the recesses for the braces may need to be recut slightly. Even sanding the top of the sides on a flat-topped guitar may mean that some further work is

needed on the recesses, but it is better to cut them at this stage as fitting the top will be easier. It is also wise to recheck that everything lines up. As stated in Chapter 2, a small error on one part of the guitar can lead to big problems elsewhere. It is also important to check the length of the braces is correct and they do not need to be forced into place since, as the late Irving Sloan once said, anything forced together wll eventually come apart the same way!

Some makers like to extend the end of the transverse brace down the side of the guitar; this is mentioned in David Russell Young's book. To do this you will need to remove the kerfing just at the end of the brace and make up the extension piece as shown in the drawing. This can then be glued into the sides before the top is glued so that clamping it is possible. The cross brace

Trial fitting the top. This one does not quite sit flat so a little more must be removed from the recess.

You can trial fit the back and mark on the sides where they need to be lowered to allow for the back arch.

then sits on this as the top is glued. Needless to say, it is important that this fits correctly and does not prevent the top sitting correctly on the kerfing.

When you are satisfied that the top fits correctly, the upper surface of the sides can be prepared. If your top is flat it is a simple matter to flatten the surface using a long sanding block or a large flat board covered with sandpaper. You will also need to pay attention to the end blocks as they may need a little lowering if you have made them slightly proud of the sides. Be careful not to remove more from one side of the guitar than from the other, and check that you are not making the recesses for the cross braces too shallow. It is easy to make these a little deeper if necessary, which is better than making them too deep to begin with. When this is done and all surfaces are level, clean off the dust and put the top to one side again. If your front is domed then fitting will be the same as for the back, and this is described below.

FITTING THE BACK

It is now time to repeat the procedure for the back of the guitar. The only differences are that the braces go across the centre line, so cutting the recesses is slightly easier as they are not at an angle, and that the back is likely to be domed. If you have chosen to make a guitar with a flat back, then fitting the back is little different to fitting the top, except that the back is likely to be tapered and so the recesses for the cross braces may have to be very slightly angled to fit correctly, although the amount needed will be minimal since the recess is only 1/8 in (3 mm) deep.

When the recesses are marked and cut, the back can be fitted. If the back is domed this needs to be accommodated. This can be done in several ways but the easiest, if you are only making one or two guitars, is to do it by hand in stages. Place the back onto the sides and

Hand sanding the side down to the mark.

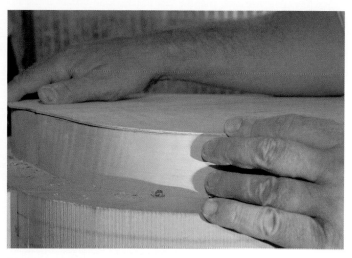

Trial fitting a back.

Using a 15 foot arch to check the
shape of the kerfing.

note where the back touches. Look also at the neck and end blocks, and you should notice that the back touches the outer ends of these.

Both the sides and the blocks will need to be shaped to accommodate the back. The way to do this is to slowly remove the areas where the back touches. As you do this, the back will lay further into its position and the area that touches will become greater. When you have the back touching all the way around, then you are very close to having it perfect. Be aware that the recesses for the back braces will get smaller as you do this and so may give a false impression of how the back is fitting. Deepen these as required as you go. You will need to be careful since the back is flexible; this must be taken into account and the back handled carefully to ensure everything remains correct.

You will also see that, since the back is domed, the kerfing will not be totally square to the side, and you will need to carefully angle the kerfing so that the back

touches all the way around. This is much easier if you have left it a little proud as suggested in the last chapter.

This process can be time-consuming and frustrating. There is another way but it requires a piece of equipment that is not readily available and so has to be made specially: a back sander. Many of the larger guitar-making companies will have something similar, as do many smaller makers. It consists of a jig with a concave dome inside it, lined with abrasive paper, which is used in a circular motion over the work to produce a perfectly domed back. The Martin company has several machines, all of which are made in-house, that do this job and they say that you can tell when all surfaces are ready from the noise the abrasive makes.

If you do want to make one of these you will need to be able to machine a relatively accurate concave impression on the back of a large piece of wood. Since the guitar is 20 inches long, your sanding disc will need to be at least 24 in diameter. It will also need to be quite

Making a Back Sander

A back sanding jig can be made from a piece of MDF (remember those safety precautions) or plywood. The one in the photographs was made from a piece of ply just over 3 ft (925 mm) wide. The centre was found and a circle of 12 in (305 mm) radius drawn using a pencil in a drilled piece of wood. The 24 in diameter of the disc is enough for most guitars that I make. The ply was only $^7/_8$ in (22 mm) thick and a careful check was made before work started that there was enough depth for the concave shape.

The concave shape can be made with a router on a pair of curved rails. The rails will need to have a curve of 15 ft (4.57 m) radius for the back and 25 ft (7.62 m) radius if you are making a jig for arched tops and they must be rigid enough not to deflect under the weight of the router, as there will be times when the rails will be unsupported by the workpiece. The router will run up and down these rails and, as the cutter is fixed at a certain depth, the router will cut more in the

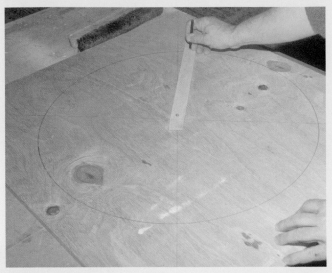

Marking the 24 in diameter.

The router sitting on the curved rails.

centre of the circle than at the edges. The ones in the photo were made to the width of the router base and then a guard was fitted either side to guide the router. By moving the jig around the circumference of the circle the cuts join up to make a concave dish.

The rails are screwed into place so the centre point of the curve is in the centre of the disc and the router is passed over this to remove the waste. Several passes may be needed to get to the correct depth which should leave the channel that is being cut ending right on the circumference of the circle that was drawn. The rails then need to be moved around the circle and the next slice of waste removed. It is important that the depth of these cuts remains the same for each pass. This is also rendered impossible if the curve is routed right to the edge of the disc, as the rails need something firm to rest on.

I used a $^1/_2$ in (12.7 mm) flat bottomed cutter and moved it round the circumference $^3/_8$ in (10 mm) for each pass.

The first two cuts were made with a rounded cutter which did not give as good a result as a flat-bottomed one.

Approximately 50 separate cuts were required to go 180 degrees around the circle and remove all the waste. For each one the rails were screwed into place about 2 inches outside the circle so the router was not having to work right to the edge.

Making a Back Sander (cont.)

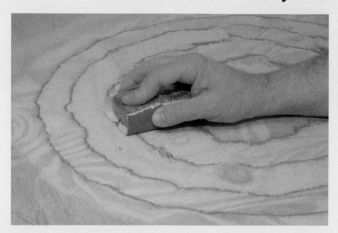

Sanding the inside of the disc.

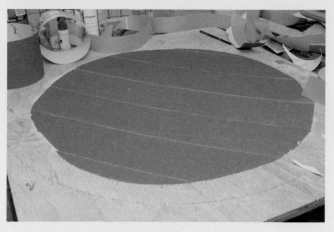

40 grit sandpaper was attached with double-sided tape.

When using the sanding disc, it is necessary to secure the sides (in the mould) to the workbench so they do not move around as the disc produces a lot of friction. Simple blocks screwed into the board work well.

If using the disc or any other method, the neck and end blocks will need to be shaped to take the back. Using the disc it is easy to see when the block has been fully sanded.

When complete the dish was not perfect in engineering terms but is more than adequate for the job. The inside was cleaned up with sandpaper and the disc was cut from the original square shape on a bandsaw just inside the positions of the screw holes used to line up the rails.

With the inside of the disc completed, segments of 40 grit sandpaper were cut and fixed into the disc using double-sided tape. The disc was then ready for use.

rigid and so will need to be made of a material that is robust and strong, and this often equates with heavy. For one or two guitars shaping the sides by hand is clearly a sensible alternative.

When you are satisfied that the back is a snug fit, touching all the way around, and the recesses for the back braces are all the right depth, it is time to clean up the surfaces to be glued, in order to remove the dust and to attach the top and back.

GLUING TOP AND BACK

Gluing the top and back onto the guitar, and keeping the guitar from going out of shape as you do so, has its own set of problems.

Even with the kerfing in place, the sides may still have enough spring in them to change shape as they come out of the mould.

Ideally, and perhaps after many years of experience, this would be the case but since we are talking about a

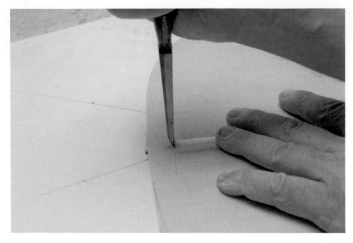

The final job before gluing the back is to ensure the back trim fits properly inside the neck and heel block.

One of the Martin factory back gluing jigs. The guitar remains in the mould for the gluing.

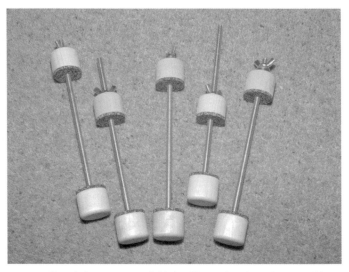

Spool clamps are available in different length and are used by some makers for clamping tops and backs.

first guitar here, it makes sense to take this into consideration and be careful.

Therefore, it seems sensible to glue the top, at least, onto the guitar while it is still in the mould, with the turnbuckle or wedged support in place to hold the sides to the correct shape.

If your guitar does retain its exact shape when out of the mould, the top and back could be glued on in a number of ways.

You could use spool clamps, as pictured, around the edge of the guitar, but these can be expensive and a lot of them could be quite heavy. Other makers wind dressmakers' cotton webbing straps around the guitar to hold the top and back in place. There are potential problems with this; if there is a small overhang on the top the webbing can bear down on this and possibly crack the wood.

One way to avoid this is to use a clamping caul. A piece of $1/2$ in (12.7 mm) fibreboard cut to the outer shape of the guitar, with the internal part cut away to give a shelf of approximately $1/2$ in (12.7 mm), will allow the webbing to bear down on just the edges and mean that the caul will not be trying to force the centre of the guitar downwards, so distorting it.

This is a very good way of doing things, but you need to be very careful not to get glue on your webbing as it can get stuck to your guitar body, which will cause all sorts of problems to remove it and repair any surface damage.

If the guitar stays in the mould then clamps, unless they are very long-throated which will be even more of a problem as they will be heavy, are out of the question. The webbing can be used but getting enough down pressure, with the webbing having to pull past the extra width of the mould, may be a problem too.

The Martin Company uses single clamps which, like many tools at the Martin plant, are made in-house. The clamp has a caul that is made to fit the guitar exactly, so a different one is required for each model, and these are pressed down with a single screw in the centre. The same press is used for top and back fitting. This is clearly too complicated for a home workshop and so an alternative needs to be found.

Using tape on the resonator guitar in chapter 24. This is sycamore so the tape sticks well; on more open-grained or oily wood this method might not be as effective.

Pulling tape over itself to prevent it lifting fibres from a guitar top.

One method that at first looks rather slapdash but in fact works well is to use tape to hold the top and back on as the glue dries. It might seem that tape is a little weak, but you will use a lot of it in small sections to glue the top into place; the overall pull of a lot of small pieces each exerting a small force is more than enough for a successful glue join.

The sides could be slid through the mould so that $1^1/_2$–2 in (33–50 mm) protrudes and the tape can be pulled down to stick onto the sides. In practice this is not necessary; the tape may tend to distort the edges of the top, in the same way as the webbing straps might and the amount of the sides that now protrude from the mould will make retaining the shape more difficult.

If the body is in the mould so that just about 1 in (25 mm) is exposed, the body can be clamped into the mould using small G clamps in several places around the edge and the tape can be pulled down and stuck to the edges of the mould. The mould would need to be clean and dust free for the tape to stick but the lesser angle of the tape over the edges of the guitar would make it less likely to damage the edges of the top. This would give a little less tension than sticking to the sides, but the important part is whether there is enough tension to hold the pieces together and if glue will seep from the join. It is wise to use a high-tack masking tape rather than some of the low-tack versions used for masking paint and, in practice, this method can work very well.

Whichever way you choose, the top should go on with minimal excess glue as this will run down inside the guitar. You should use enough that some can be seen seeping out of the join, though, all the way around. If it is not seeping then it is either not in there or the join is not good enough.

It is now time to glue the back. This can be done in

exactly the same way as the top although a little more care may be needed with the glue as any drips inside the guitar will be close to impossible to remove unless they are accessible through the soundhole.

This is an interesting time as, if the guitar has been made correctly, there may be no need to ever take it apart and so this is the last time you get to inspect your workmanship inside the guitar. I often sign the guitar somewhere on the inside at this point.

Gluing the top is often enough to hold the sides in place if there was only a small amount of spring left in them. If this is the case they can be removed from the mould and the back glued in a different manner. Be wary though, and check the sides of the guitar remain square to the top at the waist before gluing the back, and if it has moved at all, put it back in the mould and use the tape method. You can even refit the turnbuckle or wedged waist support as this can come out later through the soundhole.

If the sides do stay square you can use the jig as suggested in the late Irving Sloan's excellent book on classical guitar making. This was a workboard that was roughly the same shape as the guitar but about 2 in (51 mm) larger all the way round. It was made from 1 in (25.4 mm) board and into the edges he suggested fitting screws about $1^1/_2$ in (38 mm) long and set so that the plain shank remained visible and only the threaded portion was put into the wood. He then used webbing tape, as can be bought in a fabric store, wound over the top and around the screw heads, to pull the back down into position.

I have used a jig like this and since I could not get any webbing in long enough lengths, I used ordinary nylon cord. Enough pressure can be applied to the back of the guitar to hold it in place without damaging the edges of the back, even when using cord.

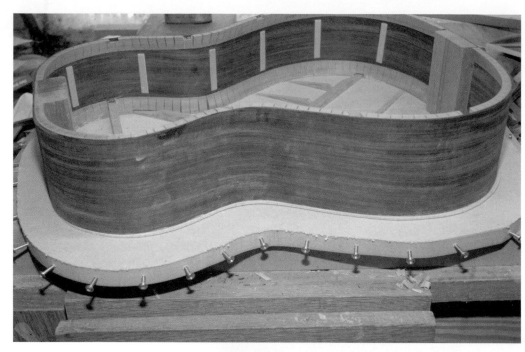

The Sloan-inspired back gluing workboard.

You can use tape, as suggested in the Irving Sloan book, or cord. Since the tension in each pass of the cord is relatively low, the back does not get damaged and the overall pressure is more than enough to glue the back securely.

TRIMMING THE BACK

Once the back is dry, the body can be removed from the mould, if the tape method is used, or untied from the board and the top and back can be trimmed to match the sides.

This can be done by hand, using a knife and sandpaper, or with a router or laminate cutter. Set the cutter to cut flush and simply run it around the edge. You need to be careful when trimming the back that the router does not tip. With the back of the guitar being arched, the router base may not sit square to the side and so could dig in in some places. A laminate trimmer with a tilting base as discussed in Chapter 3 is ideal.

If you are using a laminate cutter or a router to trim the back or top, you need to be careful that the router does not catch and tear out the grain. As the cutter rotates it can catch against the end grain and this can cause the wood to split along the grain. Such splits can be repaired, but it is not an ideal situation.

With the top and back flush to the sides it is time to clean the sides and to prepare the guitar for the binding and for the neck fitting. It is an easy job to sand the sides to remove any marks and residues from the bending iron. You should have nice, neat joins between your sides that run vertically up the end block and neck block, exactly in the centre and perfectly lined up with

Using the laminate trimmer to trim a back.

The router can lift small sections of grain such as this when the cutter is working against the grain.

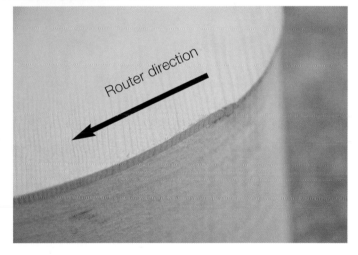

Running the router around the work backwards, or back cutting, can make for a cleaner cut.

the centre of the top and the back. Do not worry too much if you have some small gaps or the join does not line up exactly with the centres of the top and back. As long as the centres of the top and back line up together and with the neck and end block, the rest is easy as you will be fitting the neck over one end of the join and fitting in an end inlay to the other, which will hide any small discrepancies.

The most important of these is the neck to body join. What you do here is totally dependent on the style of join you have chosen. If you have decided to make the simple butt join then the area of the guitar over the neck block needs to be completely flat. The block should

have transferred its shape to the outside of the guitar, as the sides were of uniform thickness, but if there are any small bulges these will need to be removed. Use a straight edge to check that the area is flat, not just verti-cally, but across the area of the neck join too, horizon-tally and at an angle. If this is domed as part of the gui-tar's shape then the shape will need to be included into the end of the neck. This will mean cutting a concave area into the end of the neck, which will not be easy. It is far easier to make sure, even right back at the design stage, that this area remains totally flat.

With this completed, your guitar body is now ready to be bound.

Chapter 10
Binding

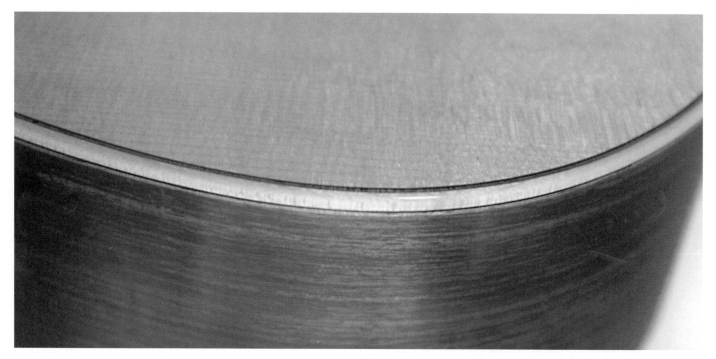

Binding is added to the edges of the guitar and serves several purposes. Firstly it is decorative. Secondly it is usually made of wood that is more robust than the top, so it offers some protection to the edges of the top – this also applies if the binding is plastic. Thirdly, and perhaps most importantly, it seals the end grain. Since end grain could absorb moisture this is a good idea. The binding is usually fitted in two parts. The larger part, surrounding the guitar body and protecting the edge, is known as the binding. The decorative piece usually inlaid inside this is known as purfling.

Binding on many factory-produced instruments is made of plastic, which is available in a wide choice of colours and styles. There is nothing wrong with plastic as a binding material in most cases, but some types can shrink in time and when this happens it can pull away from the guitar. Bindings on many top guitars are made from wood. This is not quite as as easy to fit as plastic, but the wood is a better long-term prospect and can look a little nicer: this is the way I choose, although if you want to use plastic then that is absolutely fine..

Simple but effective binding on a rosewood and spruce guitar. This is maple with small additonal strips of mahogany.

END TRIM

Before the main binding is fitted, an end trim needs to be fitted as discussed in Chapter 8. This tidies up the end of the guitar and is often made from a wood that will contrast with the sides. Maple is often used on guitars that have sides made from mahogany or rosewood, and rosewood or ebony on guitars with sides from a lighter wood such as maple. However, I also like to use an offcut from the same piece of wood as the rest of the guitar; I edge that with something so that it looks as if the sides are continuous around the guitar, with just a couple of inlaid lines at the end.

If a contrasting end trim is fitted it can also be edged to add a little more visual interest. Scrap pieces of the fibre strips that are sold for soundhole inlays and top purfling can be used. The end trim is usually made wedge-shaped, which makes it easy to fit as it can slide in until it is snug.

Cutting the edges of the end inlay recess.

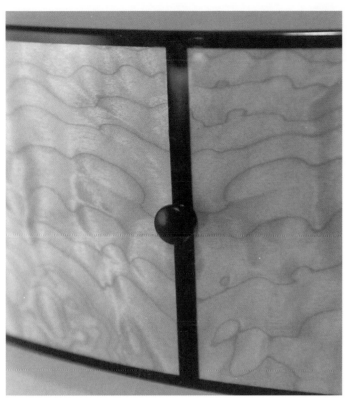

This simple ebony end inlay matches the ebony bindings on this quilted maple guitar.

This can be fitted before the top and back are attached (*see* page 81) but leaving it until later does allow a closer check that the all-important centre lines of the top, back, end and neck blocks all line up.

For the 12-string guitar in Chapter 22, I cut a wedge of pearwood taken after trimming one side to length, which neatly guaranteed it was the same thickness as the side itself. This was cut so the grain ran vertically, rather than horizontally as on the rest of the sides. A centre line was drawn on and then it was marked so that it was $1/2$ in (12.7 mm) wide at one end and $3/4$ in (19 mm) at the other. This was then bound with small pieces of the fibre binding that was also used as a soundhole inlay. These pieces were glued into place with Titebond (yellow glue) and were held in place with tape while the glue dried.

The dimensions of the inlay can be transferred onto the end of the guitar, lining the centre up with the centre line of the guitar that should run through the centres of the end and neck blocks. Once this has been marked, and has been checked, the recess can be cut. Since the thickness of the inlay is the same as the thickness of the sides, the side wood can be cut back until the end block is seen. There is a temptation to make the cuts through the sides with a sharp knife, but this will leave a V-section cut. The answer is either to cut the slot with a saw, being very careful not to stray over the line, or to cut it out close to the line and then tidy it with a sharp chisel. The sides of the recess can then

A trial fit of the inlay prior to gluing. Although this inlay is also made from an offcut from the sides, the change in grain direction makes more of a contrast with the sides. Providing a suitable offcut can be found, there is no reason why the end inlay could not have the same grain direction as the sides.

be made square so the inlay will fit snugly. With the top and back in place, a little part of these may need to be cut back to allow the inlay to fit.

With the inlay shaped to match the recess in the guitar, it can be glued into place and then trimmed so that it does not overhang the front or back of the guitar.

THE BINDING

The binding will usually be made in several parts, joined at the bottom of the guitar, as finding pieces

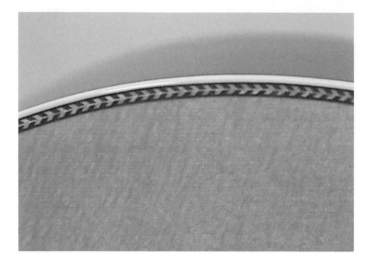
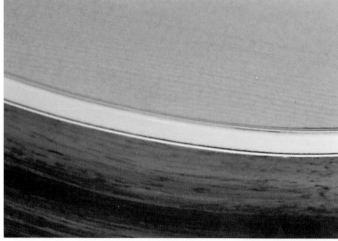
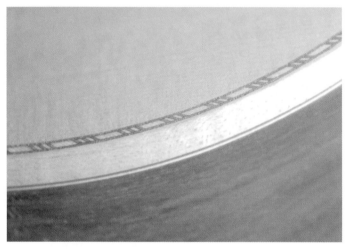

A selection of different styles of binding and purfling ranging from simple lines to elaborate inlaid abalone.

long enough to go all the way round can be difficult. Binding can be as simple or as elaborate as you choose. The bare minimum is usually a band of one wood, such as maple, around the edge with a single contrasting line inside of that. There is no reason why a contrasting line has to be used, but it does emphasise the shape of the guitar and stop the top and binding looking as if they are one piece. At the other end of the scale there are guitars bound on the front and back with multiple contrasting stripes, abalone and pearl, or even precious metals. Other than sealing in the end grain there is no structural reason for doing this, but it looks good when done well.

In all cases it is important that the pieces fit well. There is no point in spending time and money making a very elaborate binding if there are gaps around it and mismatched pieces. It does not take that much more work to do the job properly, although a well-done simple binding will look better than a bodged attempt at an elaborate one. I will deal with the basics, but there is nothing to stop you being as adventurous as you like.

The main part of the binding will be $^{3}/_{32} \times {}^{5}/_{16}$in (2.4 × 8 mm) and as long as it needs to be in order to go around half of the guitar. Inside this will be the purfling that will be glued into a recess on the face of the front. This is also sometimes done on the back, although this is not necessary. You can make up the strips of wood yourself although most guitar makers' suppliers sell a variety of bindings and purflings, both in wood/fibre and plastic, that are far easier to use.

The channel into which the binding will fit is cut in two stages; the deeper ledge that takes the main binding and a shallower ledge inside this to take the purfling. It can be cut with a specially designed hand tool that is available from most guitar-making suppliers, or with a router. Few commercially available routers have a suitable guide to prevent the bit cutting into the top, so you will need to either adapt your router, buy a specially built laminate cutter as described in Chapter 3 or use follower bits in the router. Follower bits have a bearing beneath the cutter that limits the width of the cut, and it may be possible to find a bit with a suitable bearing that is correct for the size of binding that you intend to use. Companies such as Stewart MacDonald

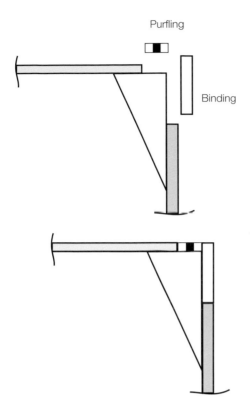

Purfling

Binding

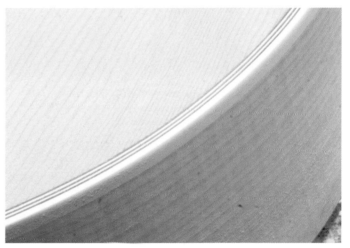

Basic binding and a simple purfling are shown in this diagram. The bindings are often the same thickness as the sides so cutting the channel to accept them may expose the kerfing. The photographs (*right*) show the channels and finished binding and purfling as in the diagram.

Guitar Shop Supply (among others) sell a variety of these and even your local tool store may have a variety of cutters and roller bearings that will enable you to find the size you need.

Guitar parts suppliers will all sell hand cutters for cutting the recess into the guitar (*see* page 37). These can be very successful if used carefully – after all, generations of violin makers used them for centuries – but all tools need to be very sharp, especially if cutting very hard woods like rosewood on the back of a guitar, and investing in a small router may be easier.

There is a problem with routers, as mentioned when discussing the trimming of backs. Routers are built with flat bases that are fine when running along a flat-top guitar, but there is a problem when they are used to cut a recess on the back of a guitar or on one with an arched front: the base of the router tips the bit so that it does not cut level with the wood of the guitar, but digs in. There are several ways around this. Some of the guitar-making supplies companies sell a variety of clever devices that can help overcome the problem. These can be bearings for small routers that are designed to keep the router running against the side of the guitar with just a small depth stop on the front. There are also more elaborate jigs that can hold a guitar

body perfectly level and which then have a router suspended above the work so that it can be raised and lowered over the guitar.

As discussed in Chapter 3, I use a laminate trimmer with a tilting base for cutting binding channels. I discovered this by searching for spare parts for my trusty Makita laminate trimmer, as I wanted additional bearings to allow me to have two points of contact beneath the cutter so the trimmer could be kept firmly up against the side of the guitar, rather than resting entirely upon the top. I was looking through the company's website (never a bad thing if you are a tool hoarder like me) when I found the tilting base. This is useful as the guitar back will mostly have a constant-radius curve, so the trimmer can be set with just enough tilt to allow for that. By watching carefully as the cut is made, any adjustments can be made to keep the slot perfect.

Whether you are machining the slot or cutting by hand, it is possible to break away small pieces of wood. These will need to be glued back and allowed to dry out before the work is resumed. One way to minimise the risk of this is to only remove a small part at a time.

It is also a good idea to test the depth of the cut on some scrap wood before setting out to bind your guitar.

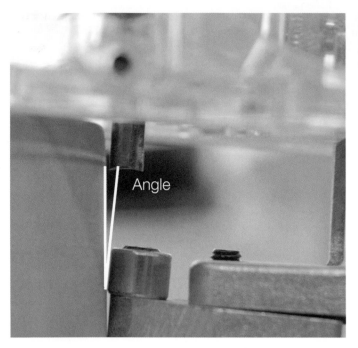

The problem with most routers is that the flat base presents the cutter at an angle due to the curvature of the back.

A binding channel being routed at the Martin factory. This machine has a cutter mounted horizontally that cuts on the same plane as the base onto which the sides rest. By holding the sides down onto this, all cuts are in line with the sides.

It will be no problem if your slot is too small – it can always be enlarged – but if you start by cutting too deeply, you may not be easily able to rescue the project and you stand a bigger chance of splitting away more wood than you intended.

As was discussed in the last chapter, one of the problems in cutting around a guitar body is the direction of the grain and how the router, or laminate cutter, affects this. This is doubly important when the binding is being fitted, because if there is a slight problem of tear-out when trimming the top, the damage will often be hidden by the binding; this is clearly not going to be the case when the binding is being fitted as any damage will be visible after the binding is glued, so cutting needs to be done as accurately and as cleanly as possible. Using downward-cutting spiral router bits, as sold in some guitar-making suppliers, will help minimise this problem. Taking off small amounts at a time and being careful with the direction of cut can be advantageous as can cutting backwards, running the router in the reverse direction to normal.

Since the sides of the guitar are very thin, it is possible that the binding channel will cut through to expose the kerfing. This is not a problem as the binding will be as strong as the wood that was there before, but only if your binding channel does not extend down the side of the guitar further than your kerfing! With the outer, binding, channel cut, the inner, purfling, channel can be cut to suit whatever purfling you have chosen. Although this channel requires less wood

Just a small selection of the binding and purfling available at Touchstone Tonewoods.

to be removed, it is still possible to damage the guitar, especially around the top, so you will need to be careful.

GLUING THE BINDING

With the channel cut the binding can be glued into place. The first stage is to cut the ends to match perfectly. These will join on the centre line at the end of the guitar and so need to be totally square. This is best achieved by cutting and then trimming with a chisel.

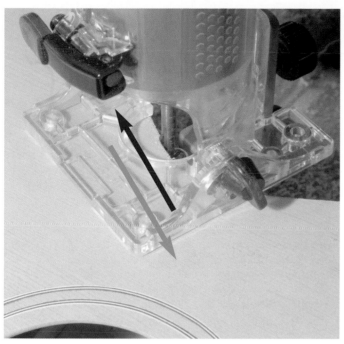

If cutting the channels by hand it will be necessary to clean them up with a sharp chisel. This may also be the case when they are machined. It is good to check before gluing that everything fits neatly.

Cutting the first stage of the binding channel on the top of a guitar. You can see from this picture that the router is cutting against the grain on this section of the top when the router is pushed in the direction of the red arrow. Pulling it, in the direction of the green arrow, will give a cleaner cut (*see* page 103).

The tilting base on the laminate trimmer in action.

The first stage cut on the back of the guitar made from reclaimed materials in Chapter 21.

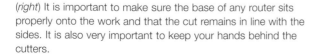

(*right*) It is important to make sure the base of any router sits properly onto the work and that the cut remains in line with the sides. It is also very important to keep your hands behind the cutters.

The electro-acoustic made in Chapter 23 has wooden bindings with a plastic purfling inside. This is the end of the binding being offered up to check the fit after the plastic parts had been superglued in place.

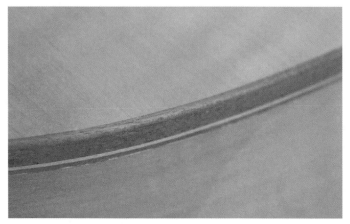

Care needs to be taken if bending layered bindings by soaking first as the glue can separate.

Wooden binding may need to be shaped on a bending iron to fit around the guitar. One advantage of plastic binding is its flexibility. The only time it is likely to need some assistance to go around a bend is if it needs to go around a tight cutaway and then a little hot water is often all that is needed. In all other cases it will conform to shape very nicely. Wooden bindings are not so cooperative and may need a little work on a bending iron to go around some of the curves on a normal guitar shape. A further problem arises when binding the backs on guitars where the binding may have to conform to the complex shape caused by the back arch and taper of the body. It may be possible that the binding needs to bend in two planes, both side to side and vertically, and this is much harder with wooden bindings. Plastic may well be a better option on a first guitar as it will give you fewer problems. If you do use

Bending the binding on the bending iron.

wooden bindings and need to use heat, be careful if you are using bindings with trim (as in the photo above), as the glue between the pieces can separate when the piece is wetted and heated. It is a good idea to lower the temperature of the bending iron and to use less water. Multi-layer fibre bindings tend to be very flexible, but these can be helped to conform to tight corners with some gentle heat.

Using masking tape to hold the binding in place. These wooden bindings are fixed with Titebond and it is a good idea not to use too much as a lot of glue squeezing out under the masking tape can become difficult to remove when it is dry, especially on the top.

Some makers suggest using webbing to hold bindings in place while the glue dries but this can be problematical. There is a lot of length to the binding that will all need to be held in place and getting the webbing to hold all this down and ensuring that it all fits correctly and snugly could be a nightmare. Not only is this a job for people with more than two hands, but any glue seeping under the webbing may well glue the webbing to the guitar. An alternative, as with the top and back, is to use masking tape. This can be very useful and some grades are even sold by guitar-making suppliers for just this purpose, but you need to be careful not to pull fibres from the top of the guitar when removing the tape. The amount of force generated by the tape need not be great: if the binding and channel are the correct size and it all fits together neatly, then the amount of tension needed to hold the binding in place while the glue dries is relatively small. A lot of small pieces of masking tape will work together to apply enough force.

As with all things, preparation is the key. It is worth trying at least part of the job 'dry' – without glue – before embarking on a 'wet run'. If using tape, it is also a good idea to have a stock of small pieces to hand so that you do not need to take both hands off the guitar to pull a fresh piece from the roll. If you are using wooden bindings it is a good idea to use a glue such as Titebond that is easy to apply. Place a little glue onto the guitar and then push the binding in. Clean away the worst of the excess by wiping away from the centre of the guitar towards the edge: if you are using masking tape, do not use a damp cloth as this will stop the tape sticking. As the tape is applied a little more glue may escape from the join, but this is easily cleaned off afterwards.

My good friend Dave King uses tape on binding without gluing first. Having put the tape on, he seeps thin cyanoacrylate (superglue) into the binding that fills the space by capillary action, although you must be careful not to allow it to also seep under the tape.

If you are using plastic binding, this can be applied without the use of any form of clamping – webbing or tape – as the plastic will stick with cyanoacrylate. There are various grades of cyano and they are useful when used correctly and next to useless if not. The key, therefore, is to take advice; buy the right one and use it correctly. It is possible to use plastic cement on plastic bindings. Some of these contain acetone that helps melt the binding surface to give a better join. Some people use good old plastic model kit cement

The surfaces need to be clean but the wood of the guitar may need to be slightly damp. Brushing on a little water will do for this, as it does not need to be dripping wet. You can also slightly roughen the back of the binding to remove the gloss finish, but all dust needs to be wiped clean before you glue. I find the best type of cyanoacrylate to use is the gel sort as it is a little easier to control or the two pack variety where the join can be assembled and held while the catalyst is sprayed on. You do not need to use much: just a thin line is usually enough, and then hold the binding in place while it sets.

MULTIPLE PURFLINGS

If you choose to use something more complicated than a single, double or triple line inside the body binding, you may need to make it up from several pieces. This is not a problem, but clearly the more pieces you use, the more difficult it will be to hold them in the correct place while they are being glued. One way is to install the inner purfling before you put on the main binding, and these strips can either be held in place with ordinary dressmakers' pins while the glue dries, or can be superglued.

Some makers like to use abalone or another type of shell around the guitar, and this is easy if you follow the normal procedure. You can cut each piece of shell by hand but sets to go around a guitar, having some straight and some curved pieces, are available from several guitar makers' suppliers. This is not glued in at the same time as the wooden part of the binding, but later as trying to fit it all at the same time would be messy and fiddly and not give as good a result. To fill the gap while the rest of the binding dries out and to prevent any glue from clogging the channel that will take the shell, it is filled with a PTFE strip. PTFE is a very slippery plastic that is unaffected by the glue and so will pull cleanly out of the slot once the surrounding binding and glue is dry. The PTFE is cut to the same size as the shell but does not stick. It can be assembled at the same time as the other parts of the binding, but when dry can be removed without damage. It is then a relatively simple job to cut the shell pieces to length and to glue them into place, as this will give a tidier finish.

Elaborate soundhole and purfling using abalone strips is very popular. It does not make the guitar sound any better, but it does look good. The normal procedure is to the fit the bindings and purfling lines first with a non-stick PTFE filler replacing the abalone. This is then removed and the small abalone pieces, which would be impossible to install at the same time as the rest of the purfling, can be glued into the gap.

This cutaway guitar has abalone inlays and a dark binding. This dark binding is also used on the fingerboard.

Of course, there is no limit to how complicated you can make your bindings. You could use all sorts of things and inlay halfway across the front of your guitar if you so wish, but that is pointless, really, as you may well have spent a lot of money on a good soundwood for the top, and to replace parts of that with fibreboard and shell is missing the point somewhat. Bindings on modern guitars rarely extend more than about $^3/_8$ in (9.5 mm) into the top of the guitar, and even this can look a little cumbersome at times.

It is also possible to add decoration to the sides and around the neck join. This is seen on some of the more expensive Martin guitars and on some hand-made ones, and requires a lot of tricky work. The binding channel needs to be accurately cut and the small pieces need to fit properly. There is no doubt that when this is done properly it can be very impressive, but if you

Scraping the bindings using a sharp cabinet scraper.

Sanding the binding.

Scraping plastic bindings is nice and easy. With all scraping you need to be sure the edge of the scraper is not digging in, especially on the top.

should ever see the ladies at Martin inlaying guitars such as these it will become clear why there is such a premium to pay on the price.

As when fitting the top, be very careful when removing tape from the front of the guitar. It is very easy to accidentally pull the grain, so you should pull the tape over itself as in the photo on page 101.

When all the tape is removed the guitar can be cleaned up ready for finish sanding. Ideally, your binding should have fit more or less exactly and so will need little sanding. One good trick here is to flick the binding with your finger and you will hear if it has stuck properly. If it has not, then dribble some thin superglue behind and, if necessary, retape it until it is dry. You may also find you will have to fill any small gaps that are left. This can be done with a wood filler of the right colour, or by the old method of glue and sawdust.

Chapter 11

Necks

Guitar necks are not difficult to make. The neck will need to be thin enough to be played, strong enough to support the strings, and so will need some form of strengthening, and it will need a join cut so that is mates with the body perfectly with everything lined up. This part is, as we have discussed, perhaps the most important part of the whole building process but it is not actually difficult; it just needs care and attention to detail. Guitar necks can be cut from a large block, which can be quite wasteful, or they can be made up from smaller pieces that use wood very efficiently.

This is going to be a long chapter as there is a lot to cover, and some aspects need to be slotted in between other jobs. Finding the right order to explain all this can be confusing, so I will try to divide it all up in a way that makes sense and in a logical progression.

The first stage is to choose your wood and get the basic block that will become your neck glued and cut.

WOOD CHOICE AND STARTING WORK

Your neck can be made from one of a variety of different woods. Many makers prefer mahogany, or one of the mahogany substitute woods such as sapele while others use maple or even rosewood, although rosewood will be expensive. There are alternatives to these. Many Flamenco guitars are made with cypress necks, and woods such as Brazilian cedar are sometimes used. The choice is easier now as many places are selling sustainable woods and know the properties of the woods they offer. Finding something that has the same weight and strength characteristics as mahogany, for example, should produce a perfectly suitable neck, provided that the wood has been stored and cut properly, and is not too oily or open-grained. Open grain will only cause problems in getting a good finish on the wood but oily woods, such as teak, should be avoided for guitar making as they will damp any vibrations and so could sound dead.

I have made guitars with Douglas fir necks and they work well provided that they have suitable support in the form of a decent truss rod. They appear to be no more flexible than many other materials as the fir has excellent stiffness-to-weight characteristics.

Gluing the neck block for the electro-acoustic in Chapter 23.

To laminate or not?

It is possible to make your neck in one piece and there is some debate as to whether this gives a better neck. There are those who argue that having no glue joins in the neck allows better transference of the soundwaves within the neck, but there is little firm evidence of this. There are others who argue that making a laminated neck produces a more rigid neck that transmits vibration better than a one-piece. Again there is little

114

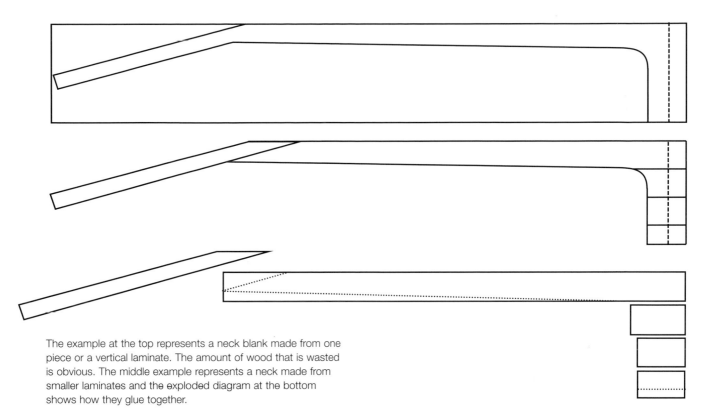

The example at the top represents a neck blank made from one piece or a vertical laminate. The amount of wood that is wasted is obvious. The middle example represents a neck made from smaller laminates and the exploded diagram at the bottom shows how they glue together.

actual evidence to back up this claim. It is worth remembering that a laminated neck can be made from smaller, and therefore cheaper, pieces of wood and that it is far less wasteful. You also do not have to find a piece that is both large enough for the whole neck and of sufficient quality throughout. This is one argument for perhaps not going for a one-piece neck as you need to find an exceptionally good piece of wood to make it work properly. There is also lot of waste.

THE NECK BLANK

The necks made for the guitars in this book vary in style to cover most of the main alternatives. These will be covered in more detail in the relevant chapters, but there are some aspects that always remain the same. The first is that you have to decide which piece of wood you are going to use and then actually start work on it.

There is an order in doing things. There is no point in tapering the sides of your neck before you have put in any strengthening or truss rods, as you will need the neck blank to be parallel when cutting the slots for these: the router will need to use an edge guide to make the cuts.

If you are making a one-piece or a neck laminated vertically to make up the correct width, then it is easy to take the measurements from your drawing in order to determine what size piece of wood you need.

Even so, if you do not have the full depth available for the heel, it can always be laminated. The guitar in

Chapter 23 had a neck blank that was able to use up some pieces of mahogany I had in the workshop that were deep enough to get a good head angle, but not quite deep enough for the heel. Therefore a small piece was added onto the heel after the face of the head was cut.

If you are laminating a neck with a separate, spliced headstock and a built-up heel, the drawing will show you how long each section of the neck will be.

Inclusive head

Most guitar necks are about $2^1/4$ in (57 mm) wide. Often this is made from three pieces each $^3/4$ in (19 mm) wide. It is not essential that the pieces are even. The resonator guitar in Chapter 24 has a neck that was made from two pieces of maple on the outside, with a thinner laminate of two pieces of sapele and another of maple running down the middle to make up the width. You can also be decorative and use contrasting wood, or even just a contrasting stripe of veneer between the laminates; this was done on the electro-acoustic guitar in Chapter 23. However, the laminates will need to be glued up and clamped in one go without slipping. The more glued faces you have, the more likely they are to slip when being clamped, so keeping it simple on a first guitar is, once again, not a bad idea.

It is essential that the pieces you make your neck from are straight-grained and free from blemishes. Quarter-sawn wood is often preferred, with the grain running vertically through the neck, but as long as the

This maple neck blank has black veneer stripes between the laminates that make clamping fun as everything tries to move.

The sapele and black veneer sandwich shown on page 114. This was not deep enough to cut the heel in one piece and so some of the scrap was used to build up the heel. Notice that the wood is not quarter sawn and the pieces are arranged so that the grain mirrors.

The front face of the neck has been planed flat and a centre line drawn on. The nut position is shown here.

grain on the piece is not too curved, good slab-sawn wood can also be used. Maple, because of the way it grows, often does not provide much in the way of quarter sawn wood and slab sawn maple has been used by many makers for years.

The laminates should be prepared by planing them flat. If you have to do this by hand it can take ages, and you will soon find if there is any uneven grain. This is one job where access to a powered planer will save a lot of time.

If you are using three laminates from the same plank, it is often suggested that the centre laminate be reversed so the grain direction is opposite to the other two. This is said to even out any stresses in the neck, and if one piece starts to move the others will hold it. I have never been fully convinced by this argument, as if one piece *is* likely to move then there is no reason the others will not move too and the neck will be ruined. After all, if one piece moves then all three are likely to have been unsuitable. As it is, reversing the centre laminate can make shaping the neck difficult, as the grain may lift when being cut in one direction on one piece while the one next to it is fine.

With the pieces ready and planed, it is a good idea to make sure that all your clamps are ready to be used and are opened at more or less the right width. It is very annoying to find that you have glued up the neck blank and you suddenly have to adjust all the clamps before you can fit them.

I tend to use Titebond when gluing up neck blanks and I have never had any problems with it.

Once the blank is glued and clamped it can be put to one side and left to dry; overnight is usually best on neck blanks. Then it is time for the most important job on the neck. All of your dimensions from your drawing will be transferred to the neck and it is important

that they have a suitable datum point. The top face of the neck blank should be planed flat and should be square to the edge. Once this has been done the marking can begin.

Start by drawing a centre line along the neck. I find it easier to measure from the heel end, marking on the tenon, if one is used, and then the neck-to-body join,

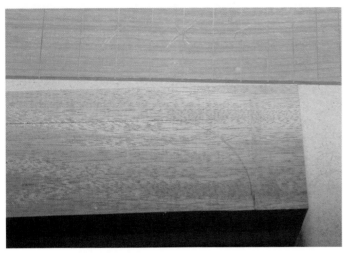

The guitar fingerboard (with a nice visible 'X' marking the 12th fret) was used to mark the positions of the neck join, nut and the heel onto the side of the neck. This neck is to be butt-joined and will also need a small piece added to make up the depth of the heel.

The head angle can be planed flat.

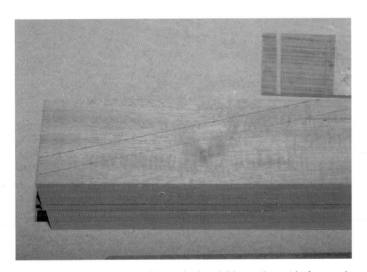

The head angle can be marked and this can be cut before work on the truss rod channel starts.

Marking the angle onto the head with a 15 degree jig. Here the depth of the head is being marked onto the neck as in the lower drawing on the next page, as the cut will be made here with the removed head portion going to make up the remaining length of the neck.

the length of the fingerboard and width of the nut; I use a square to extend these across the face of the neck. The positions can then be transferred to the sides and the side elevation of the neck drawn on.

The first stage is usually to cut the front face of the head, and I use a bandsaw for this. You can, alternatively, leave this until after the truss-rod channel is cut to allow the router a little more of a footing on the face of the neck. Either way, the excess is cut off and the face of the head planed flat. If you are using a 'head facing' (a thin layer of a contrasting wood on the head), the thickness of this will need to be subtracted from the overall depth of the head and the cut made accordingly.

FLAT LAMINATED NECKS

Making a neck as shown in the lower diagram on page 115, is an economical way of using wood. The blank needs to be long enough to cut the neck, head and the various parts needed to laminate the heel from one length. You could laminate this up from assorted sources, but making it from one piece ensures that everything is the same width, making assembly much easier.

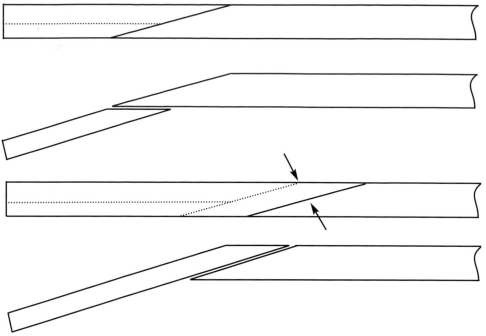

There are two ways of splicing a head laminate. Both are equally good but the lower one may give more protection for the head if the truss rod adjustment recess is at the head end of the neck.

In both cases, the head piece is cut from the main wood at an angle and then reversed and glued back onto the neck. Clamping in both cases can be a little tricky as parts try to move under pressure but can be done with care.

Since the head is thinner than the rest of the neck blank this can be planed to thickness before it is glued onto the neck. This is marked with a dotted line.

In the lower example, the arrows show the thickness of the head that is subtracted from the neck. The dotted line shows the face of the head but the solid line denotes the cut as will be seen in the drawings.

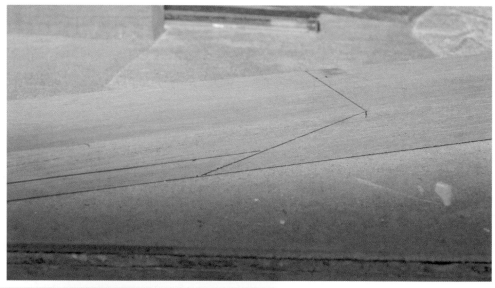

Marking the neck in the style of the upper diagram above. The line across the neck represents the nut position and the head piece will be glued under this.

Making a good join on a laminated headstock neck such as this is relatively easy. The two pieces are held together and planed so they have identical angles. As long as the piece remains square across its width, the pieces will line up perfectly.

Planing the join. The lower piece, which is the main neck piece, still has a dip which will get planed out but the line across the middle, where one piece will sit on the other, shows the face is square to the sides. The small amount of grain breakout at the bottom is not important as this part of the neck is removed when the neck depth is cut.

Just two clamps are enough to hold the join and the glue can be seen seeping from the join. This can be cleaned off with a damp cloth before it dries. It is important to stop the pieces slipping when glued. The neck is as the upper of the two styles shown on page 118 and shows how the join lies halfway down the head, leaving the face of the neck as one piece.

Gluing the head on a neck as per the lower drawing on page 118, the head in this view is on the right. Here the join will be under the fingerboard. Any planing of the face of the neck will now have to be back towards the heel to stop grain tearout on the head piece. This style has the advantage of having the grain running parallel to the face of the head and so is stronger than a head with cross grain at any point.

Another view of the join as in the lower diagram on page 118. This shows how the join should be at 90 degrees to the face of the neck.

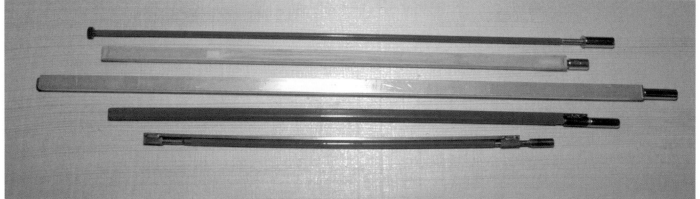

Various styles of truss rod: at the top is a simple rod that is fitted to a curved channel, beneath that two lengths of aluminium channel rod. Beneath that is an opposed rod and beneath than a two-way opposed rod.

The neck shown in the photographs was made from a piece of mahogany $2^1/4$ in (58 mm) wide and 30 in (762 mm) long. The first stage was to plane a datum face on one side so that it was totally flat. This had a centre line drawn on and the relevant positions were drawn on as for the vertically laminated neck. The end of the neck, at the 14th fret position, was marked, and the nut position marked.

Since the head is laminated from the same piece, the neck angle was drawn onto the side, in this case at 15 degrees, and the line for the face of the head drawn on.

There are two ways of joining the head, both normally termed as scarfing the head, and these are shown in the drawings and photographs. In both cases the thickness of the head also needs to be drawn on as this will determine where some cuts are made.

The length of the head can also be calculated and the remaining parts can be cut to make the heel.

The head piece can be cut using either a handsaw or a bandsaw and will need to have the head angle planed on. This is relatively easy as in both ways of doing the job it is an easy matter to clamp the pieces together and plane in one go, ensuring the angles are consistent across both faces. This is also much easier if all the pieces are the same width, having come from the same

block. The last stage before gluing is to plane the head to its correct thickness.

TRUSS RODS

The neck of any guitar has to withstand the considerable pull of the strings whilst being small enough for the player to reach around and successfully fret the strings. Many early guitars were made with thick necks that had to withstand the pressure of heavy-gauge steel strings; Orville Gibson even went one stage further and made his necks larger and hollow so the acoustic chamber went right into the neck.

During the 1920s an employee of Gibson, Ted McHugh, invented the truss rod, designed to compensate for the pull of the strings on the neck. This allowed necks to be made thinner and easier to play. Since then several styles of truss rod have been

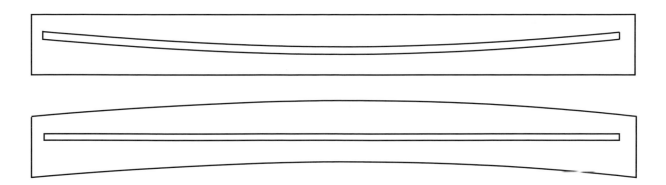

designed and used, and some of these are easier to fit than others. Some can also have an effect on the sound of your guitar, and various things have been written about guitars' necks and truss rods that are misleading. Hopefully the information here will allow you to make an informed choice for your guitar.

The need for relief

Although the neck needs to be protected from the extreme effects of the strings pulling on it, it should not be entirely flat. As the string vibrates it will naturally move more at its centre than it will at the ends, so is more likely to rattle against the fingerboard in the centre. Bowing the neck forwards slightly, so that the string has more room, allows a lower action before buzzing becomes apparent. The amount of relief needed is small, and will depend on the type of strings fitted and the tuning, but is generally about $1/10$ in (0.25 mm) at the centre of the neck. This can be seen if the string is held down at the first and last frets: the string should clear the frets in the centre of the neck by a very small amount. Adjustable truss rods allow this relief to be controlled.

Types of truss rod

The simplest form of strengthening rod predates the truss rod by many years and involves resisting the pull of the strings with a fixed metal rod or bar, or carbon fibre strips, embedded in the neck. This has advantages and disadvantages. It will make the neck stiffer, and therefore more resistant to the pull of the strings, and it may also dampen the strings less than a non-reinforced neck. The disadvantages are that the neck may be heavier and so the guitar may not balance too well on the knee, and that it is not adjustable, although as we will see this is not necessarily a problem. This type of system is used in both the reclaimed wood guitar in Chapter 21 and the 12-string in Chapter 22.

A simple diagram to show how a single curved truss rod, as invented by Ted McHugh, works. In the upper diagram a bent rod is inserted into a block. If you tension the rod it will try to straighten as in the lower diagram, bending the block back. The distances from the centre of the rod to the edges of the block remain the same.

It has been said that these rods do not allow any neck relief but while this may be true with guitars that are strung with very light strings, medium-gauge or heavier strings will generally pull the neck enough to provide some relief. If the strings are too light to do this, there is a good chance they are also too light to put enough energy into the guitar to make it sound good. They may also not provide enough relief on a guitar with a McHugh-style of truss rod (*see* below), which is generally designed to only pull the neck backwards against the pull of the strings.

Ted McHugh's masterpiece

The truss rod that McHugh designed is simple in the extreme and very efficient if installed properly. A curved rod is embedded into the neck with the centre of the rod being furthest from the fingerboard. The amount of curve is small, with only about $1/8$ in (3 mm) deflection in the centre. One end of the rod is anchored into the neck and the other end is threaded. The threaded end has an adjustment nut that pushes onto a flat plate through which the rod can pass. As the rod tightens it tries to straighten and, since it is firmly embedded in the neck, the neck has no alternative but to move also, bending backwards.

Fitting the curved rod is not difficult, but care is needed and it is not a job that can be done by hand: a router and a means to cut the curved channel are needed. However, since the rod is firmly embedded into the neck there is no air channel around the rod that can affect the sound of the guitar. The disadvantage of the truss rod is that since the rod is installed with a slight curve it is already working to bend the neck backwards, even before it is tensioned. This does not happen often – normally the inherent strength of the neck will resist it – but some very flexible necks can lay backwards and the only adjustment available will simply worsen this. Having said that, the fact that a neck will lay back with just the light tension of a slack rod could mean the neck was too flexible to be useful.

David Russell Young advocates using only metal bars in necks as he claims truss rods can cause an S-shaped warp in a neck. This is not entirely correct as the McHugh-style of rod does not compress the neck, but bends it. The amount of tension used on the rod to bend the neck is far less than is exerted by the strings. If a neck has an S-shaped warp it is more likely to be due to the neck being made from a bad piece of wood than the action of the truss rod.

I have seen articles recommending a truss rod with no curve; just a tensioning rod laid flat in a channel. The thinking is that a rod set into the back of the neck compressing the rear part of the neck will compensate for the pull of the strings. In theory this is reasonable, but wood is pretty resilient and does not take too kindly to being compressed. Therefore the tension needed on the rod would be fairly severe and far more than that exerted by a McHugh-style of rod. The only advantage of a flat rod such as this is that, not needing a curved channel, it is easy to fit. The fact that it won't work very well is a good reason not to use it, as there are much better versions that are just as easy to fit and which will work better. In practice a curved rod can be fitted even if the maker is unable to rout a curved channel; inserts in the bottom of the channel can compensate.

Aluminium channel

Many Far Eastern guitars from the mid 1970s to the present are fitted with a truss rod made from an aluminium channel with a curved rod inside it. The rod is anchored at one end and the other end pushes onto the channel. As it does so, the aluminium channel will bend and, since it has only three sides, it will bend towards its open side. With the channel being firmly fixed into the neck, the neck will move with the rod. The downside of these rods is that there is a certain amount of space around the rod, which can affect the tone. However, Martin have been using this style of rod for

Opposed rods work by having one end of each joined together. One end of one rod is threaded and a nut on this works against a collar fixed to the other rod. As the threaded rod is shortened, it will push against the other rod and bend it.

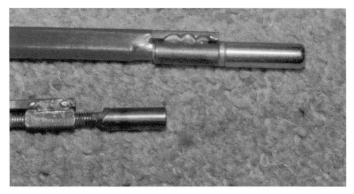

The adjuster on an opposed rod and a two-way opposed rod. The adjuster in the top rod pushes against the collar fixed to the metal bar above the threaded rod. The two-way adjustable rod beneath has a threaded section that goes through a threaded collar and so can lengthen as well as shorten the lower rod, bending the upper rod in either direction.

some years with excellent results, and the kit-built guitar in Chapter 20 has one.

Opposed rods

Another style of rod is made up of two rods, one above the other. The rods are joined at one end and one rod is threaded at the other end. As the adjustment nut is turned on the thread, it pushes against the other rod, causing it to bow, and since the lower rod is being shortened and the upper one will remain the same, the whole assembly will bend backwards.

The opposed rod has been used in many guitars and was originally seen in Rickenbacker electrics. It is easy to fit, being fitted into a flat-bottomed channel, and it does not seem to affect the tone of the guitar as much as the aluminium channel rods.

The Hot Rod

Stewart MacDonald Guitar Shop Supply sell a wonderful device called the Hot Rod. This is a twin rod that is

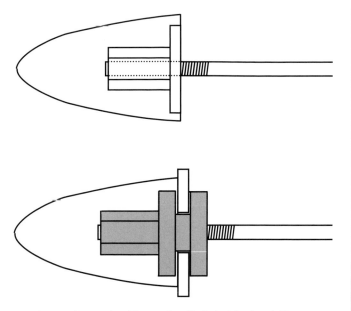

A normal curved rod is usually adjusted at the head. The threaded portion of the rod is passed though a small metal plate or washer onto which the adjustment nut pushes. In the case of the 'double McHugh' below, the adjuster is made so that it can push or pull on the metal plate. This has to be slotted, rather than drilled, so that the adjuster can slot over it. The curved line represents the adjustment cavity.

Making truss rods

A simple McHugh truss rod is not difficult to make. You just need to be able to cut a thread onto the rod. The choice of what thread is usually determined by your truss rod adjuster.

Companies such as Stewart MacDonald Guitar Shop Supply sell truss rod adjustment nuts and these usually have a 10-32 thread. This is designed to work on material that is $3/16$ in diameter and so may not work as well if you can only get metric stock, in Europe for example. $3/16$ in is roughly 5 mm and it is possible the thread may work on the metric stock but it may be that an M5 nut on a metric thread may be more suitable.

As we have disussed, the rod is simply threaded at one end with an anchor at the other. The anchor can be as simple as a nut threaded onto the end and then fixed to stop it coming undone. It will need a washer or a small metal plate to anchor it into the neck and spread the load over a wider area. The width of the nut alone is not usually enough.

Start by cutting your truss rod to the correct length so that the adjustment is where you want it at the head end and the anchor is embedded in the heel.

Cut a thread of approximately 1 in (25 mm) at the adjustment end and $1/4$ in (6 mm) at the anchor end. Thread the anchor bolt onto this and either braze or peen it to stop it moving. 'Peening' is simple; if one or two threads protrude past the end of the nut, the rod can be splayed, by careful application of force, to stop it turning.

Start by making a few hits with a centrepunch in the free end of the rod while it is held in a vice. Two or three firm applications of mild violence will be enough to splay it. The end can then be rounded over by tapping it with the rounded part of a ball peen hammer. (It is called a ball peen hammer as it is used for peening and it has a ball on one side of the head.) The free end of the truss rod will end up looking like a rivet.

The small plate at the anchor end, used to widen the bearing surface can be as simple as a small piece of thin metal drilled to accept the rod or a suitably sized washer. This can be slid into place on the bar. At the adjustment end a similar plate will be needed to spread the load of the adjustment nut. I often use a suitably sized washer for this too.

adjustable both ways and so can be used to add a forwards bow, to add string relief, as well as a backwards bow to straighten a neck. It has another advantage in that it can be adjusted both ways: this means that it can be fitted to the neck upside down, so that the adjustment nut is not set as deeply into the neck as it would normally be. The adjustment works in the opposite direction to normal, which is hardly a problem as you will soon get used to it.

With the Hot Rod installed upside down, less wood needs to be removed from the head to make space to adjust the neck. This removal of wood is a well-known source of weakness on guitar heads and has contributed to many neck breaks. Many of the guitars made by Dave King have this style of rod fitted and he has had excellent results.

Other manufacturers also make double adjustable rods, and truss rods of all styles are available from most guitar parts suppliers.

Double McHugh

The McHugh-style of rod can also be made to operate in both ways. If the adjustment nut is machined in the same way as on the drawing, then it can be used to pull and push the rod. This style has been used for many years by my good friend Roger Giffin, who makes excellent electric guitars, with good results.

Most adjustable truss rods are made from mild steel.

Harder materials such as stainless steel could be used, but they are less flexible and, as we have seen, the truss rod works by being flexible.

The steel bar

One inherent problem with any truss rod is that it in order to act it needs to be free to move within the neck; it therefore acts like a spring and can absorb some of the energy from the strings' vibration. Certainly using one type of truss rod over another can alter the sound on otherwise identical guitars, although in some cases this change will be minor. Very little research has been done into this, so all opinions are subjective, but it does suggest that using an old-style fixed rod in a guitar neck may result in a guitar with a better tone, as less of the vibration is being soaked up by the truss rod.

Double steel bars in the 12-string neck in Chapter 22.

Of course, materials other than steel can be used. I have already mentioned the use of carbon graphite strips in the neck, and these are very resistant to bending in some planes. Using a $1/4 \times 1/2$ in (6.3×12.7 mm) bar set vertically in the neck may be all that is needed. This will leave the guitar lighter, and so possibly less neck-heavy, than would have been the case with a steel rod, but just as strong. Some guitar makers' suppliers will sell you carbon fibre in various sizes, and there may well be a right way and a wrong way of using it. Depending on the style of material used and the way it is laid up in the former when being made, it may have a 'grain' similar to the grain of a piece of wood. If the laminates are flat the bar will be less strong than it would if the laminates were on edge, as in a piece of quarter-sawn wood. However, in most cases the carbon graphite will be stronger than the wood anyhow and so will still adequately support the neck.

Some people claim that using carbon graphite helps avoid dead spots in the neck, when the vibration is damped by the guitar's own natural resonant frequency, although the lighter weight of the neck would serve to alter the frequency and dead spots may just appear elsewhere on the instrument.

CUTTING THE CHANNELS

If using a truss rod that is anything other than the classic curved rod, a straight-bottomed channel will need to be cut in the neck. It is a simple job to hold the neck blank in a vice, using an edge guide on a router to make the cut exactly in the centre of the neck.

The length of the rod should be marked and the router set to a shallow cut. Several passes should be used to give the final depth. This may be only $1/4$ in (6.3 mm) for a simple metal bar or $1/2$ in (12.7 mm) or a little more if using a double rod.

Which end?

Although strengthening rods will usually stop short of the head, an adjustable rod will need to be adjusted somewhere. In many cases this will be by extending the channel out onto the front face of the head and

Centering the router bit on the neck face.

Adding the curved rails to the top face of the neck allows the router to follow their shape and cut a curved channel.

The double rod on this guitar needed a small section of the channel close to the head to be made wider to accomodate the collar for the adjuster and an adjustment recess cut on the head.

The body end truss rod adjuster recess on the Martin kit.

The head facing may need to be cut to reveal a truss rod adjustment beneath.

The rod on this guitar was a little longer than the neck and so ends in the tenon. This is not a problem unless you are butt joining the neck and then a shorter truss rod would be required.

The truss rod anchor on the electro acoustic in Chapter 23 was set into a small recess in the heel.

The curved rod needs to have a fillet glued over the rod to hold it in place. This must not be so tight as to stop the rod from moving but tight enough to stop it rattling. It is a good idea to wrap the rod in plastic, heat-shrink tubing being ideal, to further prevent rattling.

Using the fingerboard to double check the neck join position, in this case, on the 14th fret.

The position of the neck join is marked on the heel as is the depth of the tenon and the final heel shape. The laminated heel referred to on page 115 can clearly be seen.

making a space for the adjustment of the rod, which is usually done either by allen key or some kind of small wrench.

Cutting a recess for the rod adjustment can weaken the head, so some makers choose to extend the truss rod under the fingerboard extension so that the rod can be adjusted through the soundhole. This is the method that the Martin company uses. It does make for a stronger and neater headstock, but it means that the neck-to-body join is a little more complicated as you need to consider where the truss rod will go, how it is inserted through the face of the guitar and how it will be adjusted. For a first guitar I would recommend using a simple strengthening rod, but truss rods are not too difficult to fit if you are careful.

You can make your own truss rods, but they are now available from parts suppliers and are generally cheap enough that buying them is much more cost-effective than making them. They are sold in a variety of lengths so, if you are not extending into the body, you need to

choose one that will be easily adjustable at the head but that will also stop somewhere around the middle of the heel, so there is not a lot of neck left that is without truss rod.

If you are going for head-end adjustment and a curved, McHugh-style rod, simply rout your channel along the centre line until it emerges out on the head. For the twin-rod or channel-style truss rods you may still be able to do this, but you might have to shorten the channel because the rods are set deeper into the neck and so the channel will extend further into the head. You may not need to extend the channel all the way to get a good adjustment recess. Both twin rods and channel rods need to be set just under the fingerboard and do not need to be embedded deep into the neck.

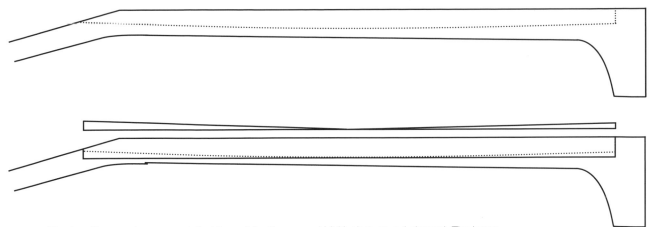

The top diagram shows a neck (not to scale) with a curved McHugh truss rod channel. The lower drawing shows the same neck shape with a full-depth channel with wedges to be inserted to make up the curve.

If you are using a McHugh-style of curved rod, then some means of cutting the curved channel will be needed. I use two rails made from mahogany that were sawn as one piece on the bandsaw, to give them the curve, and then split down the middle to give two identical pieces. These are fixed to the face of the neck with double-sided tape while the channel, which will follow the shape of the rails, is cut. In all cases the router is used to take a little off on each pass until the final depth is reached.

If you have any doubts about cutting a curved channel you could simply cut a flat-bottomed channel to the full depth of the rod and make wedges to fit into the bottom of the channel. This is not totally ideal as the channel will have a very gentle V-section, rather than a curve, but the rod will curve rather than form itself into a 'V' in the limited space available. This will certainly work better than trying to use a tension rod in a flat channel.

Depending on the style of rod being fitted, a little more routing may be required in order to fit the anchor piece or to take into consideration any parts that are slightly wider than the main rod, as is the case on some of the two-rod systems. The head facing could be glued on before the channel is cut, and the channel would simply cut through the facing, leaving a gap above the rod that would get covered by the truss rod cover that also hides the adjustment recess.

This is not normally done and the head facing covers the truss rod channel. This means the recess for the adjustmust must be cut before the head facing is glued and this means the head facing will have to be cut to match. This could be by cutting suitable hole in the head facing before it is glued or by marking and cutting the facing to meet and match the whole beneath. This would have to be done after the rod was fitted and so carving the recess would mean carefully avoiding the truss rod adjuster beneath.

With the truss-rod channel cut you could install the rod at this point or leave it until just before the finger-

The dovetail on the Martin kit.

board is glued. There is no right or wrong way; I tend to leave the rod out unless it is a McHugh-style rod or fixed bars. This is because the McHugh-style rod is embedded in the neck and the channel filled with a glued-in fillet, while fixed rods are usually glued in. Twin-bar rods and channel truss rods slot into the recess and have a habit of falling out at the wrong time as you try to work on the rest of the neck.

All of the above is pretty general as there is more detail in fitting the different kinds of rod in Chapters 20 to 24.

NECK JOIN

If you have made your neck from a deep blank, starting work on the neck join at this stage is a good idea as the block is easier to hold in a vice. If you have made it from smaller laminates with a built-up heel it is a little

Some thoughts on alignment

It is all very well making the best-sounding, most beautiful and carefully constructed guitar in the world, but if it is slightly out of line then it may be totally unplayable: if the neck is out by less than one degree, the whole guitar may be useless.

It is essential that the centre join of the top is exactly in the centre of the guitar. This is not only tidier to look at but the join will be useful as a means of lining things up. Of course, the top join should not have a nasty visible glue line, but the grain will be slightly different on either side of the join and this should show where the centre is. This centre line of the body should extend along the centre of the neck. In this way the strings will be equidistant from the centre line and the bridge will be exactly centred on the body. There is nothing particularly difficult about this. It is not, by any means, the hardest job in the world; it just needs care and attention to detail.

As we have seen, an error of half a degree on the neck-to-body join on a 14-fret, 670 mm scale length guitar (or even a more conventional 25.5in (650mm) scale length guitar) would put the centre line several millimetres out at the nut. This is enough to have the strings hanging over the edge of the board by the body join if the bridge is centred on the body.

This is all quite straightforward and if you have a background as an engineer I can imagine that you are currently wondering what all the fuss is about. The problem comes when you apply it to your guitar.

If, and this is a big 'if', all of your work is 100 per cent accurate then everything will be fine but – and this 'but' is even bigger than the preceding 'if' – the chances are that even though your work and jigs are fine, something may have moved very slightly.

A guitar is like a 3D jigsaw puzzle, and each piece affects the others. If, for example, the sides are slightly misplaced in the mould, the neck join can be affected.

If the mould, the end of the neck and the sit of the top are all out by even the smallest amount, one of two things can happen. Either all the differences will cancel each other out and all will be sweetness and light, or all the errors will combine to make a much larger, and very noticeable, error. This error may be very noticeable, yet very difficult to pin down.

You may, for example, want to line your neck and body in plan form but find the neck is out by half a degree. You can measure all the pieces and find it very hard to discover where the error is; if the top is a sixth of a degree out on the centre line, the sides are not exactly fitted to the mould and the neck is out by one sixth, then you have the basis of a half-degree shift that may be difficult to find.

Acceptance of error

What you have to do is accept the error and build in another way to compensate. The simple answer to the above scenario is that, since the top is already fixed and the sides are glued, it is only the neck that can be altered. Lining the neck up on the body will show where the join needs to be adjusted when the neck is fitted; this should be done very carefully because, as we have already discussed, each change will affect something else.

If you have to modify the end of the neck, then you should remember that doing so can affect the neck face to body face alignment. Any work on the end of the neck to correct lateral adjustment must be done with constant checks to ensure that that longitudinal alignment will remain correct.

This can be the most frustrating part of making a guitar. You may have done everything to a level of accuracy that many woodworkers only dream of and still find things are not quite right. To then have to alter things bit by bit so that everything falls into place can be time-consuming. This is doubly frustrating as it appears to be redoing work that you have already done, so you do not feel as if you are making progress. Put this out of your mind; you ARE making progress as you are adding a level of care and attention that will make your guitar far better than it would have been without.

Another view of the dovetail from the Martin kit. The bush in the heel is for the handle that is used to hold the neck while it is sprayed at the factory.

less easy, but there should be enough material in the heel to allow the vice to get a good grip.

As we have seen in Chapter 2, there are several ways of attaching the neck to the body.

Whatever style you use, the end of the neck will need to be cut very accurately. Estimating this angle is covered in Chapter 2 and it needs to be marked on the neck.

If you are making a neck with a tenon, the extra length for this, usually about $1/2$ in (12.7 mm) should have been added to your neck at the design stage, marked on the face of the neck and the line extended across. The point where the neck and body join, usually either the 12th or 14th fret, will also have been

The tenon on the resonator guitar in Chapter 24. It was an easy tenon to build as the centre three laminates of the neck were a good width which made marking and cutting easy.

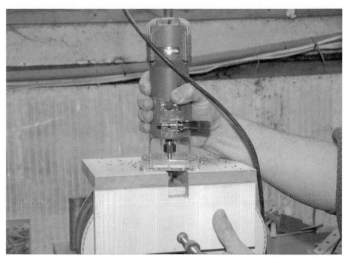

The tenon jig in use with a laminate trimmer and follower bit. Note there is also a clamp holding the jig in place through the soundhole.

A simple routing jig can also be made. This one is held in place with double sided tape and a screw. The screw hole is hidden by the heel when the neck is glued into place.

A routed plain mortice.

The mortice can be cut using drills, saws and chisels.

Checking the alignment on the neck after the tenon is cut.

Adding two pieces to the sides of a head to make up the full width. This is a Douglas fir neck.

marked on the face of the neck. It is important that this line is perfectly square across the neck as it will be the means of aligning the neck with the centre of the body. Although the tenon will hold the neck in place, the fit of the rest of the neck is more important.

Whatever angle you need to have for your neck can be marked from the 12th or 14th fret position down the side of the neck. In some cases this will be 90 degrees and other times it might be slightly different. You should also mark this angle at the end of the tenon.

The width and shape of your tenon must also be decided. The dovetail in the Martin kit guitar is harder to make but helps pull the neck towards the body of the guitar when it is fitted. A straight tenon is easier to make, but might make fitting the neck a little trickier.

The sides of the neck also need cutting down to meet the sides of the tenon. I often scribe the line into the side of the neck to help the saw take up the cut. You can use a small tenon, or gent's, and I have had good results using one of the Japanese saws. The cut should be perpendicular to the centre line as, even if the end of the body is slightly curved and the end of the neck will need to be slightly curved to match, it will be better to have a straight and flat surface to begin with and then adjust it.

With the cuts made to the line drawn that represents the sides of the tenon, the sides can be cut down. This will not be easy as you will be cutting into end grain. You could make these cuts using power tools: a well set-up bandsaw will make basic cuts that can be cleaned with a chisel, but beware if there is a neck angle as this may mean the saw blade cuts deeper in some places than it should.

Whether you are using hand saws or power tools, it will almost certainly be necessary to trim the join using

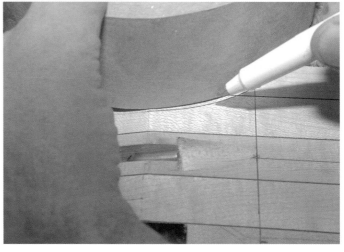

Using a convenient curved object to draw the head shape. In this case it is a roll of tape that has the correct curve.

sharp chisels; this should be done after the mortice in the body has been cut.

The body mortice can be cut using drills, saws and chisels or it can, if you are very careful, be routed. In both cases it is essential that the tools are sharp, that you do not try to take away too much material in one go and that the guitar body is held securely. This may not be as easy as it sounds: it is hard to hold the body in a vice, as the back at least may be curved, and it is easier to do the job if the body is upright. I have found that lightly holding it in the vice will work – if the body moves when you try to cut, it is a good sign that you are trying to remove too much material!

For this guitar the top of the head was also curved. The case for the closeup lens used for some of the photos in this book was ideal!

Bandsawing the sides of the head. It can seen that the neck face will rise as the head moves across the saw table, due to the head angle, until the head disappears over the edge and before the heel comes to the edge of the table also.

Since the join is morticed with one end open, I have drilled the closed end and then sawn to the drill holes with a Japanese saw before removing the waste with chisels. On other guitars I have cut through the sides with the saw and used this to line up a wooden block held to the sides with double-sided tape, and used that as an edge guide for the laminate trimmer with a bearing cutter to rout the mortice.

If you are drilling and sawing, the mortice may need to be tidied with chisels and with a little care a good job can be done.

It is possible, as with the Martin kit, to cut the tenon in the neck block before it is glued into the body, but it means that very careful lining up is needed when gluing the neck block into place. This is far from impossible – it just needs some care. If you chose to use a tapered tenon , it might be easier to buy one of the pre-prepared neck blocks as sold by Stewart MacDonald Guitar Shop Supply and make your neck to fit this. These must be glued into place in the body very accurately.

It is easier to cut the tenon before the neck is cut from its block as it is easier to hold in the vice, but it is unwieldy when you are trying to get an accurate fit onto the body and trying to line up the centre line and get the correct angle. I prefer to cut the join before the neck is cut out, so that it can be held in the vice and will move around less. Then I cut the side elevation of the neck from the block and have a second fiddle with the join as it can still be easily held in the vice as the neck is not tapered, and then I have a final tidy up after the board is glued on.

The head shape and the taper for the fingerboard can be cut at the same time on the bandsaw. Depending on the shape of your head, you may need to add pieces to the sides to make up the full width. These can be

Rosewood and ebony head facings at Touchstone Tonewoods.

This guitar had the head facing glued on after the head was shaped.

Using small spring clamps to hold the head facing in place.

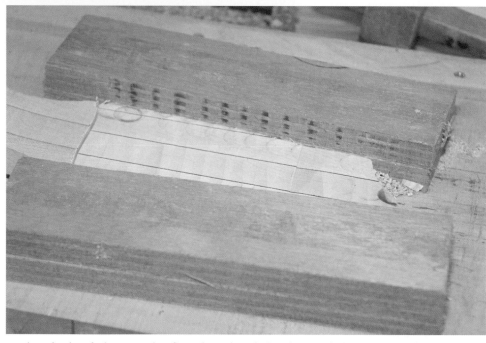

This very simple routing jig for thicknessing a head was made from two pieces of plywood held onto the workboard with double sided tape. It is very important to remember when using a jig such as this that the head must be securely fixed face down onto the workboard as, if it lifts, the whole neck will be ruined.

glued on and left to dry before cutting the head shape and neck taper at the same time. If you are using a head veneer, this can be glued on at this stage or after the head is shaped; that is a matter of personal preference. Head facings are not only decorative; since they are usually of a harder wood they help protect the face of the head and the added stiffness does strengthen it a little.

Head facings are available from guitar parts suppliers usually in ebony or rosewood and sometimes maple, although anything could be used. You can also sandwich a layer of veneer between the head and the facing if you want a contrasting stripe running around but this is not going to show if you decided to bind your head!

Since the side elevation of the neck and the head angle have already been cut, cutting the taper and head shape can prove interesting. The marks for the edges of

the fingerboard and the shape of the head are drawn onto the upper surface. Sawing to these lines will mean the bandsaw is bearing down on the neck piece, which is not fully supported on the bed of the saw, as the waste from the back of the neck has already been removed or, if this is a laminated neck, was not there to begin with. As the piece is pushed through the saw the height of the front of the neck will vary. When the end of the head is on the table, the neck piece will be angled with the face of the neck slightly facing you and this will drop away as the end of the head passes over the edge of the saw table. The opposite happens when getting close to the heel, as this needs to be raised to sit on the table, which pushes the neck face away from the saw table and against the natural tendency of the saw blade to push down as it cuts.

It may be necessary to trim the back of the head after it has been cut from the blank as the original cut may not have been totally straight given the problems of moving a large block through the bandsaw.

It would be easier to make this cut before the waste at the back of the neck is cut, but this then gives a problem when the side elevation of the neck is cut which, if anything, is more difficult to control.

One alternative is to re-mark all the relevant lines on the back of the head and neck but this requires very careful measuring so that the lines on the front, that you have been working to all along, match the lines on the back. Marking on the back is especially useful on the head where the end is usually perpendicular to the face. Sawing from the top would match the head angle with the angle of the end looking a little strange and keeping the head face down on the bed of the bandsaw will make an easier, and safer, cut. I find that cutting the end of the head and then the sides with the face of the head down on the bandsaw bed and then following with the face of the neck down to cut the taper and the part where the taper splays out to make the head is the best way.

If you do mark the lines for the taper of the fingerboard onto the back of the neck it is important to triple check they line up as fixing mistakes is not going to be easy. It is a good idea to cut outside the line and clean the edges of the neck to match the width of the fingerboard at a later time.

The head shape may need to be tidied up with sandpaper, scrapers, or planes and if the neck has been cut from a deep block, the back of the head may need to be thinned. Once again, there are various ways of doing this and over the years I have tried sanding drums and routers as well as hand tools. Cutting by hand is fine if the head has not been cut too deep, which can happen if trying not to cut too close to the line (as cutting too thick is much better than cutting too thin), but can be hard work. Whichever way you choose, the back of the head needs to be flat and an even thickness.

Using a drum sander with a fixed board behind it to sand the back of the head to a constant depth. The rosewood packing piece is to allow for the depth of the fingerboard that is already glued to this neck.

Head binding

If you are going to bind the head it is essential you do this before the fingerboard is fitted, as the fingerboard will get in the way if you use a router. Binding the head is the same as binding the body except that the head is much smaller and not as deep, so the router has less to sit on and it is easier to make mistakes!

Since the head is angled, it is usual practice to continue the binding channel under the fingerboard, so the fingerboard and head need to seamlessly join. You will need to make sure that your neck is exactly the right width for the end of the fingerboard, so that your head binding aligns with the neck binding.

I use the laminate trimmer for any head binding, and do not cut the channel to the full depth of the

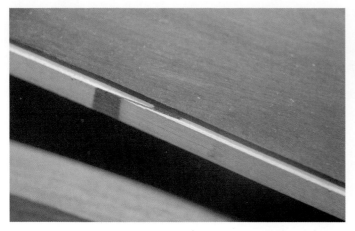

A routed binding channel on a head.

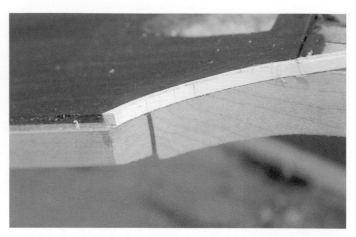

The binding trimmed and cut so the second piece fits exactly.

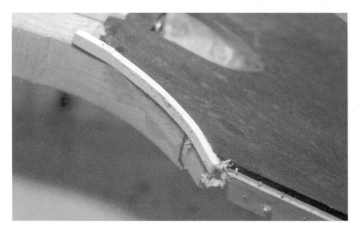

The first piece of binding glued on and in the process of being scraped and sanded back. Body binding is oversize for most headstocks.

The binding around the curve on the end of this head needed a little help to remain in place while the superglue dried. Four piece of binding were used for the complete head.

binding. Gluing a $1/4$ in (6.3 mm) deep binding onto a head that is only $1/2$ in (12.7 mm) deep would look a little unbalanced, so I cut the binding down so that it is about $1/8$ in (3 mm). There are usually sharp corners on headstocks, so the binding may need to be made in several pieces with joins between them. The better these joins are, the better the final job will look, so taking time over them is worthwhile.

As with the rest of the guitar, these joins are glued using either cement, superglue or, in the case of wood binding, Titebond and left to dry before being scraped and sanded back to a perfect finish.

The neck is now ready to have the fingerboard installed.

Chapter 12
Fingerboards

It is now possible to buy pre-slotted fingerboards in a variety of scale lengths and in various woods. These are sometimes sold flat and sometimes with a profile or camber; it depends where they are bought. They will save a lot of work, but there may be times when you want to make your own. In the case of the reclaimed wood guitar in Chapter 21, I had to cut the board as it was the only way of getting it for free!

If you do buy a pre-slotted board you need to check that the wood is straight-grained and shows no signs of the grain lifting on the face of the board: this would make it difficult to work on when you have to level it. Even if the board is supplied profiled and ready to go you may still have to do some work on it, and that is much easier if it has no wild grain.

It is also worth checking the edges of boards. Check that the grain is running through parallel to the face and not at an angle through the board. Only a few weeks before this part of the book was written I used a very nice, dense and very black ebony fingerboard on a guitar. It looked superb and was of very high quality. Sadly the density of the wood and the lack of any discernible grain meant it was impossible to see that it had quite a lot of grain breakout on the surface. This was not even apparent when I curved the surface, as I did not use cutting tools such as planes but the method I show later in this chapter, with sandpaper. The grain became very apparent when I started trying to fret the guitar, with small pieces of wood chipping out of the board at the edges of the fret positions. This was annoying and while careful use of filler and glue could have made the guitar workable, it would have been a nightmare to re-fret, so I decided to remove the board and fit another. This is a lot of work and not something any sane person would want to do willingly. Had it been possible to see the grain before starting work, I would not have used that board.

Some pre-slotted boards are supplied parallel with the slots neatly perpendicular to the edge. Others can be more randomly shaped making it necessary to find a centre line. This can be done by using an engineer's square against the last fret position. Some boards are sold cut so that the end of the board is the nut position cut and others with the nut positions cut into the board,

Scribing the edge lines onto the underside of a pre-slotted board.

and it is sometimes a little hard to work out if this is the first fret or the nut position. Often only some careful measuring will make it clear which is the case! Once a centre line is found and drawn onto the board, the width of the board at the body and nut can be marked and the board is ready for shaping.

If, on the other hand, you have an unslotted board then you need to be doing things slightly differently. Exactly what you do will depend on the method chosen for cutting the fret slots. There are some jigs available from parts suppliers that hold the board in place and allow you to cut through slots and into the board, and some of these are made to accept rectangular boards of a given dimension. Alternatively you can use a simple jig, using a hand-held square to position the saw blade, but you will need to accurately mark the board before you start.

In all cases, accuracy is the key. Start by drawing a good, thin and visible centre line on the fingerboard. You could lightly scribe the board, since you will be adding the radius after you have cut the fret slots and the scribed line will be removed; on an ebony or rose-

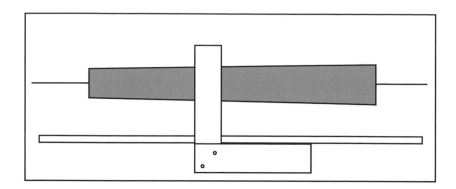

The Irving Sloan-inspired fret slotting jig.

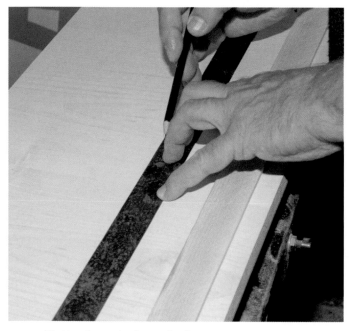

Marking the centre line on the jig.

The board lined up on the centre line.

wood board some chalk rubbed into the scribed line will make it more visible.

The jig I used for the guitar in Chapter 21 is simplicity in the extreme and I first saw this in a book by the late Irving Sloan (*Classic Guitar Construction*, Sterling Publishing 1984). It consists of a flat board onto which the fingerboard is fixed over a marked centre line, and on one edge is a raised bar parallel to that centre line. An ordinary marking square held against the bar will be perpendicular to the centre line and the fretting saw, of which more in a moment, is held against this to start the cut.

The board needs to be marked very accurately. This is much easier if the centre line is clean and visible. You will need to have a good ruler that is clearly marked and a sense of adventure!

The first stage is to mark the nut position at one end of the board. Scribe a small mark on the centre line at the point you want the fingerboard side of your nut to

be. From this point measure the distance to your first fret position. You will notice that your ruler will not have enough marks on it to make it accurate enough to measure the fret position to engineering accuracy, but you can judge the position within those marks to get very close. If your ruler did have enough graduations to be totally accurate they would be close to impossible to see, and so hard to use. You also need to be referring to the table of measurements that has the cumulative total, or nut to fret distances, as this will help avoid some basic errors.

There will be some very small errors and these will be so small as to be almost irrelevant. For example, if you cut the third fret position on a $25\frac{1}{2}$ in scale $^4/_{100}$ in out of place, then your fret will be 0.18654 per cent out of place. ($^4/_{100}$ of an inch, or 40 thousandths of an inch, is the diameter of many light gauge 'A' strings, or about the same as two box cutter blades, and well within most people's capabilities to work.) To give you an idea how small this is, hook a guitar up to a tuner and

Scribing the fret positions using the square.

Cutting the slot with a small saw.

try to bend a string and hold it a whole one per cent out of tune. It is not easy, and that is over five times more than the error you have in your board. Now just press a string hard and see how much the tuner alters on that. Pressing hard on frets can be far more variable than a slight mistake in fretting. Of course, the closer your frets become, further up the board, the more this small amount will matter, as it will be a bigger percentage of the total distance between the frets. By the time you get to the 12th fret that percentage difference for a 40 thou mistake has risen to almost one third of 1 per cent, so still not that much and still less than the variation you can get just pressing your fret hard or waving the neck around. Clearly work as accurately as you can, but you *can* make reasonable fretboards by hand.

So, measure and mark the first fret position. Then measure and mark the second fret position using the cumulative table mentioned above, so that the position is marked from the nut rather from fret to fret. If you have made a small mistake on a fret this will ensure that it is not repeated all the way up the neck, and whilst one fret may be out of position, the others will be fine. When all the fret positions are marked it is time to measure them all again to check them.

Before I start cutting I prefer to scribe the actual fret position onto the board. The square is butted up firmly against the bar on the side of the jig and lined up with the mark on the board, and this is extended either way to show the fret position.

Once these have all been marked the actual slots can be cut. It is a good idea to make sure the jig is held down firmly on the workbench as you do not want it to move when you are working on it. One good way to do this is to fix a bar to the bottom of the jig and place this in the workshop vice.

The saw cuts are made by lining up the sawblade with the scribed fret position and holding the saw blade against the square to start the cut. With some practice

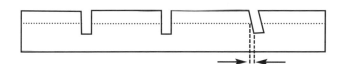

As can be seen in this diagram, slanted fret slots will make an inaccurate board. The dotted line shows the depth of the board after radiussing and the arrows show the relative movement of the fret slot.

it is quite easy to make everything line up correctly. Once the first part of the cut is made, the square can be dispensed with and the saw will align itself with the first part of the cut. I used a sharp Japanese or a wooden-handled gent's saw for this. It is important to ensure that the saw cuts remain vertical and do not wander off to one side or the other. If they do, fretting the guitar will be difficult and you may have problems when the board is radiused, as the slots will appear to move in the direction of the slant.

The depth of the slot depends on your chosen fretwire, but need not be finalised at this stage. The board is still going to require a lot of work and the slots can always be made deeper or slightly wider. It is more important not to overcut them or, worse still, cut through the board. Once the fret slots are cut the board can be radiused.

Profile/radius/camber

There are several ways to refer to the cross section shape of a guitar fingerboard. When I published the second edition of *Make Your Own Electric Guitar* in 1998 there was some discussion on the Internet about the correct terminology. In fact there is no 'correct' terminology, but there are several ways of describing it. Some people will

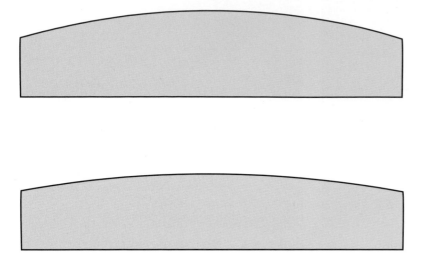

7 and 12 inch radius curves.

refer to the radius of the board; this is partially correct and I will come to that later. I have referred to the camber and this is also correct. Camber is usually used to describe the cross section shape of roads that have to be higher in the centre to allow rain to drain off and this has been around since Roman times. The raised centre of the board is a camber, though other people will refer to the profile.

The amount of curve you have across the board, whether you call it radius, camber or profile, is a matter of personal taste. Some people prefer a flat fingerboard, as on classical guitars, but others prefer a curve as it is more comfortable for the fingers, which are naturally bendy! A more pronounced curve may feel more comfortable, within reason, but may produce other problems.

Generally the amount of curve is fairly small. It is often quoted in terms of its radius and this will be between 7 and 14 in (177 and 355 mm). This may seem a lot when written in black and white, but anything with a radius greater than 14 in will feel very flat.

The relative merits and demerits of greater- or smaller-radius boards are not as significant on acoustic guitars as they are on electrics, as they are unlikely to be strung with light strings and a very low action and used for lots of string bending. As the string is bent across the board it can choke against frets further up the board, killing the note. This is not too much of a problem with the higher action and heavier strings that are normal on an acoustic guitar, but it is a factor if you want to replicate the feel of an electric guitar on your acoustic.

Compound radius

This problem has led to some manufacturers and makers offering compound-radius necks. These have a steeper curve (smaller radius) at the nut end of the board so that fretting chords is easier, and a flatter

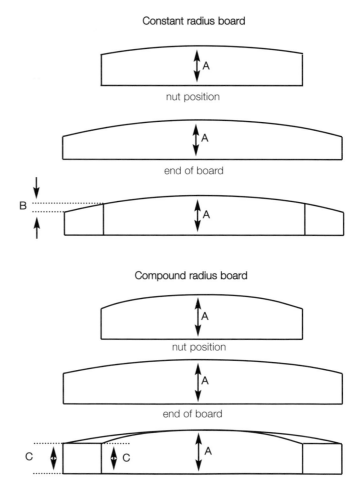

Constant radius board

nut position

end of board

Compound radius board

nut position

end of board

In the above diagrams, the boards have a constant thickness denoted by the dimension 'A'. In the upper diagram, the board has a constant radius. When the board is tapered, the edge of the board at the nut will be deeper than the edge of the board at the end of the body, denoted by the measurement 'B'. On the lower diagram, the board is made so the edges of the board remain at a constant thickness, denoted by the measurement 'C'. This gives a greater radius at the nut than at the head end of the neck.

Using the sanding stick to camber the board.

The first passes will be along the board.

Passes across the board will even the camber and show any high or low spots. When the board is marked evenly across and along its length, lighter grades of paper can be used to remove the scratches and finish the board.

profile (larger radius) at the bridge end of the fingerboard so that strings can be bent. When introduced this was seen as a massive advance, but it had been happening for years without people realising.

If you cut a fingerboard so that it has an even radius along its length and it is made parallel, then the thickness of the board will be the same all the way along the line that is parallel to the centre. The centre of the board will be the full depth and the sides will be lower by whatever factor the radius introduces.

If, however, you then taper the board so that it is narrow at the nut and wider at the body end, as on most guitars, the thickness of the board will remain the same in the centre but the edges will differ. The edge will be deeper at the nut end as you have cut into the radius to make the board narrower.

Large, commercial guitar-making companies that use machinery to cut the curve on the board will produce an even curve. Few small makers, on the other hand, radius their fingerboards before tapering them. Therefore, if they taper their boards so that the sides remain a constant depth, then the amount of curve across the board will vary provided that the depth remains the same in the centre. Many people have been doing this without even thinking about it!

You could camber the board before cutting the fret slots. However, this may make the process of actually cutting the slots more difficult unless you are using one of the jigs that actually guides the saw blade: if you are using such a jig, it is a very good idea to do this.

If you cut the slots before you curve the board you cannot easily use a plane to remove material from the board as it may well chip out along the fret slots – something you really want to avoid. You can use a plane before the slots are cut, but it needs to be set on a very fine, very sharp cut and you need to watch for any areas on the fingerboard where the grain may not

be in the optimum direction. A little swirl in the grain, that may not even be visible when inspecting the board, will mean the plane blade digs into the end grain and lifts it, and you will have to deal with this to remove the damage. If you have set the plane blade deep then the damage will be correspondingly deep and you will need to remove more wood to get below the damage.

If you have any swirly grain or if you have lifted a little of the grain with the plane then there is always Option B. Option B is quite simple. Even when using a plane to remove the main part of the camber, the board will need to be finished off with sandpaper, and if it is particularly difficult to plane then it might be good to do the whole job with paper.

You will need a good sanding stick as described in Chapter 3. You can then either hold sandpaper under this or attach it with double-sided tape. Use 80 grit that will be plenty harsh enough to remove the waste without being too fierce, and be sure to keep the block flat

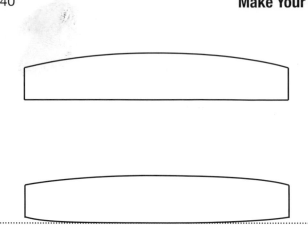

With a pre-profiled board it is a good idea to check to see it has not dished. This could render the board useless if it is too bad.

onto the board so that it does not create dips or humps in the board.

Work on each side in turn and check frequently that the board is remaining flat along its length. You should also wear a dust mask, as most fingerboard materials are very abrasive and unpleasant. You may also have to change the paper frequently. Ebony tends to be very dry and dusty, but there is a lot of oil in rosewood that will clog up the abrasive on the paper.

Using either the plane or the sanding stick will not create an even curve across the board, so you may need to sand across to achieve this. Sanding across the board also serves as a double-check that the board is being worked evenly: sanding the board along its length will create scratches, and these will be removed and replaced with scratches across the board when the block is used to even out the camber. If any area is higher or lower than it should be, this will show up as the scratches will not be even.

When the board is suitably cambered these scratches can be removed by repeating the process with a lighter-grit paper. Start with 120 grit to remove the last cross-scratches and then go to 220 or 400, and finally 600 grit to give the board its final sanding. You could leave the final sanding of the board until after it is glued to the neck and the neck to the body if you are leaving your fretting until then.

There are radius blocks available that are designed to produce an even radius along the board but these must be used with care. If using one by hand it is wise to remember that when moving arms and hands around, as you would be when you are pushing a block along a board, there is a natural tendency for the arm to move in a curve, so the block may not always be held at the best angle and may not sand as evenly as it could. The curve on the underside of the block will also attack the board at differing angles and so may remove more waste at some points than others. This is less likely when using a flat board!

It is easier to profile the board before it is attached to the neck. Some pre-cut boards, such as those sold by Stewmac, will be pre-radiused (these are sold unrapered, so have a constant radius rather than a compound camber) but may others will not. One thing to watch on boards that have been bought pre-cambered and on boards that you make yourself but left a while before using is that they do not dish after being worked on. Some boards will do this, especially if the atmosphere is damp; the thinner edges will curl up a little, making the underside of the board curved as well as the front (and, of course, lessening the curve on the front). If the amount of curl is very small it may be possible to remove it when gluing the board down, but if it is severe it might be that the wood was not dry enough or stable enough, and should be discarded.

Having successfully radiused the board then it is a good idea to check the depth of the fret slots. The act of radiusing the board will lessen the depth of the slots at the edges of the board; if these get too shallow for the fret tang, then trying to deepen them when the board is glued to the guitar, especially at the upper fret positions where the board lays over the guitar front, can be a problem. It will also be a problem if you bind the fingerboard (*see* below) as you will not be able to see the end of the fret slot once the board is bound and it will then be very difficult to fix. You also need to check now that the fret slot is not too narrow or wide for your chosen fretwire. Check now and the world is a brighter place.

If all goes well, and it does most of the time, then you will have a tapered and cambered board that has been successfully slotted for the number of frets you will be fitting, but it will be bare wood. The next stage is to add any decoration you may require.

BINDING

Many acoustic guitar fingerboards are bound. This is to seal the fret ends and prevent ingress of moisture that could lift the fret, as well providing decoration. The binding is often made of plastic, but wood is nicer-looking and just as easy to apply on a home-built instrument. The fret slots do not extend through the binding, so the fret tang needs to be cut back so that only the bead sits over the binding. This is covered in Chapter 15.

The board needs to be radiused before the binding is applied, and it will need to be cut so that it is narrower than required by the width of the binding, which is usually $1/16$ in (1.5 mm). The binding is then attached to the fingerboard after the radiusing using a light smearing of wood glue (for wooden binding) or cyanoacrylate (for plastic binding), being careful that excess does not seep into the fret slot, which could cause problems later on. In this case the edges of the board may need to be moistened so that the glue adheres properly. There are some cyanoacrylates that do not

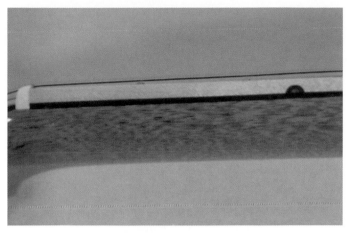

A nicely designed wooden binding with half round position dots.

Binding does not have to have a big contrast in colour to look good, as this Everett guitar shows.

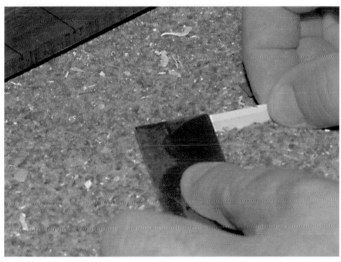

Measuring the width of the binding to check the overall width of the fingerboard.

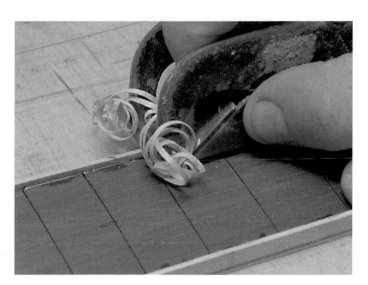

Using a small plane to cut down a wooden fingerboard binding. Care is needed not to mark the board or damage a fret slot.

Adding extra superglue to fully seal a wooden binding.

Trimming the ends of the binding.

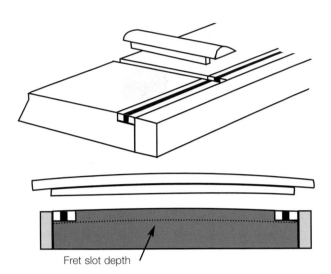

Fret slot depth

More elborate binding may require the slots to be cut through part of the inlay so the frets can be seated properly.

A simple abalone fingerboard dot with a paste dot on the side of this unbound fingerboard.

need to have the wood dampened, so reading the directions on the glue and following the safety instructions is a must.

Elaborate binding

Some guitars go one stage further than just having a simple wood binding and also have contrasting lines or even pearl or abalone inlaid along the fingerboard edge. In these cases the width of the binding might be too great to allow the fret end to sit over it without raising and causing a sharp edge. In this case it is wise to inlay the extra layers in the board and cut the slots through them before adding the outer layer as before. Start by cutting the board to width, then cut the channel for the binding so that it is the right depth when the board is radiused. Radius the board and then inlay the binding before allowing it to dry and extending the fret slots through. The outer binding can then be added.

Inlays and markers

Guitar fingerboards are generally inlaid with markers at the 3rd, 5th, 7th, 9th, 12th, 15th, 17th and 19th fret positions. On many guitars this is done with simple dot markers made of pearl or even plastic. Since the 12th fret position marks the first harmonic point and octave, double dots are provided. More elaborate inlays can be added either to emphasise these fret positions or just to decorate the fingerboard. In both cases the dot markings are repeated on the side of the board or in the binding, so that the player can see where they are on the fingerboard.

Dots are by far the easiest form of inlay to install and can be purchased from guitar parts suppliers in a variety of diameters. To install, simply drill a hole of the

It is a good idea to pilot drill the position marker holes.

correct size and to the correct depth and glue in the dot. It can then be sanded flush with the front of the board.

More elaborate inlays can take considerably longer. Simple shapes such as the diamond-shaped snowflakes seen in Chapter 20 are inlaid by drilling a hole that is slightly smaller than the body of the diamond shape and then using a sharp, small chisel to enlarge the hole so that the diamond fits. The inlay is then glued in using a filler that is the same colour as the fingerboard; the glue will seep through the small saw-cuts that make the edges of the snowflake so as not to leave a gap.

Block markers are one stage on from these. The majority of the area can be opened with drills or with careful use of a small router, such as the Dremel router. The shape can then be finalised with small chisels and any slight imperfections can be filled with the correct colour of filler.

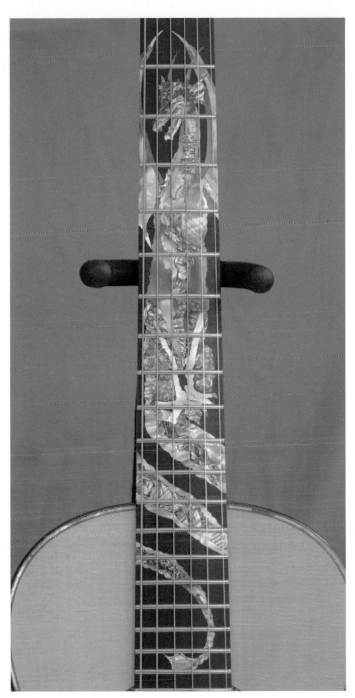

Excellent inlay work on a guitar by Dave King.

A simple drilled hole can be used for a dot.

Using a small chisel to make the round hole into a rectangular one.

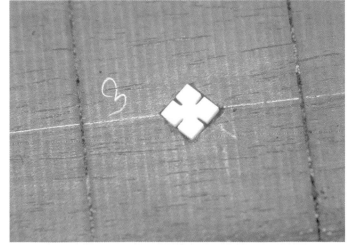

The diamond marker inserted into its hole. More observant readers may note this was installed after the fingerboard was glued to the neck. This is far from ideal but book production deadlines sometimes mean that jobs get done in the wrong order! The fret number is also marked as it would be a disaster to fit it on the fourth or second fret.

Some makers like to use elaborate inlays such as the tree of life or other forms of artwork. This can look very impressive if done correctly, but can look terrible if it is done carelessly. It is certainly not recommended for a first guitar, but I have included a fine example of one of Dave King's inlays just to illustrate what can be done. In these cases the basic shapes are cut from pearl and their positions marked on the board. The excess material on the board is then removed with routers,

A filler made from a mixture of ebony dust and glue was used to fill in the gaps of the inlay and then sanded smooth.

The four stages of installing side dots: firstly the hole is marked and then drilled.

chisels and knives so that the inlay pieces fit perfectly. Although pearl or abalone is used for many of these inlays, silver or gold wire is sometimes used for fine lines. Inlays such as these can take many days to cut and fit, and are not for the faint-hearted. If you have ever had any doubts about why these inlays are so expensive when added to custom guitars, have a go at making one yourself and it will all fall into perspective!

The use of lasers to cut out material for inlays and to cut the board to fit them has been increasing as laser cutters have become more available. They are still expensive and not for the average home builder, or even small company, but access to them is sometimes possible by the usual combination of borrowing, begging and payment – all processes that most guitar makers are familiar with.

The actual use of one will depend on what software is driving it, but producing accurate artwork is important. The amount of cut the laser is capable of and the type of material that can be cut will also vary with the laser type, so it is best to find the capabilities of the machine you have access to and then decide whether it is capable of doing the job you want to see. Many top-end and even lower-end guitars have extensive inlay work done on laser machines and the possibilities are almost endless but, once again, this might be a step too far on a first guitar.

A far easier proposition are the smaller position dots that are fitted along the sides of the fretboard in the same positions as the main dots. Small pearl or abalone dots are available for this and most guitar makers' suppliers will also sell small lengths of plastic rod, usually in white for dark wood, unbound fretboards, and black for guitars with lighter binding. I have also seen brass rod used and even small brass tube with black filler in the centre.

These dots can be installed by drilling a hole of the correct size, inserting the dot or plastic rod, and cutting

Next, the dot, in this case a small length of plastic rod, is glued in and, if necessary, cut to length.

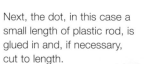

Finally the dot is sanded flush (*above*) and (*right*) the finished dot.

Trial fitting the neck on the Martin kit, in this case before the binding and fingerboard inlays are fitted.

Lining up a simple tenon.

Before the neck was tapered this gutar had a thorough check to make sure all pieces, such as the fingerboard and nut, all lined up and were in the correct place relative to the centre line of the neck.

it, or sanding it, flush with the board. The main thing to watch out for is that the holes line up along the length of the board. Normally one dot is fitted at the major positions with two at the 12th fret.

Some people would now choose to fret the guitar, but I prefer to wait until after the board is glued to the neck.

GLUING THE BOARD

As stated in Chapter 2, the most important factor in making a good guitar is that everything should line up. Fitting the neck can be a time-consuming and frustrating part

of the guitar-making process, but it is very important that it is accurate and it is worth taking whatever time is required.

Since the neck does not have to be out by much in order to throw the alignment of the guitar way off and since the fingerboard is an essential part of the neck this too needs to be fitted accurately. Therefore some very careful preparation is required and this will also involve trial fitting the neck with the body of the guitar.

By now you should have spent a fair amount of time working on your neck join to a level of accuracy that should, rightly, make you proud. It is always worth double checking that the neck lines up with the body centre line and also that the face of the neck lines up correctly with the body. This includes the all-important neck angle. If a straightedge is placed on the face of the neck, the distance this is above the top of the bridge position should match the distance you calculated when drawing, as discussed on page 30. If all is correct then you should be fine to glue the fingerboard onto the neck. There will be some opportunity to fiddle with the neck join a little before the neck is glued, or bolted, onto the guitar but it would be sad to overlook a minor mistake at this point, before the board is glued on.

What work you need to do at this stage depends upon your chosen neck join. Start by dry-fitting the neck. If you have a bolted join or a tenon this is relatively straightforward but if you have chosen the simple butt join it can be difficult to line the pieces up. You need to check that the centre line of the neck lines up with the centre line on the body and when this is so, that the join between the body and neck has no gaps around it. A tiny gap is not the end of the world if you

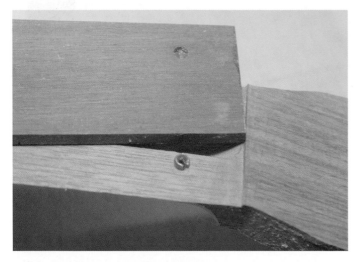

These small fittings are factory installed at Martin to line the fingerboard up exactly.

are using a tenon or bolt-on neck but if using a butt join the pieces need to fit together more accurately. If there are any high spots these can be gently pared down with a chisel and cleaned up with sandpaper, taking care to ensure that the neck remains in alignment and that all dust is cleared away. A very small adjustment at the heel can result in a considerable shift in the centre line of the neck at either end. The trick is to be methodical and slow. Remove a little at a time until the join is completely flush.

When you are confident that the alignment of the neck is as good as you can get it, clamp the fingerboard to the neck using clamps that are light; heavy clamps will make the neck difficult to handle. Lightweight plastic clamps are fine as they are only holding the board in position temporarily. Take care to line up the centre line of the board and that of the neck. Check the neck fit again and note if the board is sitting flush over the front of the guitar. On some guitars the combination

Applying the glue to the Martin kit neck. (Yes, I had run out of titebond.)

A thin film of glue can be spread over the entire area.

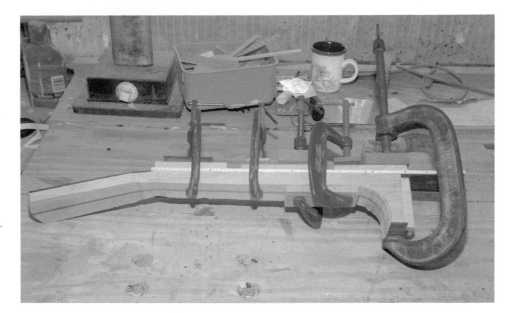

The fingerboard clamped in place. Note how everything was readily to hand, the clamps were adjusted, the box of spare wood for clamping cauls and an essential coffee were all nearby.

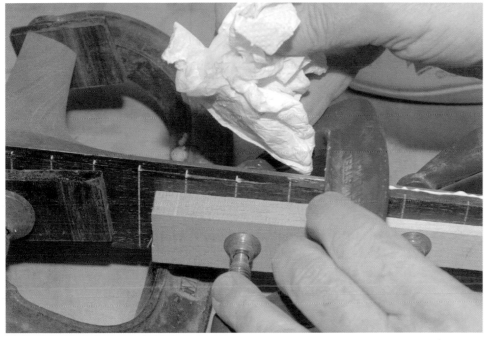

Cleaning off the excess glue.

of fingerboard thickness, bridge height, top arch and neck angle mean the board will sit flush to the front of the guitar. On others the neck angle and flat front of the guitar might mean a very small difference in the angle that will mean that by gluing the board to the front of the guitar a slight downward pitch of the board will result as it reaches the body. This is generally not a problem. Alternatively, a small wedge may be needed to support the board and keep it level. Place a straightedge over the board and check the height at the bridge position. The frets will add some height to the board, usually about 1/16 in (1.5 mm), but this should all correspond to the drawing you made. There will still be some room for adjustment when the neck is finally fitted but at this stage you want to get everything as

accurate as you can, as it affects how you glue the board onto the neck.

If all has gone well, you will find that your board is exactly lined up with the centre line of the neck and with the centre line of the body, and that the neck angle is correct. You now need to glue the board onto the neck without it moving out of alignment and, since the glue will serve as a lubricant when it is being clamped, you need to stop it all moving around.

There are tricks you can use. You could leave one or two position dots out of the front of the board until after the board is glued to the neck and extend the centre of the holes to accept a small screw or pin that can stop the board sliding as it is clamped. This can then be removed and the dot installed. This method will not work if you have an opposed rod truss rod, as you will be trying to screw the positioning screws into the metal.

Another method is to use small brads that are cut off and which act as pins on the underside of the board. Unclamp the board after carefully marking exactly where it was. Then knock in some small brads, cut them off about $1/16$ in (1.5 mm) from the face of the neck and file them to a point. Reposition the board and press it down onto the brads so they mark the underside of the board. If necessary, drill these positions a little deeper with a small drill bit and be certain to recheck the alignment of the neck. If it has moved, take out the brads and add some more at a different point, but get it right!

Then as you clamp, the brads will stop the board moving. The Martin kit (Chapter 20) has small pins fixed into the face of the neck and holes in the underside of the board to accept them. Since these necks are made on computer-controlled machines they are very accurate. What you are attempting to do is to match that accuracy by eye!

When you have checked and double-checked you can spread some glue over the face of the neck and glue the board into place. Be careful when spreading the glue, as the sharp brads can damage the world's best glue-spreading devices (fingers).

Clamp up the board using as many clamps as you need with cauls to protect the face of the board, and triple check that it is still in alignment. If it is not, do not be scared to take it off, clean up the glue and try again later.

Before the glue sets, it is a good idea to make sure you have removed any that may have dropped down in the area of the neck-to-body join so that the tenon and the angle between the end of the neck and the underside of the fingerboard are clean, and then leave the neck overnight to dry off properly.

The next stage depends on personal preference. You could choose to fret the neck at this point before it is shaped, while it is still flat underneath and easier to deal with, but that does trust that everything will be fine when it is glued on, or you can fret it after it is shaped and before it is fixed, or after it has finally been fitted to the guitar. For the purposes of this book I will carry on in the order that I normally do things.

Chapter 13
Neck Shaping

The shape of the neck is a matter of personal preference, but it does serve a purpose. The neck should be not so large that playing is uncomfortable but not so small that it is too weak. A larger neck may well make the guitar sound better as the greater mass may damp less of the string vibration, and there are many players who prefer a larger neck because they find a smaller one does not give the hand enough support when playing.

For me it is not the overall size of the neck that makes a difference but the shape. Again, this is a matter of personal choice, and necks can vary from a shallow D-shape through V-shapes to a deep semi-circular shape. My own preferences are for V-shape or a shallow D-shape. The difference between a comfortable neck and one that is 'not quite' can be very small. I once reshaped the neck of a guitar for an old friend who watched while I did it (something I do not normally like, but he was buying the takeaway for lunch). He was finding the neck a little too big and so I shaved off about $^1/_{16}$ in (1.5 mm) from an area roughly $^1/_4$ in (6.3 mm) from the underside of the fingerboard. He was amazed at how such a small change could make a big difference to how comfortable the neck was to play, but all I had done was to remove a small amount from where it mattered most. It just happened that he and I share opinions of what makes a good guitar neck and I could see that the neck was just a little too square.

Quite rectangular section necks are a common sight on guitars made by relatively inexperienced makers. Over the years, since my electric guitar making book was released, I have spoken to many people who would like to make a guitar, either electric or acoustic, and whose only concern is shaping the neck. They are quite happy to do all of the complex parts but shy away from the part that I think is the most fun. It is quite possible to remove too much wood but, as mentioned above, a little removed from strategic places will make a big difference without substantially altering the strength of the neck. The most common area where I find necks to be a little large is the same as that on the neck I reshaped, giving them a slightly 'square' feeling.

Various makers have various ways of shaping necks and I use a combination of surforms, spokeshaves and scrapers, finishing with various grades of sandpaper.

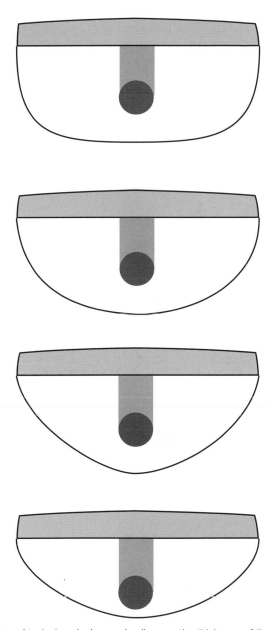

A variety of typical neck shapes. In all cases the thickness of the fingerboard and the depth of the truss rod and fillet are the same. The top example is very square and would feel uncomfortable to play. The second is almost semi-circular and the third is a V-section. The bottom example is a shallower curve and shows how the truss rod can end up close to the back of the neck.

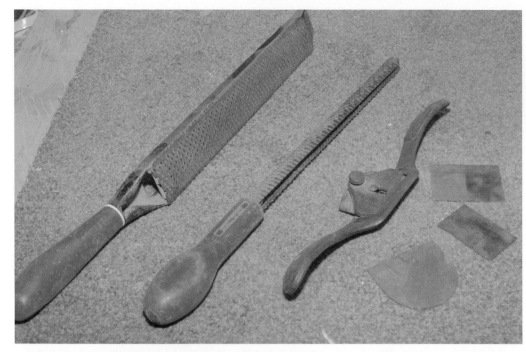

My normal neck shaping tools; two surforms, a spokeshave and scrapers.

Using a suitable curved template (in this case the filter box again) to mark the heel ready for shaping.

A heel rough cut with the surform.

Shaping an acoustic neck always, to me, seems more awkward than shaping electric guitar necks, but although I have made a large number of acoustic guitars, I have made many more electrics and so this could be expected. In either case the process is much the same. I start by shaping each end of the neck and then join the two areas up.

I know of some makers who shape necks before the fingerboard is glued (*see* Martin kit Chapter 20) but I prefer not to do this. Shaping a neck obviously removes material and therefore the neck will become a little more flexible. It is perfectly possible to glue a fingerboard onto a neck that is pre-shaped without building in a forward or back bow (and it is possible to bow an unshaped neck, too) but it is a little easier

with a neck that still has the extra 'meat' on it to keep it straight. Clamping the board in place is also easier with the back of the neck still flat. Having said this, I do sometimes part-shape the heel of the neck before fitting the board. Gluing the fingerboard before shaping does mean that when you come to shape the neck there is an overhang of fingerboard at the body end.

You could clamp the neck to the workboard or bench with the end of the neck overhanging in order to give access to both sides of the heel, or you could made a jig to hold the neck.

Using a rounded surform, I carve away the end of the neck as shown in the photographs. At the heel end I try to keep the shape rounded. This shaping can also

The end of this Douglas fir and sapele neck has been marked ready for shaping.

The 12-string neck from Chapter 22 rough carved with surforms.

With the head of the guitar clamped to the workbench, the curves of the shape at either end are joined with a series of flats.

The first of the flats, represented by the red line (*below*), is shown on the electro-acoustic neck.

extend down the heel, but care must be taken not to damage the edges. At this stage rough shaping is all that is required – just the main part of the excess can be removed.

With this partly done the neck can be unclamped and turned so the head is protruding from the work-board and the area under the nut can be shaped.

The neck shaping needs to flare gently into the head shape without any abrupt changes in direction and, again, the first stage is only to remove the main part of the waste.

With this done the relative positions at each end of the neck need to be joined in lines along the neck. I sometimes remove the main part of the waste with a surform and then tidy with a spokeshave. The impor-tant thing to remember is that the neck should not bulge or dip along its length, so the lines between each

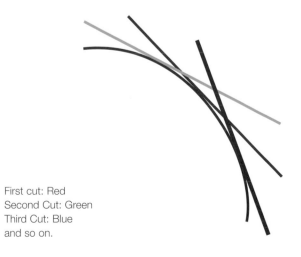

First cut: Red
Second Cut: Green
Third Cut: Blue
and so on.

By joining the curves at the ends with a series of flats, the eventual curve will appear. Here the spokeshaving has done its job and only a very small amount of unshaped wood can be seen along the centre of the neck. From here scrapers and sandpaper will finish the job.

Sandpaper over a block will help remove high and low spots and even the shape. Finer grades of paper remove scratches from the previous grades.

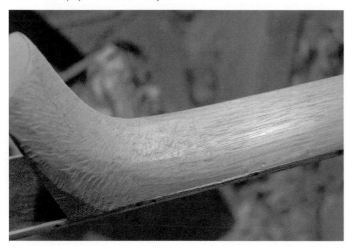

At the heel end, the neck shape needs to be blended into the heel. The clever way is to remove a little at a time and feel for lumps and dips as you go.

Using a small scraper to remove surform marks from the head to neck area.

The partially finished neck.

A simple neck holding jig (not to scale)

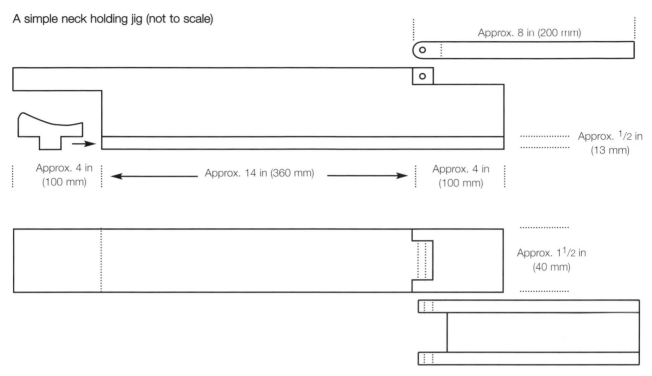

Approx. 8 in (200 mm)

Approx. 4 in (100 mm)

Approx. 14 in (360 mm)

Approx. 4 in (100 mm)

Approx. 1/2 in (13 mm)

Approx. 1¹/2 in (40 mm)

A simple neck holding jig is easy to make. The block needs to be a similar width to the neck to be shaped, or even slightly narrower. The underside is cut so that the jig can be held in a vice. At one end the block is cut away to allow clamping of the fingerboard extension and at the head end a pivoting piece is made that can be adjusted for the head angle for clamping the head in place. This is pivoted on a simple coach bolt. The main bed of the jig needs to be roughly the same length as the distance from the nut to the body join on the neck.

My prototype neck holding jig was made from a piece of scrap sapele. The head piece was not inset in, as on the drawing above, and tended to get in the way when the jig was being used. Using this jig gives much more support to the neck over clamping the head to the workbench.

corresponding part of the curve at either end should run straight between those points. To hold the neck while this is being done I have made a jig onto which the neck can be clamped and which, in turn, can be either clamped to the workbench or held in the vice.

Some makers use drawknives, but I have never even owned one so cannot comment on how good or bad they are. It is much simpler to say that if you use the tools you are comfortable with carefully and in the way they were designed, and you keep them sharpened

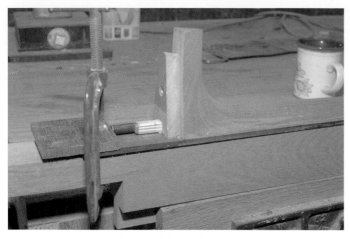

Clamping the Martin neck from Chapter 20 into the jig.

The adjustable head piece allows for any head angle and can be adjusted to deal with different fingerboard depths.

The head sanded and ready to be marked for the machine head holes.

properly, then it should present no problems. I tend to use a spokeshave as it was designed to be used but will also sometimes use it on the 'pull' stroke, like a drawknife. It is almost like a drawknife that has a cut limiter on it!

It is worth taking your time on the neck shape. This is the part of the build process that I enjoy most, as it can make such a difference to the finished guitar.

Many woods used for guitar making are very interesting to look at but have grain that makes carving necks a challenge. It is not unusual to find that the grain runs perfectly straight along part of the neck but then tears out in one small area, so you always need to be ready for this and not try to remove too much in one go.

I use the spokeshave until the neck shape is almost right. It will leave small ridges running along the neck and these get removed, and the final shaping done, with scrapers. I have said elsewhere in this book how useful a properly sharpened scraper can be, and in neck shaping they really come into their own.

Once satisfied that the neck shape is fine, I change over to sandpaper used over a cork block to remove any remaining shaping marks and to finally even out the shape, sanding out any remaining high or low points.

Once this is all done the neck is finish-sanded and the neck-to-body fit once again checked. Remember that removing wood from the neck can make a previously totally stable piece of wood move. It is rare, but it happens. Check that the alignment and neck angle are correct.

MACHINE HEAD HOLES

The neck can then have its machine head holes drilled. How you drill the machine head holes depends, in part, on what heads you have chosen to fit. Many modern-style machines have screw-in bushings and most are made in the Far East and so are made to fit a 10 mm hole. If you are in the United States you can drill a $^3/_8$ in hole and open it up, if needed, with a peghole reamer.

If you are using one of the types with a separate, push-in bushing you could measure the diameter of this and use an appropriate drill. You could drill the hole for the achine head shaft to one size and then re-drill to open out the front of the head to take the push-in bushing or you could drill the hole all the way through at the bushing diameter as the bushing will support the shaft through most of the headstock.

In all cases accurate drilling is essential as misplaced machine heads, even if only slightly out of position, will look nasty.

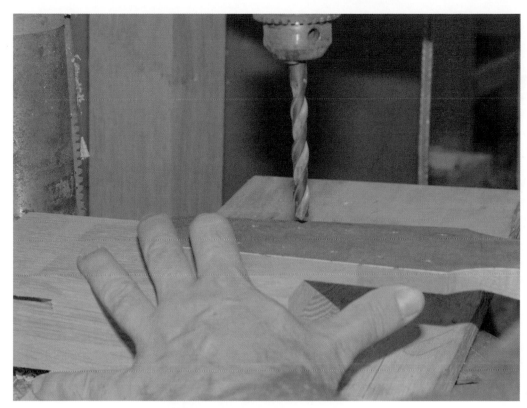

Drilling the machine head
holes on the 12-string in
Chapter 23. The head
is resting on a piece of
plywood which is also drilled
giving a cleaner
exit hole on the rear of
the head.

A finished head.

I centre punch the hole centres and use a drill with
a pointed centre.

It is also good practice to support the back of the
headstock on a piece of scrap and drill all the way
through the head and into the scrap. This will help prevent breakout around the edges of the holes at the
back.

It is also essential that the holes are drilled vertically;
they will simply not fit properly if the holes are at an
angle and so using a drill press (pillar drill) is the ideal
way to do this.

The neck can then be readied for either finishing or
gluing to the neck, depending on which you intend to
do first. Some makers choose to finish the neck and
body separately, others prefer to join the two and finish the whole guitar. This is deal with in more detail in
Chapter 18.

Chapter 14
Neck Fitting

It is a good idea to clamp the neck and body to re-check alignment before fitting. Minor adjustments now will save a lot of problems later.

For many years fitting the neck to the guitar before the finish was applied was the convention. After all, if a Spanish guitar has a slipper heel and the neck is built in, then anything else is impossible, surely! One problem that arises if the neck and body are finished together is that there can be a build-up of lacquer around the neck join and it can be hard to polish the area as well as the rest of the guitar. This is because reaching in around the neck join to get a good finish is not easy and the pieces are easier to handle if not assembled. A number of makers now finish the body and neck separately and join them afterwards, and this is what the CF Martin company do.

Each method has its supporters and I will not try to influence your decision. If you are using a butt-joined neck it is sometimes easier to glue the neck on at this stage and finish the complete guitar, but for tenon joins and bolt-ons many people prefer to finish the guitar before final assembly.

Much of the actual fitting work will already have been done, certainly to a basic stage, when checking that everything is in line. You may need to tidy things up at this stage, to make the join even better, and triple-check the final alignment, as if there was even the smallest movement in the fingerboard as it was being clamped this could affect the alignment of the bridge. While your neck may be totally in line, a small discrepancy between the centre lines of the neck and fingerboard could put the final position of your bridge a little out. This is not ideal, but also not the end of the world; if it is $1/16$ in (1.5 mm) or even $1/8$ in (3 mm) off the centre line, you can deal with it now by adjusting the neck the small amount that will bring the centre line of the fingerboard to where the bridge lines up on the centre line of the body.

GLUING OR BOLTING

The actual gluing process will vary depending on what style of join you have. As discussed earlier, the bolt-on neck is really a composite join, with the neck bolted to the body and the fingerboard glued to the front of the guitar. The join is not meant to be dismantled often; it is designed to be semi-permanent with the option of taking things apart available if, for any reason, the neck of the guitar should need to be adjusted.

It might be easier to insert the captive nuts before the neck is shaped as it can be held more accurately for

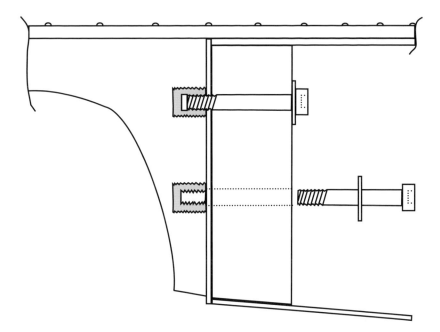

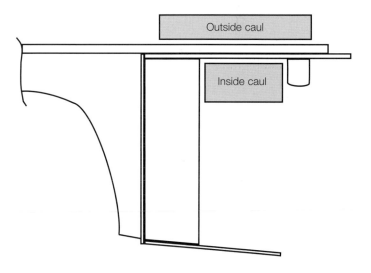

A diagram showing how the bolts are installed into captive nuts in the end of the neck. Clearly the bolt holes need to be drilled accurately and be positioned so that it is possible to tighten them from inside the guitar without fouling any part of the internal structure.

Clamping the fingerboard extension requires cauls both inside and out and care to avoid the internal bracing.

drilling; the method is included here just to be with the final fitting of the other necks. When bolting necks the captive bolts inserted into the heel of the neck must be installed very accurately so the neck lines up and the join is not under any undue stresses caused by forcing bolts into holes that are not quite aligned. The bolt-on method will work equally well on a guitar with a butt-joined neck or one with a tenon.

The length of the bolts used is important as they must be long enough to pass through the neck block with a washer under the head – to distribute the force over a wider area – and to secure themselves in the captive nut, but they must not be so long that they extend out of the far side of the heel. Two are usually used, arranged vertically along the centre line of the neck block. It is important that they are positioned so that it is possible to tighten the nut from inside the guitar. Allen-headed bolts are most commonly used as it is easier to get an Allen wrench inside the guitar.

The upper bolt should be clear of the main cross brace that runs under the end of the fingerboard, so positioning this $1^1/8$ to $1^1/4$ in (28.5 to 32 mm) below the top surface of the guitar should be fine, although be sure to check this. The lower one must be able to be adjusted without fouling on the back braces, so the distance between the two bolts will depend on the depth of the guitar.

Both the end of the neck and the neck block should be marked and the holes drilled very carefully. Remember that any drifting off the centre point when drilling these holes will cause all sorts of problems, and will be very untidy and difficult to rectify. Once this has been done the inserts can be fitted into the heel, the bolts inserted through the neck block and the neck attached.

You will need to clamp the fingerboard extension to the face of the guitar and make sure that the clamps do

not mark the wood of the guitar front (or the finish, if that has already been applied) or the wood and finish around the soundhole and the inside of the guitar. This is especially important as the clamp needs to push against something solid in the inside of the guitar. If it sits half on and half off a brace it could do all sorts of damage. The face of the fingerboard will also need to be protected, so you could find yourself having to fit one clamp with a caul beneath the board, inside the guitar where it is hard to position and impossible to see, and one on the board, which will require all three of your hands. You will also need to do this without spreading glue from the underside of the board all over the face of

Test clamping the neck with a caul inside and outside. The outside caul is an offcut of fingerboard.

your guitar. Clearly this is one area of the guitar-making process that calls for at least one dry run to ensure that everything works. The dry run can also be used to mask the area around the fingerboard extension.

There should be no gap around the end of the neck where the neck and body join. If there is, it is likely that your drilling was not as accurate as it should have been.

TENONS

Depending on how you have designed your tenon, it can be easy to fit or quite tricky. The most common design is a dovetail, as seen on the Martin kit. These can be adjusted quite easily for fit; the ideal situation being to have the tenon adjusted so that it is tight in the slot with the face of the neck exactly matching the edge of the body. Any variance in this and the tenon would need to be adjusted. This is shown in the Martin kit chapter. If the neck needs considerable force to make it level, then the slot may be too tight and fitting the neck might force all the glue out of the slot. Too loose and it may not stand the strain of life as a musical instrument.

Once the tenon is perfect the neck can be glued into place. If the guitar has already been finished great care will need to be taken not to damage the finish while gluing the neck. The same notes as written above apply as regards protecting the guitar and the fingerboard extension when gluing and clamping.

Tapered tenons do pull themselves into place and so need less clamping onto the body. A clamp to hold the fingerboard extension, with suitable cauls, and one holding the tenon into its block may be all that is needed.

If your tenon is simpler and straight-sided it may need to be pulled into the mortice.

You could try to clamp it, but a clamp big enough to go from one end of the guitar to the other to hold the neck in place is not going to be easy to find and fitting it will be a nightmare. It may have to bear against the elegant point you have designed into the lower part of your heel, which could damage it. The clamp would have to be firm enough to hold the neck but not too firm to damage the guitar and you would need to be able to hold everything in place and tighten it up at the same time, which is not an easy job for people with only two hands. This is the point in the process where you may suddenly agree that bending sides or fretting is not the hardest part of the job after all!

The method I use was gained from David Russell Young's excellent book and uses no clamp, but a piece of twine, tensioned by twisting, that pulls on one screw set into the heel and one set into the end block.

The neck is usually glued before the trim that covers the end of the heel is fitted, as this will later hide the screw hole. In some guitar designs this hole can be used to mount the strap button, if one is fitted, although of course this implies the neck is unfinished. A 1 in screw is inserted into the heel so that about one third of it is proud. Another screw is fitted into the end of the guitar where the end pin will eventually go.

A piece of thick string or twine is wrapped around the two screws and tied to be relatively tight. The edge of the guitar at the bottom end, where the string passes over, and any area around the neck where the string appears to be sitting on the guitar will need to be protected, then a small slat of wood can be pushed through the string and rotated to tension it. If the fingerboard extension has been glued down and is held by a clamp, the string is all that is needed to complete a good join, as it is more than capable of producing enough tension. Once again, a dry run is essential before attempting it with glue.

When it is glued all the excess should be carefully cleaned off.

BUTT JOINS

This same method can be used on guitars with a butt-join neck, but they are a little trickier as there is nothing to keep the neck from sliding around as it is glued. In this case I check very carefully that all is well before clamping the fingerboard extension to the front of the guitar. With this checked for alignment, the string is then tensioned and the alignment again checked. The area around the heel can also be checked to ensure that there are no gaps. Once this is certain I mark the edge of the binding where the fingerboard extension passed over with two very fine pencil lines; these will help when realigning the neck when it is glued. At this stage you could also add a couple of small brads and file them to a point, as was done under the fingerboard, to stop everything sliding around. The process is then repeated with the neck being glued into place and

A screw in the heel of the neck, the screw hole will be hidden by the heel cap.

The endpin hole can be used to temporarily hold a screw.

The tensioning on this guitar was done with some old electrical cable. The block, previous seen wedging top and back halves together, is used to stop the cable or twine sitting too low on the back of the guitar and allows the tensioner more space to work. The tensioner is simply a piece of wood used to twist the cable. The fingerboard extension is clamped down and the guitar was placed face down on two trestles so the weight of the guitar helped the join. Excess glue is still seeping and someone should stop taking photographs and clean that off!

hopefully, if your preparations are good, everything will go smoothly.

Although David Russell Young advocates using epoxy to glue the neck, I have had good results with Titebond and similar glues. You do not need to use too much glue as it can seep and drip everywhere, but the underside of the fingerboard extension and the neck tenon and/or butt join need to be thinly coated. As with all gluing there should be some seepage and the clamps should be tight but not too tight. With everything glued, the excess should be wiped away with a damp cloth and pointed drinking straws to keep the joins as clean as possible. The guitar can then be put to one side so that the glue can set. It may seem a little obvious, but it is wise to make sure the guitar is not resting in any way that exerts a negative force on the neck join, as this could undo a lot

of very hard work if it cause the neck to misalign while drying. Placing it face down on trestles, as in the photograph above, keeps a positive pressure on the join.

When the neck is dry the joins can be further cleaned up and the fingerboard checked for straightness. It is also a good idea to again double-check that the centre of the neck lines up with the centre of the body. It is not a problem if this is very slightly out. As I have said, having the centre of the bridge a little off the centre line is not going to matter too much, and most people will not notice, but if it is any more than about $1/8$ in (3.5 mm) then your preparation was not good enough. If you have epoxied the neck into place it might be time to start building your guitar again. At least with Titebond or hide glues you could, if necessary, take it apart and have a second try.

Chapter 15
Fretting

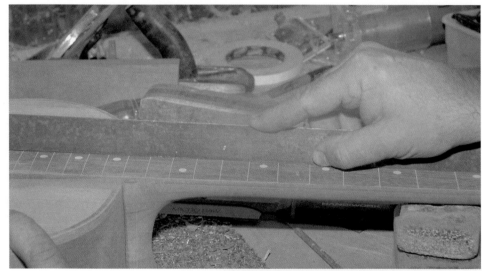

Checking the board is level.

Removing any high spots with the sanding stick and 120 grit paper.

Fretting the guitar can be done at several stages in the build, but I prefer to have the neck fitted to the guitar so that I can be sure that everything lines up and the board is flat along its length. You could fret it before gluing it to the guitar neck, but this may cause problems if there are any lumps and bumps in the guitar. In theory the join you will make between your guitar neck and body will be perfect and in line, so there is a seamless transition from the perfectly straight neck onto the body and there will be no problems when gluing it all up, but in the real world things can go wrong. My approach means that the face of the fingerboard can be inspected for any small knocks or marks that may have occurred in the making of the instrument.

All of this can be dealt with by some careful application of the sanding stick. I usually start by running a straightedge along the fingerboard to check the main alignment and then gently sand the board along its

Using 280 grit paper to remove the sanding marks.

Removing dust from the slot with a saw.

Using a former dental implement to remove waste from the slot on a bound fingerboard.

length with the sanding stick. This will show up very quickly if there are high or low spots. If the work on the neck and the board has been properly completed, there will not be much adjustment needed and it will be a straightforward job to remove the sanding marks and get a good final finish to the board.

BOARD FINISH

It is not enough just to have the board flat along its length and evenly radiused. All marks from the sanding should be sanded out and the board given the best surface finish possible, since this will affect how the guitar feels to play.

If needed, I flatten the board with 120 grit and then remove the marks from this with 180, 280 and 400 grit. I

will, if the board is very dense, also use 1200 grit wet and dry, which leaves a semi-gloss finish on the wood. Once I am happy with the finish and sure that the scratches from coarser papers are fully removed and not just polished, I will clean the worst of the dust off with some lemon oil, which is sold as a fingerboard treatment.

Slots

The sanding will have introduced some dust into the slots and this needs to be removed. The fretting saw can be used to do this on unbound necks, but you must be careful on the high-fret slots not to mark the front of the guitar. A high-pressure airline is a good way, but even this may not remove all the dust. I also have a selection of old pointed tools, some of which once saw

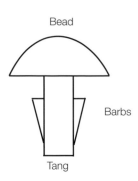

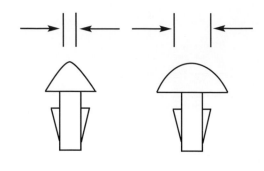

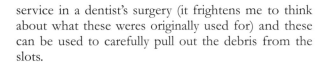

Fretwire terminology.

Diagram showing a standard fret on the right and a Petillo fret on the left. The narrower, and more pointed, Petillo fret clearly has less area on top and so the string should start its vibration right over the centre of the fret rather than to one side, which is possible on a standard fret.

service in a dentist's surgery (it frightens me to think about what these weres originally used for) and these can be used to carefully pull out the debris from the slots.

Installing the frets

It is easier to fret a guitar if there is some mass behind the neck, and this is not the case when the board is fretted before gluing it to the neck. When making electric guitars I often leave the neck unshaped until after the frets are fitted as the rectangular neck is easier to support and with something very firm and, preferably heavy behind it, is much easier to fret. This is not usually possible on acoustic guitars as shaping the neck after it has been fitted is much harder: you cannot easily shove an acoustic into a vice to hold it while shaping a neck like you can on an electric, but fretting a board that is not attached to a neck has its own problems. If you do chose to do this I would suggest fixing it onto something solid, such as a large block of flat wood, with double-sided tape before attempting to knock the frets in.

One advantage of pre-fretting the board is that if the board bends back significantly after fretting, it may be because the frets are too tight: in this case it is time to remove then and slightly widen the slots. This may not have been apparent if fretting onto a board that is glued into the neck, although with some experience this can be felt.

You could fret the board after it has been glued to the neck and before the neck is shaped. It will be slightly easier to support the neck when it is like this and the end of the fingerboard will need to be fretted carefully with something suitable underneath to support it but, again, this does not allow for any minor changes when the neck is glued on.

However, regardless of whether you fret before or after you have glued it into place, you will have already decided what fretwire to use.

FRETS AND FRETWIRE

Guitar frets are usually nickel silver and come in a variety of sizes. Not only will the bead vary in size, but the tang, which is the part that is inserted into the fretboard, can vary in size, too, so that cutting the right size of slot is essential (*see* Chapter 12). Martin offer a number of different sizes of tang on their standard fretwire and will use oversize or undersize frets to correct distorted necks, so it is logical to assume that forcing a fret into a slightly small slot will cause the neck to lay back. In many years of guitar making I have only had this happen a couple of times: the warning signs that the slots were too small were all too obvious and this will be covered shortly. It is more likely to happen on a stiffer wood such as ebony rather than a more pliable wood such as rosewood and, as there will be more 'give' in the rosewood and the slot, width will not be as critical. I have been using one or two saws for years, have never measured them and have made a lot of fingerboards: I have rarely had any problems fitting whatever size fretwire I was using.

Some players prefer a higher fret so that they can feel the fret as they play, while others prefer a smaller fret for precisely the opposite reason. Higher frets often feel better if the player is trying to bend notes. Some prefer a wide fret, as is found on some Gibsons, and others prefer a narrower one. Phillip Petillo, a guitar maker from New Jersey, patented a thin, triangular fret that gave better intonation, but this has not been widely adopted.

The thinking behind the Petillo fret is clear, but in practice normal frets are preferred by many people. There are enough other factors that can cause a guitar's intonation to wander, such as the finger pressure on fretting and neck flexibility, to name just two, that will affect the note more than the fret shape.

Jim Dunlop fretwire sizes

No		A	B	C	D	E
6000	mm	3.250	2.990	0.910	0.530	1.470
	in	0.128	0.118	0.036	0.021	0.058
6100	mm	3.180	2.790	0.810	0.530	1.400
	in	0.125	0.110	0.032	0.021	0.055
6105	mm	2.990	2.290	0.790	0.530	1.400
	in	0.118	0.090	0.031	0.021	0.055
6110	mm	2.640	2.920	0.910	0.510	1.270
	in	0.104	0.115	0.036	0.020	0.050
6120	mm	3.000	2.900	0.950	0.600	1.300
	in	0.118	0.114	0.037	0.024	0.051
6130	mm	2.790	2.692	0.914	0.508	0.914
	in	0.110	0.106	0.036	0.020	0.036
6140	mm	2.800	2.700	0.950	0.600	1.000
	in	0.110	0.106	0.037	0.024	0.039
6150	mm	2.743	2.591	0.787	0.510	1.067
	in	0.108	0.102	0.031	0.020	0.042
6155	mm	2.870	2.616	0.787	0.533	1.168
	in	0.113	0.103	0.031	0.021	0.046
6160	mm	2.800	2.700	0.950	0.600	1.000
	in	0.110	0.106	0.037	0.024	0.039
6170	mm	3.280	2.500	1.220	0.600	1.100
	in	0.129	0.099	0.048	0.024	0.043
6180	mm	2.570	2.720	0.890	0.500	1.100
	in	0.101	0.107	0.035	0.020	0.043
6190	mm	2.390	2.130	0.740	0.510	0.990
	in	0.094	0.084	0.029	0.020	0.039
6200	mm	2.540	2.000	1.140	0.600	1.100
	in	0.100	0.079	0.045	0.024	0.043
6210	mm	2.540	2.000	0.860	0.500	1.100
	in	0.100	0.079	0.034	0.020	0.043
6220	mm	2.400	2.000	0.960	0.500	1.100
	in	0.097	0.079	0.038	0.020	0.043
6230	mm	2.480	1.990	0.900	0.520	1.080
	in	0.098	0.078	0.035	0.020	0.043
6240	mm	2.388	2.032	0.787	0.483	0.940
	in	0.094	0.080	0.031	0.019	0.037
6250	mm	2.413	1.905	0.914	0.508	0.762
	in	0.095	0.075	0.036	0.020	0.030
6260	mm	2.800	2.000	0.950	0.600	1.000
	in	0.110	0.079	0.037	0.024	0.039
6265	mm	2.800	2.000	0.950	0.600	1.000
	in	0.110	0.079	0.037	0.024	0.039
6270	mm	2.540	1.905	0.914	0.508	0.762
	in	0.100	0.075	0.036	0.020	0.030
6290	mm	2.337	1.981	0.787	0.508	1.016
	in	0.092	0.078	0.031	0.020	0.040
6300	mm	1.940	1.600	0.960	0.600	0.640
	in	0.076	0.063	0.038	0.024	0.025
6310	mm	2.311	1.346	0.940	0.559	0.787
	in	0.091	0.053	0.037	0.022	0.031
6320	mm	2.159	1.194	0.711	0.533	0.737
	in	0.085	0.047	0.028	0.021	0.029
6330	mm	2.388	1.092	0.787	0.508	0.787
	in	0.094	0.043	0.031	0.020	0.031
6340	mm	2.235	1.829	0.838	0.508	0.889
	in	0.088	0.072	0.033	0.020	0.035

Note: 6340 flat topped, 6180 brass
Used with permission from Dunlop Manufacturing, Inc.

For a first guitar a medium fretwire, such as Dunlop's 6120, is ideal. The Dunlop company make an impressive range of wires and many manufacturers use them. The chart above shows the range and sizes, and those most commonly used for various applications.

There are two accepted ways of fitting frets: compression fretting and glued in. Both have their supporters and both are valid, but in either case the fret needs to be seated properly into a properly cut fret slot.

The main problem with fret slots is that the saw does not run through the slot cleanly on each pass, and so widens the ends of the slot. This can mean the ends of the fret may not sit properly into the slot, but this is not the end of the world and there are ways around it. It is a good idea, especially if you are going to bind the fingerboard, to cut a few fret slots in an offcut of the fingerboard material and fret those as you would with the board. You will get a good idea of the ease of fretting and of whether the slots are too wide or too narrow.

GLUED-IN FRETS

Most frets are installed by what is known as the compression method, when the tension of the wood holds the fret in place. Some makers prefer to set the fret in glue. Glued-in frets need to have the slot cut so that it is as near as possible the same size as the tang. If the slot is any wider then it may not glue properly and may waggle around in the slot: this can mean it will lift or it could rattle.

If gluing in, it should be possible to push the fret into the slot with just a small amount of pressure. This is to overcome the resistance of the barbs on the fret, which will still be wider than the slot and will help to keep the fret in the slot.

The glue that you use for this is a matter of personal choice since there are few glues designed specifically to fit frets (generally made of metal) into wood (generally made of wood). The glue is not there to fix the fret permanently into place but to seal it and stop it moving. If and when the fret needs to be removed for any reason, heating the glue by holding a soldering iron onto the fret will normally make it an easy job to remove. Some people use hide glue, others Titebond or white glue and others use cyanoacrylate. The downside of using glue is that is can get messy and you need to be able to keep your fingerboard clean.

You also need to be able to hold the fret in position while the glue sets enough to do the job for you. Clearly with cyanoacrylate this is not going to be a problem as you can hold the fret in place for the short amount of time the glue needs to go off, but you need to be very careful that you do not splash the glue around or glue yourself to the guitar.

Prior to fitting the frets, it is wise to double-, and even triple-check, the board to make sure it is flat along its length and has not acquired any lumps and bumps.

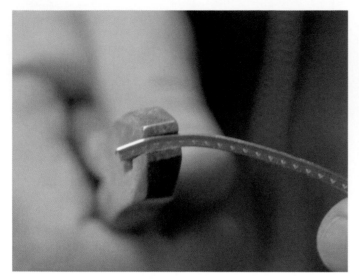

Using pliers to bend fretwire.

Using a fret tang cutter for frets that will sit over the binding.

Next the fretwire will need to be curved to match the radius of the fingerboard. It will not matter that much if the radius of the fret is a little more that the radius of the board, as there will be some resistance from the barbs on the tang and the centre of the fret is less likely to pop up. Having a fret whose radius is less than the board can mean the ends of the fret will pop out.

Start by gently bending the fretwire to the required radius. There are tools available designed to do this, but you can do it by gently bending the wire a little at a time. There is no need to bend it much. If you work across a length of fretwire, moving perhaps half an inch at a time, a very small amount of pressure will give you the radius you need. The main thing to watch for as you do this is not to twist the wire. Since it is a T-shape it will try to find the path of least resistance and bend at an angle; you simply need to keep control of it and ensure you are bending the bead.

Once this has been done the frets can be cut to length. Cut each one to be slightly longer, by about $^1/4$ in (6.3 mm), than the fret slot and then apply a little glue to the slot. Place the fret into place and push it down. If the slot is the right size then this should be easy and the fret should go down properly. If the radius is not enough you may have to remove the fret to start again, as the ends are unlikely to stay down. If the fret is very slightly over-radiused then a small mount of pressure in the centre will hold it down while the glue dries.

If the guitar has binding, the tang of the fret needs to be cut away to allow the bead to sit over the binding. This can be done with one of the specialist tools that some guitar parts suppliers sell, or even with a file. The tang will need to be cut back so that it is just a little shorter than the slot, as this will allow for any glue that may have seeped from the join between the binding and the fingerboard. It is also worth ensuring that the

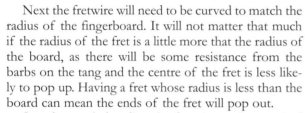

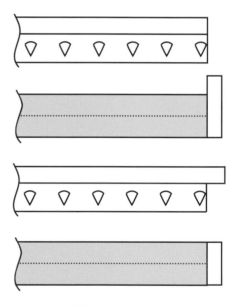

There are two ways of fitting binding to a fingerboard. In the upper example, the fret sits inside the binding which is then carved to the shape of the fret end. In the lower example, the binding is flush with the board and the tang is cut away so the fret bead sits above the binding. On both cases the boards are shown flat for illustration only.

radius on the fret continues into the part of the bead that is now tang-less, as this will ensure it sits down onto the binding properly.

If you are using cyanoacrylate then you will not have to wait long, but if you are using a slower-setting glue you may need to fashion some sort of clamp; with up to 20 frets to deal with, this could take some time.

Once the frets have been glued into place and the glue is set, any further cleaning of the board can be done and the ends can be clipped to length with flush-cutting end nippers. These can be bought from guitar

Cutting the fret ends flush with the edge of the board.

parts suppliers or a pair of almost flush cutters can be ground down to make them cut exactly flush. If doing this, remember that grinding the metal will make it hot, which can make it brittle so that it will chip easily.

With all frets trimmed the ends can be tidied. This is done with a long file, taking care not to bash the end into the guitar body or headstock. The file needs to be used along the frets to make them flush with the edge of the board. Be careful not to let it dig in if it comes up against a fret end that sticks out more than the others. Special care also needs to be taken not to mark the top where the fingerboard sits on the guitar front. This can be nasty as the file is usually quite sharp and you don't want to have this moment to remind you just how soft the top can be! A simple answer is to make a mask from plastic or card to protect the top.

The first couple of passes will get the ends of the fret flush with the edge of the fingerboard, but the file can also be used to bevel the ends of the fret.

COMPRESSION FRETTING

Guitar fretwire is generally not designed to be glued in. It is made with small barbs on the tang, the part that goes into the board, so that they grip. Knocking the frets in and allowing them to stay there is a method that has been used successfully for many years. We have already discussed the size of the slot in the board; when you fret in this way you quickly get a good feel for how well the fret is going into the board. The trick is to not try too hard and to take things slowly at first. You should also wear some form of ear protection, as knocking frets into a board makes a fair amount of noise and can damage your hearing.

Supporting the neck with a shaped block. This one is padded with several layers of masking tape.

The frets are prepared in a similar way to when gluing except that the wire is bent just a little more. The ends need to be cut back if they are to go over binding on the neck, and it is essential that the underside of the neck, beneath where you are fitting the fret, is adequately supported. I like to use a big lump of hardwood with something on top of it to protect the neck wood. It is also essential that constant checks are made under the neck to ensure that nothing has crept between the support and the neck itself that could mark it.

It is also a good idea to double-check that the fret slot is nice and clean and free from any sanding dust.

There are specialist hammers available for fretting guitars but I have been using a small pin hammer for years and it works fine. I do tend to hold the handle

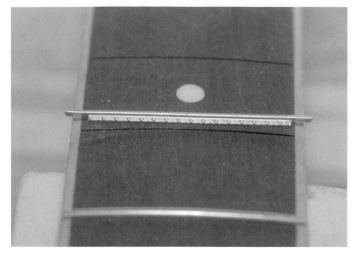

The fret will need to be cut a little longer than the slot and if binding is fitted it may need to have the tang cut back as here.

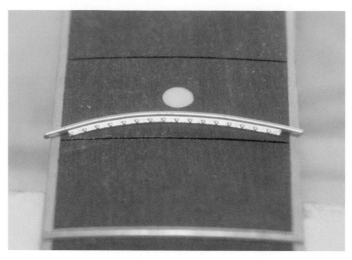

The fret is curved slightly more than the curve of the fingerboard.

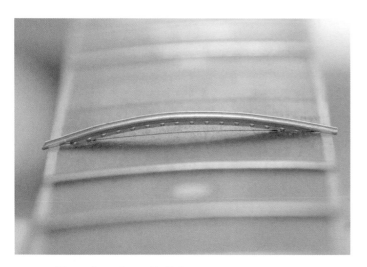

The ends are tapped in first.

The fret is then slowly worked into the slot working all the way across it. Care must be taken to keep the ends bedded down.

The fret on this unbound fingerboard is almost in. There is just a small gap beneath the centre of the bead.

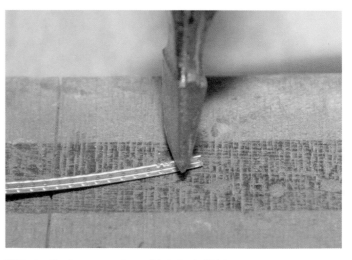

Widening the tang on a piece of fretwire to fit into an oversized slot.

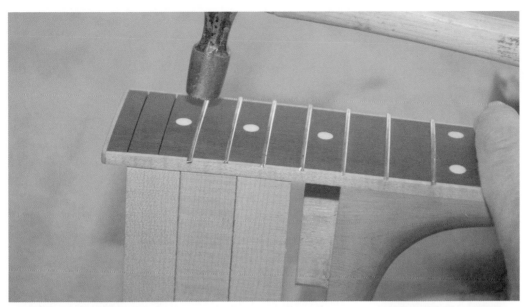

Fretting the fingerboard overhang can have its own problems. If the neck is fretted before it is fitted to the body, a suitable block of wood, in this case an offcut from an old neck blank, can be used to support the underside of the board and provide suitable mass to absorb the hammer blows.

If the board is fretted after the neck is fitted a support will be needed inside the body to absorb the blows. This panel beaters' shaping block fits neatly inside the guitar and has enough mass.

The metal block is held with one hand inside the guitar while the fret is hammered in. Attempting to fret the overhang without any support beneath can damage the guitar and the frets will not sit as easily.

Filing the fret ends flush with the board.

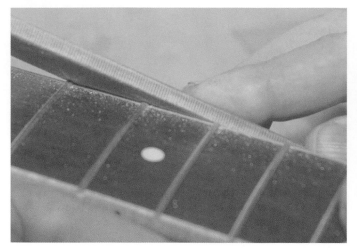

Filing a 45-degree angle onto the ends of the frets.

The angled fret end will require more work but this can be done at the setting up stage.

close to the head and use it relatively gently, but that is just personal preference.

Position the fret into the slot, making sure, if the tang has been cut back, to allow the bead to sit over the binding: the remaining part of the tang will then fit between the bindings and not force it off the side of the neck as the fret is hammered in. Then gently tap each end into place.

The trick now is to go backwards and forwards over the fret, knocking it gently, so it sits properly into the slot all the way along its length without the ends popping back out. Gentle taps are all that is required and if the neck is supported properly beneath, the frets should go in well.

You can sometimes have problems if the board has been cut by hand. I have already mentioned that the natural movement of the human arm is in a curve and so it is possible that when cutting the fret slot there may be a very slight variation in width at the ends. This can cause the ends of the fret to not sit properly, but is not a problem.

If the fret does not go down into the board properly, it can be removed with some flush-end cutters, which you should have to trim the ends of the fret, and the tang can be adjusted. This is simply done by holding the fret face-down on something solid and tapping the underside of the tang with something hard – some people use an old file and I use the pointed side of my pin hammer. This splays the bottom of the tang very slightly and will make it just that much wider that it should fit into the slot properly.

If you take your time, have done your preparation properly and support the neck properly, it should not be too difficult to fret your guitar in this manner.

Life does get interesting when you get to the fingerboard extension over the face of the guitar. This also needs to be supported underneath by something that has sufficient mass. I have used an old builder's hammer held inside the guitar and under the fret position. This weighs

Using the 'Jaws' press.

about 4 lb (1.8 kg) and provides enough mass to absorb hammer blow and allow the fret to take the full force.

Once the frets are all in, their ends can be trimmed and shaped as described for the gluing method.

PRESSES

Some makers like to use a fret press. These can be very good, but can only really be used on a board that is not yet attached to the guitar.

The fret is prepared in the same way as above and then a solid metal caul with an inside radius the same as the surface of the fret is inserted into the press; this is used to push the fret into place. Clearly some effort has to go into ensuring that the radius on the board matches that of the caul, but the end result is often excellent, with the frets needing little or no work after they are fitted.

Chapter 16
Bridges

The bridge on a
Martin OM28VR.

Some basic design work on the bridge was covered in Chapter 3. This chapter covers further design work and the making of the bridge.

Guitar making has evolved to the point where most guitars will have a bridge that is very similar in size to most others, that is $1^1/2 \times 6^1/2 \times {}^3/8$ in ($37 \times 165 \times 10$ mm) and this is a good starting point if you are designing your own: start at that size and then add your own design touches

Some smaller-bodied guitars, or parlour guitars, have much smaller bridges and there is nothing wrong with this, provided that there is room to fit the strings and space to fit the saddle.

There is nothing to stop you making your bridge asymetric, and the guitars made with the Kasha bracing system will have this as standard. The theory is that the different-sized parts of the bridge allow the treble frequencies to radiate out to their part of the body more effectively. Of course, this suggests that the vibrations will follow the path set out for them in the design and not just do their own thing, and that different parts of the top look after different frequencies.

The saddle is normally $^1/16$ in (1.5 mm) to $^1/8$ in (3 mm) thick. It is arched across the top to match the arch of the fingerboard and is set about halfway down into the bridge in a routed channel. On steel-strung guitars it is usually angled to compensate for the difference in stretch between varying thicknesses of strings, so that they do not go out of tune when fretted.

The bridge on this Goodall is small and curved. The saddle is a little close to the bass string bridge pin which will be trying to force the saddle forward.

Because the compensation needed to keep each string in tune is not even across the strings, any one-piece saddle on an acoustic guitar will be a compromise as no individual adjustment of the string length is available, although careful shaping of the top of the saddle

169

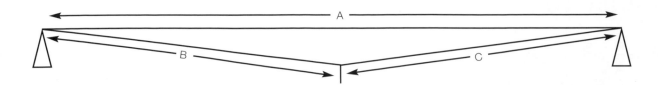

Many small-bodied parlour guitars have a simple rectangular bridge.

A simple geometric pattern than explains compensation. If a string (A) is suspended between two points that are raised above the fingerboard, pressing the string down to a fret position stretches that string as it is, in effect, making the other two sides of a triangle. The sum of (B) and (C) will be greater than (A) and since stretching a string will raise its pitch, the first octave position, half way along the string's length, will appear sharper than it should. Moving the bridge away from the nut a little will allow for this, and since thin plain strings stretch less than thicker wound strings, the amount of compensation needed will be greater on the bass side of the bridge than the treble.

A complex but interesting bridge on a Breedlove guitar. This is also unusual in that it is not a pin bridge but has the strings slotted through the rear of the bridge.

A nicely elegant bridge on a Taylor 612CE guitar. The top of the saddle is carved help intonation.

can help. One alternative is to use a two-piece or even three-piece saddle that can be fitted into separate slots in the bridge to allow for the different amounts of compensation needed on the wound and unwound strings.

Some guitars have a wider, $1/4$ in (6.3 mm) wide saddle that is designed to fit over a bridge transducer. These saddles are wide enough to be shaped to intonate each string. Other guitars have standard-sized saddles still with a transducer beneath. To enable the saddle to transmit the best possible vibration to the guitar top, it

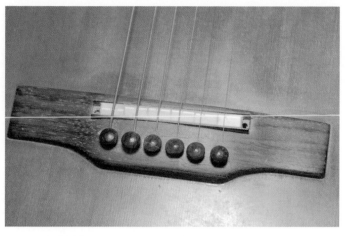

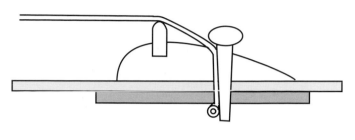

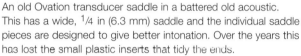

An old Ovation transducer saddle in a battered old acoustic. This has a wide, 1/4 in (6.3 mm) saddle and the individual saddle pieces are designed to give better intonation. Over the years this has lost the small plastic inserts that tidy the ends.

A cross section of a guitar bridge. The top and bridge plate beneath are shown shaded. The bridge pin holds the string in place by friction and so needs to be a good fit.

needs to be firmly bedded down onto the bottom of its slot in the bridge, with its base resting flat on the flat bottom of the channel (or on the acoustic pickup, if one is fitted). This means it must be cut carefully and accurately; more details of this are in Chapter 19.

The bridge is made separately from the guitar and is not glued into place until the guitar is finished, as the area around it is otherwise impossible to polish to a good gloss. The bridge is usually not finished but is left as natural wood. The saddle slot is also often left until after the bridge has been glued onto the guitar so that the proper saddle position can be found – the bridge can slip very slightly when it is being glued - or it can be cut before if you are confident of the saddle position.

As we discussed in Chapter 2, the overall height of the bridge and saddle is determined by the neck angle, or lack of it, by the thickness of the fingerboard that runs over the body and by the height of the strings above this.

A low bridge with a high saddle may not transmit the vibration of the strings to the top effectively and the string pressure will always be trying to push the saddle over, towards the nut. A higher bridge with a lower saddle may not have a steep enough angle over the bridge to stop the string vibration successfully. A certain amount of down-pressure is required to make the bridge work and to stop the small amount of string between the saddle and the bridge pin from rattling, as the string vibration is not stopped at the saddle.

For some years it was quite fashionable to find acoustic guitars with tailpieces, where the strings were anchored onto a frame that was fixed to the end block and not into the bridge. There are good and bad points to this design, the good being that, since the strings are not fixed to the bridge, there is no rotational force on the bridge. The tension of the strings is taken by the whole body of the guitar, not just the top. This could

allow a lighter bracing for any guitar as the braces are not protecting the top from dipping in front of the bridge and rising behind it. The downside of these bridges is that the extra unsupported string will act to dissipate some of the string's energy and the guitar will not sound as bright. The pressure on the bridge may also be less and so less vibration may be transferred to the top. Many highly regarded but pretty cheap guitars in the 1920s and 1930s featured tailpieces and some 12-string guitars still do. It is a matter of personal preference.

BRIDGE PINS

Most acoustic guitar bridges are what is known as pin bridges. In these the strings are held in place by friction pins that fit into holes in the front of the bridge. The ball-end of the string pulls up underneath these and forces them to grip the sides of the hole.

There are two ways of fitting the pins. One is to make a tapered hole that is an exact fit and to cut a slot in the front of this to take the string. The other way is to make the hole slightly oversize, although still tapered, and allow the string to pull the pin into place. A hole that is too wide may cause the pin to fall out and, since this may not happen while the guitar is being strung, it is bound to happen at an inopportune time and may fling the bridge pin far out into your stunned audience. A hole that is too tight might cause your string to jam the bridge pin into place, making it difficult to remove.

Bridge decoration

Just like the fingerboard, the bridge can be decorated with inlays or can be carved. Early Martin guitars had pyramid carving on the edges of the bridge and some more elaborate guitars have had all manner of things

An ebony block and rosewood bridge blank.

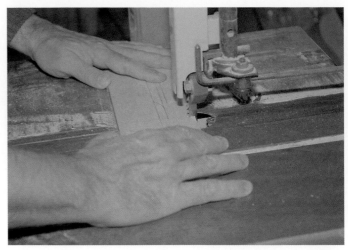

Cutting a template from $^3/_{16}$ in (5mm) plywood.

carved into their bridges. The simplest inlay is often one or two dots either side of the saddle. These are sometimes a little more than pure decoration – some cheaper guitars have been made with bridges that are screwed and glued into place and the dots cover the heads of the screws.

Another use of dots is to cover up an early form of transducer. The Barcus Berry company was one of the first to make piezo-electric pickups for acoustic guitars and one of their products was known as the 'Hot Dot'. This was a simple transducer that fitted into a hole drilled through the bridge. The unit itself was pushed through and glued into place with its wire coming out on the inside of the guitar. The remaining hole above the Hot Dot was filled with a small pearl dot. The Hot Dot has now been superseded by more advanced pickups, but in its time it was the industry standard. However, adding carving or decoration is entirely up to you.

MAKING THE BRIDGE

Guitar makers' suppliers will often supply bridge blanks. These are usually ebony or rosewood and often are rough-cut. Start by flattening the top and bottom and planing one side flat to use as a datum. You could mark directly onto the bridge but it is a much better idea, even if only making one guitar, to make a template of your bridge from thin plywood; this will allow you to spot any mistakes and rectify them before you start. Mark a centre line across the piece that will be used as a basis for the measurements of bridge pin and saddle position. The saddle position should not be too close to the front of the bridge as it needs to be supported adequately. The treble end of the saddle will be further forward than the bass side and this should be about $^3/_{16} - ^1/_4$ in (5–6.3 mm) back from the front edge of the bridge. The angle of the saddle will leave the bass side about $^7/_{16} - ^1/_2$ in (10.5–12.7 mm) back from

Cutting out the bridge shape. It is much easier to see the lines if they are drawn onto masking tape.

the front edge. If the pins are $^3/_8$ in (9.5 mm) back from this, it will mean they are $^7/_8$ in (22 mm) back from the front edge. This position can be marked across the template. The bridge pin holes can also be marked and could be drilled to $^1/_8$ in (3 mm) to be used as a basis for drilling or marking the actual bridge. The overall shape will also need to be cut out and sanded to shape so that it can be used to mark the actual bridge piece.

Since most bridges are made of a dark wood I often find it easier to cover the face of the bridge with masking tape so that any lines and positions transferred from the template are easily seen.

With the plan of the bridge marked, the first stage is to drill the bridge pin holes. This should not be left until after the bridge is shaped as drilling accurate holes will be more difficult. These should be drilled on a drill press (pillar drill) and the holes should be centre-punched to assist accurate drilling. The underside of the bridge should also be supported on a block of wood and the hole drilled through the bridge and into

Drilling the bridge pin holes. By fixing a guide on the bed of the drill table, centre punching the hole positions and drilling with a pointed bit, accurate holes are much easier.

Double checking the height of the bridge.

the block beneath; this should prevent any breakout on the underside of the bridge. With all the holes drilled, the bridge can be shaped. I usually use a $3/16$ in (5 mm) drill as this is just a little smaller than the bridge pins need and it is easy enough to open the holes out a little with a reamer. With all the holes drilled, the bridge can be shaped.

The angle of the neck and the thickness of the fingerboard extension over the body should have been designed to give a bridge of approximately $1/2$ in (12.7 mm) overall height, with the saddle being about $1/8$ in (3 mm) above the bridge that is $3/8$ in (9.5 mm) thick. This will need to be checked on the guitar as there may be some small variations in the way the guitar has gone

together, compared with how it was planned. Since the angles are so small a very small difference can be important, so it does need to be checked.

Remember that the action of the guitar is usually measured at the 12th fret which is halfway along the string length. Since the string is only very slightly above the height of the frets at the nut, there is a slight angle between the string and the tops of the frets. If the action is planned to be $3/32$ in (2.2 mm) at the 12th fret this relative height above the frets will double by the time it reaches the bridge. Therefore if the face of the fingerboard lines up with the top of the bridge, the saddle height will need to be $3/16$ in (5 mm) above the bridge to give the $3/32$ in at the 12th fret. If the straight-

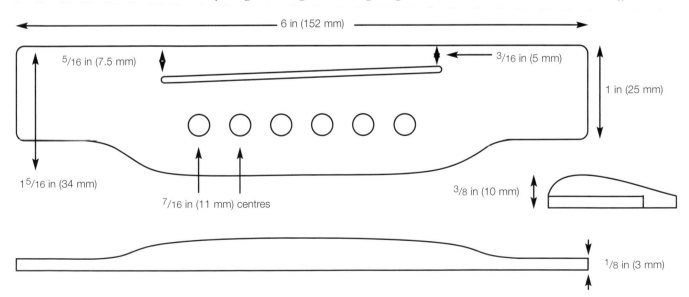

A typical bridge, drawn full size.

The ends of the bridge are bandsawn off.

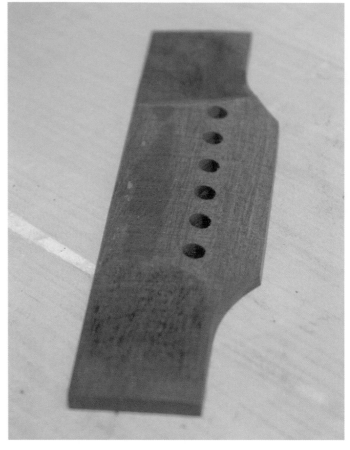

The basic shape is belt sanded and scraped.

edge touches the bridge blank about $1/16$ in (1.5 mm) under the top face of the blank then the saddle will be roughly $1/8$ in (3 mm) deep. If the straightedge clears the bridge by a significant amount, your bridge is likely to have a very high saddle and you should either check the integrity of your neck join, as the angle may be wrong, or make a bridge from a thicker blank.

BRIDGE DIMENSIONS

The ends of the bridge are thinner than the centre when viewed from the front. The ends are usually about $1/8$ in (3 mm) deep and so the excess needs to be cut away and the bridge shaped to give an even, flowing curve (*see* drawing page 173). I start by bandsawing off most of the waste and then get to work on a belt sander.

The shape of the upper surface cross section of the bridge is designed to have the saddle at the highest point of the bridge with the area behind this falling away, so the bridge pins are a little lower than the base of the saddle. This helps the string angle over the saddle that will stop the dead string – between the pin and the saddle – vibrating. This can be carefully sanded on a small belt sander, checking all the time that not too much is being removed and that the curve is even. The bridge can then be scraped and sanded to make all the lines flow and to remove any marks from the belt sander.

If the top of the guitar is arched, the bridge will need to have its underside shaped to fit. This can be done by carefully scraping and sanding the underside until there are no visible gaps. One thing that helps is to lay some 120 grit paper over the bridge area of the body and to move the bridge up and down over this, so that it takes up the shape of the top.

When you are certain that the underside of the bridge is fine, mask the area under the bridge and

Bridges waiting for finish sanding.

transfer your centre line and the saddle position onto the masking tape. Next, clean off any dust and place the bridge over the masking tape in its final position. Double-check your measurements to ensure that the distance from the nut to the 12th fret on the neck is the

The saddle position is marked with a tapered jig that represents the outer edge of the fingerboard extended to the bridge.

With the saddle position marked and checked, the front edge of the bridge is marked on the tape.

Masking the bridge area.

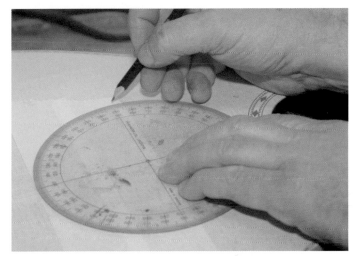

Ensuring the front edge of the bridge will be square to the centreline.

Checking the bridge is in the right place.

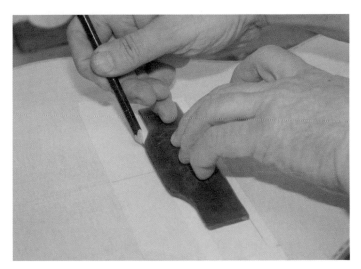

The bridge can be placed into position and drawn around.

Cutting the masking inside the pencil line. The finish will extend under the bridge for a short way making for a tidier join.

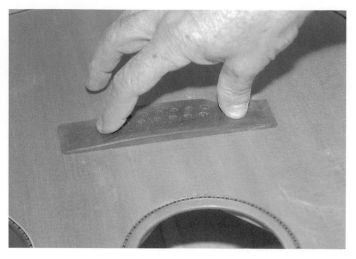

Test positioning the bridge.

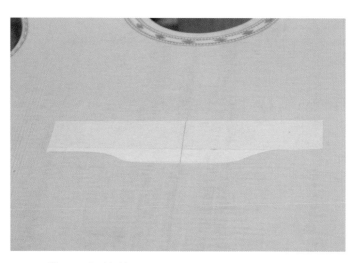

The masked bridge area.

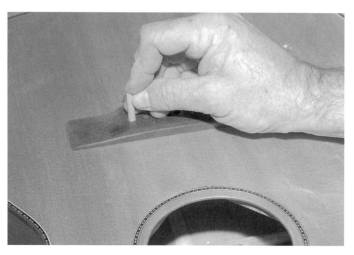

Tapered dowel plugs can be used to stop the bridge moving as it is glued. The outer holes are drilled through and the dowels inserted.

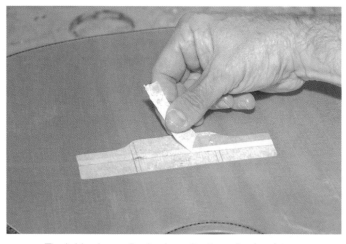

The bridge is usually glued on after the guitar has been finished. The masking tape will need to be pulled over itself to avoid damaging the fibres of the top or the finish.

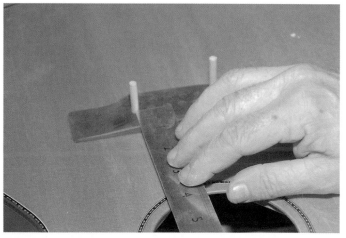

Before gluing it is advisable to recheck the bridge is correctly located. This is your last chance to alter it easily if you have made a mistake.

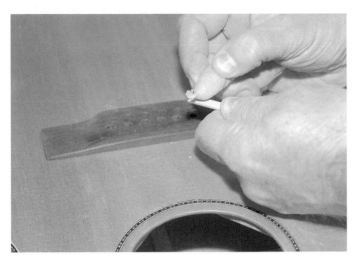

Waxing the dowels with a candle so they can be removed.

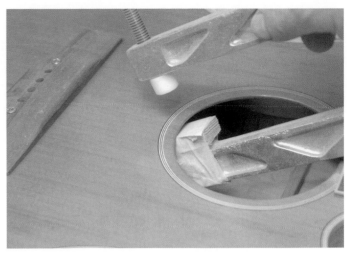

Test fitting a bridge clamp. This has the ridge temporarily screwed to the top to stop it moving around. Packing pieces have been added to the clamp to clear the bracing inside and a caul will protect the top of the bridge.

same as the distance from the 12th fret to the treble side of the saddle position. Also double-check that your bridge is located exactly on the extended neck centre line, which should clearly also be the centre line of the body, and that its front edge is square to the centre line. It may be a good idea to use a bridge clamp to hold the bridge in place so that it does not move, before gently drawing around the edge of the bridge with a fine pencil. Be careful not to use too much pressure and mark the top. Once the bridge has been marked, it can be removed and the masking cut away to leave just the bridge shape in the centre. You could scribe around the bridge and cut the masking tape to the exact outline of the bridge, but it is better to make the masked area fractionally smaller than the bridge. That way, when the bridge is glued on, all the gaps will disappear and the finish will appear to disappear tidily under the bridge while there is still plenty of wood-to-wood contact for affixing the bridge.

GLUING THE BRIDGE

When the guitar is finished and polished, this masking tape can be carefully removed, leaving an area of wood beneath for you to be able to glue your bridge directly in place. Needless to say, the gluing and clamping should be done carefully as any misalignment at this stage will be very annoying, and very difficult and time-consuming to put right.

Clamping the bridge into position requires long-necked clamps. These can be found in engineering supply catalogues but will often be quite heavy. This is not ideal as the guitar top is quite thin and you do not want to distort it when gluing on the bridge, so buying specialist bridge clamps may be a good idea. These are aluminium and so lighter and, since they are designed for the job, are just the right size. You can only fit a maximum of three of these through the soundhole to

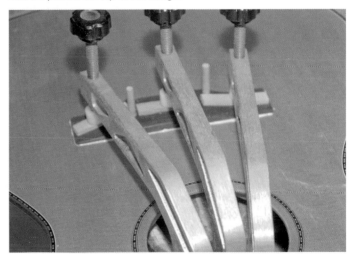

You can just about fit three bridge clamps in a normal sound-hole but you need to be very careful not to damage the guitar.

It is possible to clamp the bridge with just one clamp. This has a caul that is clamped in the centre and two wedges are inserted at each end to add more pressure.

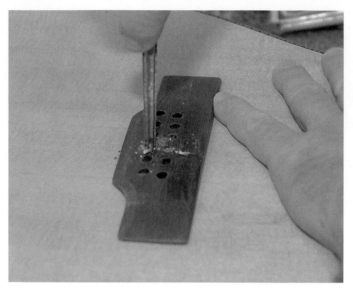

Clearing the bridge pin holes with a tapered reamer.

hold the bridge in place, but if you are careful in the way you use them you can get away with using fewer. It is possible to get enough downwards pressure using just one, but you need to be able to spread that pressure out over the whole area of the bridge. Making a caul to fit the top of the bridge is one way or using a caul and wedges, as demonstrated in the photograph, is another.

The bridge will need to be prevented from moving around when it is glued. I have used several methods. One is to drill the outer two string holes before the bridge is glued on, whilst it is held in place during the dry fitting, and then fit small plastic or wooden dowels to hold it in position while it is being glued. These will need to be waxed to stop them becoming a permanent part of the guitar. They are easily removed when the glue is set and the holes may still need to be further widened to take the bridge pins.

Another equally suitable method is to accurately mark the centres of the outer string holes and drill these to $1/8$ in (3 mm). Small countersunk screws can then be used to hold the bridge in place. The countersunk head will automatically position the bridge accurately over the hole if care has been taken to insert the screw completely vertically. The screw will also add some downwards pressure on the bridge to help clamping. I tend to use this method when using just one clamp and wedges.

As with any other stage in the building process, the excess glue will need to be cleaned off before it sets and once the glue is dry, the clamps can be removed. Do this carefully as they can damage the finish around the soundhole.

The remaining holes for the bridge pins can be drilled through the top of the guitar. A good tip here is to use

a bridge clamp to hold a piece of wood under the bridge to support the underside of the bridge plate: this way, the wood will not break away when the holes are drilled. If you have access to a peg hole reamer, this can be used to taper the holes to match the pins for a better fit.

FITTING THE SADDLE

The final stage is to fit the saddle. You will need to cut a slot in the bridge approximately $1/8$ in (3 mm) wide and with a totally flat bottom. This is clearly a job for a router of some kind. You will need to make up some kind of jig to support this, but the first stage is to check your saddle position.

Two-piece bridge saddles were discussed earlier, but for a first guitar I would suggest a simple one-piece saddle, as you can always get clever on your subsequent guitars (and there probably will be more than one). One-piece saddles have been used successfully on many hundreds of thousands of guitars and work well enough.

You can estimate the compensation needed on the saddle. I often position saddles so that the exact end of the scale length on the treble side of the saddle is on the fingerboard side of the saddle slot. The saddle will be $1/8$ in (3 mm) wide and so can have the top shaped to adjust this a tiny bit if necessary. On the bass side I usually allow $3/16 - 1/4$ in (4.5 − 6.5 mm) in compensation.

If working by guesswork does not appeal to you, or if you want to make a multi-piece saddle, then you can find the exact position by stringing the guitar temporarily and making a false saddle to show you where the real one will end up.

To find the best position you should string up your guitar with the gauge of string you wish to use and your false saddle will need to be the same height that your final saddle will be, so that the string action is the same. Any differences in this will affect the amount of compensation needed and you might as well just guess! If you are making a one-piece saddle, just use the top and bottom strings. Incidentally, this is the point where it all comes together for the first time and you amaze yourself that the box you have built actually sounds like a guitar. It is a fun moment.

The temporary saddle can be made from some scrap hardwood. Place this beneath the strings in the area that you have marked for your saddle and tune the guitar to pitch. If you have measured everything correctly you should find that when you play a harmonic at the 12th fret and compare it with the note, they are almost the same. If the fretted note is higher than the harmonic, move the 'saddle' backwards slightly, towards the bridge pins, and try again. Do the same with the bass side and you will find the optimum angle.

If you are using a one-piece saddle you can then mark the points on the bridge where the intonation is correct and join them with a line. This will be the cen-

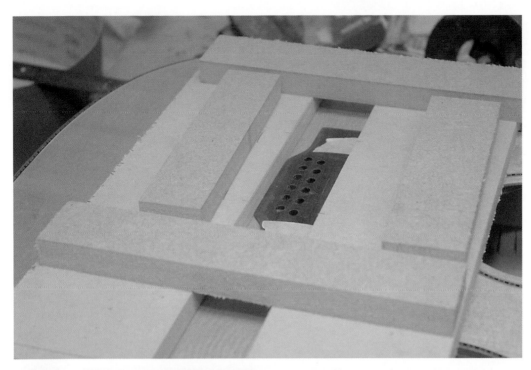

A very crude but effective jig for routing the saddle slot. This is strips of MDF fixed with double sided tape.

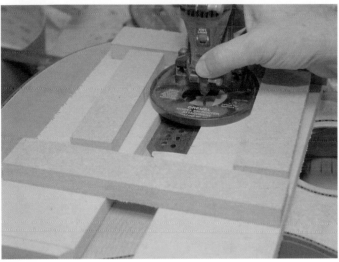

The jig is designed to allow the router to only move in one direction with end stops to prevent it cutting past the end of the required slot. With come careful measuring this works very well.

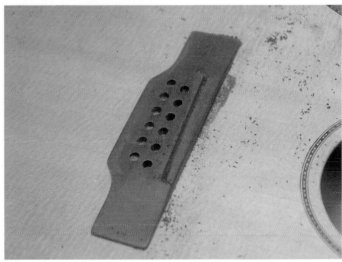

With the slot cut to depth, the jig can be removed and the saddle made.

tre of your saddle slot. If you do chose to make a two- or even three-piece saddle you will need to string the guitar completely and make several false saddles.

Jig

You now need to make a jig that will allow your router, be it full size or mini, to cut the saddle slot. If your guitar has an arched top then the easiest way is to make something that will be supported on the edges of the guitar and that will give you a flat surface just above the

bridge. This will mean that although your guitar top may be arched, the bottom of your saddle slot will not be, which is what is required. You will also need to make an edge guide so that the router runs in a straight line. Do not be tempted to try this freehand: the router will try to pull into the direction of the cut and you will not end up with a straight saddle slot.

There are commercially available jigs that can be purchased to do this job, but you can also make something yourself. The jig in the photo is made from off-cuts of MDF and is held together with double-sided

Saddles come in a range of sizes and widths. Blanks in both bone and synthetic materials are usually available.

Testing the saddle for fit. The first stage is to make sure it is the correct length and will fit into the slot without binding on any part. It needs to be free to slide in and out but not be too tight.

tape, as it may not be worth making a permanent jig if you are only making one or two guitars. The two pieces of MDF that run across the front of the guitar, in front of and behind the bridge, are shaped and positioned so they touch the bridge itself, which helps stop them from moving. They are also attached to the front of the guitar with a small piece of double-sided tape.

The ends of the slot are determined by the cross pieces that join these two blocks. Two pieces of masking tape were stuck onto the bridge where the ends of the saddle slot were to be so that they were more visible, and the cross pieces were positioned so that the router was stopped at this point. The remaining pieces were taped down so that the router was only able to move in one direction and so that the router bit was running along the marked saddle position.

You should try to cut about halfway through your bridge. You do not want to cut right down to the top as this will separate some of the string vibration from the guitar top. You may need to go a little deeper if you are using an under-saddle transducer in order to make room for the saddle and the transducer, but you do not want the slot too shallow as the strings will try to pull the saddle over and it will not sit upright.

The saddle itself can be cut to length to fit into the slot, without being too short; it then need to be adjusted to be the correct height. This is covered in more detail in Chapter 19.

BRIDGE-MOUNTED PICKUPS

Fitting a bridge-mounted pickup would also be done at this point. The problems of amplifying acoustic guitars so that they can be heard in today's decibel-soaked concert arenas is one that has haunted designers for many

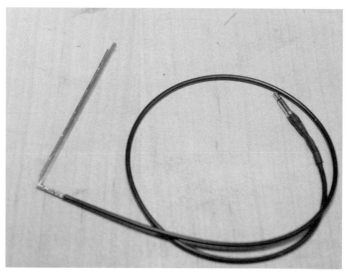

A relatively simple under saddle transducer. Although very slim, the height of the transducer will need to be allowed for when designing the bridge and cutting the slot. As can be seen, the connecting wire goes straight through the top of the guitar and so care must be taken to ensure that it does not foul one of your main braces.

years. It was, after all, the problems of amplifying acoustic instruments that led directly to the solid electric guitar, which has become an instrument in its own right and which will rarely, if ever, replicate the sounds of a true acoustic guitar.

The problem is that a lot of ambient noise, as is found at concerts, can itself cause the body of the guitar to resonate, which in turn is picked up by the microphone and fed back to the amplifier to create a loop. This feedback can be very unpleasant and is difficult to avoid. Picking up the vibration of the strings directly from the bridge and passing this into the PA system is one way to lessen the feedback problem, and over the last 20 years the science of these pickups has developed until many of them are now excellent. For high-volume applications, such as playing a guitar with a full band, they may not be suitable, but for amplifying acoustic instruments in reasonable-sized venues they can be very good.

Most systems have a small transducer that fits into the bridge slot beneath the saddle, which will have a wire running from it that will be fed through a hole drilled in the end of the saddle slot. This, in turn, may be fed into a pre-amp unit that is fitted either inside the guitar, with the controls mounted on the side of the guitar, or externally. Many systems are powered by a small battery and it may be necessary to add a battery box inside the guitar.

The transducer will take up some space and so the saddle slot will need to be routed a little deeper or the saddle made slightly thinner, or a combination of both. The width of the slot, and of the saddle, will be determined by the width of the transducer. The transducer relies on the pressure of the saddle on it and so a thin saddle balancing on a slightly thicker transducer will not give the best results. All this needs is some simple planning to make sure that everything fits together. Further details can be found in Chapter 23, where a transducer system is fitted to the guitar, and most manufacturers will include detailed fitting instructions.

Some Taylor guitars use a Fishman system that has the pre-amp controls mounted on a plate fixed into the side of the guitar.

Chapter 17

Top Nuts

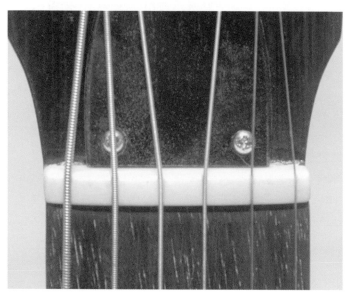

A finished top nut.

Marking a nut blank prior to cutting it to width.

The top nut on the guitar acts as one end point of the active part of the string. It separates the strings, holds them at the correct height above the first fret, to stop buzzing, and is cut to allow the string to move across it when tuned without sticking but to stop it rattling when the guitar is played. Over the years I have seen many guitars with all sorts of problems caused by having a badly made or badly cut nut.

It was traditionally made of bone or ivory although, in more recent years, plastic and even brass have been used. Plastic is generally too soft and brass is really too dense and can mark easily, causing string breakages, but there are now some substitutes that are very good. These modern plastics are a world apart from the soft white stuff used on cheaper instruments a few years back. Martin and many other large makers use synthetic nuts and saddles.

I like to use bone, which is a by-product of the meat industry, but some people are uncomfortable with this and so products like 'Tusq', a synthetic material sold as guitar nuts and saddles, is ideal.

A pencil was also run along the top of the fingerboard to show the curve. This will help when sanding or filing the nut down to its correct height. It may leave a mark on the end of the fingerboard that will need to be removed.

Belt sanding the nut to the correct height. This can be done with a file.

Test fitting the nut.

The nut on the Martin kit from Chapter 20.

It is a good idea to fit the nut before the guitar is finished. It may need to come off again when the guitar is set up, but this is no problem. If held in place with superglue it can be removed easily with a small hammer and a small piece of hardwood: put the wood against the fingerboard side of the nut and tap it gently. Since superglue has excellent tensile strength but little shear strength the nut, which has been perfectly secure until this point, will break free very easily and not take any wood with it. In the days before superglue was widely available nuts were often epoxied onto the guitar. This is not a good idea as if you do have to remove it you can also remove some wood.

By gluing the nut on before the finish is applied you do not get a build-up of lacquer around where the nut will be, which can be difficult to trim back successfully, and the nut will be the best form of masking for where it will eventually end up.

Most guitar makers' suppliers will sell blank nuts made from bone or one of the synthetics; blanks are normally $1/4 \times 5/16 \times 2$ in (6.3 × 8 × 50 mm) and the first stage is to cut it to length. Place this on the end of the fingerboard and mark the width of the board. The nut can then be cut, filed and sanded until it is exactly the same width.

You may also notice that at $5/16$ in (8 mm) the height is more than you need, and this can be cut, filed or sanded down until it is the right height. You will need about $1/8$ in (3 mm) above your fingerboard. This may be adjusted later, so do not finish the nut off at this stage.

Chapter 18
Finishing

A good finish will bring out the true beauty of the wood.

The finish on the guitar serves two purposes: it is decorative but it also serves to protect the wood from minor damage, moisture absorption and from simply getting dirty. The art is to get a finish that is thick enough to protect the guitar but thin enough not to damp the vibration of the instrument.

The earliest finishes were shellac-based. Shellac is made from the shells of beetles that are melted in methylated spirits to form an emulsion; when the spirit evaporates the solid material is left as a thin film on the surface of what is covered. The best-known form of shellac finish is probably French polish, which is just the shellac and spirit. Applying this and getting a good gloss finish, especially on a guitar with its curves and corners, is a very skilled job and can take years to learn.

Another shellac-based finish is varnish. Many violins are finished in an oil-based shellac varnish, and these can take a long time to dry. Violin makers will tell you, often at length, about how this is the only finish that will replicate the characteristics of antique violins, despite the fact that what they use is different to what was used many years ago – they are also inclined to tell you that Stradivarius used to knock trees with his knuckles and, as we have discussed, this is complete nonsense!

In general, varnishes are too soft for use on guitars since the oil does not evaporate completely, as the spirits in French polish do, so the final finish can be quite soft. This prevents a really high gloss being attained.

In a production environment French polishing, or even time-consuming varnish, is clearly uneconomical and so alternatives have been found. The earliest, and in some people's opinion still the best, is a nitrocellulose finish which uses, as the name suggests, cellulose as the body material. This is melted in a solvent, which is often based on toluene, a particularly nasty chemical that is both poisonous and carcinogenic. It can be handled safely with the proper equipment but can also be damaging to the environment. Some states and countries will not allow its use unless very strict guidelines are followed, which can make it very expensive to use.

Cellulose (often referred to as nitrocellulose, or just nitro) gives a good, durable finish that feels nice when used on guitar necks. It is not sticky and, since it is quite flexible, it can take knocks well without chipping and is still capable of taking a good gloss. It is easy to apply, providing you have the correct equipment and adhere to the safety guidelines. Depending on it's mix it can take several weeks to dry properly in normal temperatures before it can be polished; this means it is still quite expensive to use in a production environment.

The drying time can be brought down by using ovens to gently heat the guitar after it has been finished, in the way that the Martin company do (*see* page 274), but this is costly in capital terms.

If you choose to use nitrocellulose you will find a confusing array of varieties. Some makers swear by one type and others by a different brand. There are different grades of material, some harder than others and some more transparent, and it is best to take advice from the technical department of the company you are buying from. Or, and this is much easier, get your material from a recognised supplier of guitar finishes and take their advice. It is also essential you read and understand the safety information on the product.

During the 1960s and 1970s, some companies started to use a polyester finish. This is a two-pack system that cures rather than dries. A catalyst is added to the material and it hardens by chemical reaction. There is little or no evaporation, so less material has to be sprayed. When using cellulose, for example, the thinners that form the solution with the solid material account for about 70 per cent of what is sprayed and most of this just evaporates. With a two-pack system all of what is sprayed stays on the guitar. The upside of this is that less material needs to be sprayed and so costs are lower; however, this has to be played off against several factors, not least of which is that the material can be even more dangerous than cellulose and so expensive equipment is needed to deal with the airborne dust.

Another downside to the early polyesters was their hardness. They were very hard but also quite brittle. This meant that a minor knock that might cause little or no damage on a cellulose-finished instrument could result in an ugly chip out of the polyester. Also, marks that might just dent cellulose could give ugly scratches on the polyester. Thinner coats on more modern factory-produced guitars are a little more resilient and many modern finishes are not as brittle as the ones from years ago, but getting rid of small dings and marks is still just as hard.

When multiple coats of, for example, cellulose are used, the thinners in the spray coat act on the previous coat to soften the surface and allow the new coats to bond. This does not happen with a chemically cured finish. This means that a two-pack of any type is very hard to patch in the event of minor finish damage. A cellulose-finished guitar can have the area of the damage locally touched-in as the new finish will melt into the old one. This does not happen on polyester, so repairs are often ugly.

In recent years the technology of paint has been driven, at least in part, by the environmental lobby. New materials have been developed and tried, and not all two-pack finishes are as brittle as some of the early ones were and so are a little more durable when used on a guitar. The finishes can also be applied in thinner coats, but they do have to be used very carefully and should not be applied without the proper equipment for dealing with the spray dust. There are now a lot of water based finishes available and more products are being developed and introduced all the time; what is available as I write this book could be out of date by the time I finish my next coffee.

PREPARATION

Regardless of the finish you choose, the key to a good result is the preparation that goes into it. You cannot use finish to hide problems or bad workmanship. The finishing process will, if anything, emphasise these little problems.

Your guitar needs to be checked over very thoroughly to ensure that there are no gaps under any of the binding, that all areas of rough wood have been sanded smooth and that the surface is free of scratches. When you have done this, do it again! Small gaps around the binding can be filled with glue and dust, or a suitable filler, and several applications might be needed.

Some people will tell you that the wood should be sanded as smooth as possible before the finish is applied. You could start by sanding with 120 grit, before going to 220, 400 and then 1000 grit to get a very silky-smooth finish. There are other people who will tell you this is not a good idea as you are making the surface too smooth and that the lacquer then has problems adhering to the smooth surface. I know of several makers now who sand to 120 or 220 grit only before finishing, as they say this gives more surface area for the lacquer to bond to. This may be the case but the sanding must be done with the grain, otherwise ugly marks will show. They do not seem to have these problems though.

Gulfoss waterfall in Iceland. This is far more interesting to look at than a photograph of someone finish sanding a guitar.

When masking the fingerboard it is a good idea to push the tape down around each fret so no finish can seep under and onto the board.

Finish sanding is really quite boring work but it is necessary. However, there is little point in showing photographs of someone sanding a guitar so I am including a photograph of the white water above Gulfoss waterfall in Iceland, which is much more interesting.

Equally important in making the lacquer stick to the guitar is the removal of any sanding dust. This will sit in the pores of the wood and prevent the lacquer making contact. When the sanding is complete the guitar should be dusted with a tack rag (available from most paint suppliers) or with a cloth dampened with thinners. This should pick up a lot of dust and you should keep doing this until the cloth comes away clean.

On guitars that are sprayed before the body and neck are joined, the areas that are to be glued should be properly masked.

Masking

If you have chosen to finish the neck and body separately, the areas that will eventually receive glue should be masked so that the finish does not adhere. You could spray over these areas and then scrape the finish back to bare wood, but the scraping back needs to be done very carefully because if any residues of finish remain in the grain the glue joint could be weakened; it is better not to have glue there than to have to remove it.

With the area that will be under the fingerboard and the neck area masked, the corresponding parts on the neck itself need to be masked.

In all cases the fingerboard should also be masked and it is a good idea to ensure that the masking tape stays close to the fret and matches its shape, as if it merely lays over the top some of the finish and polishing compounds can find their way onto your fingerboard. This can be cleaned off but it is much easier if this is avoided.

The area on the body where the neck will sit will also need masking. Here the neck is held in place and the end of the fingerboard drawn around. The masking can be cut just inside this line, as when gluing the bridge, so that a small amount of finish extends under the join.

Preventing overspray or finish drips inside the guitar can be done either by masking the soundhole, as seen here, or by putting newspaper inside the guitar to pack the soundhole area. If this is done, care must be taken to ensure the newspaper is clear of the soundhole and so does not stick to the finish.

The excess grainfiller can be rubbed off across the grain with another towel. Wiping across the grain will leave the maximum amount in the pores of the wood, in this case, mahogany.

Using a paper towel to apply grainfiller on a rosewood guitar. This is rubbed into the grain.

Plastic bindings can be cleaned after grain filling by scraping them with a sharp blade. Wooden bindings should be masked as the grainfiller can stain.

Grain filling

Some woods require no further preparation than sanding. Maple or sycamore, for example, are very close-grained and so can be finished without needing grain filling. Other woods, however, will require some sort of grain filling.

Grain fillers are pastes that are compatible with the final finish. If you use a filler of one type and a different finish you can end up with problems, so make sure that what you have is compatible. Fillers will also often come in various colours to match the wood being filled, but beware: some of the colours can be a little fanciful.

I have yet to see any piece of mahogany as red as the fillers that are sold as 'mahogany' colour! I tend to use a generic brown for all brown woods – a slightly darker one for rosewood and a light one for everything else.

The stain in the coloured fillers can also be pretty fierce if it touches white wood bindings or plastic. It is best to mask all of these before you start filling.

The filler is rubbed into the wood along the grain so that the paste fills the pores. Before it dries the excess is wiped off across the grain to remove all of what is left on the surface and to keep the pores filled. When this has dried thoroughly the surface can be sanded to remove any residues that have escaped the cloth.

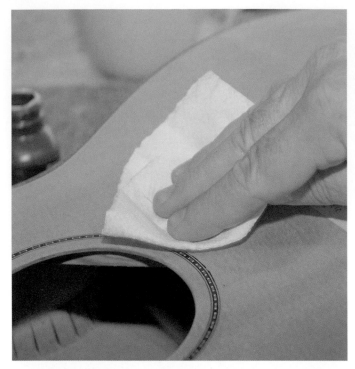

Using a paper towel to apply Tru-Oil. The trick is to keep the coats very thin and build them slowly.

Lightly flatting back the finish between coats to remove any unevenness.

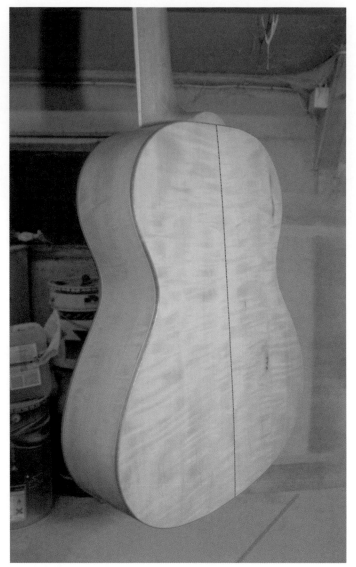

The 12-string from Chapter 22 was coated in Tru-Oil and hung between coats.

The guitar should then be dusted with a tack cloth to remove any dust without pulling the filler from the wood and the masking should then be removed from the bindings. Any areas that have slightly discoloured can be scraped clean or sanded lightly.

The guitar should then have a final, final inspection before finishing (a triple-final inspection can also be a good idea).

TYPES OF FINISH
Tru-Oil

One finish that is used extensively by amateur makers is Tru-Oil. This is sold as a gunstock finish and is a tung

oil varnish that can be wiped onto the wood. This builds up and a substantial finish can be had with careful application. It is similar to French polishing and a lot of care needs to be taken. The trick is not to apply too much at one time as you can get drips, which can be sanded back when they are dry but this will take time. It can also be difficult to apply around a neck join, for example, so using a separate neck method may be best if you are Tru-Oiling.

One advantage of Tru-Oil is that it is very easy to repair little areas of finish that get knocked. You simply flatten the area around the damage and apply more Tru-Oil.

I chose to finish the 12-string in Chapter 22 in Tru-Oil with a wax topcoat as it has a good amber colour that will look good with the pearwood on the guitar.

I chose to leave the 12-string semi-matt and so polished the finish with very fine wire wool and wax polish.

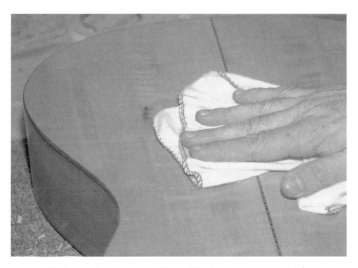

Polishing the wax to a shine, this gives a nice satin look.

If you do not have access to spray equipment, a Tru-Oil finish on a guitar is a good alternative. It can be applied with a soft cloth, or even paper towels, and if you are patient a good finish can be had.

The first stage is to shake the bottle as it will separate out a little if it has been standing on a shop shelf for a while. Some open-grained woods will benefit from being grain filled before using Tru-Oil, but on the 12-string I applied it directly.

The guitar was finish sanded and a hook was made with a bent coat-hanger so that the guitar could be hung to dry.

Tru-Oil is an interesting finish. The first coat always looks great because the colour of the oil will show up the grain of any wood that it is applied to. After that it is tempting to think that there is not enough material being applied at each go, as it does not appear to build very quickly. Do not fall into the trap of trying to rush

it as it will look worse; things will suddenly start to get better as more and more coats are applied.

How often you can coat the guitar depends on the ambient temperature and moisture levels in the atmosphere. In summer it will dry quicker than in winter and you may get two, or even three coats on in a day. In winter or in cooler climates you might manage only one per day.

It is perfectly possible to build up Tru-Oil with a cloth so that the finish is thick enough to polish to an acceptable gloss when it has dried out completely.

For the 12-string I wanted something less 'flashy'. I gave the guitar about 15 coats, using just over a small bottle of Tru-Oil, and then flatted it back with 600 grit wet and dry before polishing it with good wax polish and 0000 grade wire wool, and buffing with a soft cloth. This gave it a very nice satin sheen that protects the guitar well.

Brush coating

Brush coating is, in some ways, very similar to finishing with Tru-Oil as you are attempting to put very thin coats onto the guitar without leaving too many marks from the means of applying the lacquer, in this case a brush. You also have all the same problems of getting the lacquer around the difficult-to-reach parts of the guitar and holding it while you do so, avoiding drips and not letting lacquer build up around the guitar edges.

It is worth making sure that your brush is of good quality. It is not only really annoying to have to pull stray bristles that have been shed by your brush out of your finish, but it can make unsightly marks in the finish that you have to then deal with, usually by waiting until the coat is dry and sanding them out.

There are no real hard-and-fast rules about brush finishing. What you do is dependent on the material you are using, as you can use two-pack, nitrocellulose or water-based lacquers, and how much you thin them will depend on the finish itself, the ambient temperature and the softness of your brush.

As with Tru-Oil, the trick is to build up a lot of thin coats and not to try to rush the procedure. If the lacquer appears to be spreading away from the brush it could be too thin; if the brush marks are very obvious it may be too thick. You will need to sand between coats, perhaps even more than you would when using Tru-Oil, and you will certainly need to allow the guitar to harden completely before polishing it.

This may seem like avoiding actual instruction on my part, but it is really best to try the finish out on something before you commit to your guitar, as each finish and set of circumstances is different, the make of lacquer and type of brush is also variable, and so it will be time well spent. You can even do this experiment while waiting for some of the other parts of the guitar to be ready.

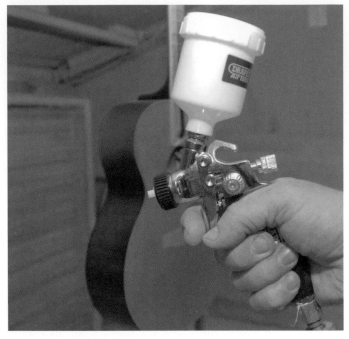

An economical top-feed spray gun.

Using a larger bottom-feed spray gun.

Spray

Assuming that you have access to spray equipment and the correct safety equipment, or you are simply prepared to risk your health, there some basic spray rules.

The most important thing to do is read the manufacturer's safety sheets relating to the product that you are using. The second most important thing is to keep everything very clean. Clear lacquer is very easy to contaminate with dirt and all sorts of nasties that will make your guitar look not so good. If the spray gun has been used for another colour, at any time, it should be disassembled before use and cleaned thoroughly. I do know of people who keep one spray gun for colours and another solely for spraying clear finish.

The compressor should be of adequate size to maintain the necessary pressure at the gun. Too large is not really a problem if you can regulate the flow, but too small will mean that you will get pressure drops and the spray pattern of the gun will vary.

Compressing air also compresses any moisture in the atmosphere and this can condense, creating water droplets in the air hose. If these get anywhere near the guitar your finish is going to be ruined, so installing a water trap in the airline is not just a good idea but pretty well essential.

Most lacquers will need to be thinned before use. There is a tendency to over-thin in order to make spraying 'easier' but, again, the manufacturers will have details on how much to thin their product and even how much pressure to use at the gun. If you use a water trap it will probably also have a pressure regulator built in.

The more pressure you use, the more suction is created in the gun and therefore the more liquid it will suck through the pipe. Higher air pressure also equates to higher-speed airflow, so using a very high pressure will blast your guitar with lots and lots of liquid. Spraying too much at one time may cause sags and drips in the finish, which is not a good thing as they are notoriously difficult to remove without leaving any trace. I like to use a relatively high pressure and a slightly thicker consistency lacquer, but a good rule of thumb is about 40psi (2.75 bar).

Some manufacturers will suggest a certain viscosity for the paint but this will mean nothing unless you have something to measure it against. If you put a set amount of liquid into a container and let it drain through a hole of known size in the bottom, the time this takes will indicate how viscous the liquid is. This will vary with temperature, so several makers I know check each batch of paint they mix every time they go to spray.

If you do not have access to a viscosity checker, then you need to guess how thick or thin to have your paint. As already stated, thinning too much may cause the paint to run. Remember that the idea is to get a thin film of solid material onto the surface of your guitar. If you thin the lacquer too much there will be fewer solids in each coat and so it will dry thinner, and you will need to spray a lot of coats onto the guitar. Attempting to spray lacquer with the consistency of molasses will also give problems. It will require much higher pressure at the gun and will form larger droplets

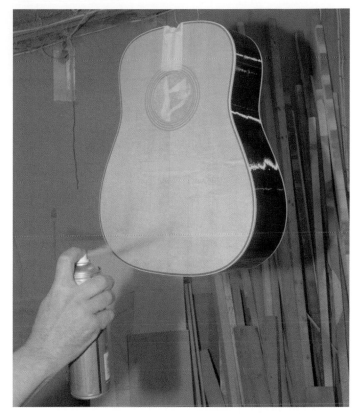

Using an automotive clear laquer from a spray can.

in the air, giving an 'orange peel' effect to the guitar. You may also find that it dries before it reaches the guitar and so does not stick properly. As mentioned previously, the thinners act to melt the previous coat.

If you are using a pressure setting of about 40psi and your paint is too thick, it will be readily apparent, as it simply will not want to come out of the gun. You can then thin it a little more until you get a good spray pattern.

HVLP

HVLP is a high-volume, low-pressure system that is used by a number of makers and can be less expensive than conventional guns and compressors. It can produce excellent results if adjusted correctly and its operation understood. There are some very informative websites, many of them from custom car enthusiasts, where the ins and outs of spraying are discussed at length and there is some very good information. Remember, however, that not everything on the internet is necessarily true and not everyone writing is necessarily an expert, but with this in mind there are some very good tips to be found if you look carefully.

Adjusting the gun

Most spray guns have an adjustment to control the amount of air going through the gun, the amount of paint that is pulled from the reservoir and the spray pattern. Getting the air and paint mix right is a matter of practice and will depend on the nozzle size on the gun, the consistency of the paint and the air pressure. Having too much pressure can cause too much lacquer to be pulled from the gun, and in the same way the correct pressure and too much paint can give an identical effect. Practise on something other than your guitar before you commit to working on the real thing – it will be time well spent.

The pressure and amount of paint may also affect the spray pattern from the gun. Higher pressure can cause a wider fan of lacquer and this may not be ideal if, for example, you are spraying a neck where most of the fan will miss the neck and you will simply be painting in mid air. The orientation of the fan is also adjustable with the nozzle rotatable by 90 degrees, allowing the paint to form either a vertical or a horizontal fan (*see* box).

Clearly, getting to know the equipment and materials is worthy of a book in itself and an online search might yield several that are worth reading, but becoming familiar with what you are using is also important. The best way to do that is to practise.

Spray cans

It is possible to buy cellulose and acrylic clear lacquer in spray cans. These are never cheap and getting enough to cover a guitar and get a good finish may cost as much as buying a small HVLP system. Some clear lacquers are simply not designed to build into a thick coat. They are for sealing artwork, such as pastel drawings, onto paper and so are totally useless for guitars. I have found some clear lacquers sold for automotive use to be fine and others that are terrible: you need to test anything you find to see if the thickness of the

If using a colour coat, the bindings should be masked as much as possible. Masking the binding on the fingerboard separately to the face of the board means that just the binding mask can be removed.

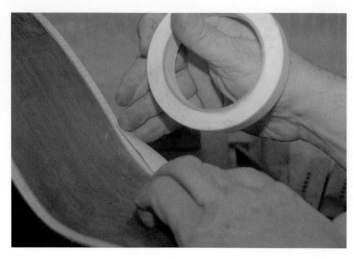

Masking the bindings. The top edge is close to impossible to mask and so will need to be scraped clean.

covering increases as you spray more coats. In the UK much of the paint sold in automotive stores, including the clear lacquer, is acrylic and not cellulose. This is fine and in some cases works very well, but I have found that is it very susceptible to humidity and have had one case where the paint refused to ever harden sufficiently. It is also very hard to get off if it all goes wrong (as in the case where it would not harden): using any form of paint remover, either chemical or a hot air gun, simply turned the acrylic into a thick liquid again and made it almost impossible to remove, rather like tar. The simple answer is, again, to buy some and try it on something other than your guitar.

Colour coats

If the guitar is to have any sort of colour there are several ways of achieving this. You can paint the guitar if it is to be in a block colour, which is unusual, or you can stain it or tint the lacquer.

Some finishes will have a certain amount of tint built in – Tru-Oil, for example has a nice amber colour – but most clear lacquers are exactly that, clear. If you want to add some colour to the guitar, either as a one-colour tint or a sunburst, then you need to decide this in advance.

As mentioned above, painting acoustic guitars a block colour is not that common compared with other finishes. When this is done the most common finish is pure black. Gibson's Everley Brothers guitar was black and this is not a problem to do, but you have to mask the bindings and the soundhole inlay before colouring the guitar.

Masking the bindings only does part of the job: it is quite easy to mask the edges of the binding, as we will see shortly, but the top surface is a little more complicat-

ed. You can try to mask it but the problems of getting the masking tape to conform to the shape of the binding will make life difficult. It might be easier to spray over it and then scrape the paint back with a scalpel blade or something similar to remove the colour. If done carefully this can be fine, although scraping paint from wooden bindings is not the easiest of tasks since the paint will soak a little way into the binding. This can be prevented by spraying the guitar with a few coats of clear lacquer, before adding the colour, to seal the binding and prevent the colour coats from sinking in.

Masking or scraping back the soundhole inlay is a lot more difficult as it is not possible to use the edge of the guitar to support your hand while you are working. Doing it badly could ruin the look of an otherwise fine guitar, so proceed carefully.

It is possible to make a jig that will help with this. The diameter of the soundhole is known, so if you make a base that has an arc of this size routed in, it can be used to mount an adjustable scraper blade. This can run around the inside of the hole with the scraper blade being adjusted to scrape a small amount from the binding as it goes round. This would take some time to make, but not as long as stripping and refinishing the front of the guitar if you slipped while scraping by hand.

This problem also exists on guitars with tinted lacquer and sunburst, but for some reason the block colour guitars always show the mistakes more clearly.

Tints and stains

Adding an overall transparent colour to a guitar can be done in two ways. You could stain the guitar the required colour and then clear-lacquer it, or you can add a tint to the lacquer, spray several colour coats and then finish with clear. Of these I prefer the second, as

A sprayed on suspended colour coat, in this case the basis for a sunburst.

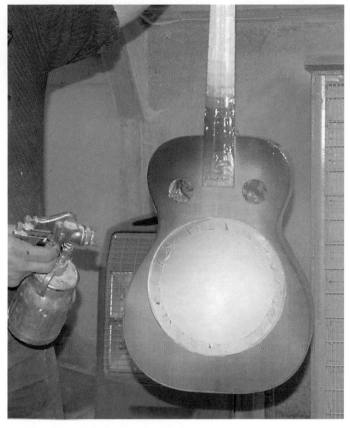

Lightly spraying the edges of the Resonator guitar to build the sunburst. The electric fire in the background is only used to take the chill off in the mornings and it not part of the normal sprayshop equipment!

the lacquer has less tendency to be patchy. Staining directly onto the guitar works for some people, but if you have any sanding scratches (of course you would not, but...) or if the surface of the guitar is more absorbent in some areas than others then the colour can be patchy. The stain will also tend to soak under any masking applied to the bindings, and while this is not a problem with plastic bindings it can be a real headache with wooden ones.

If you do stain the wood directly, the stain, like the grain filler, has to be compatible with the other finishing materials. If in doubt, grain fill, colour and lacquer a test piece. Time spent doing this is far better than time spent trying to strip a bad finish from your guitar before trying again.

The stain should be applied with a cloth and any excess on the surface should be cleaned off. This will help give a more even colour. Once this has been done the colour will generally look a little flat and boring. This will change when the guitar starts to get its clear coats. The problem is that it is when it starts to get these, some previously unseen blemishes may appear. This is why checking the guitar after sanding is so important.

Before the clear coats can be applied the bindings and soundhole inlay will need to be cleaned up. Once this has been done it is even more important than normal that the clear coats are not so thick that they might drip, as not only are drips always hard to get rid of, but they may drag some of the stain out of the wood and remain visible even after the drip has been sanded flat and the finish completed. Spraying on thin coats and letting them build up in thickness slowly is the best way to go.

The other method for a tinted finish is to suspend the stain in the lacquer to make a tinted lacquer. This can then be sprayed onto the guitar until the required depth of colour is achieved, and then oversprayed with gloss. The bindings will again need to be masked and cleaned after the colour coats have been applied, but this is a little easier as there is more substance to the tinted lacquer than there is to a stain by itself. This method also has less tendency to stain the wood.

Suspended tints are used when finishing a guitar in a sunburst. The first stage of this, after masking the parts that need masking, is to spray the base colour onto the guitar where it is needed. If only the front of the guitar is to be sunburst then only that needs the

Peeling the masking on the binding on a tinted neck. The front of the fingerboard remains masked. The masking is being pulled over itself to get a cleaner line.

The area under the masking may well need to be tidied with a scraper.

base colour. If the sides and back are to be sunburst also, then these will need the base colour too.

Spraying a sunburst is almost an art in itself. The spray gun will need to be set for a fine spray and it is essential that there are no drips. It is far better to spray a little to begin with, let that dry and then add to it than to try to put all the colour on in one go and get drips. It is also better to set the gun to a small fan, as this will be easier to direct so that the colour only goes where you want it. It is also important that the lacquer is thin enough not to form large droplets and therefore a 'splattered' sunburst, yet not so thin that it will run off the guitar and cause even more problems.

The sunburst will mean that more of the top colour will be needed around the edges of the guitar, leaving the centre with the base colour. One way to achieve this is to spray the guitar at an angle, so that the gun is aimed at the edge of the guitar; although most spray will hit the edge, the overspray will form the sunburst. If this is done slowly and carefully, the sunburst will form gradually. With the resonator guitar in Chapter 24, the area around the end of the neck needed special attention because the height of the fingerboard, which was raised slightly to get the right angle at the bridge, acted as a mask when the spray gun was pointing across the end of the neck, leaving an area that did not get colour. This had to be touched in later using a very fine spray.

Once the sunburst is done the masking gets removed and the bindings and inlays cleaned; the guitar can then be clear coated.

Needless to say, sunburst finishes cannot be done if the guitar is being finished in any way other than with a spray gun. You cannot get a good sunburst finish from an aerosol (even if the colours you are interested in existed in aerosol form) as the spray pattern from these is just too coarse. If you have not got access to a spray gun of decent quality, then a clear guitar or a stain tint is the only way to go.

Wire wool and wax used to get a semi-gloss finish on the electro-acoustic in Chapter 23.

Clear coats and finishing off

If the guitar is coloured, tinted, sunburst or natural it will have to have clear lacquer applied to give it its final finish.

The electro-acoustic in Chapter 23 was finished in a 40 per cent gloss satin nitrocellulose lacquer and had four or five good coats before it was waxed with beeswax applied with 0000 grade wire wool, like the Tru-Oil guitar, to give it a satin finish; if you want a high gloss the lacquer needs to be polished.

It is essential that a guitar that is to have a high-gloss finish has had time for the finish to harden properly before any attempt is made to polish it. A nitrocellulose

Flattening the finish using 600 and then 1200 grit wet and dry paper, used wet over a block. Adding soap to the water helps stop the wet and dry paper from clogging.

finish can reach full hardness in a matter of days if the conditions are right, but may take several weeks to fully harden if the weather is cold and damp. If the finish is not fully hard then it is not only more difficult to get a good gloss, but you stand more chance of rubbing through the finish to the bare wood underneath as you polish. A good guide is that if you can smell any trace of thinners, it is not ready.

The first stage is to completely flatten the finish with 1200 wet and dry paper used wet. If your finish is a little 'orange peely' and thick enough, you could use 600 grit and then use 1200 grit to remove the marks from that. Some soap or detergent in the water will help to stop the paper clogging up, which will mark the lacquer as you work, and it is not advisable to let the guitar get too wet. Any excess water should be soaked up as it may find its way into the soundhole where it can leave nasty stains inside your guitar. Keeping the guitar very wet as you work on it can cause water to get absorbed by the wood of the guitar, which can then swell and damage the finish, and your guitar.

If you find any small dips in the finish around the bindings or inlays these can be filled before the guitar gets its final shine.

It is possible to use superglue for this, either the gel type or one of the two pack varieties, as these have the advantage of hardening very quickly.

The downside is that they are usually harder than the surrounding finish and so can be difficult to flatten back to the level of the existing finish without rubbing through what was already there. If you do use superglue, it might be necessary to spray a coat or two of finish over the flattened superglue so that it acts as just a filler rather than part of the finish itself.

Another way is to thoroughly inspect the guitar before flatting the finish and dribble unthinned lacquer

Sanding the edges and the bindings requires care so as not to cut through the finish.

into the gaps and allow it to dry out before flatting and buffing. One again, the better the preparation, the better the end result.

Polishing

Once all unevenness in the finish is gone and the surfaces are uniformly sanded, the gloss can be restored by polishing out the scratches caused by the wet and dry paper. There are many different products on the market to polish paint, but not all are suitable. Some are simply too abrasive: if you put some of the compound on your finger and rub it between your fingertips you should not feel any abrasiveness or grittiness at all.

It is a good idea to flatten the finish and then leave it for a day or two to further harden.

Polishing the lacquer with a soft cloth and buffing compound.

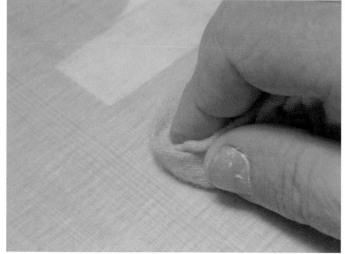

It is important to get to all of the edges when polishing. The masking tape is still on the bridge area of this guitar so that the polishing can get right to the edge of where the bridge will be, without putting polishing compound on the bare wood beneath the bridge.

With the body fully polished, the masking can be removed.

You also need to ensure that your cloth is clean and has not picked up any grit. Old T-shirts could be used, but if you find you are not able to remove all the scratches caused by the flattening with wet and dry paper, then it could be because you are actually adding them with the cloth. I know of one maker who only uses cotton wool to polish his guitars. This is not a bad idea.

You need to put some force into the polishing as you are trying to use a combination of the cloth, or cotton wool, with the compound to remove the thinnest top layer of the lacquer. If you have too much polishing compound then all you are doing is swirling

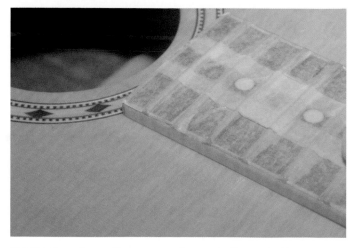

The fingerboard now sits over a small amount of lacquer making for a much cleaner join.

it around the surface and not achieving very much. You need to feel some resistance but you also do not need to press way too hard. This is another of those jobs where you learn by doing it and by feel.

There are also things to watch out for. You may find that if you have a two-pack finish the lacquer will be very hard indeed and may need a lot of very hard work to remove the scratches.

You will notice that your finish gets a nice shine quite early, but if you hold the guitar up and angle it so light hits it from different directions the reflections may well show lots of small, swirly scratches on the surface. Work until these are gone.

Properly hardened cellulose is sometimes a real joy to polish, but if it is a little soft then you will notice that it is difficult to get the wet and dry marks off the guitar. This is a very good clue that the finish may still be too soft, and if this is the case it will be very easy to polish right the way through to bare wood beneath. This is something that you have to be very careful of at all times as it is easy to spoil a lot of good work; it is much better to wait until your finish hs properly hardened to avoid the risk of damage.

One little trick that is useful is something that I picked up from a vintage guitar forum. Apparently Gibson did not flatten the sides of the headstocks on various of their guitars as this area was prone to being polished through. Instead they left it un-flattened and just polished it. Therefore, if you look at the sides of the head on many old Gibsons you will see that the lacquer still has some blemishes from the spraying process underneath the polished shine.

Once all the scratches have been removed you can carefully remove the masking tape over the fingerboard and from the soundhole, and clean up any rough edges on the lacquer, lightly sanding and rebuffing as necessary.

With this done it is time to give the guitar its final shine. You can use a good furniture polish to remove any residues on the guitar, but remember never to use silicone polishes on guitars as they will leave residues that can make any finish repairs very difficult. Wax is always best.

You can now finally set up and assemble your guitar. We have already covered gluing the bridge and cutting the saddle slot, and you can install your machine heads and get the guitar ready to be played.

Chapter 19
Final Assembly

It is one thing to have made your guitar, but it will need to be set up carefully to get the best from it. There is no point in just throwing some strings on and hoping.

At this stage you have a nice-looking guitar with a bridge glued into place. The first stage is to go all around the guitar and check for anything that looks wrong. If you have been careful there should be no big and nasty surprises, but there may be small items – the edge of the fingerboard may need some attention where the masking tape has allowed the lacquer to build up a little. This sort of thing is no problem, but you also have to do some more major jobs.

The first is to level the frets. In an ideal world these will have gone into the fingerboard perfectly and will be sitting entirely flush with the board so that each one is exactly the same height as the others. In practice this is rarely the case (although a good fret press will get them almost to this point) and they may need a little dressing. This is sometimes called 'filing the frets' and some people do, indeed, use a file, but that is a very harsh way of doing things. It is much better to use a fine oilstone but, again, you have to beware. Not all oilstones are suitable for the task. Many of those sold in DIY chains are soft and will just make a mess. Many are also not flat and, since you will be relying on the stone being flat to level the frets, this is not good.

A good India oilstone with a fine cut is going to be more expensive than the average DIY store stone, but it will do the job properly and will be useful in sharpening all sorts of tools which, sadly, many of the DIY store examples are pretty useless at also.

The guitar will need to be well supported while tackling the frets because if it moves around, the job will not be as good and the guitar might get damaged. If the neck is unsupported below, any pressure exerted on the neck could force it out of shape just enough to make the job harder than it should be.

So, the guitar needs to be placed on something soft with the neck supported from beneath and the truss rod, if one is fitted, should be adjusted to make sure the neck is as straight as possible. The front of the guitar should be protected and something should be placed over the soundhole to stop any dust from the process getting into the guitar.

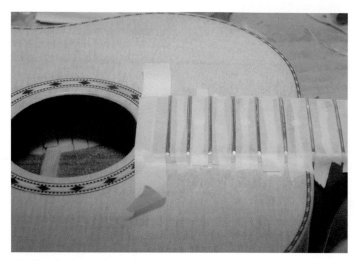

Masking the fingerboard when stoning the frets will prevent most, although not all, of the residues and polishing material reaching the fingerboard.

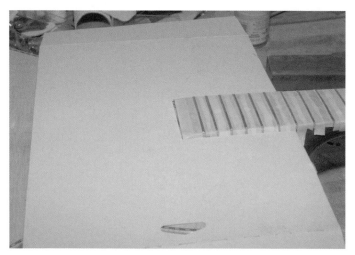

Making a card, or thin plastic, mask for the front of the guitar will prevent dirt from entering the soundhole and also protect the top from any accidental damage. This can also be useful when filing the fret ends after fitting.

It is not a bad idea to remove the top nut from the guitar when stoning the frets as this allows better access to the first couple of frets. Since the nut is only held on with superglue it will be easy to get off. The nut

Using a good oilstone along the neck. The paper towel will help keep your hands clean. Supporting the neck is doubly important when stoning the frets.

When the tops of the frets are all marked by the stone it is time to start across the board.

can be persuaded back into its slot using a small hammer to tap it in and possibly some superglue dropped carefully beneath it. If it is really high then it might be necessary to take it out and carefully refit it.

It should not be necessary to use much downward pressure on the stone. Ideally it should glide along removing just a small amount as it passes. If you press too hard you can bend the neck and get a false idea of how flat your neck is.

The stone should mark each fret equally, replacing the light scratches made by the wet and dry with scratches going in the other direction. If this is the case you need do no more but if there are areas where the scratches made by the wet and dry paper remain, the fret is clearly a little low at that point. Because the first set of scratches on the fret, made by the paper, were across the neck and the stone is being used along it, the scratches will reflect light differently and it will be easy to see. If some are very slightly lower than others, some more attention with the stone will be in order. Remember that the stone is removing some of the fret on each pass and even the fine side will remove more than you intend to if you are not very careful.

Once the tops of all frets have been touched by the stone it is time to use the stone across the board. This will scratch the frets along their length and remove the scratches made when stoning along the neck, again making it easy to see where you have been successful. By alternately going along the neck and then across, the frets will be levelled and the radius of the fret will be maintained. As stated above, you should not need to do too much of this, a couple of passes in either direction should be enough, and you should finish with a very light stoning along the board to leave a final set of scratches across the fret. The stoning process will remove a little of the fret crown and leave a small flat area on top of the fret that will need to be recontoured. This is easier if you leave the frets marked in this way.

This process is also going to make a mess. Some of the abrasive from the stone will get worked off and there will be nasty dark marks made. It is a good idea to clean this debris away frequently, but do not rub it with cloths as it is an abrasive and can scratch your new paintwork. I have an old paintbrush I use to dust it off (wear a face mask) or you could vacuum it away. It may also leave some staining and will make your hands very dirty, but this can be dealt with by wearing disposable gloves, and some careful repolishing of the guitar afterwards. If you have any doubts about why you do not do this when the guitar is bare wood, cleaning the mess up will make it all clear. It would stain terribly.

Recontouring

There are several ways of dealing with the flat on the top of the fret. One is to simply ignore it, especially if it is not too bad, and to polish the scratches from the top of the fret. This is not ideal. Another alternative is

can then be cleaned up ready to go back on the guitar; it will already have served one purpose in being a very effective mask to prevent lacquer going onto the point where it would be glued.

Before you start with the stone it is a good idea to lightly mark the tops of the frets so that you can see if they need much levelling. This can be done with some 320 grit wet and dry paper, used dry on a cork block and used across the board so that it marks along the top of the fret.

Most oilstones come with slightly different grits on either side. Starting with the coarser side, which should be a lighter grit than the 320 used on the fret to mark the surface, make long strokes along the neck. If you hear any clinking noises you should check the board to see if it is straight; if it is, you need to investigate as one fret may have popped out of its slot. If this is the case it is not too hard to see which one it is, as there may be some dust from the oilstone next to it. The errant fret

Using a fret file to restore the contour of the bead.

Marking the top of the fret wih a marking pen.

to use a fretfile to restore the profile of the fret. These are concave files that vary in sharpness, radius and uniformity and can be used to recontour the top of the fret. Martin, on the other hand, do not use them and prefer to use triangular files with the corners polished smooth to recontour the tops of the frets. There are good and bad points with both. Fretfiles vary enormously and as I write this I am trying to remember if, in over 30 years of making guitars, I have ever used two that are similar or even one that has a uniform cut along its length. I am not sure I have.

Using a modified triangular file requires some skill but can be very good as the files are often better made than many fretfiles and give a more controllable cut; your aim is to not touch the top of the fret, but to reshape it.

The marker pen will highlight how well your recontouring is going.

When I was writing *Make Your Own Electric Guitar* I was told of a useful trick when recontouring frets. If you use a felt pen to mark the top of the fret, the use of the file, in fact any file, on the fret will remove the ink and the fret will shine through underneath, making it clear when you have got close to, but not too close to, the top of the fret. If you leave a thin line of felt pen along the top you have not lowered it too much (thanks Marty).

Whichever method you use, the frets will need to be cleaned and polished, and their ends rounded over. For this I use an old needle file with a diamond shape that I have had since I first started making guitars. It may not be the best tool but it works and I get good results. The fret ends are rounded to lose any sharp edges and then polished in the next action along with the rest of the fret.

With most of the residue from the stoning removed, the frets can have their shine restored by successive grades of wet and dry paper. I generally use 600 grit on a cork block along the fret and the flexibility of the cork allows the paper to wrap around the fret a little, so polishing the sides of the fret too. Once the marks from the stoning and filing have been removed I use worn 600 grit paper over my fingers and along the neck to put more, very small, scratches across the fret; these are then

Using my trusty old diamond-shaped file to round over the fret ends.

Removing the worst of the scratches with some old 400 grit paper. Successive grades are used to remove all the marks.

Using a wadding metal polish on the fret to give it a final shine.

Using a small scraper blade to remove the small ridge of lacquer that may be left by the fingerboard masking.

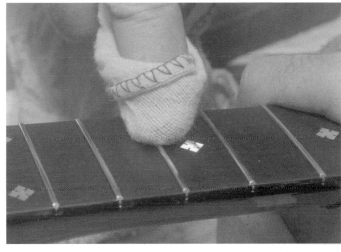

Polishing the fret and cleaning the board.

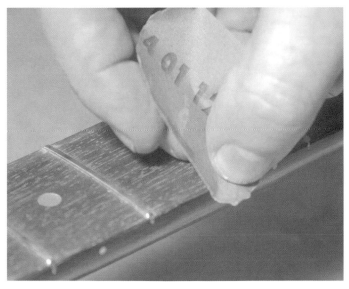

Cleaning up the edges of the board and the ends of the frets.

polished out with 1000 or 1200 grit paper over the cork block, working across the board and so along the fret.

The last stage is to use metal polish to get the final shine. Some people recommend masking the board before using any polish on the frets as it can soak into the board. This is broadly true, but in practice it tends to sit on the board and is easy to clean off. On some good ebony it can also polish the wood very effectively and make that shine, too.

Once all this has been done, I use a good lemon or orange oil (I have no idea why, but they are sold for the job and do it perfectly well) to clean the board right off. As much of the oil as possible should be cleaned off but any residue should be allowed to dry before the guitar is strung; there are other jobs to do beforehand which will allow time for this.

The end pin will need to be fitted. If you are using an ordinary strap button then a simple hole of the correct diameter for your chosen end pin's screw will need

Machine heads positioned to mark and drill the mounting holes.

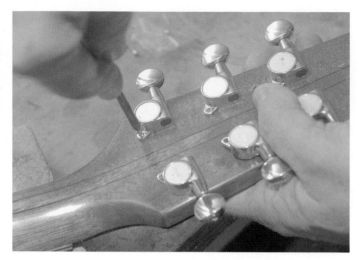

Installing the screw. These are not used to hold the machine heads in place, they are just to stop them turning and so should not be over tightened. They can break easily.

Drilling the holes for the machine head fixing screw. Accidentally drilling all the way through the head is going to ruin your day so proceed with care.

Tightening the bush on the machine head. Using the correct size tool will help prevent damage to the head.

to be drilled into the end block through the centre of the inlay. The larger, tapered end pins traditionally used on guitars will need to have a pilot hole drilled and the hole then opened with a tapered reamer of the correct size so the pin is a tight push fit. End pin jacks, for pre-amps, are usually fitted into a hole either 3/8 in (9.5 mm) or 1/2 in. (12.7 mm) diameter. Holding the guitar while drilling these is really a two-person job as the guitar will be hard to hold and drill by yourself.

INSTALLING THE MACHINE HEADS

Since the holes for the machine heads were drilled before the guitar was finished, it is possible that some of the finish may have dribbled into the holes and they may need to be opened out a little. The easiest way to find out is to try a trial fit with one of the heads and see if it slides neatly into its hole. If not, the hole can be cleaned out with careful use of a file or, better still,

a small reamer. I have one that was sold for making tapered holes in violin heads to fit tapered violin tuners, but it is exactly the right size for this job.

If your chosen heads have separate ferrules that fit into the front face of the heads, these should be fitted first and then the heads installed from the rear. If they have screwed-in bushings, the heads will need to be fitted and the bushings screwed in from the front. Do not tighten them fully at this stage as the holes for the mounting screws behind need to be drilled.

Align the heads as you want them, either symmetrically or not, and then mark the screw holes and remove the heads again. The mounting screw holes can then be drilled. It is a good idea to put some tape on the drill to act as a visual depth stop, so that you do not drill out of the front of the head. With a new drill bit this is far too easy.

With the holes drilled the head can be refitted, the mounting screws inserted and the bushes tightened. Do

Another view of the saddle on the Breedlove guitar shown on page 170 showing the partially intonated saddle.

not tighten the mounting screws too much. I have seen far too many guitars with these screws broken off in the head from being over-tightened and there is no need: the bush is there to keep the head in place and the screw is there just to stop it turning, so it only needs to touch the surface of the head, not to push it into the wood.

THE SADDLE

The saddle needs to be a firm, but not overly tight, fit in the slot made for it in the bridge. Most guitar makers' suppliers will have a choice of blank saddles in a variety of materials and you should have cut the slot in the bridge to match the saddle you have already bought; this needs to be cut to length and the ends rounded as the slot in the bridge is likely to have rounded ends from the small router bit.

The bottom of the saddle must remain flat to make contact with the bottom of the saddle slot all the way along its length while the top will need to be shaped.

The top surface will be curved to roughly match the contour of the fingerboard. In theory this will give an even action – the height between the string and the fret – across the curved fingerboard, but in practice the top strings may well be closer to the frets than the bass strings, so the curve may not be even.

Put the saddle into the slot and place a long straight-edge onto the saddle and over the fingerboard. The further the straightedge can be placed back towards the nut and still sit on the saddle the better. Contact between first fret and saddle is ideal.

Check the distance between the straightedge and the 12th fret on the treble side. If this is less than the action you planned at the design stage then your saddle is too low. This is not often the case as saddles are usually generously proportioned and there is usually plenty of height available.

If the action is much higher than planned, start by making a curve across the top of the saddle. Take the saddle out and file or sand the contour on the top. I either hold it in the vice and file it to shape, finishing with sandpaper, or belt sand it. The deciding factor is

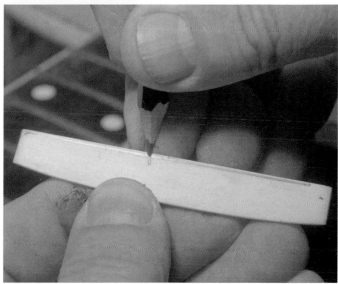

Marking the bottom of the saddle prior to lowering the action.

Removing the waste making sure to keep the bottom of the saddle flat.

whether there is anyone else in the workshop to complain about the awful smell that bone makes when it is belt sanded.

Put the saddle back into its slot and again measure the action at the 12th fret on both the treble and bass side. If this is still much too high you can estimate the amount of saddle you need to remove and mark this as a straight line on the bottom of the saddle and sand or file this off, keeping the bottom of the saddle flat. If it is close to being correct and only needs final adjustment, leave this until you string the guitar. For final adjustment the nut will have to be cut and then the saddle adjusted.

This is one of those cases where the order of things to do comes quite naturally when you are doing the work, but is hard to explain in writing!

Bridge pins

It is now time to fit strings to the guitar for the first time. You will need to use these when cutting the nut and for the final action checks. You will have already made the bridge with the holes drilled for the pins and may have used the two outer ones to locate the bridge when gluing. Each pin is held in place by friction and so the hole needs to be just large enough so that it is not a struggle to get the pin out when changing strings, but not too large that it does not stay in. Start by drilling them with the same size drill you used when drilling the bridge and then widen then, if necessary, with a small tapered reamer. Fitting the top and bottom strings is useful when setting the action and all six (or however many you designed your guitar for) when cutting the nut.

THE NUT

The nut, as we have discussed, supports the strings over the first fret and holds them at the right spacing to make playing comfortable. The strings sit in slots cut into the nut; these have to be wide enough to allow the string to move freely so that tuning is not difficult, yet narrow enough so that the strings do not rattle in the slot. They have to be cut so that the string stops vibrating at the fingerboard side of the nut, not half way across it, and they have to be just deep enough to allow the string to pass over the first fret with minimal clearance. Easy, really. In truth it is not that difficult if you follow some simple guidelines and take care.

The first stage is to mark the nut positions. The outer strings should not be too close to the edge of the fingerboard, and this was one of the items that was planned when drawing the guitar to begin with. These positions can be marked and the remainder of the space divided by five to give the six string positions. These are first marked with pencil and then a small triangular file or even a razor saw blade can be used to notch the positions. The strings can then be positioned to check that the spacing is OK.

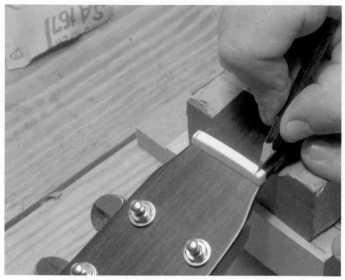

Marking the outer string positions.

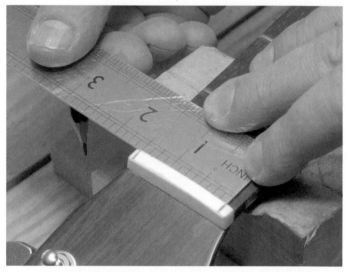

Measuring the space between the outer strings.

Marking the positions. As with the bridge pin holes, the space between the outer strings is divided by five to give six string positions.

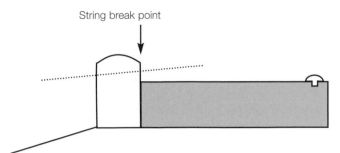

String break point

The nut slot is cut on a slight angle downwards, as shown by the extended dotted line.

Using a small razor saw for the thinner strings.

The slots can be cut with a razor saw for the smaller strings and a junior hacksaw for the larger ones, but saw blade teeth are splayed so that the saw does not stick in the cut. This will give, at best, a flat bottom across the slot or, at worst, a ridge running along the centre of the slot. You could also use ordinary needle files if you can find any of the right size, or any of the specially made nut-cutting files that are on the market.

Many of these files are sold at exact sizes that match the string sizes you may fit, but in practice this often gives a slot that is too narrow and will not allow the string to move through the nut when being tuned, causing it to stick. There needs to be some space to allow the string to move, but not so much that it rattles. Many guitars with tuning problems can be cured simply by using the next size of nut file on the nut slots.

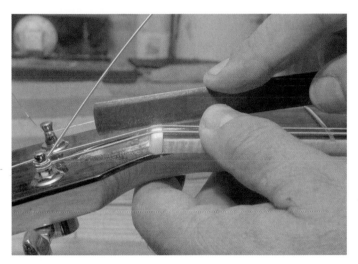

Using a nut file.

Cutting the slot to size

The slot will need to be cut with a flat bottom along its length and at a slight angle so that the string vibration starts at the fingerboard side of the nut. It will also need to be just deep enough so that the string misses the first fret by a very small fraction when the guitar is

When fretting between the second and third frets, the string should just clear the first fret.

fretted between the second and third frets. If you take it stage by stage and check frequently, a good job is quite easy.

As each string slot is cut you will need to tension the string to pitch before checking the nut height, as otherwise the flexibility of the string might give a false impression of how the slot is progressing.

Ideally, the string should not be buried in the slot, but just under half should be proud. Any less than half and the string could slop out of the slot; any more and the vibration might be damped. When all the slots have been cut deep enough for the strings to clear the first fret, the overall height of the nut can be reduced so that the strings are partially revealed. Once again, be careful not to remove too much. The nut can then be finally shaped.

The front face of the nut, facing the fingerboard, needs to be kept vertical to the end of the board, but the rear part can be shaped and all corners rounded off a little.

Bone can also be polished to a high gloss with metal polish, so the nut can be sanded with 280 grit to remove the scratches made by the file or sandpaper, then 600 and then 1000 wet and dry, and then polished before being glued into place.

The very last stage is to lubricate the nut slots. Graphite from an ordinary pencil is very good for this and a little rubbed into the slots will help the strings move freely. If you do hear creaks and the strings stick when tuning, the nut slots will need to be opened out just a little.

With the nut slots cut, saddle fitted, bridge pins adjusted and strings fitted you will get a first hint of what your guitar will sound like.

Final action adjustment

At this point the action should be a little too high. Final adjustment of this is a matter of trial and error. The trick is to work out how much you want to lower the action at the 12th fret, then double this amount at the saddle and remove it; but it is not a great idea to do this in one go, just in case the measurement is flawed. You also need to play each note on each fret to ensure that the guitar is free from buzzes and rattles.

You will need to remove the strings each time you remove the saddle and tune the guitar to pitch each time you restring it and test the action.

With care you can get the action down to what you require, but be careful not to take it too low. Acoustic guitars simply do not sound as good with very low electric guitar-like actions.

INTONATION

Once this has all been done the intonation can be checked. Play the harmonic at the 12th fret and the fretted note, and compare them. If your measurements have been good then they should be very similar. If the

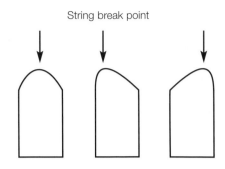

String break point

Changing the shape of the saddle can alter the intonation. The diagram on the left shows a saddle with an evenly rounded top with the string break point being in the centre. The two others show the amount that the break point can be moved by shaping the top differently.

Adjusting the truss rod. Depending on the style of truss rod you may need to use a wrench, allen key or screwdriver to make the adjustment but it is important to use the right tool.

fretted note is a little sharper than the harmonic, you can move the break point on the saddle back a little by careful contouring of the top as shown in the diagram.

Once this has been done the saddle can come out for one last time to be polished, then put back into its slot and the guitar restrung.

TRUSS ROD

With the guitar strung to pitch, it might be necessary to adjust the truss rod very slightly to compensate for the pull of the strings. You need a little relief in the neck to allow the strings room to vibrate. Fretting at the first and 14th fret should give you a small amount of space under the string at the mid position, usually no more

Making a paper template of the scratchplate.

The scratchplate was cut out using heavy duty scissors and finished with scrapers and sandpaper before being placed into position on the guitar. The masking tape on the guitar is placed to just touch the scratchplate so that it can easily put back into the same position when the self-adhesive backing is removed.

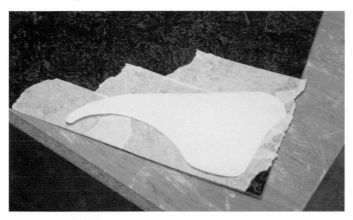

Transferring the shape of the scratchplate onto the scratchplate material. This has been covered with masking tape to make the lines easier to see.

The completed scratchplate.

than $^1/_{32}$ in (0.75 mm). The amount of relief you will need on the neck will depend on the neck, scale length and string tension so do not be afraid to experiment a little. A neck that is too straight will tend to have rattles on the lower fret positions.

Adjusting this with the truss rod is really not rocket science but do not be surprised if no adjustment at all is needed. The rod is quite stiff and the neck will have some natural resistance, so the tension of the strings may well be automatically balanced by the tension that is inherent in the springiness of the wood.

If it does need adjustment, it is a simple job. Many people are almost afraid of touching a truss rod, as so much has been written about them that they almost have a folklore of their own. This is ridiculous as they are very simple and if you adjust a little at a time and do not crank them really tight, then you will have no problems.

SCRATCHPLATE

Your guitar is now very nearly complete. The choice of whether you fit a scratchplate is entirely up to you, but the use of a pick and even fingers may damage the front of the guitar, so a scratchplate can be a good idea. I have fitted these to a couple of the guitars I have made for this book; they were made from commercially available materials sold for exactly this purpose and were cut to shape after a template had been made from paper or card. The material is self-adhesive, so once it is cut and the edges are cleaned up the backing can be removed and the scratchplate stuck down. Note that this is a 'one go' operation, so make sure it is in exactly the right position before sticking.

A small cover may be needed for the truss rod recess if this is in the head; this can also be made from any of the commercially available scratchplate plastics and fixed with a couple of small screws.

A truss rod cover made from some pearl plastic.

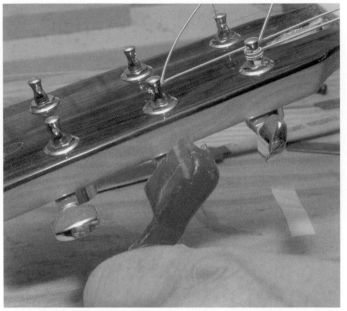

A stringwinder is a very useful tool and will save a lot of time and arm ache.

It is a good idea to trim the ends of the strings.

AND FINALLY...

The guitar is now complete, but it may sound a little thin at first. For some reason, guitars tend to improve very quickly after first being strung up. The electro-acoustic in Chapter 23 was quite disappointing when first strung, but after being played for a while has developed quite a bit of character. With a flat back and a cutaway it was never going to be a truly great acoustic, which was not the intention, but it is far from being a bad acoustic and it continues to improve.

You may also find that an early change of string will help the guitar. During the setting up of the nut and saddle the strings will have taken something of a pounding, and playing the guitar for a while with a new set may make it sound much better.

The guitar will also settle a little and it is quite possible that a few minor adjustments may be needed after a few weeks of playing. This is quite normal and they are generally very minor.

Having covered most of the main processes involved in making the guitar, I will now show some examples of how these can be applied.

Chapter 20
Guitar Kits

The rise in the popularity of guitar making as a hobby has spurred several companies into offering guitar kits. These vary in style and in how much work has already been done, but they can be an ideal introduction to the skills of guitar making. With all kits there is a considerable amount of work still to be done, though: you will need to have access to a suitable work space and will need to make some of the jigs and workboards seen elsewhere in the book.

The kit that is to be made in this chapter is one that can be bought from Martin Guitars. They not only make some fine guitars, but also have a related company, Guitarmaker's Connection, that supplies wood and parts to makers across the world. Guitarmaker's Connection is actually based in the original Martin guitar factory on North Street, Nazareth, Pennsylvania, that was opened in 1836 by C.F. Martin and which is now a United States national monument.

Martin supplies kits of most of their standard body shapes. I chose to make a rosewood D28 kit as this is one of the most popular of the kits they sell. This also comes with a free copy of Martin's Dreadnaught guitar plan and a very useful booklet, written by Martin's own Dick Boak, that gives some good hints and tips on how to put the guitar together.

The first stage is to check that everything is present. Martin provides all the parts, right down to the strings, and these should all be checked against the packing list. Many of the parts are quite small, such as the position dots, and others are quite fragile, such as some of the bracing pieces, and they need to be carefully stored until they are needed.

The back comes partly thicknessed, although I felt it could be made thinner, but not joined and so the first stage is to glue this together. A central inlay is also provided and this need to be glued between the back halves.

The back was joined on a workboard with wedges as described in Chapter 7 and left to dry overnight.

The excess glue and any unevenness in the back were then sanded out. This unevenness should be very small if you make sure that everything is laying flat against the workboard. With the two halves already thicknessed this was not a problem.

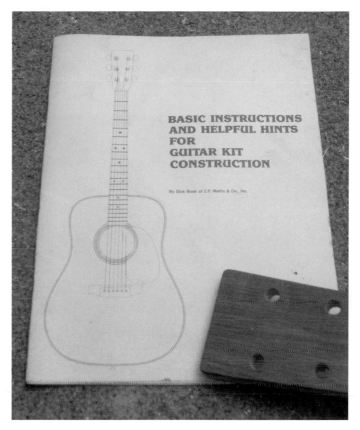

Dick Boak's excellent book is included with the kit.

The back comes with an outline of the guitar chalked onto it but this is not to be relied on for measurements; it is just a guide to where the back should fit on the piece of wood. To get a better idea it is worth tracing the shape from the supplied plan and transferring that to a thin piece of plywood, so that a jig can be made. Marking the shape on the back with chalk is, however, a good idea as it is visible against the dark wood.

The back was sanded to remove any marks on the inside and then wiped with a cloth dipped in spirit to remove some of the oil from the rosewood: this is to help make a good glue join with the braces and back trim along the centre of the back.

Using a thin piece of metal to protect the back while shaping the back trim.

The braces positioned before gluing.

The finished back trim.

Gluing a back brace. These are pre-shaped and profiled so careful clamping and shaped cauls may be needed.

Martin supplies a number of strips of cross-grained spruce for the trim that strengthens the back join. These need to be measured to find their centre line and then glued accurately over the back join. It is wise to double-check that you are gluing them on what you have chosen to be the inside of the back, not the outside. Remember that mistakes like that are only funny if they happen to someone else.

These were glued into place and weighted down. I decided not to use the bar system as I wanted to make this guitar with the minimum of tools. This is not the ideal way as you need to use a lot of weight and the parts can slip but, in this instance, all was well and when the glue was dry they were radiused to make them look tidier. Since the grain runs across the strip, planing a radius may well pull some of the grain out. You can partially shape the strip with a sharp chisel but you need to be careful not to slip and mark the back.

Murphy's Law states that if something bad can happen, it will and Murphy's Law applied to the insides of a guitar can be amended to state that if any mistakes are made they will be in a position that is visible through the soundhole!

The back trim was then finish sanded and the positions of the cross braces marked. These had to fit snugly into the slots cut into the back strip. The wood was removed carefully with a sharp chisel (taking note of the Murphy's Law statement above) checking frequently to ensure that the brace was a good fit. The braces were then glued using clamps and a curved caul underneath to match the radius of the brace.

Once these had set, were inspected and any remaining glue spots were removed. Last but not least, all parts were carefully sanded along the grain with 180 and 220 grit paper.

Soundhole inlays installed using a very thin superglue. Martin recommends plastic model cement, but either is suitable.

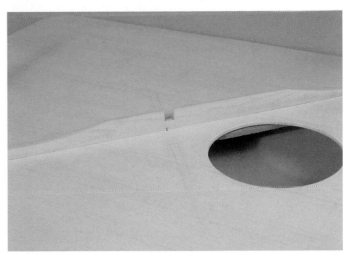

Marking the first brace so that it will line up correctly when glued.

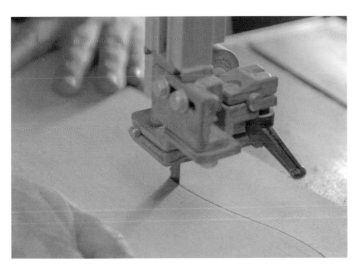

Bandsawing the top. The pencil marks made at the factory to show the brace positions can just be seen.

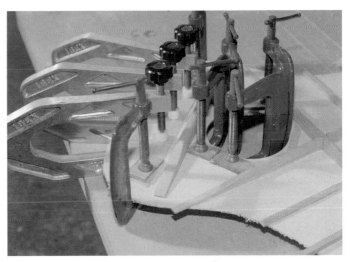

A little bit of 'clamp overkill' when gluing the braces. The bar system would have been much easier!

THE FRONT

The front of the Martin kit comes glued and thicknessed with the soundhole and soundhole inlays already cut. The Dick Boak instruction book says to install the inlays with plastic model cement and care needs to be taken not to damage the raised portions between the grooves, as these are very fragile. The innermost ring of inlay needs to be fitted very carefully as it is visible once the fingerboard is glued; it had to be cut exactly to fit the groove so that there was no gap between the two ends of the plastic. An alternative to model cement is superglue and this, too, needs to be used very carefully; for some glues the wood should be dampened before it is applied. Many different types of superglue are available and it is better to have one of the slower-setting ones.

Once the inlay was complete it was left to dry thoroughly and then the excess was sanded back. This is a little easier when dealing with plastic inlays as they sand well, but the paper must be supported over a block to stop it digging into the top.

The inside edge of the soundhole also needed some attention and this was sanded to give a small radius.

The top and back were then cut out using a fine and thin blade on the bandsaw. Cutting them out is not essential before the bracing is fitted, but it is easier this way because it allows more leeway for the clamping of the braces as the clamps do not have to reach over wood that will be removed later. This would not be the case if the dowel bar system (*see* page 69) was used. Between $1/4$ in (6.3 mm) and $1/2$ in (12.7 mm) was left outside the line.

The bracings come ready cut and shaped, and the first to be fitted were the main cross braces. These are

Cutting a form from MDF to hold the sides.

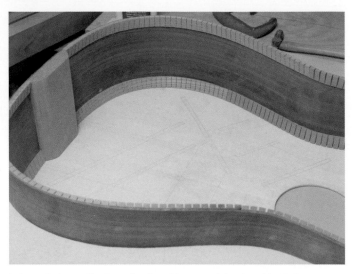

I chose to brace the top after the sides were joined and kerfed. This meant I could check the brace positions before they were glued.

pre-notched, as they are made in large numbers in the factory on computer-controlled machines, so that they fit together in the centre. These were clamped with a long-throated C clamp.

Martin recommends that you should next glue the transverse brace and top plate, then the bridge plate, the two tone bars, the four side braces and finally the soundhole reinforcements. These last pieces needed to be cut from the spare bracing stock.

After the bracing had dried, the inside of the top was cleaned up and sanded. The ends of the transverse brace and cross braces were already shaped but were cleaned up and checked to confirm they were $1/8$ in (3 mm) deep. The tone bars and side braces on the top were cut so that they tapered to nothing before reaching the kerfing.

SIDES

The sides for the Martin kit come pre-trimmed to shape and taper, and are pre-bent. This saves a lot of effort but it is always possible they may have moved slightly from their original shape as they may have sprung back a little.

You could make a complete mould to ensure they are exactly to shape as described in Chapter 3, but this is a lot of effort to go to for one guitar, especially as most of the work on bending the sides has already been done for you! I chose to make a simple form just to keep them more or less in place and to the right shape. This was cut from a piece of $3/8$ in (10 mm) MDF using a tracing from the supplied plan to give the shape. I used a bandsaw to make the cut, being very careful to stay close to the line.

The first stage of making the body was to check which was the top edge and back edge of the sides. The Martin sides come pre-cut to accept the back, so if

you lay one side on your workboard and it rocks you have the back side down. If it stays still then you have the flat, top side down. These were marked so that no mistakes were made in gluing them.

Not all of Martin's kits come with a full-size plan and so for other kits the shape can be taken from the shape that is pencilled on the inside of the top. It is also possible the sides may need to be trimmed to length; for this, make sure that your line is drawn perpendicular to the edge that you have determined is the top. If the sides do have to be trimmed, make sure the underside is well supported when cutting, as it can split.

The end blocks are supplied from the factory fully shaped except for their height, which will need to be trimmed. I measured and marked the centres with a pencil and continued this line around all four sides so that the centre line was visible not only when gluing the sides to the end blocks, but also from inside the guitar, to line it up on a centre line on the drawing, and along the top and bottom edges to help in locating the top and back.

The neck and end blocks were glued to the sides with the excess protruding from the back of the guitar. There is a temptation to trim these to length but avoid this, as you will need the excess when fitting the back to make a snug join. Clamping cauls were put under the clamps to stop them damaging the sides, and paper was put between the cauls and the guitar to stop them getting stuck. This is a good alternative to waxing the cauls as it leaves no residue on the wood; also, it is far easier to get a stuck piece of paper from the guitar side than it is the caul.

Martin provides the kerfing ready slotted and this needs to be cut to length as described in Chapter 8. This was glued on using small clamps and clothes pegs, and is probably the only thing done on the kit that uses exactly the same method as the factory!

Gluing the back kerfing. The extra height on the tailblock can be seen in this picture. This will be cut to size when fitting the back.

Once the back and top were glued, the excess can be trimmed away with the laminate trimmer.

GLUING TOP AND BACK

Dick Boak's book on constructing the Martin kit suggests gluing the back on first. This is not the normal way of doing things, although in this case it is quite sensible. You can glue the top on first, which means you can pay more attention to the inner finish around the kerfing and the end blocks, but gluing the back on first will make attaching the top easier.

The top kerfing was levelled using a sanding stick and the positions of the braces marked. These were slotted and prepared as in Chapter 9 and then the top was trial-fitted until the fit was perfect and properly aligned.

With this complete, the top was removed and put to one side while the back was fitted. The first stage was to line it up, mark the brace positions and start fitting them. Once this was completed, the kerfing and sides were shaped to accept the curved back as shown in Chapter 9. The back was then glued into place.

Back Gluing

Once the back glued onto the guitar, it should be double-checked to see that it is sitting properly. It is far easier to remove it and correct the problem when the glue is wet than it is when it has had time to dry. Any excess glue can be cleaned off while it is still wet.

When the guitar has been allowed to dry out, the inside of the body can be inspected prior to gluing the top. You will need to ensure that you to remove any glue drops that have fallen inside when gluing on the back, as these will be very unsightly.

Gluing the top

With the back cleaned, the fit of the top should be double-checked. It is possible that the guitar may have

distorted slightly, and it might need a small adjustment. The face of the kerfing can be brushed to remove any sanding dust that could weaken the glue join.

Holding the top in place while it is glued is a little easier than holding the back as it is largely flat. There is a slight bow in the front of the guitar and this can be easily dealt with by making a thin caul to sit around the edge of the guitar as described on page 101. It is a good idea to wax this before you attempt to glue the top onto the guitar: if glue does get into the wrong place and sticks the caul to the guitar front, then the whole body may be ruined.

The body of the guitar can remain in the form until after the top is glued to ensure that it stays in shape, although with the kerfing in place and the back on, it will not distort too much if the form is removed. The top is laid face-down on the workboard and the glue applied to the kerfings as for the back. By placing the top face down, no glue will drip down into the guitar and be visible. Try not to use too much glue, yet not so little that there is not enough to stick.

This is another operation where the late Irving Sloan's method of strapping the top works well (*see* page 102), although you could weight the top around the edges, or use clamps or even use tape.

With the top in place and the glue dry, the body can be removed from the form and the glue cleaned up from around the sides.

BINDINGS AND PURFLING

Martin supplies its standard plastic bindings and the kit that I have chosen to make has the optional herringbone purfling that was used on some of Martin's more famous guitars.

Test fitting the herringbone purfling into the slot.

Trimming the end inlay that was fitted after the inding channels were cut.

Before the channels were routed, the end inlay was inlaid. Martin supplies this as a piece of V-shaped plastic with two strips of black and white plastic that can be glued either side to give some contrasting lines. These were glued together with superglue and then the inlay was measured, the guitar marked and the slot cut with a dovetail saw.

The binding and purfling channels were cut with a laminate trimmer using the tilting base on the back of the guitar, and several passes were made to make a clean cut and keep it the right size.

With the channels cut and checked, the binding and purfling were glued into place. As with the soundhole inlays, Martin recommends using plastic model cement for fixing these, but superglue works just as well. I chose to use the plastic binding supplied with the kit together with a commercially-available herringbone purfling very similar to that used on the classic Martin D-28s. The bindings were held in place with masking tape while they dried and the two ends were butt-joined at the end inlay taking care to keep the join on the centre line.

When this is all in place, you can check for any areas that are not fixed properly and superglue can be dribbled in to hold them. With this done the guitar can be finish sanded first with 120 grit then going down to 280.

TEST FITTING THE NECK

The neck in the Martin kit comes part-shaped with the dovetail and the channel for the truss rod pre-cut.

The first stage is to open up the mortice in the neck block. This has had the sides glued over it and so they need to be trimmed to match the mortice beneath. I started by drilling a hole to locate the mortice and then used chisels and files to remove the waste. If the body

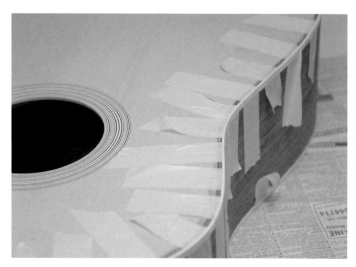

The binding was held in place with tape while the glue dried.

has been assembled accurately around the centre line ,the mortice should be in the correct position.

The dovetail on the neck is oversize and needs to be cut back so that the neck is at the correct angle to the body and aligned along the centre line. Using a file or rasp, the edges of the dovetail were trimmed so that the neck sat flush with the face of the body. Both sides were worked at the same time to keep everything even. This can be time consuming and frustrating, but it is the most important part of the guitar-making process.

Don't worry if you remove too much material as you can use thin veneer shims to pack out the joint if you need to. It is not ideal, but it will work and some very expensive hand-made guitars have had to have veneer shims too!

The Dick Boak book and the Martin plan state an angle of 1.5 degrees is needed and the neck is already

The neck block comes pre-cut and so the mortice needs to be found through the sides. The first stage is to drill a hole and remove the waste.

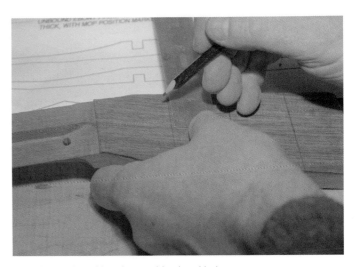

Measuring and marking the machine head holes.

Test fitting the neck. It should be a firm fit with the top surface of the neck lined up with the top surface of the body and everything at the correct angle.

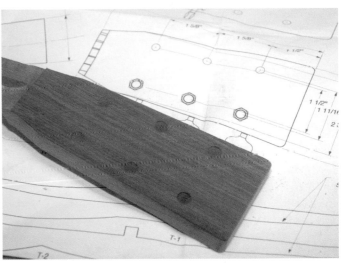

The finished head.

cut to this, but do not assume it will automatically line up and be at the correct angle as there are a host of other factors that could have affected the neck fit while the body has been assembled. The same methods used in Chapter 14 can be used to check the fit.

Some small adjustments were needed and were made to both sides of the neck, and either side of the tenon, to keep the neck aligned with the centre of the guitar.

The body was then put to one side while work on the neck proceeded.

THE NECK

The neck comes from the factory with pins inserted into the face of the neck to properly locate the fingerboard. The board itself is pre-slotted and has the holes for the locating lugs computer-routed into the under-

The installed truss rod.

side: this means that not only is locating the fingerboard into place no problem, but the board does not slide around while it is being glued.

The head-to-neck transition area needs to be shaped to include the diamond-shaped head reinforcement.

The heel is cut to length. This view also shows the truss rod extension under the fingerboard.

Shaping the diamond using 120 grit paper and a block. The back of this block has been used as a handy place to mix some filler.

The heel cap was glued and sanded to shape.

The first stage is to prepare the neck. The neck join has been done but a head facing is supplied and this needs to be glued on. Unlike the other guitars in this book, the Martin kit has the truss rod adjustment at the body end of the neck accessible through the soundhole, so the head facing does not need to be cut to make an access recess for the truss rod adjustment. The head facing was glued on and left to dry before being trimmed back and then marked for the machine head holes. These were positioned as on the plan and drilled to $3/8$ in (9.5 mm), taking care to support the back of the head to prevent any grain from breaking out.

The truss rod on the Martin is a box-section type and has a small plastic strip that sits over the top of the rod in the channel. Unfortunately I managed to damage this in the workshop and so a small length of veneer was substituted. The channel is cut into the neck on one of Martin's computer-controlled machines and has a curved section at one end where the machine tool has entered the wood. The rod needs to be positioned so that it does not sit in this curved section, which would make one end higher than the other. The overall length also needs to be checked to ensure that it will end at the right point under the top.

Before the board is glued on, it is a good idea to inlay the side inlays at least, as these can be difficult to reach once the board is glued and it is easy to fit them with the board edge-on in a vice. Martin supplies a short length of white plastic rod that is inserted and glued into $1/16$ in (1.5 mm) holes and chopped to length. The front inlays were also glued and in this case I chose, to ignore the dots supplied with the kit as I had some snowflake inlays that I wanted to use.

These were inlayed into a hole that was first drilled to $1/4$ in (6.3 mm) and then opened out with a small chisel to accept the diamond-shaped inlay. They were glued in using a mixture of epoxy and ebony dust to make some black filler, which filled the small cuts on the edge of each snowflake and matched with the board (*see* page 143). When the inlays were dry, they

The truss rod channel extends into the body. This needs to be routed so the neck will fit.

To suspend the guitar while it was finished I screwed a small hook into the neck block.

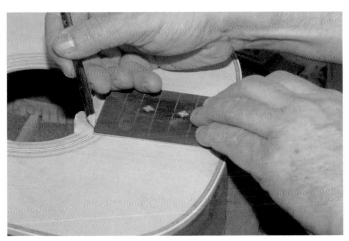

Marking the position of the fingerboard on the masking that will protect the area while the guitar is being sprayed. The masking will be cut back slightly inside of this line so a little of the finish extends under the edge of the board as shown in Chapter 18.

were sanded flat with the front of the fingerboard and the board was glued to the neck.

Martin very kindly part-shapes its necks and so there would appear to be little to do. However, the area around the diamond that is shaped at the back of the neck behind the nut and the area where the neck joins the underside of the fingerboard both need a little shaping, but this is quite straightforward.

Once this has been done, the truss rod needs to be fitted into the front of the body. This is quite straightforward to mark and cut, and the channel stops short of the transverse brace that runs in front of the sound-hole. When the neck is glued, the adjuster is fed into the hole provided in this brace and the truss rod slips neatly into the slot cut into the body.

With the neck finish sanded, I decided to finish the body and the neck separately so I did not glue the neck

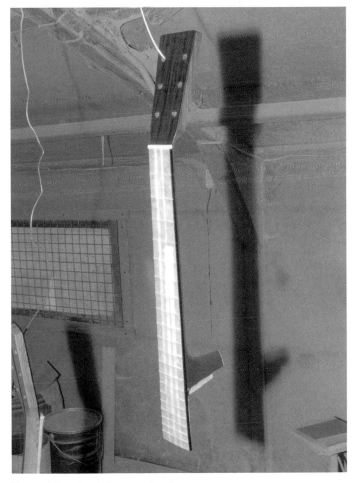

The neck hanging in the spraybooth.

on at this stage. The bridge position did need masking so the neck was temporarily fitted to the body while the bridge position was worked out and masked.

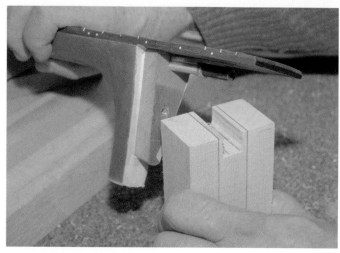

Because the truss rod extents under the fingerboard overhang, a cut out was made in a block to support the board.

Reaming the bridge pin holes.

The fretted overhang.

The bridge comes part finished, with the bridge pin holes part drilled and the saddle slot ready routed, and so great care needs to be taken in fitting it. It has to align with the centre line of the neck and also be at the right point to allow the guitar to play in tune.

Very careful measurement was taken to make sure that it was square to the centre line and also that the saddle position was correct on the treble side. While the neck was in place, another check was made to ensure the fingerboard was at the correct angle from the bridge and that the neck was level.

The area under the fingerboard was masked and I decided to mask the area around the neck join at the same time so the neck was not being glued onto grain filler, but just wood. This did risk having a slight build up of filler around the join but unmasking, careful sanding of the join, and then remasking dealt with this.

The masking of the heel area was done by masking the edges of the area so that the neck would still fit into the mortice and then cutting just inside the line with a sharp scalpel blade. The rest of the mortice could be masked inside this area.

The grainfilling was straightforward with the top protected to prevent any staining and the bindings masked. These were scraped clean after the guitar had been sanded to remove any sign of the grain filler.

Fretting

The last job before finishing was to fret the neck. This was straightforward using the fretwire supplied by Martin and because the neck was unbound. The neck was checked for straightness before the frets were fitted, and the main portion of the neck was fretted using the very useful 'Jaws' fret press supplied by Stewart MacDonald Guitar Shop Supply. The fingerboard overhang was supported on a block made with a cut-out for the truss rod while it was fretted conventionally.

The fret ends were trimmed and shaped and the nut, which of course comes with the kit, was fitted before the fingerboard was masked, the neck grain-filled and then sanded.

Finishing

The guitar was finished using spray cans of clear lacquer brought from an automotive store. In all about five large cans were used.

Once this was dry, the guitar was left to harden completely, the lacquer was polished to a high gloss and the neck was readied to be glued to the body.

Although handling the body and neck separately when finishing them is easier, it makes fitting them a little more complicated as there is a constant fear of

Lining up the scratchplate.

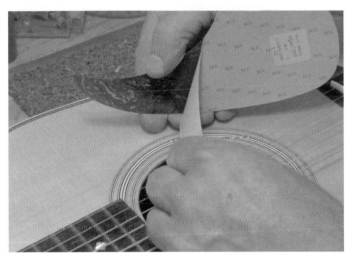

Peeling the self adhesive backing. Remember you only get one go to get this right!

The kit is an excellent way to get started.

knocking something with a clamp: therefore, a lot of care is needed when putting the guitar together. This was not too much of a problem, even for someone as untidy in the workshop as me, but the job did require a couple of dry runs and some careful arranging of things so that they were close at hand when needed. This included the glue, the clamps and useful things like damp paper towels to remove the glue seepage.

One advantage of the dovetail neck join is that it pulls the neck towards the body when it is fitted accurately. As the neck is pushed down into the socket, the sides of the dovetail should pull the heel into the body. This makes clamping much easier as only one clamp under the neck block and one to clamp the fingerboard are needed. Once the neck was dry, the clamps were removed, very carefully, and the area around the neck-to-body join and the fingerboard extension was polished to remove the remains of any glue.

The bridge was glued on and the string holes drilled through before the frets were levelled, the saddle was fitted, the nut was cut and the strings, which were included in the kit, were put on using the bridge pins that also came with the kit!

I was impressed by the quality of the Martin kit and the results that could be obtained. I purposely made it with as few tools as possible: after all, it was not important to see if I could complete a guitar using all the tools I normally have at my disposal, so completing the Martin kit with the minimum seemed like a good idea. If you have any worries about any of the major 'lumps' of the guitar-making process, such as fitting the truss rod, making or fitting the neck or bending the sides, I would honestly recommend starting your guitar-making career with a kit such as this; Dick Boak's book is also well worth reading.

Chapter 21
Reclaimed Materials

The planks that made the top were hardly inspiring to look at.

There was a time, not that long ago, when books such as this would recommend using materials that were already in short supply and which, today, would not be considered 'politically correct'. This has now changed and people are generally more aware of the impact that the modern world is having on supplies of some woods and materials. Alternative woods are now used, often with very good results.

Another alternative is to use what could be called 'pre-owned' materials: reclaimed or second-hand wood. This has added advantages in that old wood can often be very high quality and is just the sort of thing that is not available on the open market anymore. The downside is that there can be damage and screw holes to deal with, but with a little effort fine guitars can be made using wood that can be surprisingly good value.

As an example of this, I chose to make a guitar from reclaimed materials. The intention was that everything on the guitar would be recovered from somewhere although I knew that it was likely that the frets, possibly, and strings, certainly, would have to be new.

For the rest a little searching around, a few questions in the right places and some lateral thinking worked wonders, and I have managed to get everything I needed for next to no outlay.

THE TOP

For the top of the guitar I used some pine that came from the roof of an old shed that was demolished some years ago on a farm near to where I live. The wood was far too good to just be burned and so, in the manner often found on farms, was put away until such time as another use could be found.

I discovered this when my friend Tim Smith, who had demolished the shed with his father, asked to use my thicknesser to turn some of this wood into door frames for the cottage he was rebuilding. I was pleasantly surprised at the quality of some of the wood and also how much there was. Needless to say, very little of it was suitable for guitar making, but a search through a very large pile turned up a couple of interesting

Planing revealed close straight grain on some pieces beneath the years of grime.

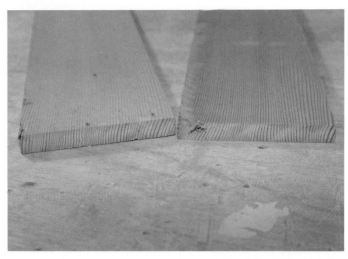

The two pieces chosen to make the top had almost quarter sawn grain.

pieces. This all looked very uninspiring, as it was very weathered, but the experience of seeing Tim planing the wood he had used made me sure that what was underneath the patina would be fine. None of the pieces were wide enough for a two-piece top, but that was not really a problem.

The first stage in the selection process was to find boards with a close grain and not too many splits or nail holes. Those boards were then inspected to see if the end grain was perpendicular to the face. A few of these were then chopped into useable lengths (meaning lengths that I could get into my car) and taken back to the workshop.

The first stage of preparation was to remove anything that was not wood, such as nails and any staples that may have been used to hold things in the old shed. With this done the wood was planed to remove the old weathering and to show its true beauty.

The boards were all about 6 in (155 mm) wide and 1/2 in (12.7 mm) thick, so a four-piece top was required and the boards were split lengthways on the bandsaw. The four pieces were then chosen and positioned so that the guitar shape could be fitted avoiding any of the nail holes. This was just personal preference, as it would have been possible to have simply repaired the nail holes. Several makers have made well-publicised guitars from reclaimed woods and have repaired any major blemishes. The guitars have been fine and have sounded good.

The only thing that I found, and that I will admit caught me out slightly, was that there was some splitting along the grain near the nail holes: although the holes were not on the guitar top, the splits were and so needed to be opened and glued. This could have been a problem if they had been old and had accumulated dirt and dust, but they were still fresh and so were easily glued up.

The two planks were sawn, not split, in half. The nail holes from the boards previous life can be seen top right.

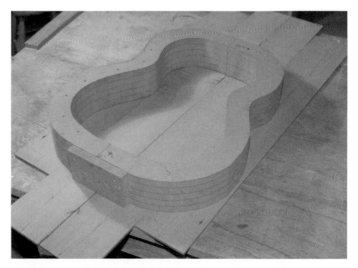

The mould was used to mark the shape and ensure that the nail holes were missed.

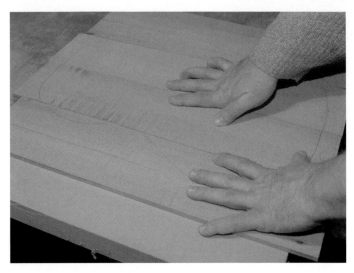

Lining up the boards ready for gluing.

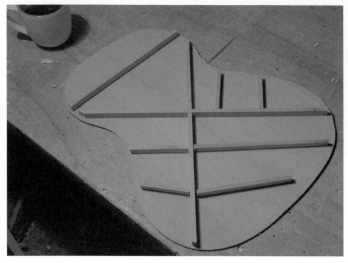

The bracing was cut and placed onto the top to check position and size.

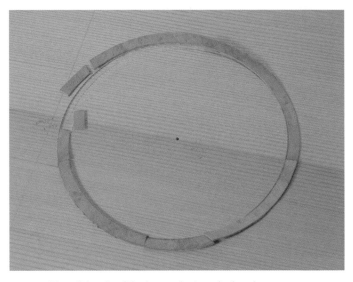

The wild grain of the burr walnut made the pieces very fragile but they were easily mated when glued in.

Gluing the four-piece top was no different to gluing a two-piece, except that there was a little more planing needed to get the edges square and flat. The work-board was marked with the join positions, the area was waxed to prevent the boards sticking, and the boards were glued using the wedge method described in Chapter 6. What was nice about gluing four pieces was that the smaller widths of the board made them less prone to bending across their width. With the top glued, it was sanded to thickness and marked ready to be cut and glued.

The shape of the guitar is the one shown in the design chapter. This guitar was designed to be a 14-fret model and so the soundhole, bridge positions and the bracing positions were marked accordingly.

In keeping with the 'anything as long as it is free' nature of the guitar, the soundhole inlay was a simple ring of burr walnut. This was left over from some veneering work on an old car dashboard (a 1935 Lagonda Rapier for those who may be interested) and a number of pieces were cut that had a $2^1/4$ in (57 mm) radius on the inside and $2^3/4$ in (70 mm) radius on the outside, making a ring $1/4$ in (6.3 mm) wide. The recess for this was cut with the small Dremel router and only needed to be $3/64$ in (1 mm) deep. Two passes were needed as the cutter was only $1/8$ in (3 mm) wide and, once cut, the segments for the inlay were fitted. There was little point trying to match the grain too well as the burr on these pieces was quite wild and the nature of the grain on the burr meant that it tended to break when handled! I had intended to make the ring from four pieces, but the final count was considerably higher.

The walnut was glued into place with Titebond and left to dry out. Once this had been done and the glue on the inlay was dry, the Dremel router was again used, this time to cut the soundhole. The edges of this were then sanded.

The next stage was to brace the top. The braces were also made from pine from the shed roof. There was one board that I selected that had good, close grain, but this was running parallel to the face making it unsuitable for the top but perfect for the bracing. This was sliced and planed into the various thicknesses that were needed and these were cut to size prior to being glued, and then shaped as described in Chapter 6. The bracing was a fairly conventional cross brace and the bridge plate was made from a piece of purple heart that I found lurking in the back of my father's shed.

THE BACK

The back and sides of the guitar started their working life as the top of a bar in a London pub. This was

The well worn bar of a well worn pub proved to be excellent material.

Although not perfectly quartered, there was enough wood for the back.

The piece chosen for the sides was almost perfectly quarter sawn. The sides were bandsawn from one piece so the grain remained bookmatched. The remaining old varnish was removed when thickness sanding. Note the red push stick ready to be used.

stripped out during some refurbishment and simply thrown out. I was lucky that my neighbour spotted this and rescued it. It was very good quality mahogany and examination of the end grain showed that there was just enough with good grain to make the back and sides. There was not enough width to make a two-piece back, but a three-piece was no problem. This was cut, planed and glued and, when dry, thicknessed.

Many guitars with three-piece backs will have the centre section tapered, but I chose to keep the sections parallel as there is no advantage in tapering them. Since the guitar was to be kept relatively simple I also chose not to inlay the join at all, but to glue the pieces together with no contrasting material between. The quality of the wood was such that the joins are barely visible on the finished guitar.

Once the sections were glued, and the back was cut out, the cross-grain strips that cover the joins were made from mahogany that was left over from the back. Once dry they were shaped as in Chapter 7 and then the positions of the back braces were marked. The back braces were made from the shed roof. I decided to make this guitar with a flat back to keep things easy and it was therefore straightforward to make the braces.

THE SIDES

The sides of the guitar were also from the pub bar top. There was one plank that was about 8 in (203 mm) wide with an extra trim piece glued onto one side. There were also some screw holes in the plank but once the piece had been inspected for any other screws or foreign objects, it was machine-planed to remove the old varnish, revealing a particularly nice piece of mahogany. In fact, the bar has yielded some of the best mahogany I have ever used. Some careful positioning

Thicknessed sides ready to be cut.

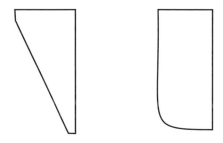

Most commercially-available kerfings are triangular, as on the example on the left, the kerfing for this guitar was made with a simple radius on one edge and this is perfectly acceptable.

The walnut block from the back of an old neck that was used to make the end and neck blocks.

The neck block clamped in place.

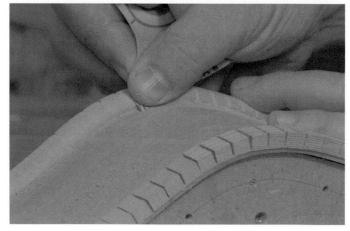

Sanding the kerfing.

meant that all the nail holes could be avoided, and the sides were cut on the bandsaw and then thicknessed to $^1/_{10}$ in (2.5 mm), ready to be bent.

Once they were bent into the mould, the sides were sanded and then the neck and end blocks were prepared. These were made from walnut as there hap-

pened to be the scrap cut from the rear of an electric guitar neck lying around. This was cut to size and glued into place.

Other guitars featured in this book have had kerfing that is factory-produced as it is cost effective and easy

A trial cut was made under the end of the fingerboard to ensure the purfling channel was the right size for the inlay.

The purfling inlay was made by marking the shape of the guitar onto sections of the veneer and then marking a line $1/4$ in (6.3 mm) inside this and cutting with a sharp knife.

The inlay was held in place with tape until the glue, in this case Titebond, dried.

The oak binding on the back of the body.

to use. For this guitar I decided to make it myself, from yet more of the shed roof. This was cut to $3/8 \times 1/4$ in (9.5 × 6.3 mm) and slotted on the workbench. For this I used a piece of wood clamped to the workboard to act as a backstop, positioned so that it was short of the edge of the workboard. This allowed me to cut into the kerfing material using the edge of the backstop as a guide and the edge of the board as a measure. By positioning the previous cut on the edge of the board and cutting against the backstop, each segment was the same size.

With all four pieces cut, the kerfing was glued into place, sanded and carved to shape and the positions of the braces marked so that recesses could be cut for them. The kerfing was not made fully triangular, but was rounded on the inner edge.

The top was fitted first, taking care to ensure it was lined up correctly, and then the back was prepared. The sides were easy to sand to accept the flat back, and this too was glued into place. Once this had been done the mould was split and the complete guitar body removed.

The inlay on the end of the guitar was made from another piece of purple heart. In retrospect it would have been nice to have used a piece of the red wood that was used for the bridge, fingerboard and head facing, but this was not found until after the body of the guitar had been made and time pressures meant choosing something to get the body finished. The wedge was cut and thinned, and a wedge-shaped cut out was made to accept it. The wedge can be fitted before the binding channel is cut, but in this instance I did it afterwards and cut the wedge to fit. If you prefer, it can be fitted and trimmed by the cutter that makes the binding channel.

The binding and purfling channels were cut using a laminate trimmer as described in Chapter 10. The

The two square-section steel rods that were used in the neck.

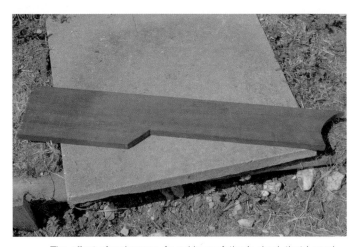

The offcut of mahogany, found in my father's shed, that I used for the neck.

binding was oak strips that were cut off the edge of a piece that was being prepared for some furniture made in the workshop I share. It had been given to me in lengths about 10 ft (3 m) long and measured about $^3/_{32}$ × $^5/_{16}$ in (2 × 8 mm) so was the perfect size for the job. It appeared to be flexible enough but the grain on oak is really a little short for anything that has to bend this much; another wood would have been better, but the oak was free and therefore it was used, and I put up with the odd crack.

Before the binding was fitted the purfling around the edge of the guitar was cut and fitted. After experimenting with several materials to make clever stripes for the inlay around the top, I decided that I would replicate the soundhole inlay around the edge and so carefully cut strips of burr walnut $^1/_4$ in (6.3 mm) wide to a variety of curved shapes. These were fitted into a routed channel just $^3/_{64}$ in (1 mm) deep, so gluing them in was difficult, but the result was pleasing.

The final stage before gluing on the binding was to tidy the edges of the inlay to make it flush with the edge of the top, so that the binding would not foul it. The binding was then glued into place and left to dry.

THE NECK

The neck on the guitar was originally going to come from the same mahogany as the back and sides, but the piece I had proved big enough to make the neck for the 12-string in Chapter 22 and so I searched through piles of scrap wood at my father's house to find a piece of mahogany $^3/_4$ in (19 mm) thick that I had discarded there about 25 years ago. I know it is one that I had cut as the standard of workmanship was about as bad as I remember in that period! It was, however, perfectly seasoned, straight and, like almost all of the rest of the guitar, free.

It was taken to the workshop and cut to give a piece $2^1/_4$ in (57 mm) wide. This gave enough to make a laminated neck as shown in Chapter 2 with pieces being used to build up the heel and make up the head.

Since the guitar was to remain fairly simple I decided not to use an adjustable truss rod, but to brace the neck with steel bars. I was pondering what to use for

The unidentified, but very free, wood used for the fingerboard, bridge and head facing.

this when my old friend Dave Tasker, with whom I share a workshop, pointed out some steel bar samples that had been given to him some time before. Two pieces of this were about 2 ft (610 mm) long and $^1/_4$ in (6.3 mm) square, so two channels were cut into the face of the neck and two pieces of the steel were glued in with epoxy. Two pieces is a little on the overkill side, but the neck will be fine.

THE FINGERBOARD

The fingerboard was proving to be a problem. I had discovered an old pallet in a corner of the store room

When cut and planed it provided the fingerboard, bridge and head facing.

Pushing the filler into the holes drilled in the scrap plastic to make the position dots.

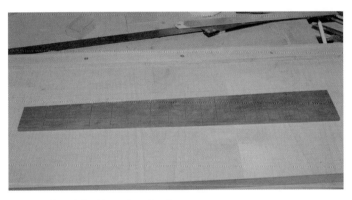

The slotted board on the jig.

Gluing the dots into place.

attached to the workshop that appeared to have some interesting tropical hardwood as one of the slats. I pulled the pallet apart and found this was actually a pretty nasty piece of red softwood that was split and very fibrous, totally unsuited to life as a fingerboard. I tried a few other sources of scrap wood but found nothing that was useable until I went to buy some for another guitar. At the woodyard the foreman understood my need for interesting but free wood and found a piece of an unknown hardwood. It is red in colour, has a close grain and is very hard. I have no idea what it is: it came into the country used as a spacer between boards of Sapele and was long enough to yield a reasonable fingerboard, bridge blank and a head facing. It was at this time that I also realised that I could have used it for the inlay at the bottom of the guitar, but that had already been made.

The fingerboard is not the best piece of wood I have seen but it is straight and hard enough, and with some careful work has turned out OK. It was, however, very good value.

The board was slotted by hand as described in Chapter 15 and the decision had to be made as to what type of dots were to be installed. I looked for various inlay materials and thought about inlaying a veneer, but

the contrast would not have been great and so I opted for dots very similar to those used by Fender on their early rosewood fingerboards. These are known as 'clay' dots and are a distinguishing feature of some early Fenders. I found a commercial wood filler that was about the right colour, which had been bought to cover up some previous 'restoration' on an antique rocking chair my partner had bought. A little of this could be spared to make some dots.

It is not a good idea to just drill, hold and gloop in filler, and then sand it as the filler will tend to seep along the grain and look untidy. Instead, a piece of scrap plastic was found and a series of $1/4$ in (6.3 mm) and $1/8$ in (3 mm) holes were drilled into it. Tape was placed over the back and the filler was spread down into these holes. When dry, the excess on the top was removed with a scraper and the tape was removed from the back of the plastic. The dots were then simply pushed out of the holes using the end of the drill bit

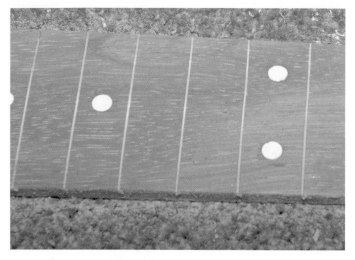

Completed and sanded dots.

Rough shaping the heel.

Gluing the head facing.

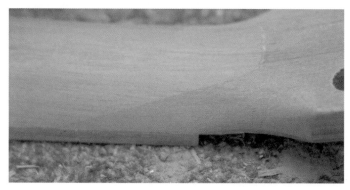

With the neck shaped, the join between the neck and the spliced head can be seen. This is as drawn on the lower diagram on page 118.

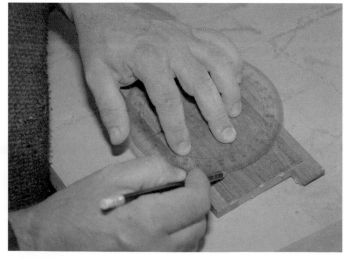

Marking a curve on the top of the head using a protractor.

that made them as a punch. The dots were then glued into holes in the face and sides of the board, and sanded flat.

Although it can be done either way round, in this case the board was radiused before the dots were fitted. This was done so that I could see how much depth I had left on the sides of the board to fit the side position dots. The final thickness of the fingerboard was determined by what could be salvaged from the wood available rather than the ideal depth. In practice this worked out just fine, but had it ended up too thin, I would either have had to discard the board or pack the underside using veneer, which would have been quite acceptable and could have given me contrasting stripes beneath the board.

Before gluing the fingerboard onto the neck, the sides of the head were widened with two pieces of wood and a head facing was added, made from a thin slice of the same wood that had been used for the fingerboard. The head shape was also cut and the thickness of the head checked so that it was uniformly $1/2$ in (12.7 mm) across.

Clamping the neck to the body to check alignment, the neck angle and the fit of the butt join.

Double checking the height of the bridge.

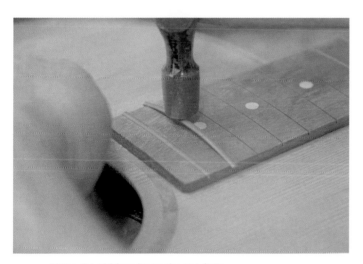

Using the old fretwire on the top frets.

Checking the string alignment.

The neck angle was checked and the measurement transferred to the heel, and then cut before the board was fitted. The fingerboard was then glued onto the neck.

Once this had been done, the heel was first partially carved to give its tapered shape and the fit to the body was once again checked. The neck was then shaped using a variety of tools before being finished with scrapers and sandpaper.

The final job before fitting to the body was to drill the holes for the machine heads. To keep with the spirit of the guitar, these were bought from an internet auction site and, although new, did seem to be made up from a couple of different sets!

The neck join was a simple butt join, attached as shown in Chapter 14, before the fingerboard was once again checked for straightness and the board prepared for fretting.

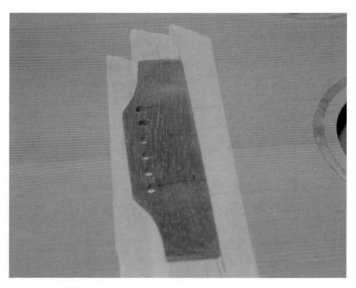

Masking the bridge area prior to spraying.

Masking the sides of the fingerboard prior to grain filling. Only the face of the fingerboard was masked while spraying.

FRETTING

I had thought the fretwire would have to be bought new, but I found some lurking in the back of my own shed that had been bought at least 20 years ago. It was a little tarnished, but a quick attack with some wire wool had it looking fine. The board was fretted as shown in Chapter 15.

The bridge for this guitar was taken from the same wood as the fingerboard and was cut to $6 \times 1^3/8 \times {}^3/8$ in ($152 \times 35 \times 10$ mm), drilled, routed and finally finish sanded. Masking tape was then applied to the front of the guitar as shown in Chapter 16 and the bridge placed and its position marked so that the tape could be trimmed.

The last piece to be added to the guitar before spraying was the top nut and this was made from an offcut of Corian that I obtained from a kitchen-making company.

With this all done, the fingerboard was masked, the mahogany of the guitar grain filled and the guitar readied for spraying. Even the lacquer used was a leftover, in this case from the rebuild of an aeroplane, although I will admit that some had been used on guitars before.

The guitar was sprayed, left to dry and then buffed, the bridge glued into position, the string holes drilled through the top and the saddle slot routed. The inside of the guitar was then vacuumed to remove debris and dust, the heads were fitted and the guitar was strung. The saddle on this guitar was another piece of the Corian from the kitchen company, and this was shaped and then fitted.

The top has proven to be good sounding but a little soft and some early playing marked it, so a scratchplate was made of plastic that proved to be the most expensive part of the guitar other than the strings. The

The finished guitar after some months playing.

scratchplate, machine heads, bridge pins and strings were the only things paid for.

The guitar played reasonably well when first strung, but with a little setting up it has become a very nice little guitar with a rich, balanced sound and quite loud for its size. Because of its parentage, with half coming from a farm and half from a pub, it is nicknamed 'The Drunken Farmer'.

Chapter 22

12-String

The 12-string guitar has a sound all of its own. This is due to it having paired strings, the top two strings being pairs of equally tuned strings and the remaining four pairs being tuned an octave apart. This causes several problems on the guitar. First, and most important from a structural point of view, the extra strings mean extra tension on the neck and across the fingerboard that has to be supported by making the top and neck stronger, but not so strong that the top does not vibrate properly. The extra strings also need to be playable in pairs without making the fingerboard too wide, which means careful design on the fingerboard and bridge. The tuning heads need to be positioned so that the strings do not foul each other, and with 12 strings to deal with this can be tricky without making the head too big.

I have chosen to make a 12-string version of the guitar designed in Chapter 2. There was a time when all 12-strings seemed to be based on big guitars, presumably with the idea that a big guitar will have the bass response to compensate for the extra treble frequencies generated by the octave strings, but this idea has fallen from favour and smaller 12-strings are now much more common, and many of them are very good. They also do not lack in bass response provided that they are made well and some attention is given to not making them too stiff. Having had some good results already with this size of guitar, it will be interesting to see what a 12-string version sounds like and I also have the chance to experiment as I acquired some figured pear wood that will hopefully make a guitar that sounds as good as it looks.

This guitar is to have a $25^1/2$ in (650 mm) scale and a 14-fret (to body join) neck. The neck will be mahogany with a spliced-on head and ebony board bound in maple.

The main difference between this and the other guitars made for the book is that the bracing is made just a little thicker; this is to support the extra tension on the top. There are really three ways of strengthening the top: the top itself can be made thicker or the bracing can be made stronger, or both. Making the top thicker is going to alter the way it will vibrate and a very stiff top may not vibrate as well as one a little thinner. Making the bracing bigger will support the top but

allow the various sections of the top to vibrate in a more normal manner, but the thicker bracings may have a dampening effect on the top and they may not transmit the vibration from the bridge to the top in the same way as thinner ones might. This is an area where little proper research has been done, so the best approach is to try things and develop your own ideas. Needless to say, thickening the top and the braces may give a very strong but bad-sounding top. I have chosen to beef up the bracing but leave the top able to vibrate.

TAPER

The width and taper of the fingerboard is very important if the guitar is to be playable, as the string spacing on 12-string guitars can cause problems. They need to be close enough together to be able to be fretted together but not so close that they rattle against each other. The problem of spacing the strings on the nut is shown in the diagram on page 232. The nut needs to be wide enough so that the strings do not end up almost equally spaced, making it difficult to fret pairs cleanly, yet it does not want to be so wide as to be too much of a stretch to fret anything.

Before starting work it is a very good idea to plan everything full size. This will not only help in deciding the width of the fingerboard at both nut and body end but will also be invaluable in helping plan the string spacing at the nut and bridge.

I have planned for a nut width of $1^{15}/16$ in (47 mm) and the fingerboard will be $2^9/16$ in (64 mm) at the end of the board with the spacing at the bridge being the same; $2^9/16$ in between the outer pairs of strings.

Keeping $1/8$ in (3 mm) between the centres of the strings at the bridge is going to be enough to stop them vibrating into each other but the nut may need some minor adjustments. Having a $1/8$ in string spacing between each pair will use up the available nut space very quickly. Keeping the overall distance between the outer strings the same and slightly varying the space between some pairs will make the guitar more comfortable to play.

With a $1^{15}/16$ in (47 mm) nut width the strings can be inset from the edges by about $1/10$ in (2.5 mm) this

The distance 'A' between any pair of strings on either of the two sets of six will be the same.

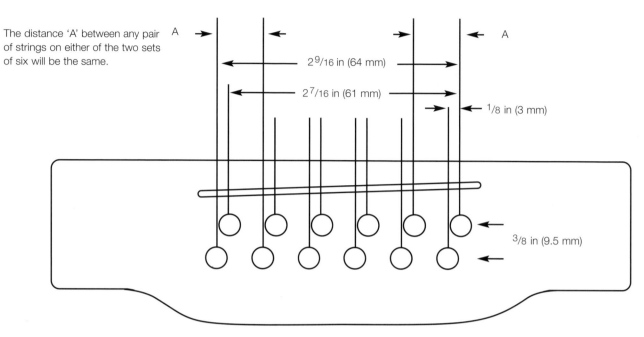

2⁹/16 in (64 mm)

2⁷/16 in (61 mm)

¹/8 in (3 mm)

³/8 in (9.5 mm)

This bridge drawing shows the changes to the bridge shown on page 173. The overall depth of the bridge has been increased to account for the extra bridge pins. These are spaced in two rows ³/8 in (9.5 mm) apart. Finding the distance between the strings is straightforward and easier if you think of them as two sets of six, rather than one set of twelve. Measure the distance between the outer strings and subtract the distance between one set. This will give you the distance between the outer strings of one set of six. Divide this by five to give you the spacing. The spacing will be the same for the other set of six but will start ¹/8 in (3 mm) from the start of the previous set.

is a little less than the ¹/8 in (3mm) I would normally use. This gives 1.65 in (42 mm) between the outer strings. If the pairs of strings were all ¹/8 in apart, then the centres of each pair will be 1¹⁷/32 in, or 1.525 in, or 39 mm apart. This would give a fraction over 0.3 in or 7.8 mm between the centres of each pair. In practice, the pairs can be closer together at the nut than they are at the bridge, with the bottom pairs being 0.1 in (2.5 mm) apart and the treble strings even a little closer, perhaps 0.08 in (2 mm) apart. This will give centres of each pair of 0.31 in (7.9 mm) as can be seen in the nut diagram (*right*).

STRING SPACING ON THE BRIDGE

Working out the positions for the strings and the bridge pins on the bridge is a little more complicated on a 12-string than it is on a six-string guitar. Working out where the outer strings of the outer pairs lie is no different to doing so for a six-string, as the outer strings will be in from the edge of the board in the same way as they are on a six-string; it is just the spacing in between that is different. Instead of dividing the total distance by five you need to separate the two sets of strings.

You could work out how far into the edge of the board the centre of the pairs of strings will be, measure

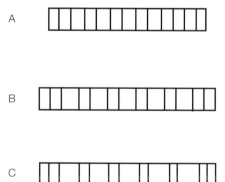

The examples above show the problem of nut spacing on 12-string guitars. Example 'A' has a nut width of 1 ⁵/8 in (42 mm), common on many 6-string guitars. Insetting the strings from the edge of the board by ¹/8 in (3 mm) gives almost uniform string spacing between each string and no discernable difference between the pairs. Clearly playing this would be difficult. The centre example, 'B', has a nut width of 1¹⁵/16 in (47 mm) with the outer strings also ¹/8 in (3 mm) from the edge of the board. The pairs are far easier to separate. The final example, 'C', has been modified to have the outer strings ¹/10 in (2.5 mm) from the edge of the board, with the bass string pairs having a slightly wider spacing than the treble pairs. The centres of each pair remain equidistant.

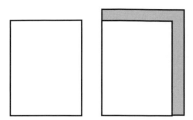

On the left is a rectangle representing the $^3/_8 \times ^1/_2$ in (9.5 × 12.7 mm) cross section of a brace. On the right is a rectangle representing an increase of $^1/_{16}$ in (1.5 mm) on both dimensions. This gives over 30 percent more cross sectional area.

The back trim was maple to give a good contrast with the pearwood.

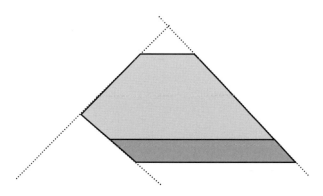

The bridge plate on the 12-string will also need to be bigger. Since the extra set of string pins are $^3/_8$ in (9.5 mm) away from the other set, it really only needs to be this much longer. The inside edges of the brace positions are shown by dotted lines.

the distance between these points and divide by five to give you the centres of each pair and then mark $^1/_{16}$ in (1.5 mm) either side of this point to give you the string positions, or you can take the total available width and subtract the distance between one pair of strings. This can then be divided by five to give the distance between the lower (or upper) of the pairs. The distance between the each string in the other pair will be the same as this but will start $^1/_8$ in (3 mm) past the outer of the already marked positions. This is one of those things in guitar making that is far easier to do than it is to explain. By marking one set from one side and then going back the other way means that a double check is made on the dimensions as the pairs should be equidistantly spaced; if they are not when the last one is marked then there has been a mistake.

MAKING THE GUITAR

The top of the guitar is spruce. It was joined in the normal manner and then sanded on the thicknessing belt sander until it felt right. I would love to give you an

exact measurement but on this piece I can genuinely say it was done by feel: there just seemed to be a point where it was just right. The soundhole inlay was made from some offcuts of coloured purfling material edged with coloured fibre to match the body binding exactly, and was inlaid into a recess cut with a Dremel router.

The main cross braces were made about $^1/_{16}$ in (1.5 mm) larger in width and depth. This may not sound much but if normal ones are $^3/_8$ in (9.5 mm) by $^1/_2$ in (12.7 mm), then adding $^1/_{16}$ in (1.5 mm) to these dimensions gives almost 30 per cent more cross-sectional area and a considerable increase in mass along the main braces.

The main cross braces were made from Douglas fir and they were left rectangular rather than being shaped. The smaller braces were also left rectangular in section. The bridge plate was made slightly larger, from maple.

Back and sides

The back and sides were thicknessed and the back was joined with a piece of the same binding material as used around the soundhole. Because this is thinner than the wood that makes up the back, it is necessary to make sure that it sits correctly in the join. As the three parts are brought together, the inlay must be pushed down to rest against the workboard, so that it sits flush with the rear surface before the wedges and the clamps are finally tightened to join the back.

Once dry, the back was cleaned and the join strengthened with a line of maple; maple was chosen as it looked good against the natural pink colour of the pearwood. The back was braced with a 15 ft (4.7 m) radius and readied to be glued to the sides.

The sides were interesting to bend. I had never bent pearwood before so it was something of an experiment,

Testing the fit of the bent sides in the mould.

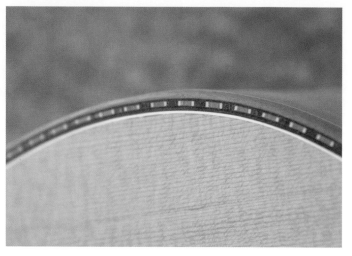

The purfling matched the soundhole.

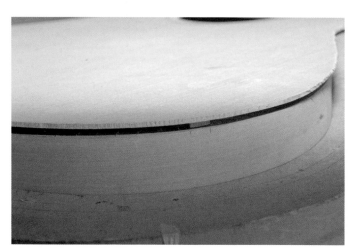

Marking the brace positions.

one of mahogany added to the bottom. When sliced up to make strips of binding it gives a maple stripe inset into the edge. The mahogany was chosen because the colour looked good with the pearwood.

The neck

The neck on the guitar was laminated from mahogany. This is shown in Chapter 11 as an example of how a neck can be made from a small-ish piece of wood. The mahogany used was reclaimed and very good quality. Laminating a neck with a spliced-on head is useful on a 12-string guitar as it removes the need to make a very thick neck blank, as would be the case if the neck was to be cut from a single piece, and it also means that the string tension is parallel to the grain. The neck also has a built-up heel, and this was glued up and then band-sawn to shape.

The neck was not fitted with an adjustable truss rod, but was made with two metal rods for strength. These were $^1/_4$ in (6.3 mm) square, from the same stock acquired for the Drunken Farmer guitar, and epoxied into routed channels that were centred $^3/_{16}$ in (4.5 mm) from the centre line of the neck; thus the inside edge of the channel was $^1/_{16}$ in (1.5 mm) from the centre line and the total width of the strengthening was only $^5/_8 \times ^1/_4$ in (16 × 6.3 mm), so there was no danger of exposing the rods with normal neck shaping.

This head on this guitar was designed so that the strings did not foul any other machine head. The head was drawn full size on a piece of paper and a tapered head design was used to bring the machine heads in towards the centre at the far end of the head. The head is 9 in (229 mm) long, $2^7/_8$ in (75 mm) at its widest point and tapers to $1^7/_8$ in (48 mm).

The head is also faced with two pieces of veneer; one piece of black-dyed veneer on the outside and a piece of maple on the inside giving a thin white stripe

but it bent well and showed no signs of splitting even though there is a small amount of flame in the wood. Once the sides were safely in the mould, the end blocks were fitted and the kerfing added. The bottom inlay was made from an offcut from the sides, edged with more of the binding material, and it looks as if the side goes all the way around the guitar and just has a couple of small inlays at the end. The top and back were then fitted as discussed in Chapter 9.

Binding

With the top and back glued, the binding channel was cut, partly by router and partly by hand, and the binding glued in. The same coloured material used in the back join and the soundhold inlay was used around the top, along with the black/white/black fibre inlay also used around the soundhole. This was then edged with a mahogany binding, made by cutting strips from a block of mahogany that had a veneer of maple and

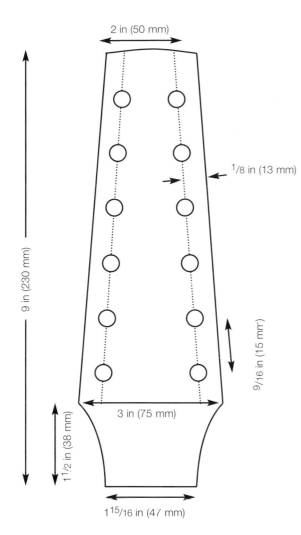

2 in (50 mm)

1/8 in (13 mm)

9 in (230 mm)

9/16 in (15 mm)

3 in (75 mm)

1 1/2 in (38 mm)

1 15/16 in (47 mm)

The head design. It is a simple taper design and this allows the strings to miss the other string posts.

The head marked ready for drilling the machine head holes.

Unlike other guitars in the book, the head facing on the 12-string was not structural but purely decorative being made of a layer of black-dyed veneer with a layer of maple veneer beneath to give a contrasting stripe.

around the side of the head. The head veneer also hides the join across the head where it was laminated as in the upper example shown on page 118.

The fingerboard was cut to width and radiused before being bound with maple strips.

Before gluing the fingerboard to the neck, the neck angle was carefully checked and any adjustments made. Since this was to be a butt join, as some other guitars for this book, this has to be cut before the fingerboard is glued as otherwise any adjustments can be very difficult.

With the board glued onto the neck, the neck was shaped, finish-sanded and double-checked to ensure that it was still lined up correctly. Small brads were knocked into the area where the heel would attach to the body to stop the neck from sliding around when glued, and then it was glued and clamped, with one clamp in the soundhole and a sash clamp holding the rear of the neck.

Once this was dry and with the clamps removed, I decided to fit the board with abalone dots. This would

normally have been done before this stage but I do like guitars with no dots and had thought about making this one that way. Then I found the dots in the box of parts for this guitar and I remembered that I was going to fit them, so they were added late.

The guitar is fretted with quite a thin wire, with the tang cut back to fit between the binding, and once this had been done, attention passed to designing the bridge.

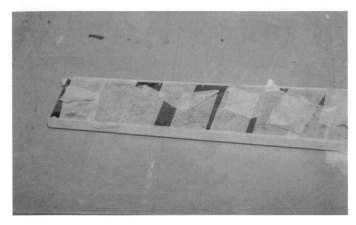

The fingerboard was bound with maple and this was glued on with Titebond and held in place with masking tape until the glue set.

Cutting the nut slots; this can get tricky as there are a lot of strings to deal with. Good marking out at the start is essential.

The finished guitar.

The string spacing had already been decided when designing the guitar, so transferring these measurements to the bridge was not a problem. The bridge was made from a large block of ebony that was bandsawn down to the correct size and finished with a belt sander, scrapers and sandpaper.

Finishing

The guitar was finished in Tru-Oil with a wax polish over the top. The Tru-Oil was applied with paper towels as shown on page 188 and the guitar left to dry out before the wax was applied and the bridge fitted.

The saddle on a 12-string is even more of a compromise than on a six-string, as the compensation difference between the octave strings would mean that the saddles were ideally staggered. This could be done but would be complicated and could look pretty ugly. In practice most 12-strings have a simple one-piece angled saddle, and few people have problems with this.

With frets dressed, tuners fitted, and bridge and saddle made, the guitar was strung and the nut cut. This too is a little more complicated than on a six-string, partly because there are simply more strings to deal with and they can get in the way of each other. The strings were fitted and the outer strings lightly notched into the nut to check the position. The centre of the pairs can be marked on the nut in pencil, with the actual string positions located either side of the marks. It is always a good idea to lightly notch the nut and to let the strings sit in these notches to check the spacing.

With the nut cut, the guitar was strung and the action checked. A little was taken off the saddle to lower the action a little and the guitar was given its final polish.

It is a nicely rounded guitar that is not too harsh and my conclusions are that pearwood not only looks good, but makes good 12-string guitars.

Chapter 23
Cutaways and Electrics

The third guitar has the same basic shape as the 'Drunken Farmer' but is being made with a cutaway and with a built-in pickup and pre-amp.

Cutaways on acoustic guitars are a source of argument among builders and players. They are designed to allow easier access when playing the upper areas of the fingerboard, but some people will argue there is a trade-off in tone and that a guitar with a cutaway will never sound as good as one without.

Since there are so many factors affecting the sound of a guitar this argument is far from cut and dried. Certainly a badly made guitar with no cutaway can sound worse than a nice one with a cutaway, but this will not affect the guitar being made here as it is also going to be compromised by being fitted with various types of electronics.

Electro-acoustic guitars are far from a new idea. It was the need to amplify an acoustic guitar, and the compromises that were necessary, that led to the invention of the solid electric guitar. The solid guitar has, apparently, gained a popularity of its own but there is still a need to amplify an acoustic guitar when playing in large venues or with other, somewhat louder, instruments.

The problem is that the acoustic guitar can be difficult to amplify by using a microphone alone and the guitar can feed back badly if a transducer system is used. For many years a combination of close micing, transducers fitted into the guitar or into the bridge and magnetic pickups have been used.

The introduction of the Ovation electro-acoustics in the early 1970s changed this. The system they used, with separate under-saddle transducers for each string and a pre-amplifier that helped tailor the frequency response of the system, was developed quickly and successfully, and led to other companies putting more research and development into the problem.

By the end of the 1990s, there were a number of systems on the market and some makers had built guitars that were purposely designed not to be as acoustically live as would be the case if they were not relying on pickups for their sound. Gibson marketed the Chet

The uninspiring looking, but very nice, cedar top.

Atkins nylon-stringed guitar that was far closer to being a solid-bodied guitar than a true acoustic, but which was designed to sound like a true acoustic when amplified.

The guitar in this chapter is a combination of ideas. It has a top, back and sides that are not that different to any other acoustic. However, it is made slightly thinner, parallel and with a flat back; this is because its acoustic tone is not so important, as its pickup is in the bridge and is picking up the vibration of the string directly.

The guitar was made in the same mould as the Drunken Farmer with a cedar top, a cherry back and sides, a laminated mahogany neck, a bound rosewood fingerboard with no inlays, a cutaway and a high-quality bridge saddle pickup. The top and back were joined as normal with the back having an inlay along the centre join. The centre trim along the inside of the back was maple.

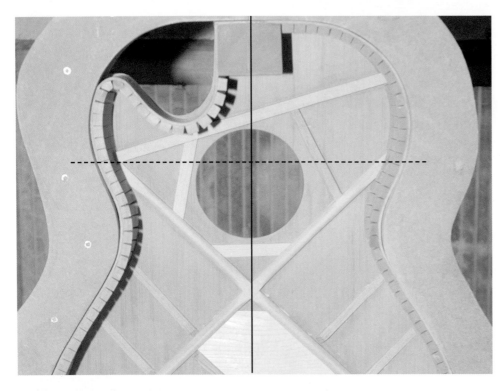

With the transverse brace repositioned to miss the kerfing in the cutaway, the cross braces were also repositioned so that the treble side was pulled back to join the transverse brace. Repositioning the bass side brace to also touch the transverse brace would have been very untidy so a compromise has it roughly in the positoin it would be normally. The join of the cross braces remains over the centre line.

The bracing of the top (which was braced entirely flat) had to be redesigned since the cutaway made it difficult to fit the standard cross-bracing. Instead, an asymmetric bracing system was fitted. The transverse brace, that normally goes across the top just in front of the soundhole, was repositioned at an angle to clear the cutaway. This also meant that the main cross braces were also slightly asymmetric. All internal bracing was made from Douglas fir.

The back was also made flat with three cross braces. These were cut to fit inside the sides.

SIDES

The sides of the guitar were easy in some ways since they were parallel and there was no back arching. However, the inclusion of the cutaway meant that the sides, and the way they were attached to the neck block, had to be altered.

The sides were thinned on the thickness sander and whilst the upper half was bent into the mould one end of the other half was soaked for several hours in a bucket of water. This was to ensure that the part that was to be bent for the cutaway was very wet before work commenced.

The top half of the sides was made slightly longer than normal so that it extended past the centre line and to the edge of the neck block. The neck block was made with a taper to match the fingerboard and was the same width. This was to allow the side to form part of the cutaway flush with the underside of the fingerboard. The join between the two sides was at the edge of the neck block.

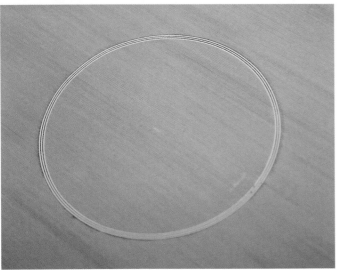

The simple plastic soundhole inlay. This was made of three pieces of plastic binding to make up the full width.

TOP AND BACK

The top was cedar. This had been lying around at home for over 20 years since I bought it – I knew I would use it one day! It had a very simple six-ply plastic inlay around the soundhole. This was made of three pieces of a black and white plastic inlay bought at a parts supplier. The recess was cut with a Dremel router to a diameter of $1/16$ in (1.5 mm) and the plastic was installed and sanded back. Once this had been done the soundhole was cut out to 4 in (102 mm) diameter and the outer shape of the top was cut on the bandsaw.

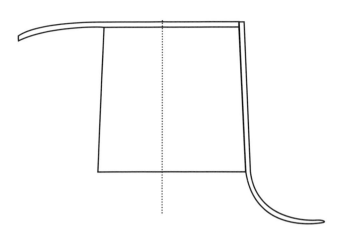

The neck block was tapered to allow the side in the cutaway to match the fingerboard taper. The upper side was not joined to the lower on the centreline but at the edge of the neck block.

The neck block was glued in and the side trimmed to the edge of the block.

The non-cutaway side of the body was extended past the centre line.

The cutaway was bent freehand.

Now, I will admit that the inclusion of the cutaway was a last-minute decision and not something I do that often. Therefore I decided to try making the cutaway freehand rather than drawing and adapting the mould.

With the first side bent into the mould, the second was carefully bent from the lower bout to the waist, ensuring that it conformed to the shape of the mould. With the waist bend complete, the side was carefully bent to the maximum possible with the bending iron. The side was then reversed and the bend that forms the inside of the cutaway made. Both of these bends were fairly severe and the sheet metal backing was used to support the wood on the outside of the bend, but the cherry took the bend well and there was no grain-splitting.

With the side almost complete, the mould was reassembled and the neck block was clamped into

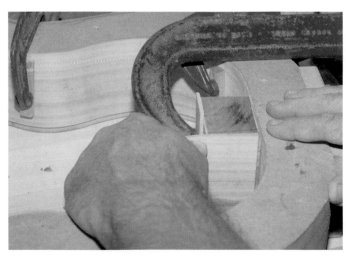

Fitting the cutaway side onto the side of the neck block.

Gluing the cutaway side onto the neck block was interesting. The mould was placed on it's side and two long and sturdy clamping cauls were used to clamp the side to the block using clamps at either end. This meant a certain amount of preparation, to ensure everything was to hand and properly adjusted, and someone was needed to help fit the clamps as one had to be held while the other was tightened.

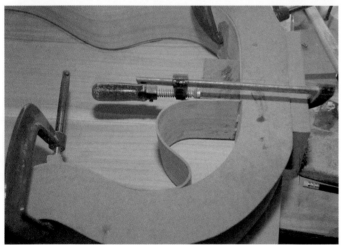

The finished cutaway, still with some glue (that was inaccessible when clamped) to clean off.

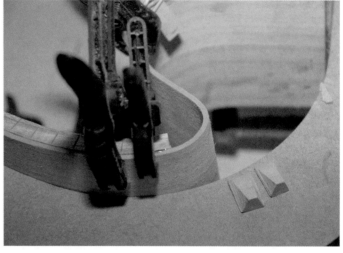

The kerfing in the cutaway had to be modified to fit.

position on top of the upper side. The lower, cutaway, side was then trimmed so that the end butted against the other side on the edge of the neck block and the cutaway remained smooth and even.

This really was a case of 'doing it by eye' but presented no problems. Needless to say, each alteration to the cutaway had an effect on the rest of the side and so constant attention was needed to keep the rest of the side the correct shape, but patience and time, and the occasional cup of coffee while I thought about things, worked wonders.

With the side trimmed, the neck block was glued onto the first side, the first side clamped into the mould and the second side installed carefully; then the end block was glued and the lower side glued to the edge of the neck block.

One aspect of this guitar that needed to be watched was a tendency for the cutaway to pull the neck block at an angle, away from the mould. The remedy for this was to keep it clamped into place.

Kerfing

The kerfing was simple to install over most of the guitar, but was interesting inside the cutaway. I used commercially available pre-slotted kerfing but had to separate each block, reshape them and glue them in around the cutaway. The few that were inside the cutaway 'horn' had the glued side curved to sit comfortably, and had to be trimmed at an angle on the inside so that the pieces did not foul. This also made for problems gluing them into place as, being separate pieces, they

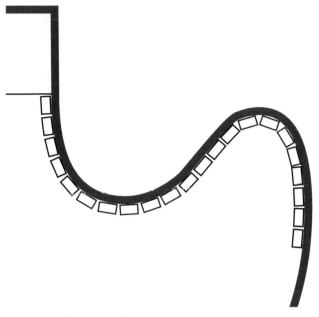

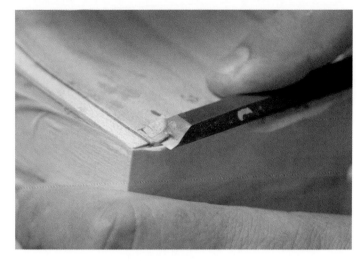

Using a sharp chisel to remove some wood prior to fitting a trim on the join between the sides.

Kerfing is essentially a series of flat-backed blocks that are glued onto a curved surface. The relatively small radius of those curves causes no problems but tighter curves may cause the kerfing to not sit properly or to foul on the next piece. In the diagram above, the red coloured kerfing in the convex part of the cutaway can be seen to have gaps where the radius is too tight while the red marked kerfing in the concave part of the cutaway is fouling on itself and also not sitting correctly.

The finished trim piece.

had a tendency to slip and the pegs and spring clamps used to hold them in place tended to overlap: this meant that only a small part could be completed before it had to be left to dry prior to the next piece being added.

One advantage of making acoustic guitars is that having to wait in this way is not usually a problem as there are plenty of other things that can be done while the kerfing is being glued. In this case, by starting with the sides, the work on the top and back was done while waiting for the kerfing to dry.

ASSEMBLY

With the top, back and sides complete, it was a simple job to join them together. The flat back and top made fitting easy and the guitar seemed to go together almost too quickly.

Once the body was complete, end inlay was fitted and the binding channels were cut and the maple binding bent. Although on some guitars I will happily bend wooden binding without water or heat as the curves are quite gentle, the binding for this guitar was bent around the bending iron so that it would go around the cutaway and horn. In practice this was about the most time-consuming part of the build as the binding kept

cracking. Eventually the time-honoured way of swearing at the guitar and drinking coffee until it behaved itself worked and the binding was glued. This guitar has a similar inlay to that fitted around the soundhole added to the binding. This was plastic and was held in place with superglue while the wooden binding was glued with Titebond. All of this was held in place with tape while the glue dried and the bindings were then scraped and sanded flush with the body.

The join between the two sides on this guitar was not on the centre line – and therefore hidden by the neck, as on many guitars – but was on the edge of the body where the cutaway starts. I decided to inlay this with a small piece of maple, so the area was cleared with a chisel and the inlay glued in.

The last job on the body was to cut the holes to fit the pre-amp that is an integral part of the pickup system.

The two mounting holes for the pre-amp controls.

The finished body.

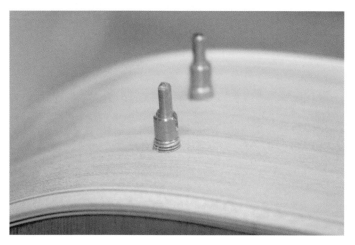

Test fitting the controls into the holes. Enough thread is showing on the shafts to make fitting the nuts easy.

This comes complete with the under-saddle transducer, the pre-amp box, battery clip and end pin jack. The controls can be fitted in a number of places, but the most common are on the upper edge of the guitar close to the waist or on the upper bout close to the neck join, and this is where I chose to put them. The holes were drilled 1.2 in (31.5 mm) apart and were centred on the centre line of the body. The holes were drilled to $^9/_{32}$ in (7 mm) and the unit test fitted.

NECK

The neck on this guitar was laminated from two large pieces of mahogany either side of a central core of mahogany with two pieces of black veneer glued in between. This gave two contrasting stripes along the neck. The block was not quite deep enough to make the heel (*see* p 116) and so an offcut from the block was added beneath the block to make up the extra piece. This offcut came from the piece cut off to make the angle at the front of the head; it was planed flat and the neck was made ready for the truss rod.

This guitar has a single curved rod as invented by Ted McHugh at Gibson in the 1920s. These are not difficult to fit provided that a little time is spent making a jig. The channel was cut in stages and the depth checked at each end and in the centre. Once it was deep enough at the ends to take the rod and the filler strip that holds it all in place, but not too deep at the centre, the slot for the anchor was routed and the recess for the adjustment was made in the head. The rod was then fitted and the curved maple filler strip was glued in to hold the rod in place.

Once this was all dry, the neck shape was bandsawn from the block and the sides of the head were built up with small pieces of mahogany.

The head on this guitar was similar to the 12-string made in Chapter 22, being a slight V shape with three machine head holes per side. Once the side pieces were dry the head facing was glued on, with the position of

The truss rod fillet glued into place.

Bandsawing the head to depth.

Gluing on the sides of the head.

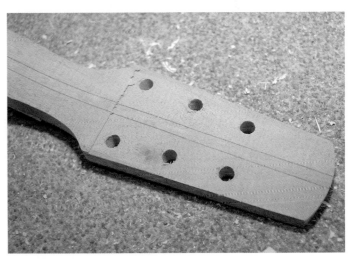

The back of the head ready for sanding.

The partly shaped neck heel.

the truss rod adjustment recess measured and clearly marked before it was glued, and the head shaped. The recess for the truss rod adjustment then needed to be found and cut through the head facing. This could be partially cut before the head facing is glued, but cutting through the head facing to the existing hole often gives a better finish.

Since this guitar was predominantly to be played electrically, the neck was built to be more like an electric

The neck ready for fitting.

The two pieces of rosewood that made up the bridge.

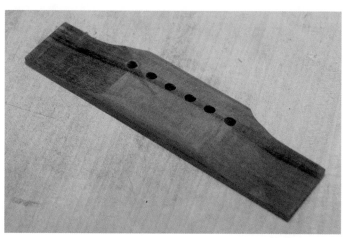

The rough sanded bridge.

The neck was stopped from sliding around when being glued by some small brads filed to a point. Positioning the neck for the first time is important as the holes the brads make are not easy to move!

guitar neck than an acoustic one. This meant a nut width of $1^{11}/_{32}$ in (42 mm) while the fingerboard radius was made to 12 in (305 mm). The board on this guitar was made from a piece of old rosewood and was cut for $25^{1}/_{2}$ in (650 mm) scale. It was bound with the same binding material as the body, and dots were fitted to the edge of the board before the board was glued to the neck.

With the board glued on, the neck was shaped and finish sanded and everything was double-checked before the neck was glued on. This was a butt join, and a couple of small brads were used to position the neck and prevent it from slipping while it was clamped overnight.

The fingerboard was double-checked for levelness before it was fretted. The only problem in fretting was that holding the block inside the guitar, to absorb the impact of the hammer blows, was made a little more difficult by the cutaway.

BRIDGE

The bridge on this guitar was made from rosewood to match the fingerboard. The fingerboard had been made from some old stock Rio rosewood that had been in the workshop for many years; this came from a small batch of fingerboard blanks that were seconds. The one used on the guitar was fine but there was

Wet sanding the guitar with Danish Oil and 1000 grit paper.

The back prior to spraying.

The whole guitar was Danish Oiled.

another that was bent. This was useless as a fingerboard, but since Rio rosewood is, rightly, in short supply, I decided to ensure the bridge and fingerboard on this guitar matched by making the bridge blank from a laminated block. Two pieces of the rosewood were cut from the slightly bent fingerboard blank and glued together, and the bridge made as described in Chapter 16. It is not normal practice to laminate a guitar bridge, but I was feeling revolutionary and it has worked perfectly well.

FINISH

In order to show a variety of finishes, I had decided to spray this guitar in semi-matt lacquer and wax polish it. Since the cherry used on the back and sides was close grained, it did not need grain filling but I sealed it with Danish Oil. This sets in the wood and also brings out the colour of the grain. The guitar was hung and liberally coated with the oil and left to dry overnight. It was then flatted back with 1000 grit paper used wet with

To personalise the guitar it was signed with a gold pen, normally used for writing greetings cards, in between lacquer coats so the final coats sealed it into place.

The pickup and pre-amp as supplied.

Polishing the beeswax with a soft cloth.

The end block was drilled to ¹/₂ in (12.7 mm) to accept the endpin jack.

more of the Danish Oil. The excess was wiped off leaving a very smooth and satin-like finish to the wood that was ideal to spray over. The fingerboard was then masked, the guitar sprayed with 40 percent gloss lacquer and when everything was dry, it was waxed with beeswax and very fine wire wool, and finally polished with a cloth.

FITTING THE PICKUP

The pickup unit on this guitar was made by Headway Electronics in the UK. It is known as the 'Snake' and is supplied with very comprehensive fitting instructions. The pickup itself looks like a short piece of shielded wire and it is important that the wire does not get bent at a sharp angle. This meant that once the saddle slot

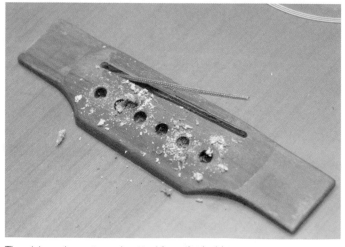

The pickup element was inserted from the inside.

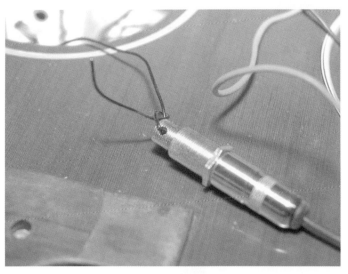

The endpin jack was fitted by inserting a wire into the hole in the end block and tying that to the jack so it could be pulled through the guitar.

The thread on the endpin jack was held in place with a sharp tool while the nut was attached.

The guitar strung and ready to have the scratchplate fitted.

was routed into the guitar, a hole had to be drilled at an angle of no more than 50 degrees through the top. The entire unit comes pre-wired, which makes life quite easy. With the saddle slot routed and the hole drilled, the pickup was pushed into the hole from the inside of the guitar. The small box containing the controls was mounted on the previously drilled holes and the endpin jack was fed through a $^1/2$ in (12.7 mm) hole drilled in the end block.

The battery box is a small leather pouch that is attached on the inside of the guitar with very sticky double-sided tape that is supplied. The only tricky part

is the fitting of the endpin jack. This is fitted at the furthest point fom any access on the guitar and needs to be held while the nut is tightened. The easiest way to get the endpin into place is to feed a wire into the guitar through the endpin hole and pull it out of the soundhole. The endpin can be tied to this and carefully pulled through the guitar so that it emerges out of the hole, taking care not to get anything tangled inside. Installing the nut can also be fun. This needs to be threaded onto the endpin without pushing the endpin back inside the guitar. I find that holding a sharp tool onto the thread as the first couple of turns are made

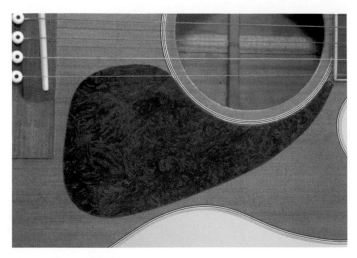

The scratchplate.

with the nut will help a lot. The next stage is to tighten it and the only way is to reach inside the guitar and hold it while the nut is tightened. If you are of heavy build it might be sensible to get someone with smaller arms and hands to do this for you. This was the only time I regretted making the guitar quite as thin as it was. Needless to say this was the guitar's fault for being too thin and not mine for having gained some weight. Once this has all been fitted, the wires inside the guitar can be taped onto the braces or sides to keep them from rattling around.

Headway recommend that either bone or one of the harder man-made materials be used for the saddle, and this has to be a good fit in the slot. If it is too loose the sound of the pickup will be compromised. With the saddle installed, the tuning heads were fitted, the frets were dressed, the guitar was strung and the nut cut.

As with the guitar in Chapter 21, I also decided to make a small scratchplate for this guitar as the cedar on the top is quite soft and might get marked. This was made firstly as a paper template and then cut from scratchplate material with heavy-duty scissors, lightly sanded around the edges to clean up the cuts, and then polished with a soft cloth and metal polish.

This has turned out to be a fun guitar. It is easy to play and because it is relatively thin it is comfortable to play standing up on a strap. It is also very pleasant sounding and well-balanced.

What started as something of an experiment has proven to be a useful guitar and is now gathering a few battle scars.

Chapter 24
Resonators

The Dobro-style 'spider' bridge where the string vibration passes to the edge of the cone.

The National-style 'biscuit' bridge where the string vibration passes to the centre of the cone.

Not all acoustic guitars rely on the vibration of the guitar to produce the sound. During the early years of the 20th century – an interesting time in the development of the guitar – the guitar was moving from being a solo instrument used for accompaniment to being a part of the orchestra. As it did so the need to produce more volume became apparent. This was eventually to lead to the development of the electric guitar and to the high-quality means of amplifying more traditional acoustic guitars, but in the early days this was not an option.

One way to produce more volume is to increase the amount of air moved by the top and to make the guitar bigger. Orville Gibson's attempts to produce hollow necks were all part of a desire to get the guitar to be heard when played with other instruments. The line of evolution shows the flat-top guitar getting bigger, with the Gibson J-200 as the definitive design, and the development of arch-top guitars. These were built as they have greater internal volume, and their f-hole design projects sound from the guitar better than the round-hole, flat-top guitar. People did try to amplify

guitars, but the technology did not really exist for this to happen without howling feedback or problems when the tone of the guitar was lost.

One answer could have been a dead end, were it were not for the fact that these guitars attained a sound all of their own that was perfectly suited to styles of music that were not imagined by the designers. The Dopyera brothers reasoned that a spun aluminium cone installed into the guitar would produce more volume, as the cone would act like a loudspeaker. This is known as a 'resonator' and guitars of this type are often referred to as resonator guitars. The history of these guitars could, and indeed has, filled entire books and so I will not repeat it here, but basically there were two ways of transferring the string vibration to the cone, and these are the result of some extended lawsuits and general bad feeling.

The first guitars had the cone with its apex pointing upwards. It was supported in a circular well within the guitar. The strings were attached to a tailpiece and fed over the bridge, which was a simple wooden saddle attached to what was known as the 'biscuit'; a small,

Sanding the sides in the mould after the end and neck blocks were fitted.

Cutting one of the formers for the sound ring.

circular piece of maple that sat in the centre of the cone. This transferred the vibration of the strings to the cone.

The brothers' National company made wooden- and metal-bodied guitars but a legal dispute with investors led to the Dopyera brothers starting their own company, making similar guitars. Due to the patents for their own invention no longer belonging to them, the brothers had to find an alternative way of using the cone. This was done by attaching the bridge to an aluminium frame, known as the spider, that sat on the edges of a cone with its apex pointing downwards. The new company was known as Dobro (for Dopyera Brothers) and it too made metal- and wooden-bodied instruments, although some people confuse things and refer to all metal-bodied guitars as Dobros and all wooden as Nationals – this is not the case.

There were other designs, such as the National Tricone which, as its name suggests, had three cones, but the main bulk of the instruments made were fitted with either the biscuit or spider style of resonator. Some of these had f-holes in the upper bout or round holes with covers, and some had square necks for playing on the lap.

The resonator guitar did not really sound 'pure' enough to find a lot of use in an orchestral or big-band environment, but the upsurge in popularity of Hawaiian music in the 1930s was to secure its future. When played with a bottleneck or metal slide, the tone of the resonator was perfectly suited to Hawaiian music.

The relative cheapness of the guitars also made them ideal for impoverished blues players and since then, the distinctive sound of the resonator guitar has had a well-established place in popular music.

MAKING A RESONATOR GUITAR

A resonator guitar is actually quite simple to make. Since all the sound comes from the cone, the top is not required to move at all and so it need not be carefully braced. The sides of resonator guitars are also not tapered and both back and front are usually flat, so they are far easier to fit than a domed back or front guitar. The only potentially difficult part is making the circular well into which the cone is placed, but these are available from the same suppliers that make the cones - or you could be clever and make one yourself.

I chose to make a Dobro-style guitar with the spider bridge. The top is spruce and the back and sides are sycamore. This is plain and unfigured as I wanted a very plain-looking, retro-styled instrument. The neck is mahogany and the fingerboard is rosewood. There is no binding along the neck and the fingerboard inlays have been kept simple. Although the top is spruce, it is braced with a $^1/4$ in (6.3 mm) plywood frame inside to stop it vibrating.

The first stage was to make the mould as was detailed in Chapter 3. Each side is made from four pieces of $^3/4$ in (19 mm) MDF, making a total depth of 3 in (77 mm).

The sides of the guitar were made $3^3/8$ in (86 mm) deep. They were cut to depth on the bandsaw and the ends were squared to make fitting into the mould easier. Bending plain maple is relatively simple and with care the body can be produced quite quickly. Once the sides were in the mould, the end blocks were fitted and the kerfing added.

I chose to make the sound ring myself and there are various ways of doing this. One way would be to make the ring from layers of plywood. This is how many

The two halves were fitted with spacers to make up the full depth of the ring.

Bending the first maple laminate. The sapele for the second laminate is waiting it's turn on the workbench, already soaked.

The sides were checked to ensure they were square before the two pieces were screwed and glued together.

Using ratchet straps to hold the laminates in place.

drum shells are made and $^1/_{16}$ in (1.5 mm) ply is usually used. Since the finished ring will have close to $^3/_8$ in (9.5 mm) wall thickness, six pieces will be needed. I chose to make mine from alternate laminates of maple and sapele for no other reason other than that that was what was available as I was making the guitar; I only needed four laminates as they were thicker than $^1/_{16}$ in (1.5 mm). In retrospect, plywood would have been easier.

The first stage is to made a mould for the ring. In this case the ring will be made on the outside of the mould. The inside diameter of this needs to be 10 in (250 mm) for the spider-style cone, so a router was used with a circle-cutting attachment to cut two pieces of $^3/_8$ in (9.5 mm) MDF. The first of these then had four spacers screwed to it so that the final height, with the other circle, would be $3^9/_{64}$ in (80 mm, this being

one case when working in metric is actually much easier). This is so that the ring will fit inside the plywood strengthener as that is $^1/_4$ in (6 mm) thick.

It is possible to make the mould so that the ring is made on the inside. This works for some drum makers but requires very accurate cutting and fitting of the plies, because if they do not fit exactly into the mould the laminates might not be fully circular.

With the mould ready to go, the four laminates were cut. These need to be different lengths since the diameter of the piece will alter as each one goes onto the mould. The lengths are simple enough to work out as a 10 in circle will require 31.41 in (10 x Pi (3.141)), although if making them, as I did, from solid wood you might want to make them slightly longer and cut them to length as they are fitted onto the mould. This is not

The workboard was marked with eight lines that represented the centres of the holes that were to be drilled.

The positions were marked on the side of the ring and the line extended, using a square, to the centre of the ring.

A circle cutter was used to cut the eight holes, taking care not to cause any grain breakout on the inside.

just because you can get a better join, but also because it is not easy to bend all the way to the end of a piece and having the extra will prevent the ends from being too flat.

The laminates were also made slightly deeper than the 3⁹/₆₄ in (80 mm) needed for the guitar, so that they could be trimmed to fit.

The first laminate on the guitar was made from maple. This was just over 0.9 in (2.2 mm) thick and was bent to shape using the bending iron. Making a true circle with the bending iron is not easy, but with some care it is possible to get close enough as it will take up its proper shape when put onto the mould. As with bending the guitar sides, the wood will spring back a little, so it is best to bend to a tighter radius so that it springs back, when cold, to roughly the correct diameter.

The first laminate was left to dry and cool with clamps holding it to the tighter radius while the second laminate was bent. This was made from sapele and was a little thinner as it was from a piece that had been sanded down for use as guitar sides, but for which I could not find a matching back. As a result I decided to use the sides in the ring.

With the first two laminates bent, dried and cooled, they were cut to length and then glued. The ends of the laminates could be bevelled to make a cleaner join, but they can also be butt-joined. In this particular case, the fact that the mould is not continuous, but has a top and bottom piece with spacers between it, would make it difficult to make the bevelled edges lie flat. Whichever way is chosen, it is a good idea to stagger the joins of each laminate around the mould, so if the first is at 0 degrees, the second can be at 180 degrees, the third at 90 and the last at 270 degrees: this way each pair of laminates has joins that are at least 90 degrees different.

As with gluing anything against a mould, the first stage is to make sure that only the pieces you want to glue get glued, so candle wax was rubbed onto any area that might get glue spillage. The first laminate was then placed onto the mould and glue spread on its outside. The second piece was then placed onto this and clamps applied.

There are several ways of clamping the piece. For this guitar, which I will admit is the first of this type I have made, I used webbing ratchet straps. These apply a fairly even pressure over most of the circle, but the ratchet makes it difficult to get the final part completely flat. An alternative is to use hose clamps. These can be bought in a variety of diameters, and using three or four on the mould is a better way of applying the pressure than using ratchet straps.

The first two laminates were left to dry out overnight and then readied to take the third laminate. This too was glued and clamped. The final laminate was then glued and when it was dry, the laminates were trimmed back to the edges of the mould using a smoothing plane.

Making a plywood ring is a little easier as it is possible to cut the plywood so that it is bent across the grain, rather than along it as was the case with the wooden plies. My good friend Andy Morris, the drum maker, uses an inside mould and this is just as simple to make as the outside mould that I used. Two pieces of MDF are used with the hole cut using a router. The sizing needs some thought. When drum making what you are interested in is the outside diameter of the drum. For a tone ring it is the inside diameter that is important, so the diameter of the circle needs to be estimated. If the inside diameter of the ring needs to be 10 in, then the outer diameter needs to be 10 in plus the width of the plies. Six pieces of $1/16$ in (1.5 mm) ply will give a ring with a wall thickness of $3/8$ in (9.5 mm) and since this is added to both sides of the circle, the diameter will need to be 10 in plus the two sides, making a total diameter of $10^3/4$ in (275 mm). Again, cutting the plies to length is a simple case of multiplying the diameter by Pi.

Andy makes his drum moulds with a top and bottom piece of $3/4$ in (19 mm) MDF, and these are separated by spacers that are cut to length to give the correct height for the drum, or tone ring, on the inside faces of the mould; they are then screwed into place so that the spacer also acts as a support for the edge of the ply that is being glued. These are positioned at 90-degree intervals, as Andy usually uses four plies in his drums, so that the joins can be staggered.

The plies can be cut roughly to length and placed into the mould. The point where they overlap can be marked and a little extra, perhaps $1/8$ in (3 mm) added to allow for the fact the ply will not fit exactly into the mould when just being held in place. The piece is then cut to length and, in theory, if the two cut edges are placed together the piece will just snap into the mould exactly circular. In practice it may need a little trimming, which can be done with a very sharp knife or small saw, and the piece fitted again, taking care to keep all cuts square.

Once the ring had been allowed to dry, it was removed from the mould and cleaned up. It was then marked to take eight holes around the diameter. These allow the sound out of the ring into the rest of the guitar and were cut to 2 in (51 mm) diameter. The first stage is to mark the eight positions around the ring. For this a datum line is drawn onto a workboard and another line at 90 degrees is drawn on to intersect this. The 45-degree positions can also be drawn on so that eight lines radiate from a centre point. The outer diameter of the ring was measured and this distance halved. This measurement was then transferred to each of the four diagonals so that the distance from the centre to the mark was the same all the way around. The ring was then placed onto the workboard using these marks on the diagonals to centre it. The positions of the lines were then marked onto the ring to give eight equidistant marks around the circumference. These were then

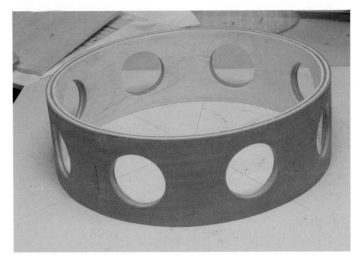

The ring with all eight holes drilled.

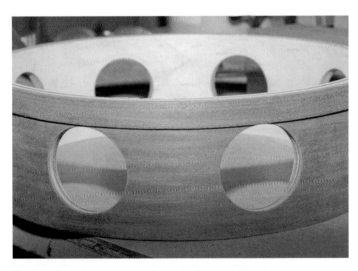

The top of the ring was strengthened with an additional piece of sapele, bent and glued.

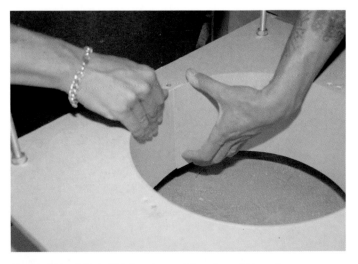

My good friend Andy Morris using an internal mould to make a plywood drum shell. The plies have to be cut very accurately.

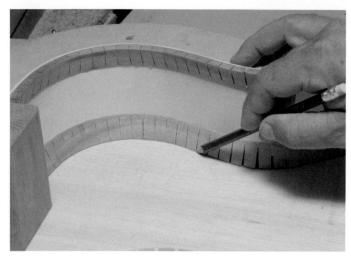

Marking the inside of the kerfing onto a piece of plywood that will strengthen and support the top.

Using a variety of clamps and cauls to glue the plywood to the top.

extended across the side of the ring using a square, and the centre of the ring was measured and marked half way up this line. These are the centres for each of the eight holes.

The holes were made with a circle cutter in a hand-held electric drill. The trick is to take things easy and not to try to force the saw through the wood. The centre drill bit will break through long before the saw has cut through the piece, and this hole can be used to help prevent splitting on the inside. Simply remove the hole saw from the drill chuck and use it by hand from the inside of the ring. It is not easy to rotate and takes some effort, but by cutting part way from the inside as well as the outside a cleaner hole will result.

With a clear indent on the inside, the hole saw can go back into the chuck to complete the cut from the outside. Once all eight holes have been cut, they can be cleaned up with sandpaper.

The top, and sometimes the bottom, of the tone ring may need to be thickened a little. The cone will sit in a recess made into the top of the guitar and, since there will be a small amount of play around the cone, the recess in the top will come very close to the edge of the ring. It is a simple job to add an additional ply around the top that is only $3/8$ in (9.5 mm) or $1/2$ in (12.7 mm) deep to strengthen this area. Doing the same on the back will give more gluing area between the ring and the back.

The additional piece was glued onto the ring using a number of small spring clamps and left overnight to dry.

THE TOP

The next stage was to make the top. This started as a normal guitar top bought from a guitar parts suppliers. It was glued together and sanded to depth, but for

some reason never got used and spent over ten years sitting at my home.

The mould had been used to mark the shape before the sides and kerfing were installed and the shape was cut out using a bandsaw. As the top on resonators is not designed to vibrate in the same way as on a normal acoustic guitar, it was strengthened with a backing piece of $1/4$ in (6.3 mm) plywood. This was marked by using the mould with the sides and kerfing in place, so that the plywood would fit inside the kerfing. The top and its plywood strengthener were then glued together; this gave a top that is almost $3/8$ in (9.5 mm) thick. The top was then glued onto the sides.

The next stage was to mark the front to accept the cone. The guitar was to be a 14-fret model and so the fretting tables were used to give the remainder measurement, the distance from the neck-to-body join to the bridge. Since the bridge is right at the centre of the cone, the centre of the circle would be the bridge position. In theory. In practice I moved the centre of the cone back about $3/32$ in (2 mm) so that the cone and spider could be rotated to give better intonation when the guitar was played conventionally. This would allow the treble side of the saddle to rotate close to the $25 1/2$ in (650 mm) point while the bass side moved back about $3/16$ in (5 mm) for better intonation.

With the bridge position marked, a router was used to remove the waste. The first stage was to rout a circle with $10 1/2$ in (266 mm) diameter to a depth of $1/4$ in (6.3 mm) to take the lip of the cone. The circle fence was then adjusted to give a diameter of 10 in, and this corresponded to the inside diameter of the ring.

This circle needed to be cut very carefully. Since the circle fence was fixed to the centre of the piece that would end up being waste, it is a little like sitting on the branch of a tree while you cut it close to the trunk! As the final cut is made, the piece the router is attached to

Drilling a pilot hole in the centre of the cone position.

The cone and spider were also placed in to check all the measurements.

Preparing to rout the hole; a deep breath was needed before starting this.

The ring was clamped to the top using spring clamps through the soundholes.

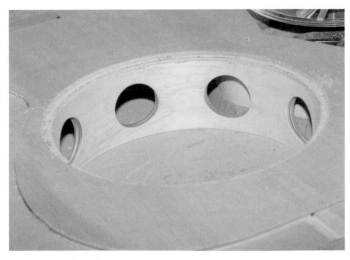

The ring was positioned into the hole to ensure that everything lined up.

Marking the top bout to take the soundholes.

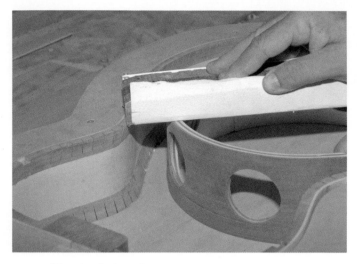

Trimming the tone ring.

Bracing the back was simple as there was just one transverse brace.

will break free, and you can make a nasty mess of the guitar if this happens suddenly. You could use the circle fence to make a routing jig that is basically a 10 in diameter circle. A follower bit can then be used to cut through the top with no danger of digging in, but the router may be difficult to balance on the edge of the jig. Both methods have potential pitfalls.

With the holes cut, the ring can be glued onto the inside of the top. It is a relatively simple job to line this up with the hole and I used spring clamps to hold it in place. Eight of these placed through the tone holes were enough to give a good join.

The final job on the top is to mark and cut the holes for the soundhole inserts that are a feature of the guitar. These are $2^1/8$ in (54 mm) in diameter and were cut with a hole saw. The inserts for these holes were bought at the same time as the cone and other hardware, and are a simple push fit.

THE BACK

Before the back can be glued on, the tone ring needs to be trimmed so that it is exactly the same depth as the rest of the guitar. A straightedge can be used to highlight the high points: these can be trimmed with a smoothing plane and finally with a sanding stick used across the sides and tone ring.

The back of the guitar is as simple as the rest. There is no centre inlay and the wood is a plain piece of maple. Just one cross piece was added, across the upper bout of the guitar, and this was trimmed to fit and the kerfing recessed to accept it.

Gluing a flat back onto a guitar is pretty easy. Tape was used around the edges, but the guitar was placed face down on a workboard with a weight on the back over the tone ring so this too would glue well.

Cutting the binding channels on a flat and parallel guitar is about as easy as it gets. The first pass cut the

Cutting the binding channels was easy; the binding was maple and mahogany with a black/white/black purfling. Cutting the channels is much easier if it is done before the cone well is cut as the router will have more area on which to sit.

recess for the main binding, and the only piece of decoration on the guitar – a simple black/white/black fibre purfling – was installed into a second recess. Once the glue on this had dried it was scraped and sanded smooth, and the guitar body was finish sanded.

THE NECK

The neck design on many resonator guitars differs from normal acoustic practice as the neck will often pass right through the instrument, to be anchored at the tailblock. On this guitar I chose to make a conventional neck join with a tenon into a slot on the body.

The neck was laminated from a central core of maple with sapele either side, making a central core of $5/8$ in (16 mm) with mahogany either side making up

The tone well of a metal-bodied National-style resonator. This does not extend all the way into the guitar as on the Dobro-style made in the book. The neck extension, that carried on to the end pin, can also be seen.

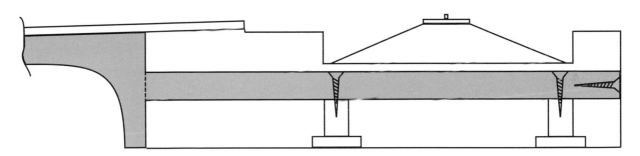

The diagram above shows how, on some resonator guitars, the neck is extended through the body and supported on wooden blocks.

the rest. This was glued and left overnight, and then faced on the planer. The piece was deep enough to accommodate the head without having to splice it. It was not quite deep enough for the heel, although this was not a problem as a small piece of the scrap could be cut and glued on to match.

The first stage was to mark the side elevation of the neck and then cut the front face of the head. This was then planed flat. The head shape was also marked and the centre line, nut position and fingerboard taper marked on the face.

The truss rod on this guitar is a twin rod that required a slot $1/4$ in (6.3 mm) by $3/8$ in (9.5 mm). This also needed to have some additional depth where the adjuster is, but this was routed into the face of the neck without any problems. The access hole in the front of the head was left until the head facing had been glued on, and this could not be done until the head had had a small piece of mahogany glued to each side to make up the full width after the neck had been bandsawn from the blank. The side elevation had been marked

onto the neck earlier and this was followed with the bandsaw. The two pieces required to make the head full width were cut from the waste removed when the side elevation was cut. The taper of the neck and shape of head were also cut on the bandsaw.

NECK ANGLE

The resonator cone on the Dobro-style instrument requires a fair amount of down-pressure from the strings. The only way to achieve this is to angle the neck back a little further than would normally be the case, so that the strings form as sharp an angle as possible over the saddle. In practice this angle is limited by the cover plate that sits over the resonator, as this has a raised hand rest that the strings pass underneath.

Checking the neck angle using a block the same depth as the fingerboard and frets at the neck join, a straightedge between that and the bridge, and an angle gauge to check the angle and transfer that to the neck.

The neck mortice was cut through the sides using a Japanese saw to cut into some drilled holes.

Gluing the 0.1 in (2.5 mm) block onto the end of the fingerboard. This was tapered to a wedge when it was dry.

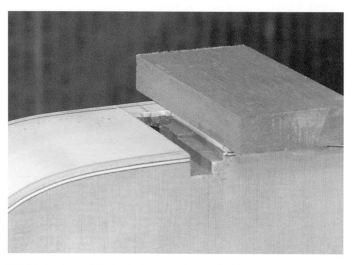

The block of wood that acted as an edge guide. This would have been impossible to use if the guitar had not had a straight portion on the sides leading up to the join.

Having the saddle too high and the neck angle too great would mean the strings would foul on this.

In order to work out the optimum angle, I made a false bridge saddle from a piece of wood and placed the resonator into the well on the body. The fingerboard for this guitar was a pre-slotted rosewood board and this was used to estimate the angle. By placing a straightedge on the fingerboard and placing the fingerboard so that it joined the body at the 14th fret, the board could be angled back to give a suitable height at the bridge. The height of the frets and the eventual string action needed to be taken into consideration, but I estimated that the end of the fingerboard would have to be raised above the face of the guitar by 0.1 in (2.5 mm) to give a good break angle at the bridge. I then removed the fingerboard, placed a

block 0.1 in (2.5 mm) high at the proposed end position of the fingerboard and measured the angle between this and the end of the guitar. This gave me the required angle that had to be cut into the heel to allow the neck to sit back properly.

This angle was marked either side of the heel in the correct position and the neck angle was sawn using a sharp Japanese-style saw. The cut was not made all the way through the neck, but stopped at the centre three laminations in the neck. This gave a ⅝ in (16 mm) wide tenon to fit into the body.

The slot to accept the tenon was marked onto the end of the guitar. It is possible to cut this using hand tools, but I made up a very simple jig to allow me to rout the channel. This was nothing more than a block of wood with a straight edge fixed to the guitar with

Resonators

259

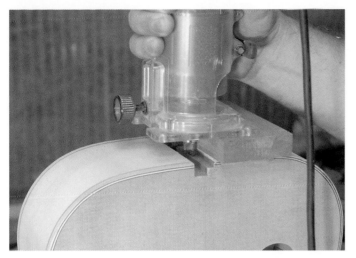

The laminate trimmer with a follower bit was used to deepen the mortice into the neck block.

The neck angle was also checked before the neck was shaped as final adjustments are easier.

Checking the alignment of the neck.

The side dots on the fingerboard extension showing the wedge beneath.

double-sided tape so that a follower bit could be used to cut one side of the slot. It was equally simple to remove the block, reposition it on the other side of the guitar and cut the other side of the slot. The whole procedure took less than half an hour and gave an accurate mortice. The neck was then trial-fitted to ensure that the centre line of the neck and the centre line of the body matched, and that the neck-to-body join was snug. Some light work with a chisel on the sawn parts of the tenon and a little work on the inside of the slot were enough to ensure a good join.

Since the fingerboard was to be angled over the front of the guitar, the underside needed to be supported with a wedge of wood. This could be cut as a wedge and glued on, but making very thin wedges is not for everyone. I find it far easier to glue a 0.1 in (2.5 mm) piece of wood to the end of the fingerboard and then to taper it. With the fingerboard held securely face-down on the workboard or bench, sharp chisels can be used to cut a good angle. Careful checking is required with a straightedge, but the job is not difficult.

The fingerboard also had its position dots fitted to the face and the sides before being fitted to the neck.

For this guitar I chose to partly shape the heel before fitting the fingerboard, as it is often easier to clamp the neck face-down on a workboard while shaping and doing so can damage a fingerboard. With this done a final check was made on the neck-to-body join and on the fingerboard angle, before fingerboard was glued to the neck, making sure to check that the alignment of the neck and body centre lines were carried onto the fingerboard.

Only the neck on this guitar was grain filled with the maple of the sides being masked to stop the dark filler staining the wood.

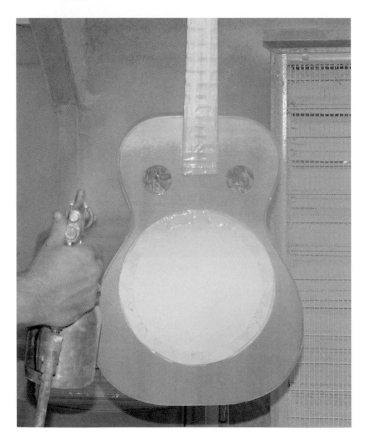

Spraying the yellow of the sunburst.

The sunburst was built up gradually.

With the fingerboard dry the neck was shaped. As is my habit, this was done with a combination of surforms, spokeshaves and scraper blades.

The final job before gluing the neck to the body was to drill the machine head holes. These were marked and drilled with a 10 mm bit on the drill press.

The neck-to-body join was made by clamping the fingerboard extension through the two small soundholes in the upper bout and, as the neck was a fairly tight fit in the neck slot, it was simply held in place with a ratchet strap with the ratchet positioned over the waist so that it did not touch the sides. All glue residue was cleaned off and the area sanded.

The next stage was to fret the guitar. This is covered elsewhere in the book and there were generally no problems, except that it was hard to keep the underside of the fingerboard over the body supported while knocking the frets in.

With all frets in and the ends trimmed, the guitar was subjected to a lot of finish sanding before the body was masked and the mahogany part of the neck grain filled. This was sanded flat and the binding was masked before the guitar was hung in the spraybooth.

I chose to finish this guitar in a vintage-style sunburst finish, so the first stage was to spray the guitar

Access to the saddle to adjust the action is not easy and requires the guitar to be destrung and the coverplate removed each time.

The soundhole covers on the Dobro are a push fit. Some models used f-holes at this position.

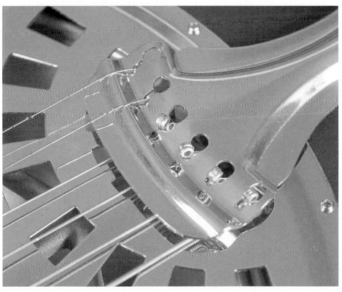

The cone needs to have some down pressure on the saddle to work at its best. This can be improved by fitting the strings as above as it increases the string break angle over the saddle.

with a clear coat to seal everything and then to spray it yellow. This does not have to be an overall coat as the edges of the top and back, and areas on the sides, will be oversprayed brown, but the front and back and the areas on the edges of the upper and lower bout were sprayed yellow, as was the centre area of the neck.

Once this was dry the sunburst was sprayed on in a dark brown stain. With both the yellow and the brown the stain was suspended in the lacquer and a great deal of care was taken not to get any drips. It is far better to

have to add a little more colour than to try to remove an ugly drip.

Once I was satisfied the sunburst was suitably vintage-looking, I left the guitar to dry out overnight and then returned to remove the masking on the binding. This is where the original clear coat proved its worth, as the front face of the binding was not masked and so needed to be scraped back using a sharp craft knife blade. Had the stain gone directly onto bare wood, this would have been much more difficult.

The area of the binding that was masked also needed to be cleaned up as there was inevitably some seepage underneath the tape. This takes time and can be frustrating, but it is worth doing a good job.

There are times when the blade will remove a little more than is required and so it may be necessary to touch up the colour in these areas.

With the binding cleaned up, the fingerboard edges were unmasked and cleaned up where necessary, and the guitar was given several clear coats, being rubbed down between.

The final stage of the finishing was to wet-sand the whole guitar with 1000 grit wet and dry, as if the guitar was to be polished to a high gloss. Once this was completed, the guitar was rubbed with very fine steel wool and beeswax to give a satin finish on the lacquer. The wire wool will leave very fine scratches in the finish and so all rubbing must be done with this in mind: the scratches must be kept going in the same direction. With a little care, a good satin finish can be achieved to create a guitar that looks as if it has been around for some time.

After a levelling of the frets, the guitar was assembled. The resonator cone was dropped into place after the spider had been bolted to it: there is a bolt that goes vertically through the centre of the spider and into the cone.

Setting up the resonator takes a little more effort as the cover plate has to come off before the saddle height can be adjusted, and the strings have to be taken on and off to allow this. Resonator guitars were not designed with ease of access in mind!

Since the spider-style of resonator requires a fair amount of down-pressure on the saddle, the angle where the string drops down to meet the tailpiece needs to be as great as is possible. Getting a compromise between a low action and a good string angle is a struggle, but since this guitar is being set up to play slide then it is not so great a problem. The angle can be helped by stringing the guitar so the string goes through and under the tailpiece, rather than being dropped in from above and taken over it. This is also not an easy option since the tailpiece sits very close to the resonator cover plate and the string is hard to get though the gap. The string slots in the tailpiece are also prone to having sharp edges, which can be filed down, and have a shape that makes them bear on the weakest part of the string, that is the winding near the ball end. This can cause the string to fail there, and on this guitar they did from time to time. In the end I came to a compromise where the wound strings go through and under the tailpiece, and the two unwound strings are fed in from the top.

All guitar set-ups are a compromise between what the guitar can physically manage and what the player requires, and somewhere between those two things there will be an optimum. With a little care, and it must be said a few broken strings, the resonator was ready to play. It was only then that I realised that I had not fitted a truss rod cover, so one was made from a piece of what is known often as 'Mother of Toilet Seat'. This is pearloid plastic that is made to resemble mother of pearl. It can look quite convincing or quite tacky, and this was one of those occasions when tacky is best!

All this guitar needs now is a bottleneck made from an old Jack Daniels bottle (although my glass bottleneck is made from a Courvoisier brandy bottle) and the player to be seated on a rocking chair overlooking the Mississippi. This is unlikely since I live near to the river Arun in England and "Arun Delta Blues" is not as widely recognised as "Mississippi Delta Blues", but the guitar does sound convincingly authentic and plays well.

The completed guitar.

Chapter 25
Martin Factory Visit

The author standing outside the old Martin factory in Nazareth in 2000. The building is now a Pennsylvania Historic Site and also the home of Guitarmaker's Connection, the Martin-owned parts and wood supply company.

The C.F. Martin factory in Nazareth, Pennsylvania produces a mind-numbing number of guitars each year, and although they use many very modern and complicated machines, they still employ a large number of very skilled people who do a lot of the work by hand. Martin guitars are not just churned out by machines: a great deal of care and attention goes into the manufacture. I was very privileged to be given access to the factory and I was fascinated to see that although they make a lot of guitars, the traditions of the company and pretty well all the old skills are alive and well, and being used on a daily basis.

Although this book is primarily about how to make your own guitar, I felt it would be useful to look at the methods employed by companies engaged in large-scale production, as there are no doubt lessons to be learned and techniques that can be adapted.

To this end, C.F. Martin and Co. was kind enough to allow me to visit the factory and ask as many questions as I pleased about its operation and processes, and I am indebted to it for its assistance in the preparation of this chapter.

Martin have been building guitars in the Pennsylvania town of Nazareth since 1859 and, at the time of writing, produce somewhere in the region of 250 guitars per day ranging from lower-priced models, some of which feature some unusual materials, to the high-end guitars such as the D-45.

Due to the volume of production, it is economical for Martin to season and prepare their own wood stocks, and a large area of the factory is given over to this. Tonewoods are stored to acclimatise and Martin has its own kilns so it can control the moisture content of all of its wood. When the wood has dried and has

Part of the extensive wood storage area at Martin.

The two rotating top and back gluing jigs. One has been at the factory for many years and was so useful another was made as a copy.

One of the thicknessing sanders used on backs, sides and tops.

had time to settle, it is rough-cut for whatever part of the guitar it is destined for. These parts are then numbered and stored in a climate-controlled room for several months to settle further. It is at this stage that the various components are inspected and selected for the level of guitar they will be used for. For example, some custom necks are made one-piece while most mahogany neck models now have the sides of the head built up. The quality of the wood needs to be assessed before the final cutting is done so that the high-end necks are cut wide enough.

The serial number of a Martin guitar is allocated very early in the build process. Model type, level of decoration and serial number are all added to a computer record that follows the guitar around the factory. Each and every process on the guitar is barcoded so that a complete time, cost and location is captured for every component.

When the wood leaves the quarantine store it is again inspected. Necks will go off to their line and the bodies will begin their journey through the factory.

TOPS

The tops are prepared for joining and the join is checked on a light box. The two halves are placed together under a little gentle pressure and the light underneath will show up any gaps in the top join. They are then glued together on a large rotating jig that can hold a number of tops. Since all tops in a batch are trimmed to a rectangular shape, the clamps on the jig are easily set.

Rosetted tops are allowed to dry in the racks behind, each one already having been assigned to a specific serial number.

Matching the colour and grain on side sets with backs.

Tops are shaped with a lug on each side to allow accurate positioning on the jigs. One of the vacuum clamps for gluing braces can be seen in the background.

Martin is constantly inspecting and updating its procedures, but this does not mean that it will discard equipment that works. The rotating-top gluing jig is a case in point. This is an old machine but it does its job so well that another, identical, jig has been made to double the production. It was so well thought-out first time around that it did not need changing. Martin also has an engineering section that designs and makes all the jigs and specialist machines that it uses.

When the tops are dry, they are again inspected and then sanded to thickness. This is done on large belt sanders that are very accurate and which produce tops of a very even thickness. The tops are then mounted into a computer-controlled router that cuts the sound-hole inlay and the overall shape, according to which model the guitar is. The top is also cut to shape but with a lug on either side at the waist with a hole through it that can be used to mount the top in jigs later in the production process.

BACKS

Before the backs are glued they pass to an area where they are laid out on a long table to be matched with sets of sides. It is impossible to guarantee that the backs and sides of one guitar will come from the same tree, and even if they did there could be considerable colour variation, so the backs and sides are matched for most even grain pattern and colour. They are then assigned to a particular guitar so that even if they travel through the factory on slightly different routes, their computer record will ensure that they meet up to become the same guitar at a later point.

Backs are also glued on the rotating jigs, but these may also have an inlay strip glued between the two

Sets of bracing material, which have been banded together by serial number, wait on top of one of the vacuum clamps to be mated with their tops.

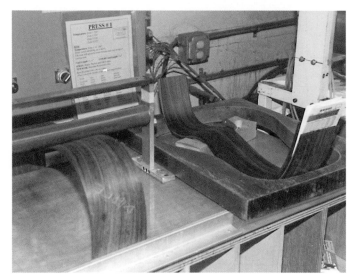

Once bent, the sides are placed in a mould.

A spring jig used for bending sides with cutaways.

halves. Once glued, the backs also go through the sanding machine and are routed to shape.

Most cutting operations are made with computer-controlled machinery, which is not only accurate but also ensures that all parts for a batch of guitars are the same, making their installation into various jigs much easier.

BRACING

As with the other parts of the guitar, the bracing material has been allocated to the guitar at an early stage and is cut accurately on the computer-controlled machinery. The bracings on the top are glued on in an operation that is typical of the way Martin operates. It has used a variety of methods over the years, but has

now settled on atmospheric pressure using vacuum bags. The bracings are placed into recesses in a jig and are glued using a roller to apply the glue, which makes sure that just enough glue is used and that it only ends up where it should. The top is positioned on the jig using the holes in the side lugs that were routed earlier, and then placed on the braces. A cover is then brought down and all the air in the jig is pumped out with a vacuum pump, giving an even 15 psi (1.02 bar) across the whole jig, which is more than adequate to hold the braces in place while they are glued. The jigs are also heated and the gluing process takes just six minutes. The backs are also braced and the central trim strip that covers the join glued in using the same vacuum method.

SIDES

Until relatively recently, the sides of all Martin guitars were bent by hand. This is still done on some custom instruments and special orders, and for guitars with cutaways. Otherwise, the sides are bent in a jig. They are sprayed with water and placed into a heated jig where they are bent to shape using pneumatic clamps. The sides remain in the jig for several minutes, after which time they cool off in a drying rack prior to assembly.

The neck and end blocks on the guitars are also made on the computer-controlled machinery. The blocks are made of mahogany for the high-end instruments,

Custom order sides are still often bent by hand.

A batch of koa sides with end blocks fitted.

A side for a custom order cutaway guitar being soaked and heated prior to bending.

Using a mixture of clamps and clothes pegs to glue the kerfing.

although high-quality ply is used on the composite X-Series models. High-end guitars have a dovetail while others have a mortice and tenon join which, because of the computer-controlled machinery, is very accurate.

The sides are cut to length and the end blocks glued into place. When these are dry, the kerfings are added.

The mixture of old and new processes at the factory is clear here. The kerfings are wiped with glue and then clamped using clothes pegs and spring clamps. Although Martin is constantly trying to update, if something works well it will not change it just for the sake of change. As clothes pegs exert the perfect pressure and are readily available, they are still used.

Because the back is domed, the sides and kerfing need to be shaped before the back will fit. Most of the shaping is included when the sides are cut, as this can

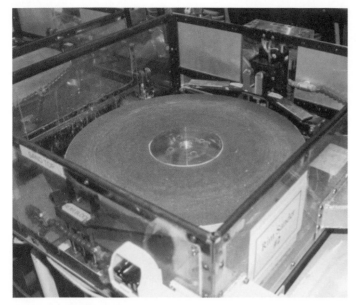

One of Martin's concave rim sanders.

Carving the braces prior to fitting the top.

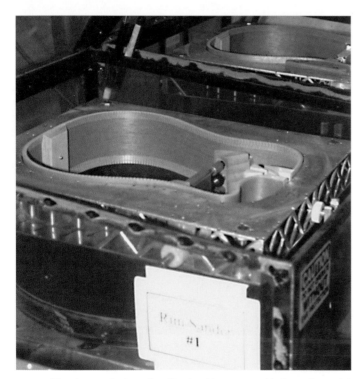

The rim sander in action. Turnbuckles are used to keep the waist of the guitar against the mould.

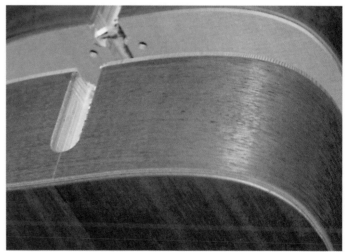

Simple binding channels.

be programmed into the computer, but the kerfings will need to be at a slight angle to the sides so that the back sits on them and the glue join is secure.

Martin uses a rotating concave sanding disc to sand the sides to accept the back. The body is placed into the jig and held securely, and the disc rotates over the back, sanding off the high points. It is apparently very easy to tell when this has been achieved, because the noise the sanding disc makes changes.

With this done, the recesses for the back bracings are cut and the back is glued on in a jig, with everything being checked to ensure that the guitar lines up correctly. The top is also glued in the same jig after the kerfings have been sanded and the recesses for the cross braces cut.

Any excess material around the sides of the guitar is then trimmed and the body readied for the binding channels. The bindings vary considerably on Martin guitars, from simple white binding with a few contrasting

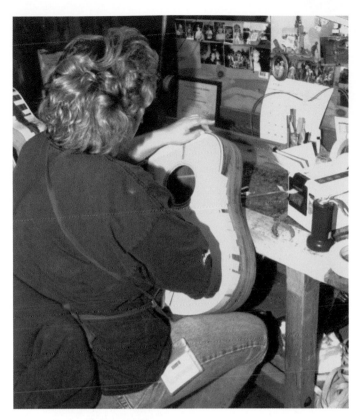

Taping binding in place.

Soundhole inlays are done at the same time as the binding.

Inlaying the abalone around the edge of a high-end guitar. As mentioned in Chapter 10, a strip of polyvinyl (or teflon) is inserted into the slot while the other bindings are glued; then removed so the abalone can be inserted into a clean recess.

inlay lines inside to complex and time-consuming multiple bindings with abalone. Some of this decoration may extend not only across the face of the guitar but also down the sides and around the neck socket, and this all needs to be cut accurately.

The main channels are cut on a table-mounted router, another ingenious machine developed in the Martin workshops. The operator can vary the depth of cut and holds the body against the router, rather than running the router around the top in the manner that is used in this book. This ensures that the channel is always correctly aligned with the face or back of the guitar, but it is a skilled job and is probably not adaptable for use in a home workshop.

The bindings are glued into place and held with masking tape while the glue dries. This is by far the most cost-effective and simple method, and certainly simpler than wrapping the guitar in binding tape, a process that is still used for sharper bent cutaways. Any abalone is not fitted at this stage, but the channel it will occupy is filled with a polyvinyl dummy strip that is not affected by the glue. This can be pulled out when the other bindings are dry and the abalone pieces installed into the resulting channel. These are cut and matched for colour before being finally shaped and fitted. This is very time-consuming, which is reflected in the price of these instruments.

NECKS

The neck also travels around the factory while the body is being made. The first stage is to glue on the sides of

A pallet of rough-cut necks.

The CNC neck carving machine at work.

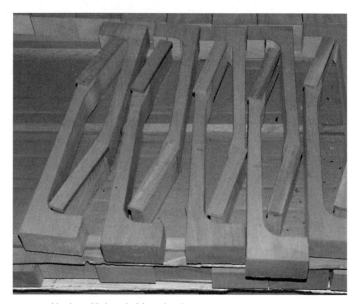

Necks with head sides glued on.

Carving a neck by hand for one of the custom orders. The clamping jig may look primitive but it works and is solid enough to give proper support.

the headstocks for the models that do not have a one-piece neck. The truss rod, or fixed strengthening rod, channel is also cut. The rough-cut necks are then placed, 24 at a time, onto the shaping jig. This is a monster of a machine that cuts all the necks uniformly and very accurately. The overall shape, neck-to-body join, the dovetail or tenon join, head thickness and rough neck shape are cut on the machine.

From here the necks go to have head facings glued on and truss rods installed. The machine head holes are also drilled, which is done in one go on a specially designed drill press.

FINGERBOARD

The fretboard will have been allocated to the guitar at the beginning and will have been thicknessed, radiused,

The specially-designed drill press that drills all six machine head holes in one go.

One of Martin's fret presses.

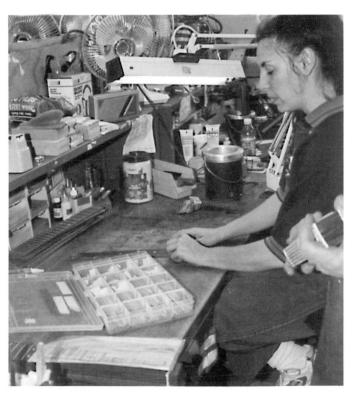

Inlaying a slotted board before fretting.

Trimming the fret ends prior to the board being glued.

Gluing the board with a pneumatic press.

Quality control is taken very seriously. Here a batch of bridges are being inspected.

Necks are fitted with a wooden handle to allow them to be handled during the finishing process.

One of the jigs used to ensure necks and bodies are in line.

fretted, inlaid and bound by the time it meets up with the neck. The fingerboard is located on the neck using two pins set into the face of the neck to give perfect alignment; the boards are glued in place on a jig and held down by pneumatic clamps.

The neck and body then come together for trial fitting. This is a critical time for any guitar, so any adjustment to the neck join is done now and great care is taken so that there are no nasty surprises when they are glued.

Not all necks are machined. Some custom orders and many prototype models are made by hand in the traditional manner. In these cases the neck is shaped using draw-knives and rasps.

Bodies are suspended for spraying by hooks screwed into the end pin hole.

Leveling between coats and final polishing are all done with air-driven sanders and polishers.

All bodies and necks are then sanded prior to being finished. The bodies and necks are sprayed separately and not joined until much later. The area around the dovetail is masked and the top is masked in the area where the fingerboard will overlay.

Martin's finishing process has evolved over the years and is described in some detail in Dick Boak's book, which comes with Martin kit guitars but is also available separately.

The first stage is to do any staining that is needed. Not all Martins are stained: the rosewood models and some exotic wood guitars are not stained, although the mahogany ones are. The stain is an alcohol-based stain that is fast-drying.

Martin first sprays a vinyl sealer over the back and sides of the guitar to seal the grain before the filler is applied. This helps prevent the filler sinking into the guitar after the finish is completed, and also protects the guitar from fingerprints.

The filler used on Martin guitars is a walnut coloured, silica-based filler and is used on all porous woods such as koa, mahogany and rosewood; it is forced into the grain and after excess filler is removed, it is allowed to dry. The top is wetted to raise the grain before being sanded again for an extra-smooth result. The entire body is then sealed with a vinyl coat to seal

Masking the fingerboard prior to spraying.

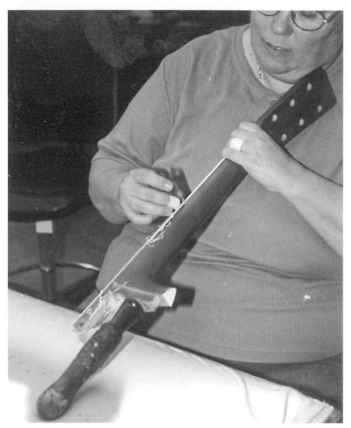

Scraping the bindings clean before the clear coats. The handle also serves as a rest. The speed and accuracy of the work is very impressive.

Bridges are glued using Martin's own design of clamp.

the wood and protect against fingerprints before the bindings are scraped clean with a sharp blade to restore them to their pristine white colour. Another coat of vinyl is then sprayed to cover the bindings and provide a uniform base for the lacquer. A lacquer sealer is used between the vinyl and lacquer to allow for the difference in materials.

The gloss coats on Martins are nitrocellulose and so their spraying facility is a very high-tech affair that is temperature and humidity controlled, and fully conforms with all environmental rules and regulations. Nitrocellulose is a highly inflammable material and needs special handling. Martin's spray booths are of the waterfall type that trap any solids in the air that could escape and settle on unfinished work, and they also serve to lower the possibility of anything nasty happening.

The guitars pass through a graduated oven that dries the lacquer quickly between coats. This not only speeds up production but also helps the solvents to escape from the lacquer.

The backs and sides of the guitars are given two to three coats of nitrocellulose and are then leveled with 400 grit paper. They are then given another two coats and sanded again before a final two coats are

applied, the last of which is left unsanded. Tops tend to get fewer coats as the wood is less porous. Once completely dry the guitars are then buffed to a mirror finish on buffing machines or lambswool pad polishers. The final coats on satin finish guitars are left unpolished.

With the neck and the body sprayed, the area under the fingerboard extension is unmasked and the neck is fixed to the body. The bridge position is marked and the finish is removed from under where the bridge will be before the bridge is glued on.

The final jobs are to fit the saddle, install the machine heads and drill through the string positions on the bridge to fit the bridge pins. All guitars are then strung and tuned, the action is set and the truss rod adjusted as needed. The guitars then go into a quarantine store for eight days so that all parts can settle. They are then inspected again and reset if needed, prior to shipping.

At the time of my visit Martin had recently completed their 800,000th guitar, although this was away being photographed, but they were already working on the designs for the 1,000,000th and this has long since been built. This is an incredible achievement for any guitar company and made all the more impressive when one considers just how much detail work is still done by hand at the factory. There are several aspects of the Martin factory that are impressive, the standard of workmanship and the dedication of the staff being just two, but the way that handwork and machines have been brought together in a sympathetic way to produce quality guitars, rather than just a lot of guitars, is very inspiring. For any guitar maker, or guitarist, a visit to Martin will yield some great ideas, and tours are run on a frequent basis.

Appendix 1
Fretting Tables

When discussing scale lengths in Chapter 2, I did discuss how to set up a spreadsheet in order to work out the fret position measurements for any scale length. I also appreciate that not everyone has the time and energy to do this so I am including the most common scale lengths here. Since measuring each fret slot from fret to fret can lead to cumulative errors, I am also including the total distance of each fret from the nut position. This can be used, with the fret to fret distances, as a useful double check that you are marking correctly. Having done this, it is also useful to include the remainder distance. This is the distance from any one fret to the end of the scale length and this is useful for estimating neck lengths and distances to the bridge and the length of a fingerboard overhang.

The scale lengths used here are shown in inches and millimetres and cover the main scale lengths used on acoustic guitars. Millimetres are shown to two decimal places and inches to three. 24 fret positions are shown even though few people make double octave acoustics.

The first scale is that used throughout this book - 25¹/₂ in or 648 mm

Fret		From nut	Remainder	Fret		From nut	Remainder
0			25.500	0			648
1	1.431	36.480	24.069	1	36.37	36.48	611.63
2	1.351	37.831	22.718	2	34.33	70.81	577.30
3	1.275	39.106	21.443	3	32.40	103.21	544.90
4	1.204	40.309	20.239	4	30.58	133.79	514.32
5	1.136	41.445	19.103	5	28.87	162.66	485.45
6	1.072	42.518	18.031	6	27.25	189.91	458.20
7	1.012	43.530	17.019	7	25.72	215.62	432.49
8	0.955	44.485	16.064	8	24.27	239.90	408.21
9	0.902	45.386	15.162	9	22.91	262.81	385.30
10	0.851	46.237	14.311	10	21.63	284.43	363.68
11	0.803	47.041	13.508	11	20.41	304.85	343.26
12	0.758	47.799	12.750	12	19.27	324.11	324.00
13	0.716	48.514	12.034	13	18.18	342.30	305.81
14	0.675	49.190	11.359	14	17.16	359.46	288.65
15	0.638	49.827	10.721	15	16.20	375.66	272.45
16	0.602	50.429	10.120	16	15.29	390.95	257.16
17	0.568	50.997	9.552	17	14.43	405.39	242.72
18	0.536	51.533	9.016	18	13.62	419.01	229.10
19	0.506	52.039	8.510	19	12.86	431.87	216.24
20	0.478	52.517	8.032	20	12.14	444.01	204.11
21	0.451	52.968	7.581	21	11.46	455.46	192.65
22	0.425	53.393	7.156	22	10.81	466.27	181.84
23	0.402	53.795	6.754	23	10.21	476.48	171.63
24	0.379	54.174	6.375	24	9.63	486.11	162.00

Martin's 25.4 in or 645 mm scale

Fret		From nut	Remainder	Fret		From nut	Remainder
0			25.400	0			645
1	1.426	36.480	23.974	1	36.20	36.48	608.80
2	1.346	37.826	22.629	2	34.17	70.65	574.63
3	1.270	39.096	21.359	3	32.25	102.90	542.38
4	1.199	40.294	20.160	4	30.44	133.34	511.94
5	1.132	41.426	19.028	5	28.73	162.08	483.20
6	1.068	42.494	17.960	6	27.12	189.20	456.08
7	1.008	43.502	16.952	7	25.60	214.79	430.48
8	0.951	44.453	16.001	8	24.16	238.96	406.32
9	0.898	45.352	15.103	9	22.81	261.76	383.52
10	0.848	46.199	14.255	10	21.53	283.29	361.99
11	0.800	46.999	13.455	11	20.32	303.60	341.67
12	0.755	47.754	12.700	12	19.18	322.78	322.50
13	0.713	48.467	11.987	13	18.10	340.88	304.40
14	0.673	49.140	11.314	14	17.08	357.97	287.31
15	0.635	49.775	10.679	15	16.13	374.09	271.19
16	0.599	50.374	10.080	16	15.22	389.31	255.97
17	0.566	50.940	9.514	17	14.37	403.68	241.60
18	0.534	51.474	8.980	18	13.56	417.24	228.04
19	0.504	51.978	8.476	19	12.80	430.04	215.24
20	0.476	52.454	8.000	20	12.08	442.12	203.16
21	0.449	52.903	7.551	21	11.40	453.52	191.76
22	0.424	53.327	7.128	22	10.76	464.28	180.99
23	0.400	53.727	6.728	23	10.16	474.44	170.84
24	0.378	54.104	6.350	24	9.59	484.03	161.25

Martin's 24.9 in or 632 mm scale

Fret		From nut	Remainder	Fret		From nut	Remainder
0			24.900	0			632
1	1.398	36.480	23.502	1	35.47	36.48	596.53
2	1.319	37.799	22.183	2	33.48	69.96	563.05
3	1.245	39.044	20.938	3	31.60	101.56	531.45
4	1.175	40.219	19.763	4	29.83	131.39	501.62
5	1.109	41.329	18.654	5	28.15	159.54	473.46
6	1.047	42.376	17.607	6	26.57	186.12	446.89
7	0.988	43.364	16.619	7	25.08	211.20	421.81
8	0.933	44.297	15.686	8	23.67	234.87	398.13
9	0.880	45.177	14.806	9	22.35	257.22	375.79
10	0.831	46.008	13.975	10	21.09	278.31	354.70
11	0.784	46.792	13.190	11	19.91	298.22	334.79
12	0.740	47.533	12.450	12	18.79	317.01	316.00
13	0.699	48.231	11.751	13	17.74	334.75	298.26
14	0.660	48.891	11.092	14	16.74	351.49	281.52
15	0.623	49.513	10.469	15	15.80	367.29	265.72
16	0.588	50.101	9.881	16	14.91	382.20	250.81
17	0.555	50.656	9.327	17	14.08	396.28	236.73
18	0.523	51.179	8.803	18	13.29	409.56	223.44
19	0.494	51.673	8.309	19	12.54	422.11	210.90
20	0.466	52.140	7.843	20	11.84	433.94	199.07
21	0.440	52.580	7.403	21	11.17	445.12	187.89
22	0.415	52.995	6.987	22	10.55	455.66	177.35
23	0.392	53.387	6.595	23	9.95	465.62	167.39
24	0.370	53.758	6.225	24	9.40	475.01	158.00

Gibson's 24⁵/₈ in, or 625 mm scale

Gibson's quoted 24¾ in scale has varied over the years and the most common variant, of 24⅝ in is shown here.

Fret		From nut	Remainder	Fret		From nut	Remainder
0			24.625	0			625
1	1.382	36.480	23.243	1	35.08	36.48	589.92
2	1.305	37.785	21.938	2	33.11	69.59	556.81
3	1.231	39.016	20.707	3	31.25	100.84	525.56
4	1.162	40.178	19.545	4	29.50	130.34	496.06
5	1.097	41.275	18.448	5	27.84	158.18	468.22
6	1.035	42.310	17.412	6	26.28	184.46	441.94
7	0.977	43.288	16.435	7	24.80	209.27	417.14
8	0.922	44.210	15.513	8	23.41	232.68	393.72
9	0.871	45.081	14.642	9	22.10	254.78	371.63
10	0.822	45.903	13.820	10	20.86	275.63	350.77
11	0.776	46.678	13.045	11	19.69	295.32	331.08
12	0.732	47.410	12.312	12	18.58	313.90	312.50
13	0.691	48.102	11.621	13	17.54	331.44	294.96
14	0.652	48.754	10.969	14	16.55	348.00	278.40
15	0.616	49.369	10.353	15	15.63	363.62	262.78
16	0.581	49.951	9.772	16	14.75	378.37	248.03
17	0.548	50.499	9.224	17	13.92	392.29	234.11
18	0.518	51.017	8.706	18	13.14	405.43	220.97
19	0.489	51.505	8.218	19	12.40	417.83	208.57
20	0.461	51.967	7.756	20	11.71	429.54	196.86
21	0.435	52.402	7.321	21	11.05	440.59	185.81
22	0.411	52.813	6.910	22	10.43	451.02	175.38
23	0.388	53.201	6.522	23	9.84	460.86	165.54
24	0.366	53.567	6.156	24	9.29	470.15	156.25

A longer 26 in or 660 mm scale

Fret		From nut	Remainder	Fret		From nut	Remainder
0			26.000	0			660
1	1.459	36.480	24.541	1	37.04	36.48	622.96
2	1.377	37.857	23.163	2	34.96	71.44	587.99
3	1.300	39.157	21.863	3	33.00	104.45	554.99
4	1.227	40.385	20.636	4	31.15	135.60	523.84
5	1.158	41.543	19.478	5	29.40	165.00	494.44
6	1.093	42.636	18.385	6	27.75	192.75	466.69
7	1.032	43.668	17.353	7	26.19	218.94	440.50
8	0.974	44.642	16.379	8	24.72	243.66	415.77
9	0.919	45.561	15.460	9	23.34	267.00	392.44
10	0.868	46.429	14.592	10	22.03	289.03	370.41
11	0.819	47.248	13.773	11	20.79	309.82	349.62
12	0.773	48.021	13.000	12	19.62	329.44	330.00
13	0.730	48.750	12.270	13	18.52	347.96	311.48
14	0.689	49.439	11.582	14	17.48	365.44	293.99
15	0.650	50.089	10.932	15	16.50	381.94	277.49
16	0.614	50.703	10.318	16	15.57	397.52	261.92
17	0.579	51.282	9.739	17	14.70	412.22	247.22
18	0.547	51.828	9.192	18	13.88	426.09	233.34
19	0.516	52.344	8.676	19	13.10	439.19	220.25
20	0.487	52.831	8.189	20	12.36	451.55	207.88
21	0.460	53.291	7.730	21	11.67	463.22	196.22
22	0.434	53.725	7.296	22	11.01	474.23	185.20
23	0.409	54.134	6.886	23	10.39	484.63	174.81
24	0.387	54.521	6.500	24	9.81	494.44	165.00

Appendix 2

Useful addresses

The following is a list of companies that trade in a variety of services allied to guitar making. Most of these companies have an Internet presence and a simple search on the company name may give you far more information. The main companies in the text are listed first followed by an alphabetical list.

Luthiers Supplies
The Hall,
Horebeach Lane
Horam, Heathfield
East Sussex TN21 0HR
England
Tel: + 44 (0)1435 812315
sales@luthierssupplies.co.uk

Touchstone Tonewoods
44 Albert Road North,
Reigate
Surrey, RH2 9EZ
England
Tel: + 44(0)1737 221064
sales@touchstonetonewoods.co.uk

Stewart-MacDonald
PO Box 900
Athens
Ohio 45701
USA
Tel: +1-740-592-3021
Fax: +1-740-593-7922

Luthiers Mercantile International, Inc.
7975 Cameron Dr. - Bldg. 1600
Windsor
CA 95492
USA
Tel: 707-687-2020

Allied Lutherie
POB 217
498 A Moore Lane
Healdsburg
CA 95448
USA
Tel: +1-707-431-3760
info@alliedlutherie.com

Guitarmaker's Connection
c/o C. F. Martin & Co., Inc.
510 Sycamore Street
P. O. Box 329
Nazareth
Pennsylvania 18064
USA
http://www.martinguitar.com

A&M Wood Specialty
358 Eagle Street North
P.O. Box 32040
Cambridge
Ontario
N3H 5M2
Canada
mail@amwoodinc.com

Allen Guitars - Luthier Supplies
P.O. Box 1883
Colfax
CA 95713
USA
Tel: +1-530-346-6590
allen@allenguitar.com

Allparts Music Corporation
13027 Brittmoore Park Drive
Houston
Texas 77041
USA
Tel: +1-713-466-6414
Fax: +1-713-466-5803

Amsterdamsche Fijnhouthandel
Minervahavenweg 14
1013 AR Amsterdam
Westpoort 3098
Netherlands
Tel: +31 -020-6828079
afh@fijnhout.nl

John Boddys Fine Wood and Tool Store
Riverside Sawmills
Boroughbridge
N. Yorks
YO5 9LJ
England
Tel: + 44 (0)1423 322370
sales@john-boddy-timber.ltd.uk

Bow River Specialty Woods
46501 Ballam Rd
Chilliwack, B.C.
Canada
V2P-6H5
Tel: +1-604-795-3462
info@bowriverwoods.com

Cocobolo, Inc.
6500 47th St. #6
Pinellas Park
FL 33781
USA
Tel: +1-727-521-0616
sales@cocoboloinc.com

Colonial Tonewoods, Inc.
4051 Bock Rd
Barhamsville
Virginia, 23011
USA
Tel: +1-757-566-8805
support@colonialtonewoods.com

Constantines Wood Center
1040 E. Oakland Park Blvd
Ft. Lauderdale
FL 33334
USA
Tel: +1-954-561-1716.
info@constantines.com

Curly Koa Guitar Wood
P.O.Box 1264
Kalaheo
Hawaii 96741
USA
Tel: +1-808-635-6256
james@koaguitarwood.com

Exotic Lumber Inc.
Annapolis:
1610 Whitehall Road
Annapolis
Maryland 21401
USA
Tel: +1-410-349-1705

Gaithersburg:
19324 Woodfield Road
Gaithersburg
Maryland 20879
USA
Tel: + 1-240-632-0385
info@exoticlumberinc.com

Exotic Woods Company
444 Erial-Williams Road
P.O. Box 532
Sicklerville
New Jersey 08081
USA
Tel +1 -609-728-5555
gulab@exoticwoods.com

Gallery Hardwoods, Inc.
P. O. Box 1515
Springfield
Oregon 97477
USA

Gilet Guitars
6 Booralee St
Botany NSW, 2019
Australia
Tel: +61 (02) 9316 7467

Gilmer Wood Company
2211 N.W. Saint Helens Rd.
Portland
OR 97210
USA
Tel: +1-503-274-1271

Firma Andreas Gleissner
Mozartstrasse 12
D-91088 Bubenreuth
Germany
+49 (0)9131 25229

Hawaiian Hardwoods Direct
Box 363
Dufur
OR. 97201
USA
Tel: +1-541-467-2610
Steve@curlykoa.com

Hancock Guitars
PO Box 425
North Tamborine
Qld 4272
Australia
info@luthiers supplies.com.au

Headway Music Audio Ltd
Units 4–5, Home Farm Works
Deddington
Oxfordshire
OX15 0TP
England
Tel: +44 1869 338 393

Hearne Hardwoods Inc.
200 Whiteside Drive
Oxford
PA, 19363
USA
Tel: +1-610-932-7400
info@hearnehardwoods.com

International Violin Company, Ltd.
1421 Clark View Road
Suite 118
Baltimore
MD 21209
USA
Tel: +1-410-832-2525

Fritz Kollitz
    Fine Tonewood and Accessories
Kairlindacher Strasse 2
D-91085 Weisendorf
Germany
Tel: +49 (0) 9135 2804
f.kollitz.tonewood.t-online.de

Le Bois de Lutherie
Fertans
25330
Amancey
France
Tel: + 33 (0)381 86 5555
Fax: + 33 (0)381 86 5556
info@bois-lutherie.com

Luthimate
10 Rue des Champs Pluviers
- ZI des Vauguillettes,
89100 Sens
France
Tel: +33 (0)3 86 67 05 95

Madinter Trade SI
Calle del Mercurio 11
28770 Colmenar Viejo
Spain
sales@madinter.com.

MapleLeaf Hardwoods
2056 Foust Hill Road
Hughesville
PA 17737
Tel: +1-570-584-5072
Fax: +1-570-584-5072
pataran@curlymaple.com

Metropolitan Music Co.
PO Box 1415
Mountain Rd.
Stowe
VT 05672
USA
Tel: +1 802-253-4814
sales@metmusic.com

Musical Forests Inc.
11 Ottawa Street
PO Box 659
Goose Bay
NL
A0P1C0
Canada
Tel: +1 201-467-4778
musicalforests@gmail.com

Theodor Nagel
Billstrasse 118
D-20539 Hamburg
Germany
Tel: + 49 40 781 1000
Fax: + 49 40 78 11 0024
info@theodor-nagel.com

North Hiegham Sawmills
26 Paddock Street
Norwich
NR2 4TW
UK
Tel: +44 (0)1603 622978

Notable Woods
342 Port Stanley Road
Lopez Island
WA 98261
USA
Tel: +1-360-468-4294
bruce@notablewoods.com

Pacific Rim Tonewoods
35811 State Route 20
Concrete
WA 98237
USA
Tel:+1- 360-826-6101
Contact@PacificRimTonewoods.com

Posono Timber
South African Office:
P.O. Box 121
Magalies View
2067
South Africa
Tel: +27(0)11. 465. 71. 02
PM@prosono.co.za

European Office:
C.P. 4 - 1025 St-Sulpice
Switzerland
Tel & Fax: +41.21.691.48.43
Albert.Monbaron@bluewin.ch

Randle Woods
P.O. Box 96
Randle
WA 98377
USA
Tel: +1-360-497-2071
roberts@lewiscounty.com

Rivolta s.n.c. di Andrea Rivolta & c.
Via Vittorio Veneto 7
20033 Desio (Mi)
Italy
Tel: +39 0362 621608
Fax: +39 0362 300734
info@riwoods.com

Santa Fe Spruce Co
129 Kearney Avenue
Santa Fe
New Mexico 87501
Tel: +1-505-983-1622

Tasmanian Timbers Pty. Ltd.
Old Beach, 7017
Tasmania
Australia
Tel: +61 429 614 453
info@tasmaniantimbers.com.au

Tonetech Ltd (Stockport)
Unit 3/5 Meadow Mill
Water Street
Stockport
Cheshire
SK1 2BX
Tel: +44 (0)7866 778208

Tonetech Ltd (Southend-on-Sea)
Unit 12 Rosshill Industrial Park
Sutton Road
Southend-on-Sea
Essex
SS2 5PZ
Tel: +44 (0)5601 147608

Timberline
Units 7 & 11A
Munday Works
58-66 Morley Road
Tonbridge
Kent
TN9 1RP
England
Tel: + 44 (0)1732 355626
Fax: + 44 (0)1732 358214
exotic.hardwoods@virgin.net

Timeless Instruments
P.O. Box 51
Tugaske
Saskatchewan
Canada
S0H 4B0
david@timelessinstruments.com

Tonewood s.r.o.
Pupavova 87
841 04 Bratislava
Slovakia
Tel: +421 2 6453 6477
sima@tonewood.sk

Tropical Exotic Hardwoods of Latin America
P.O. Box 1806
Carlsbad
CA 92018
Tel: +1-760-434-3030
anexotichardwood@abac.com

Vikwood Ltd.
1221A Superior Avenue
P.O. Box 554
Sheboygan
Wisconsin 53082
USA
Tel: +1-920-458-9351

Woodland GmbH
Hanauerstrasse 51
D-63546
Hammersbach
Germany
Tel: +49 (0) 6185 1744
info@woodland-gmbh.de

Finishes

Guitar Reranch
605 Pebble Creek
Garland
TX 75040
USA
Tel: +1-972-495-2074

Durobond Paints
65 Old Pittwater Road
Brookvale 2100
Sydney NSW
Australia
Tel: +61 2 9905 0811
sales@durobond.com.au

Inlays

Aqua Blue Maui LLC.
5805 Lower Kula Rd
Kula,
HI 96790
USA
aquablue@maui.net

Australian Mother of Pearl Co. Pty. Ltd
1 Botanic way
Wyndham Vale
VIC 3024
Australia
Tel: +61 3 9731 1607
info@mopsupplies.com

Custom Luthier
P.O. BOX 1306
Kennett Square
PA 19348-0451
USA
info@customluthier.com

DePaule Supply
1173 Berntzen Road
Eugene
OR, 97402
USA
Tel: +1-541-607-8971
andydepaule@luthiersupply.com

Shellex Klier Germany GmbH
Sudetenstrasse 15
D-64521 Gross-Gerau
Germany
Tel: +49 6152 2724
shellklier@shellex.de

Small Wonder Music Company
2 Summerhill Cottage
Chapmans Town Road
Rushlake Green
East Sussex, TN21 9PS
UK
Tel: +44 (0)1435 830509
sales@smallwonder-music.co.uk

The Rescue Pearl Company
1551 Duck Hollow Court
Rescue
CA 95672
USA
Tel/Fax: (530) 676-2770
rescuepearl@sbcglobal.net.

I have tried to keep this list as current as possible but in a commercial world, things often change. Please feel free to contact the publishers if any significant company has been left out or any of those listed appear to have gone out of business.

NBS Publications
7 Church Green
Dunsfold
Surrey
GU8 4LT

Acknowledgements

This book has taken a long while to complete between other projects and many people along the way have helped and encouraged.

This book would not have been possible had it not been for the tremendous help and generosity of David Tasker and huge thanks go to him and Juliet Brandsby Williams for the use of the workshop and to Jamie Brand who, together with Dave, owns most of the woodwork machines seen in this book.

David Dyke has been a good friend for many years as well as a supplier of wood and he happily added a lot of information to Chapter 5.

David Carroll, Neil Bond and Tony Russell from Touchstone Tonewoods have been a great help thoughout the project.

Dave King (why *is* everyone I know called Dave?) has been very generous with his time, allowing me to annoy him and take photographs.

Anton DiBenedetto for giving me the mahogany bar top and Tim Smith for giving me the wood for the top on the guitar in Chapter 21 - thank you.

Huge thanks go to Roger Giffin for being a source of information and humour for years.

C. F. Martin & Co., Inc. has been incredibly helpful and allowed me access to the factory to photograph its processes and so a huge thank you to all involved, especially Dick Boak, Danny Brown and to Joe MacNamara.

Contrast Photography in Basingstoke did sterling work on the cover pictures, Paul McConnell took the picture of me.

Ian Logan was instrumental in coming up with the cover design and is an all-round cool dude.

I also wish to thank the very many people who encouraged me to keep going on this project when other things were getting in the way and so, in no particular order; Lois Marshall, Jane Winder, Christy Roxburgh, Laurence Laurendon, Alex Bolan, Deb Hubbuck, Laura Gee. Other worthy mentions go to Marty McClary, Tunnocks plain chocolate caramel wafers, Carte Noir coffee, Gerry Budd, Micky Moody, Gwendoline Duke, Chris Bryant, Paul and Teresa at The Crossways Inn, Carol Goulden for continued support, various assorted Rummagers - you know who you all are, my Mum and Dad, Jon Saltmarsh for drawing and being cool and Chris Saltmarsh for not having gnarly hands, John at London Camera Exchange in Fareham, Andrew and Susan Mullhaupt, George Harrison, Eddie Izzard, John Martyn, Sarah Harding for emergency IT support, Sonia Hiscock and Harry, Dave Hiscock for taking some photos, Don Martin, Bryanston School for just being Bryanston School, Barry Cox, Nick Simpkin, Dick and Val at Popham Airfield for being very generous, Yan Webber, Phil Harding, Tim Wade, Pete Catlin, Sid and Toby, Alison Anderson. Nick Magnus, Gareth Tasker, Bev Lapworth, Captain Jack Sparrow, Mark Simpkin, Ashley Dacombe, Dean Markley, Ruth Martin and last, but by no means least, Sally Roots for getting this far on the proof reading without wanting to kill me.

Melvyn Hiscock, Dunsfold, 2010

Index

The boogie is innocent, it
was set up by the sunshine
and the moonlight